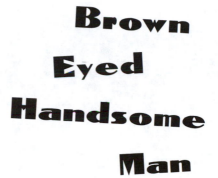

Brown
Eyed
Handsome
Man

Brown Eyed Handsome Man

THE LIFE AND HARD TIMES OF CHUCK BERRY

AN UNAUTHORIZED BIOGRAPHY

Bruce Pegg

Routledge
NEW YORK AND LONDON
OCM 50526907

Published in 2002 by
Routledge
29 West 35th Street
New York, NY 10001
www.routledge-ny.com

Published in Great Britain by
Routledge
11 New Fetter Lane
London EC4P 4EE
www.routledge.co.uk

Routledge is an imprint of the Taylor & Francis Group.
Printed in the United States of America on acid-free paper.
Design and typography: Jack Donner

10 9 8 7 6 5 4 3 2 1

Cataloging-in-Publication Data is available from the Library of Congress.

ISBN 0-415-93748-5

For my family
Suzanne, William, Carolyn, and Hannah
who lived through it,
and for my fellow musicians
Cato, Chuck, and the East Shore Allstars,
Dan and Ed of the Bards,
and Paul, Ian, and Neil of Manitou
who lived it.

Contents

Acknowledgments

Brown Eyed Handsome Man began life when I was the Director of the Writing Center at Colgate University. During the initial stages, my division directors, Jack Dovidio and Ellen Kraly, encouraged me and generously funded my research. Members of the Interdisciplinary Writing Department were also tremendously influential in helping the project along. Vicky McMillan, as department chair, also provided funding; Margaret Darby and Vincent DiGirolamo helped shape many of my ideas through their close and critical readings of early drafts; and Stacey Snyder, Trudy King, Carissa Dull, and Suzanne Bestler all helped in various ways.

Also at Colgate, Ann Ackerson, Interlibrary Loan Borrowing Coordinator, was able to locate all of my odd requests quickly and easily. Darryl Simcoe, Director of Media and Instructional Technology Services, and his counterpart Darryl Barker, Director of Media Technology, Washington University School of Law, St. Louis, were able to work a minor technological miracle and arrange the video interview with Frederick Mayer. Michael Coyle, Associate Professor of English, shared his record collection, thoughts, and tequila. And my student, John Daves, became my teacher during the project, as his open and honest discussions of race in America found their way at various points into the work.

A little over half way through the project, I left to become an Assistant Director in the Syracuse University Writing Program. Here, my friend and department chair Becky Howard also generously supported my writing, both through funding and through the gift of time. My colleagues in the program, Margaret Himley, Eileen Schell, Faith Plvan, George Rhinehart, Beth Wagner, Kristi Johnson, Mary Beth Sorendo, and LouAnn Payne, also encouraged me and either contributed to the project or patiently lived through the experience.

Mary Burtzloff, Archives Specialist in the National Archives-Central Plains Region, Kansas City, unearthed all of the existing Mann Act documents for me. Janet M. Bunker of the Lauderdale County Department of Archives and History helped me locate information on the incident in Meridian, Mississippi. Ann Morris, Doris Wesley, and Zelli Fischetti of the University of Missouri, St. Louis, were also helpful in locating items from the Western Historical Manuscripts Archive. Sharon Huffman of the St. Louis Public Schools Archive answered my questions and speedily located the picture of

Sumner High School. And Duane Sneddeker, Curator of Prints and Photographs, Missouri Historical Society, did the same for the photograph of the Antioch Baptist Church.

John Jackson, author of *Big Beat Heat* and *American Bandstand*, generously shared his thoughts and contacts with me. Fred Rothwell provided me with his huge file of English press clippings; his sterling research in *Long Distance Information* provided the foundation on which this book rests. And George Turek and Travis Fitzpatrick were instrumental in helping me locate Johnnie Johnson. Though I disagree with many of their ideas in the pages of this book, I sincerely respect and applaud their efforts to bring Johnnie into the public spotlight.

In St. Louis, Joe Edwards always went out of his way to make me feel welcome. Billy Peek, Frederick Mayer, Merle Silverstein, and Richard Schwartz each generously contributed their time and their photographs. But perhaps the most influential person in this whole project has been my great friend Bill Greensmith, who shared his time, his knowledge, his music, his photographs, his spare room, his tea, and his digestive biscuits from beginning to end. I cannot thank him, or his wife Stella, enough.

I'd also like to acknowledge the efforts of my wife Suzanne, who believed in this project from its outset. She helped in many ways, from sifting through endless court documents in the St. Charles County courthouse; to reading and debating numerous ideas before they finally found the light of day; to keeping the kids occupied when Daddy needed to write. Without her dedication and support, this book may never have reached completion.

At Routledge, I'd like to thank my editor, Richard Carlin, whose belief in this project and patience with me made the experience of writing this first book as pleasant as could be expected; my thanks, too, to Robert Byrne and Julie Ho.

Finally, several members of the Berry family, including Chuck Berry himself, were asked to be a part of this project. It is my greatest regret that they did not accept my offer.

Prologue: Grand Avenue

In the middle of a bright fall morning on October 10, 1986, a small camera crew assembled in front of the Fox Theater on Grand Avenue. They had come to midtown St. Louis to shoot a short, yet critical piece of footage for an upcoming documentary about one of the city's most well-known, controversial, and secretive individuals. A slender black man, sharply dressed and looking much younger than his impending 60th birthday, stood in their midst, the focus of their attention. Chuck Berry was back on Grand Avenue to revisit his past and savor his present.

The scene, which was to eventually appear midway in the documentary about Berry's life, titled *Chuck Berry: Hail! Hail! Rock 'n' Roll*, began with Berry walking up to and stopping at the Fox box office window. As the camera zoomed in, Berry, in a slow, deliberate voice, began a tale all-too-familiar to blacks who had lived through the Jim Crow America of the early twentieth century. "Boy," he began, staring down the camera with piercing brown eyes, "does this box office bring back a memory, a real particular memory. You know, when I was 11 years old, I came up to this very box office to get a ticket to see the *Tale of Two Cities*. My father wanted us to see it because it had a lot of artistic qualities about it. Lady said, 'Come on, we're not selling your ticket. You know you people can't come in here. Go away!'" As an afterthought, he added, "You know, it took two years for that to come to our theater in our neighborhood."

The camera followed the solitary figure of Berry as he pulled open the theater door and moved inside. Over his shoulder, on the opposite side of the road, the lens briefly picked out the imposing gray silhouette of the Third Baptist Church. Beyond that, just out of the camera's view, lies Powell Symphony Hall and a nondescript blacktopped parking lot. There, on a cold December night some quarter of a century earlier, Berry had been arrested amid allegations of sexual impropriety with a 14-year-old girl, exposing to the world the weakness that even now lay at the center of his character. It was a moment that many around him said had changed him forever.

The crew moved quickly into the theater's ornate lobby to set up the next shot of the solitary Berry, moving slowly over the marbled floor, continuing and left." Physically, the process of making the movie, the arduous rehearsal schedule, and the two shows had left him spent. Mentally, however, the day must have exacted a far greater toll. He had lived his whole life in one day, journeying from the Jim Crow indignities of his youth, through his ambitious adult years and his desire to work his way out of the Ville—the historic black neighborhood a little over a mile to the north, where he was born and raised—to his present position as rock music's honored elder statesman. Along the way, there were the controversies, musical and personal, that dogged him though the years and that would resurface even after this night of celebration. But in the end, the shadowy figure left as he had come, alone, oblivious to the turbulence generated by his own wake.

The Ville

They'd been chastened since birth by the scorn and violence the race had known. They'd been brought up on lynchings and riots, name-calling and "No Colored Allowed." The neighborhood had saved them, they thought. With the Negro-owned businesses, the hairdressers and laundry, the school teachers and the shadows of the great trees, the neighborhood had sheltered them from what they knew was on the outside: the white people.

—Ntozake Shange, *Betsey Brown*

In the early part of the twentieth century, the neighborhood known as the Ville, just a few miles north and west of downtown St. Louis and the Mississippi River, profoundly shaped the lives of all who grew up in it. During its heyday, from the early 1920s to the 1940s, the Ville was a self-contained island of black enterprise and culture in a vast white, segregated ocean. "There were restaurants, movies, nightclubs, and schools," Demosthenes Dubose, a former teacher, recalled: "There was the Amytis Theater in the Poro College building on Pendleton; the Douglas Theater on Whittier and Finney, and the crème de la crème, the Comet Theater on Sarah and Finney." There were churches and small, family-owned stores and businesses; the Poro College building alone housed, at various times, a cosmetology school, a hotel, a law school, a post office, and the headquarters of the National Negro Business League. With the opening of the Homer G. Phillips hospital on Whittier in 1937, residents of the Ville could be born, educated, trained, employed, housed, nourished, entertained, and healed both physically and spiritually all within a six-by-nine-block area. "Everybody lived in the Ville," remembered record-store owner Ted Hudson. "Teachers lived next door to steelworkers. Steelworkers lived down the street from postal workers. Your doctor lived around the corner. In fact, everything was in that community. And it stayed in that community until the mid-'50s."

It was this way by necessity; because the white culture would not admit entry, the Ville provided everything necessary for black families to survive and grow from cradle to grave. But the realities of segregation were never far from the neighborhood. Ivan James's experience seemed typical. "As children," the engineer remembered, "we were never put in a situation where we had to run up against segregation. All of our activities were limited within the family, within the neighborhood. We had a neighborhood show that was within walking distance. I never thought about going downtown."

John Wright, now an assistant school superintendent, agreed:

> When we moved to . . . the outskirts of the Ville, things were quite segregated. But we were shielded from a lot. We programmed our life around segregation. When my mother took me downtown, we ate before we left, and we ate when we got back home. We had a movie theater in the Ville so we didn't have to go to sit in the back of a white theater. We knew we couldn't go west of Grand Avenue, so all our activities—church, school, theater—were confined to the Ville.

St. Louis's attitude toward race, and the creation of the Ville itself, is rooted in the history of Missouri. Although Thomas Jefferson's purchase of the Louisiana Territory from France in 1803—that great swath of America which encompassed the country's heartland between the Mississippi River and the Rockies—did much to provide the foundations of the young nation, it also made the country once again face the contradiction of slavery in a democracy. Specifically, the government had to decide whether the territory should allow slavery or be free, and Missouri's application to join the Union in 1819 became Congress's litmus test. When the Senate rejected an antislavery bill passed by the House, the disagreement paved the way for what became known as the Missouri Compromise; the following year, Missouri was admitted to the Union as a slave state, while Maine was admitted as free. As a further part of the compromise, the remainder of the territory north of Missouri's southern boundary was designated as "forever prohibited" to slavery. In so doing, Congress had ensured an equal balance of free and slave states, although it had postponed the inevitable decision on slavery's legality for a later date.

But if slavery found a champion in the state of Missouri, it faced one of its most dramatic challenges in the city of St. Louis. In 1846—just a few years after Cellie Johnson, Chuck Berry's paternal great-grandmother, was born into slavery on the Wolfolk plantation in Kentucky, and Charles Henry Banks, his maternal grandfather, was born into slavery on the Banks Plantation in the Oklahoma Territory—a slave by the name of Dred Scott, along with his wife, filed petitions in the St. Louis courthouse charging that they had been illegally deprived of their freedoms. Although their first suits failed, a subsequent suit was affirmed by the Missouri State Supreme Court in 1850. In the next few years, the suit was overturned by the same state court; a second suit was introduced and denied by the U.S. Circuit Court in Missouri before being heard twice by the U.S. Supreme Court. On March 6, 1856, the Supreme Court affirmed the Circuit Court opinion. Chief Justice Roger B. Taney, writing the opinion, declared that Negroes could not be citizens of a state or, by implication, of the United States, because they were "a subordinate and inferior class of beings who had been subjugated by the dominant race, and . . . held no rights and privileges but such as those who held the power and the Government might chose to grant them." Negroes, according to Taney, "had no rights which the white man was bound to respect" and were "altogether unfit to associate with the white race."

The implications of the decision, of course, reached far beyond the city of St. Louis; it was, first and foremost, one of the factors that precipitated the Civil War. During the war, Missouri, as a border state, once again vacillated in its official stance on the issue of slavery. Although the Missouri militia fought on the confederate side, and Captain William Quantrill (along with future outlaws Frank and Jesse James) fought a number of bloody guerilla skirmishes on its western border against residents of the free-soil state of Kansas, the state never actually seceded from the Union. But the *Dred Scott* decision was never effectively overturned by the war. Despite the fact that slavery had been abolished and blacks were guaranteed the rights to citizenship and the vote, Taney's words shaped government policy and Supreme Court decisions on race for almost a century after they were written.

After the war, blacks in Missouri, as in many of the Southern states, initially made substantial gains. In 1870, for example, Cellie Johnson and her husband John were free to move from their Kentucky plantation to Missouri, where they rented a portion of the Bellefontaine Farm, a few miles outside the burgeoning city of St. Louis, and raised their five children. In 1890, one of those children, Lucinda, married William Berry, the son of a Tennessee slave and an Oklahoma Indian; five years later, Lucinda gave birth to Henry Berry, Chuck Berry's father. In 1894, his mother, Martha Bell Banks, was born to Charles and Lula Banks in Mississippi, the second of seven children.

But the family's progress, like the progress of all blacks born in the late nineteenth and early twentieth centuries, was effectively halted by another Supreme Court decision, *Plessy v. Ferguson*. The case, which was decided the year after Henry Berry's birth was an inevitable extension of Justice Taney's decision in the *Dred Scott* case and the almost 20 years of segregation between the races in the South following Reconstruction. It declared that, although the races were equal, as guaranteed by the Fourteenth Amendment to the Constitution, there were undeniable differences between them that necessitated segregation; specifically, the Court argued that all public facilities and institutions, providing they were equal, could be separate.

Missouri's historical ambivalence to racial issues meant that St. Louis was spared the more overt displays of racial violence that plagued other large cities at the time. However, the first half of the twentieth century was marked by quiet adherence to the "separate but equal" doctrine, and the city of St. Louis settled into a pattern of Jim Crow segregation. In downtown St. Louis, for example, blacks were simply not welcomed. The three major downtown department stores—Stix-Baer and Fuller, Famous Barr, and Scruggs-Vandevoort-Birney—employed no blacks "unless," recalled Demosthenes DuBose, "they were running elevators or pushing a broom." Two of the stores operated segregated lunch counters; at the third, "the only facility where blacks could eat," according to DuBose, "was a waist-high counter . . . where blacks had to *stand up* and *eat*." The Cardinals, one of St. Louis's major league baseball teams, barred blacks from the grandstand; in fact, the Cardinal players threatened to strike rather than play against Jackie Robinson, the first black major-league ball player, in his rookie year of 1947. The five major St. Louis movie theaters—the Loews, the American, the Ambassador, the Fox, and the St. Louis—all remained segregated until the 1950s. Hotels, too—including the Jefferson, Statler, and Chase—were closed to nonwhites.

But, as in many Southern states, blacks in St. Louis were not just separated from whites: They were seen as inferior, often as nothing more than creatures carrying disease. Until 1923, blacks traveling through St. Louis and finding themselves in Union Station for a few hours were routinely taken to a way station, where they were "vaccinated against any disease." Chuck Berry himself recalls another practice of the St. Louis police department some decades later: They would stop multiracial couples and order mandatory shots for venereal disease.

Another particularly insidious manifestation of Jim Crow was the initiation of race-restrictive property covenants. In 1910, white property owners in St. Louis began entering into legally binding agreements with other white homeowners that stipulated parties were not to sell, lease, or rent property to blacks. Essentially, the tactic employed was to encircle a predominantly black neighborhood with covenant housing, thereby stopping the neighborhood's expansion into white areas as well as decreasing the amount of housing available to minorities.

A 1947 Fisk University study of race-restrictive covenants in Chicago and St. Louis identified the main area of covenanted properties in the city of St. Louis as a quadrangle "whose sides are represented by Vanderventer Avenue on the east, Kingshighway Boulevard on the west, Washington Boulevard on the south, and Carter Avenue on the north." Because the area between Easton Avenue to the south (now Dr. Martin Luther King Drive) and Vanderventer Avenue was not sufficiently covenanted, the study noted, "openings in the buffer line of defense . . . have permitted a steady stream of

Negro families to filter in and locate themselves in better housing." This "permitted Negro settlement of the central part of this covenanted quadrangle, in blocks along Taylor, Newstead, Pendleton [now Billups Avenue], Goode [now Annie Malone Drive], Whittier, and Sarah" between Easton and St. Louis Avenue to the north; this was the area known as the Ville.

The area was originally settled by German and Italian immigrants in the second half of the nineteenth century. But the appearance during Reconstruction of Elleardsville Colored School No. 8 (which was to become the Simmons Elementary School in 1891) and Sumner High School, and of two black churches—the Antioch Baptist and the St. James African Methodist Episcopal in 1884 and 1885, respectively—signified the beginnings of a strong black presence in the area. That presence was strengthened significantly by the property covenants and the great migration of blacks into St. Louis during World War I, when St. Louis, like so many industrial cities in America, saw huge influxes of black citizens hoping to take advantage of the large number of jobs the war effort had created. By 1925, the year before Chuck Berry's birth, the Ville had become home to some 6,000 residents, 90 percent of whom were black.

One of those immigrants to St. Louis was Martha Banks. Like the many blacks who arrived in St. Louis during that time, she had decided to leave her Mississippi home in search of employment in the North, perhaps harboring hopes of teaching at Sumner High School, which, as the first black high school west of the Mississippi River, would have been a magnet for her. In the spring of 1919, the Antioch Baptist Church witnessed her marriage to Henry Berry, who had moved from rural Bellefontaine to the city, more than likely also looking for better work. In short succession, daughter Thelma was born in July 1920. She was followed by brother Henry in February 1922, sister Lucy in April 1923 and another brother, Charles Edward Anderson Berry, on October 18, 1926. They set up home in a small house at 2520 Goode Avenue, a block north of Antioch Baptist, in an area Chuck Berry was later to describe as "a nicely kept area in the best of the three colored neighborhoods of St. Louis."

Indeed, one can imagine a young Charles Berry leaving the small house on Goode and walking across the Tandy Park playground in the shadows of Sumner High, down tree-lined Pendleton Avenue, past "brick and frame cottages with well-cared lawns," to the corner of Pendleton and St. Ferdinand. This was the hub of the Ville, where Sumner High School, St. James A.M.E. Church, the YMCA, and the Poro College building each occupied a corner. Continuing south on Pendleton, he may have stopped at the family-owned Morgan's Drug Store for a soda or a penny candy before crossing Pendleton to do errands at Wardlow's Grocery, McCrary's Meat Market, Woodward's Vegetable Market, or the Velour Dry Goods Store.

Then he'd walk home east along North Market, past Dr. Cheatham's offices and the Orchid Beauty Parlor, before turning north at the corner where the Antioch Baptist Church stood and onto Goode Avenue.

So insular was this world that Charles Berry's first sight of white people was a tremendous shock. As a child of about 3, Berry recalled seeing white firemen sent to fight a blaze in a shed on Goode Avenue. The imaginative young child, incredulous that anyone could have a skin color so different, fancied that their faces had been "whitened from fear of going near the big fire." Later, of course, the white world would become more familiar to him, but it would never be welcoming. His experiences at the Fox Theater and with the white families who paid for his father's contracting work were profound influences on him. For much of Berry's life, the white world would prove to be hostile and inaccessible.

But, by his own account, his childhood seemed fairly normal. The Berry family was dominated by his intelligent, yet unschooled father; the birth of the four children, and the subsequent births of brother Paul Lawrence Dunbar Berry in December 1933 and sister Martha in 1936, was interpreted by Berry as "Daddy's strategy to have Mother at home with their own children instead of out teaching someone else's." But Berry's mother's influence was also deep. More than likely it was her decision to name the youngest Berry son after the poet, Paul Laurence Dunbar. A key figure in African-American literature, Dunbar may not have been the first poet to write in the black dialect, but he did, in the words of one critic, write "sophisticated dialect verse that located the black speaker, uniquely for Dunbar's time, at the center of experience." Significantly, his 1895 poem, "The Mask," propelled him to national fame with black and white audiences alike.

Both parents were industrious and deeply religious, Henry becoming a deacon at Antioch Baptist and Martha singing hymns while doing housework. With such a strong Baptist background, Henry and Martha Berry were also strong disciplinarians, and Berry records a number of beatings administered by them throughout his childhood and adolescence. Certainly, Berry himself proved to be a handful as he got older and seems to have been involved in a number of scrapes at Cottage Avenue School. He recounts one story of receiving a caning in second grade (for pasting letters spelling *St. Louis* on his forehead); his third-grade teacher, Melba Sweets, recalled him as being "one of the worst kids I ever knew. . . . He was so bad that he was going to take me on one day by walking out of the room. No kid had ever tried me before. I told him, in the sternest voice I could muster, 'YOU WILL BE SORRY IF YOU WALK OUT OF THIS ROOM.' It worked, and he turned around and went back to his seat."

But one teacher in particular seemed to have an impact on the young boy, as she did on everyone who came into contact with her; that teacher was

Julia Davis, who taught Berry in the seventh and eighth grades at Simmons Elementary School. Davis was a strict disciplinarian, and the young Charles Berry realized immediately that the kind of antics for which he had been noted just a few years earlier would no longer be acceptable. "She's a Baptist, but she was like a Catholic nun in the classroom," Berry recalled in 1991, on the occasion of Davis's 100th birthday. "She taught in the avenue of perfection; we tried to come close." But more important than the way Julia Davis kept her pupils under control were the lessons they learned. Davis taught an Afrocentric curriculum, remarkable for its time, stressing the history and achievements of blacks both local and national. "These were things that weren't even mentioned in our textbooks," recalled George Hyram, a St. Louis teacher and himself a former student of Davis's in the 1930s. "It was certainly a source of pride in self to find out that, even if our history books didn't mention it, we had made contributions to our country."

Quite possibly it was under Julia Davis's tutelage that Berry came into contact with the philosophy of Booker T. Washington, the great black educator and spokesman. At the end of the nineteenth century, Washington laid out a blueprint for black economic success and racial harmony in the twentieth century. If blacks concentrated on vocational, practical trades, he reasoned in his 1899 work *The Future of the American Negro*, and produced "something that makes the white man partly dependent upon the Negro instead of the dependence being on the other side, [then] a change for the better takes place in the relations of the races." It is, he argued, through "the trades, the commercial life, largely, that the Negro is to find his way to respect and confidence."

But if Charles Berry did not formally learn this through Davis's teachings, or from his mother, whose college education would undoubtedly have acquainted her with the leading black thinkers of the time, it was a philosophy that lay all around him. It lay in the businesses of the Ville, which prospered independently of the white world that surrounded them. More important, it lay at the heart of his father's contracting business. Even if Henry Berry could not articulate Washington's philosophy in the way that his wife or Julia Davis did, every day that he got into his truck and subcontracted for the white-owned Drozda Realty Company or performed house repairs in one of the nearby white neighborhoods, he lived Washington's vision of the future of black America. Regardless of where Charles Berry learned them, Washington's ideas—that blacks, in the short run, should learn trades rather than immediately striving toward middle-class professions; that they should do so independently within their own community; and that black economic success rather than political agitation would bring reform and racial equality—held great sway within the black community in the early twentieth century.

These ideas were not without critics. Black intellectuals such as W. E. B. Du Bois seized on the naivete of such a philosophy. Barely four years after Washington had published *The Future of the American Negro*, Du Bois countered with his *Souls of Black Folk*. Here, in a chapter titled "Of Mr. Booker T. Washington and Others," he argued that such thinking ignored the often insurmountable problems of segregation and racism, and that no change in American society could ever occur until political reform had removed those barriers. Even so, Washington's philosophy of compromise and economic independence remained central to black consciousness at least through the first half of the century; for Charles Berry, it was to be especially true.

Berry seemed to fall under Davis's influence quite strongly between the years of 1937 and 1939. He described his 12th year as "my most Christian and most boring of my life," although he admitted also that he was losing the struggle as puberty took hold. "I was washed around," he wrote in his autobiography, "in suds of sinful surroundings." Clearly, the sinful surroundings in Berry's mind were sexual in nature, shaped by several formative experiences in the proper environs of the Ville. The first was the visit of a white nurse after Berry fell ill with pneumonia. She "had a profound effect on the state of my fantasies and settled into the nature of my libido." Sometime later, the sexual charge of another white nurse, first "paddling me when I was into any mischief" and then feeling her lips kiss him in reward for being good, must have provided young Berry with a sense that the white world was exciting, fearful, and, above all, sexual.

Berry's sexuality also was shaped by the influence of Harry Davis, the son of Henry Berry's cousin, Harry Davis Sr. Harry Jr. was a few years older than Charles, a successful student at Sumner and a photographer with an eye for pin-ups. One of his favorite models was Charles's older sister, Lucy, and his files were full of negatives and prints of the attractive teenager. Harry also supplemented his income by developing the more salacious negatives emanating from neighborhood cameras, instilling in Berry a lifelong love of voyeurism and photographing the naked female form. When the Berry family finally moved to 4319 Labadie Avenue, a more spacious house just outside of the Ville, in the mid 1930s, one of young Charles Berry's first requests was a space in the house's basement for a darkroom.

The conflict Charles Berry's awakening sexuality created with his Baptist surroundings was to lead to an increasing number of clashes with his father. Berry's autobiography mentions two specific incidents of beatings by his father after he learned of young Chuck's encounters with members of the opposite sex. One of them, occurring when Charles was about 15 or 16, resulted in Henry Berry beating his son with a strap and, in all likelihood, was one of the incidents that eventually led Charles to move in with his more liberal sister, Thelma. At the time, Charles confessed, he "couldn't cope with the strict religious rule of his home."

The conflict in his school life, too, resurfaced, and there is plenty of evidence to suggest that Berry had a difficult time once he left Julia Davis's influence and entered high school. Given that he would have entered Sumner in 1940, just shy of his 15th birthday, his comment that, in 1944, he was "struggling to reach my junior year" suggests that he had been held back a grade not once but twice. Berry's own account of his time at Sumner does not mention academics or school-related activities, with the single and important exception of his musical debut. His account of this event, which would have occurred while he was repeating his freshman year in 1941, is a telling one not only because it suggests one of the problems he encountered at Sumner but also because it foreshadows a number of issues he would encounter later, as his musical career began to flourish. Berry recalls that he sang Jay McShann's "Confessin' the Blues" at a school program. As its title suggests, it was a blues song. In Berry's account the "school auditorium exploded with applause," and, on the song's conclusion, he was "complimented again with a tremendous ovation." However, he also indicated how scandalous the choice of song was for its time. Berry acknowledged that he was taking a liberty in singing this song, and that he performed it "without thought of how bold it would be, singing such a lowly blues at such a sophisticated affair." He went on to acknowledge the "audacity" of singing McShann's song, and said that it "startled" the audience. More significant, perhaps, was the fact that, in Berry's words, "'How dare you?' showed on the faces of a couple of faculty members."

Given that Sumner High School, with its long and prestigious history of black achievement, had become a magnet for the sons and daughters of the black professional classes, and given his own family's aspirations toward middle-class status, the choice of song was deliberately calculated to shock the sensibilities of the adults in the high-school auditorium that night. The blues would certainly not be appropriate in a school that had a strong tradition of classical music, which would go on to produce such opera stars as Grace Bumbry and Robert McFerrin, and which had already seen a promising mezzo-soprano named Lucy Ann Berry grace its stage. It was lowbrow culture, unsophisticated and decidedly lower class, received by both the black and white middle class in the same way that rock and roll would be a decade later.

By 1944, Berry's schooling had come to a halt. His name does not appear in any of the Sumner High School yearbooks of the time, and the picture emerges of a teenager adrift and isolated. "There were a lot of wealthy Negro kids at Sumner, doctors' sons who had their own cars," recalled comedian Dick Gregory, who attended Sumner in 1946, two years after Berry's departure.

"The athletes and the rich boys and the brains were the big wheels at Sumner High School." A decade later, little had changed. Anna Mae Bullock, fresh from rural Nut Bush, Tennessee, also felt that Sumner was a place she didn't belong; years later, as successful singer Tina Turner, she reflected "Sumner High was all black, but very high class—these were the children of doctors, professional people. . . . My mother was basically a maid, and the man she was living with . . . was a truck driver. . . . So in this new school, I was still feeling sort of lower class." The contractor's son, not a part of the academic or athletic cliques, must have felt similarly as he faced his junior year in 1944; consequently, the events that followed were, perhaps, all too predictable.

About a month into the new school year, somewhere in late September or early October 1944, Charles Berry decided to leave the Ville, to run away from his family and the safety of the middle-class world they inhabited once and for all. Along with two friends, Lawrence "Skip" Hutchinson and James Williams, he set out for California in a 1937 Oldsmobile; almost immediately, the three encountered the realities of segregation. Barely 30 miles out of town, in the lily-white county of St. Charles, they stopped for food at the Southern Air restaurant in Wentzville (a restaurant that would play a large role in a later scandal in Berry's life), only to be told that they would have to go around to the back and receive their plates out of the kitchen window. It was not Charles Berry's first encounter with Jim Crow—that dubious honor probably belonged to the incident at the Fox Theater box office years earlier—but it was a memory that was to stay with him for the rest of his life.

The trio's money lasted only as far as Kansas City. There, they pulled off three armed robberies in the space of five days, with Berry holding up a barbershop with nothing but the barrel of a .22 caliber handgun. Eventually, however, the three came to their senses and decided to return to St. Louis; but when their car broke down halfway across Missouri, just outside of Columbia, the threesome tried one more audacious scheme. They flagged down a passing motorist and, instead of soliciting his aid, Berry pulled the .22 barrel on him; the three made off with the stolen car and their 1937 Oldsmobile for ten miles before they were pulled over by a suspicious highway patrolman. Finally, their luck had come to an end and, after being held close to a month in the Boone County jail, the three were tried (the trial lasted 21 minutes by Berry's account) and sentenced to 10 years' imprisonment.

As Berry tells the tale, their crime spree was nothing more than adolescent high jinks; like much of what was to happen later in his life, however, the incident was not without ambiguities. Berry's actions were clearly dangerous and antisocial; at the same time, his legal advice (such as it was), trial, and sentencing were infused with the racism one would expect of a rural Missouri court in the 1940s. The sentence and judgment records from the Circuit Court of Boone County, Missouri, for November 16, 1944, corroborate some of Berry's account. The document tells us that the defendant "waives formal judgment and enters his plea of guilty" to the "crime and felony of Robbery in the First Degree." Berry's lawyer, perhaps rightly realizing that he could not defend a black teenager in Columbia, opted to take the $125 fee that Henry Berry had paid him and do nothing in return. The judge, although acknowledging that Berry had not "heretofore been convicted of a felony," had no hesitation in passing the harshest possible judgment. And Charles Berry, a month past his 18th birthday, had finally been fully confronted with the hard realities of life outside the Ville.

"De Sun Do Move"

St. Louis! The town where Scott Joplin and Tom Turpin used to play ragtime. The town that W.C. Handy made famous in his great song, "The St. Louis Blues." The town where Josephine Baker started out as a $15.00 a week waitress and ended up in Paris as one of the most glamorous stars of the international theater. . . . The town where riverboats used to run from New Orleans with Louis Armstrong's horn blasting the night away.

St. Louis, that old city of river boats and ragtime, jockeys and blues, diamond rings and glamorous women, Josephine Baker and T. S. Eliot, Old Man River and old Jim Crow, and a sun that "do move."

I swear it do!

—Langston Hughes, "In Racial Matters in St. Louis, 'De Sun Do Move.'"

For blacks in St. Louis and across the United States, the early 1950s were a time of struggle and cautious optimism. Black soldiers returning home from the war in the mid-1940s had felt acutely the contradiction of fighting oppression abroad only to return home to face Jim Crow segregation. Meanwhile, the realities of a postwar economy fueled a second migration of black workers from the rural South to the industrial North. About 38,000 black workers found their way to St. Louis during the 1940s, a figure that doubled in the first five years of the next decade, making the black population a quarter of the total city population.

At the federal level, significant civil-rights legislation began to emerge. In June of 1946, the Supreme Court ruled that segregation in public transportation was unconstitutional; two years later, President Truman outlawed segregation in federal offices and the military. But there was also much to be pessimistic about: The NAACP reported that 1946 had been "one of the grimmest years" ever for violence against blacks, and throughout the South, blacks were routinely denied the right to vote.

Back in the Ville, the Berry family bore witness to the struggle being played out in the larger world. Oldest brother Henry had returned home from a four-year stint in the army and had witnessed first-hand the realities of segregation in the armed services. ("He did climb to the rank of lieutenant in the crap crew," Berry was to observe wryly in his autobiography.) Meanwhile, Berry had served three years of his ten-year jail sentence at the Algoa Intermediate Reformatory for Young Men in Jefferson City. All of Algoa's facilities—dining, recreation, even the toilets—were segregated, and Berry recalls that the white guards were profoundly racist. One in particular—a Mr. Preston, who was in charge of the prison laundry—stuck in Berry's mind. He was from the small southeast Missouri town of Sikeston, which just two years earlier had born witness to a notorious lynching. In January 1942, Cleo Wright, a black oil worker, had been dragged through Sikeston's streets and burned alive. It was the last recorded case of a lynching in the state, one of six recorded nationwide that year, and in most Missourians' minds would forever link the town of Sikeston with the most brutal of racist acts. Clearly, Charles Berry had much to fear during his time in Algoa.

But there was much for him to learn, too. He spent much of his time in Algoa singing bass in a gospel vocal quartet, a position that allowed him a degree of freedom to travel and, on one occasion, to sing in St. Louis and see his family. Along with one of the group's members, referred to only as Po' Sam in Berry's autobiography, Berry formed another band playing secular boogie. Berry does not relate what instrument he played or what selections the band chose for its repertoire, but we do know that Sam was a guitar and saxophone player from Kansas City. Chances are that he would have been well-versed in jazz and jump blues of the kind Berry would later play in the bars of East St. Louis.

With Charles in prison and Henry in the army, the Berry family found little to celebrate in the mid-1940s. But there was one truly bright moment in the family's life. During the summer of 1944, Lucy Berry's promising career as a classical mezzo-soprano looked like it was beginning to finally take off. On July 23, at the Barea Presbyterian Church, she won the city-wide finals of a music competition and earned a spot on the bill at the Fifth Annual Negro Music Festival, to be held at White Sox Park in Chicago on July 8. It was, in the words of Langston Hughes, the master of ceremonies for the event, "an ALL STAR million dollar show." Despite pouring rain, the festival attracted a crowd in the thousands to see Hughes, W. C. Handy (the aging and legendary father of American blues music), leading black classical singers, a mass gospel choir, and Hollywood stars Don Ameche and Pat O'Brien (who were strange attractions for a "Negro Music Festival," but perhaps brought a certain star cachet to the proceedings).

Two days later, Lucy Berry and much of the entourage moved on to Sportsman's Park in St. Louis for a repeat performance. Handy, then in his 70s and almost completely blind, still managed to delight the crowd with a rousing version of "St. Louis Blues," arguably the first song ever created in that uniquely African-American musical idiom. Many in the crowd would also recall that Hughes's first published poem, "The Negro Speaks of Rivers," had been written on a train while crossing Eads Bridge into St. Louis in 1920. It was a day to celebrate black achievement and note how far black culture had reached out of St. Louis. Everyone present must have taken great pleasure in that fact, and the Berry family especially must have taken great pride in the possibility that Lucy could soon be emulating the success of Handy and Hughes.

Although Lucy did not place in the competition in Chicago, her appearance at the festival gave her musical aspirations a huge boost. Later that year, the December 8 edition of the *St. Louis Argus* carried the story of her next major appearance, her first full recital, at the Phyllis Wheatley branch of the YMCA on Sunday, December 17. The story, which carried the headline "Music Festival Star to Appear," would have given the rest of the family some consolation at the end of a year that had seen one member fighting for freedom half a world away and another, half a state away, deprived of it.

Charles Berry's return from prison on his 21st birthday in October 1947 followed hard on the heels of brother Henry's discharge from the army and was marked by two events of tremendous significance, one nationally and one personally. In October 1945, a quiet couple named J. D. and Ethel Shelley moved into their newly purchased home two blocks from the Berry's at 4600 Labadie. Within a month, the black couple found themselves named in a lawsuit. The previous owners of the house, Louis and Fern Kraemer, attempted to evict them; the purchase of the house, the lawsuit claimed, had contravened the race-restrictive property covenant that was still being recognized by the area's white residents. The court battle lasted for almost three years. First, the Shelleys won in local court; then, the Kraemers won on appeal in the Missouri Supreme Court. Finally, in May 1948, the U.S. Supreme Court, persuaded by NAACP attorney Thurgood Marshall's arguments, overturned the state ruling, effectively outlawing discrimination in housing sales throughout the country. It was a tremendous victory for blacks nationwide, but it was to have unexpectedly disastrous consequences for the Ville. Within the next 20 years, the population of the area plummeted by nearly 40 percent, destroying the neighborhood and lessening the effect of the area's black institutions that were so instrumental to Charles Berry's upbringing.

But the Ville was to play one more significant role in the life of Charles Berry that May. Almost every day, as a child growing up on Goode Avenue, he would have walked past the stately southern columns of the St. Louis Colored Orphan's Home on the block next to the Berry family home. From 1919 to 1943, the president of the home was a woman who enjoyed near-legendary status in the Ville and beyond: Annie Turnbo Malone. Born in 1869, she had risen against all probability to become one of the first black women millionaires in the country through the sale and manufacture of Poro Beauty products. So successful had she become that, by 1917, she had opened Poro College, a training facility for Poro agents and beauticians that, in its heyday, employed more than 200 residents of the Ville.

Poro College lasted only a decade in St. Louis; by 1930, Malone had transferred the entire operation to Chicago. But her legacy remained in the form of the children's home, which she had helped build with a personal donation of $10,000. On May Day, 1922, the home held a mortgage-burning celebration, beginning a tradition of May Day parades that have been a fixture on the Ville's calendar ever since. Two years later, the home and parade were named in her honor; it was at this celebration at Tandy Park in 1948, just seven months after his release from prison, that Charles Berry, in the shadow of Sumner High School and over the road from the children's home and the house in which he was born, first met Themetta Suggs.

Themetta was a small, strikingly beautiful woman; Merle Silverstein, an attorney who represented Berry in the late 1950s and early 1960s, described her as looking like "a Polynesian princess." At the time of their meeting, she was working in a dry-cleaning store, and Charles Berry must have seemed like a good catch to her, despite his prison record; after all, he was hardworking, ambitious, and, above all, handsome. Within five months, the two were married.

By 1950, Charles Berry and Toddy, as he affectionately called his wife, had moved to a small three-roomed cottage on Whittier Street, one block east of Goode Avenue and several blocks north of Homer G. Philips hospital. Not long after they moved in, in October of that year, their first child, Darlin Ingrid, was born. For all intents and purposes, the new Berry family seemed ready to enjoy a lifetime of quiet domestic bliss.

Meanwhile, the racial climate in St. Louis was beginning to change, mirroring the national impetus toward civil rights that had begun under the Truman administration. In 1947, a small group of St. Louis citizens, blacks and whites, formed a local chapter of the Chicago-based Committee of Racial Equality (CORE). Almost immediately, inspired by the teachings of Mahatma Gandi, they began a campaign of nonviolent opposition to Jim Crow segregation, especially in the downtown area of St. Louis. Their first targets, over a decade before similar protests launched a wave of sit-ins across the South and ushered in the civil rights era of the 1960s, were lunch counters. Some protests, like the one at the Katz Drug Store on Eighth and Washington, met with almost immediate success; others, such as the one at the Stix, Baer, and Fuller department store, went on for an extended period. One by one, however, the organization managed to integrate many of the lunch counters in the downtown department, dime, and drug stores in the early years of the 1950s. St. Louis's movie theaters also began a process of desegregation. The American was the first to desegregate in January 1953, in response to a slump in the motion-picture business; it was followed by the Ambassador in November of the same year.

Small wonder, then, that in May 1954, Langston Hughes marveled in his weekly *Chicago Defender* column at the changes he had seen since visiting St. Louis as a small boy. "When we changed trains there to go into Arkansas and Texas," he recalled, "we were put into a car with only colored people— my first segregated car, and from that time on in my mind, St. Louis and Jim Crow were connected.

"But this Spring of our Lord, 1954," he went on, "I was informed that I might make a reservation at any of the downtown hotels." At the Statler, he wrote, "I was never more courteously received nor more politely served at any hotel where I've stopped anywhere in the world." And, echoing the words of one of the Reverend John Jasper's greatest sermons, quoted at the beginning of the piece, Hughes related his incredulity to his audience. "All I could say to myself," he exclaimed, "was, 'De Sun Do Move!'"

The majority of these attempts at integration passed without incident; in fact, the mainstream white newspapers in the city felt that they were unworthy of any coverage at all. But one particularly ugly racial incident occurred in St. Louis at this time, when CORE attempted to desegregate the swimming pool in Fairgrounds Park, just north of the Ville. At first, the demonstration seemed to pay immediate dividends, when Mayor Joseph Darst ordered that all of the city's recreational facilities be open to blacks. But the following year, a group of white residents in the neighborhood rioted; the pool was eventually integrated by court order, although one CORE member recalls that, shortly after, the pool was filled in and tennis courts built in its place.

But if prospects for social harmony were beginning to improve, prospects for work in the black community were not. One statistic suggests that in 1950, of the 109,000 blacks working in the state of Missouri, nearly 80 percent were relegated to manual, unskilled labor. With the black population of St. Louis increasing, it was not surprising that it was difficult to find work, and Charles Berry was typical of his time. Between 1948 and 1955, Berry worked a number of jobs and eked out a living to support his family, which by that time had grown to two daughters with the birth of Melody on November 1, 1952.

Berry's occupations at the time give us a real sense of the philosophy and motivation that he carried with him his whole life. Two jobs as a factory worker, at Fisher Body Motors on Natural Bridge Avenue and at Chevrolet Shell on Goodfellow making 105-millimeter shells, did not last long. For about a year, before the two moved into the house on Whittier, Berry and

Themetta lived in an apartment on Delmar rent-free when Berry took on the position of janitor for the building.

For a while after that, Berry trained as a beautician under the Poro system. Aside from the fact that he was following his sisters Thelma and Lucy (who had, by that time, abandoned her music career in favor of the less-glamorous but more stable occupation), there was another compelling reason for Berry to consider cosmetology as a career. As Annie Malone and her former partner Madame C. J. Walker had vividly shown to the residents of the Ville and nearly every black community across the country, hairdressing was a vital means to economic independence. Indeed, as early as 1853, Frederick Douglass, the former slave and abolitionist, had noted the significance of the occupation to blacks when he wrote in an editorial titled "Learn Trades or Starve" that "a few years ago, and a white barber would have been a curiosity." One historian has argued, "Barbershops, and beauty parlors, were independent businesses with a steady clientele and, as such, were important expressions of black entrepreneurial activity." It was, simply, another extension of Booker T. Washington's philosophy of economic independence, and as such would have been a tremendously attractive occupation to Charles Berry.

Photography—inspired by his cousin Harry Davis, who had now become a professional photographer in the St. Louis area—also interested Berry as a possible career at the time. In August 1955, when his first manager Jack Hooke flew out to St. Louis to have Berry sign his management contract, he was greeted at Lambert Field by Berry, who handed him his business card. "I remember," said Hooke, "it had his picture on it, with long hair, and it said 'Charles Berry, Photographer.'" And throughout those years, between jobs or whenever the occasion demanded, Berry helped out in his father's construction business.

Late in 1950 or in early 1951, Berry added another occupation to his growing list of money-making ventures. Taking the musical knowledge he had acquired in childhood through the gospel music prized by his parents and heard weekly at the Antioch Baptist church as a foundation, adding to it the sophistication of Lucy's classical training and the illicit rhythms of jump blues learned in Algoa, Berry began to turn his attention to music. His old Sumner schoolmate Tommy Stevens had noticed that Berry, encouraged by local DJ and guitarist Joe Sherman, had become so proficient on the guitar that he was capable of playing in public. Stevens had a three-piece combo that had a regular weekend gig at Huff's Garden in East St. Louis, and in June of 1952, he invited Berry to join them and replace their guitar player.

Berry's progress in this new business venture appeared rapid. By September, he approached cousin Harry Davis about taking some pictures to be used for self-promotion, and the resulting photo session was significant for a number of reasons. First, the images were ones that would endure for many years to come: Berry in his white zoot suit, a confident smile on his face as he is picked out by a single white spotlight while cradling a small guitar. Next, and more significant, was the fact that the shoot featured Berry alone. These were not pictures of a band; Tommy Stevens is nowhere to be seen. And, perhaps most important, the negatives appeared in Harry's files as "Berry, Charles E. A. as Chuck Berryn." Charles was playing the devil's music, something that Henry Berry surely would not tolerate. Out of respect and fear that the two would slip back into the kind of relationship they had during Berry's last years of high school, before Berry had been imprisoned and smeared the family name, Berry added an "n" onto his last name and assumed, perhaps for the first time, the professional stage name of Chuck. A thin disguise, perhaps, but one that might hold weight in the unlikely event that someone from the neighborhood accidentally entered Huff's Garden and wondered if the fellow playing crude and lascivious music was Henry and Martha's boy.

A few months earlier, an unknown boogie-woogie piano player named Johnnie Johnson had arrived in town from Chicago. Born in 1924 and raised by his aunt and uncle in rural West Virginia, he had worked for a time in the early 1940s on the Ford assembly line in Detroit. After a stint in the Marines and a number of fruitless years in Chicago, where his lifelong dependency on alcohol first developed, he decided to try his luck playing piano in East St. Louis. Johnson eventually landed a gig a few blocks away from Huff's Garden, at the larger Cosmopolitan Club, leading his own threesome. The Sir John's trio—Johnson on piano, Ebby Hardy on drums, and Alvin Bennett on saxophone—began to achieve some modest success entertaining the tough crowds in the blue-collar town.

Although it lay only a few hundred yards across the muddy Mississippi, East St. Louis might just as well have been another world. It was a town built on heavy industry—the stockyards and packing plants of meat companies like Swift, Armour, and Morris and the foundries of the Missouri Malleable Iron Company and the Aluminum Ore Company—and rooted in violence. During World War I, the black population had more than doubled as blacks answered America's call for increased industrial output by migrating from the rural South to the industrial North in unprecedented numbers. When workers for the Aluminum Ore Company walked out in April 1917, the company attempted to break the strike by bringing in some of the newly arrived black workers. The action confirmed white suspicions that their jobs were threatened by the influx of migrants, and a series of racial confrontations culminated in a riot on July 2. The resulting death toll, conservatively estimated at nine whites and 39 blacks, made the incident second only to the Los Angeles riot of May 1992 as the worst race riot of the century in the United States.

For Chuck Berry, the 15-minute trip from the Ville down Easton Avenue and over the Mississippi to East St. Louis must have been quite an experience. Johnnie Johnson recalled that it was a "wide open town . . . clubs stayed open all night." Most of the bars had violent reputations. Johnson recalled the Moonlight Inn on Tudor as being a particularly rough club: "It should have been named the 'Bucket of Blood.' Somebody would get in a fight and drunk and they'd roll and all. We played right on the floor, we didn't have no stage, and they'd get fighting and knock the drums over and whatever." Even at the Cosmo, trouble was never far from erupting; Joe Lewis, a police officer and the Cosmopolitan's owner, always carried a gun with him. "He'd walk out in the middle of a crowd and fire his service revolver up in the air to break up a fight," Johnson remembered. In a park on the opposite side of the street from the Cosmo, Johnson himself, on a break during a show one evening, was stabbed by the woman who eventually became his second wife; she was jealous that he had been talking to another woman. He returned to play the gig bandaged and covered in blood, much to the band's amazement. The sights and sounds of the town must have alternately shocked and thrilled the Baptist deacon's son; compared to the refinement of the Ville, his sister's classical piano, and the black poetry and literature read by his mother, East St. Louis must have seemed like a cautionary tale in a preacher's sermon.

Stevens's and Johnson's bands could not have been more different. The Sir John's Trio played mostly pop standards from the 1930s and 1940s: "Stormy Weather," "Stardust," and "The Lazy River," Johnson recalled, were all part of the band's repertoire at the time. The standout number, at least as far as Johnson was concerned, was an instrumental virtuoso piano piece Johnson called "Johnnie's Boogie," a reworking of a piece originally recorded in 1931 by the renowned boogie-woogie pianist Meade "Lux" Lewis titled "Honky Tonk Train Blues." During the 1940s, small combos of musicians like Louis Jordan's Tympani Five had taken the arpeggiated eight-to-the-bar bass line and created a hybrid of jazz and blues called jump blues. This bass line was so versatile a musical foundation that it survived the transition of instrumentation in popular music; pianos and saxophones began to give way to electric guitars and basses, but the bass line lived on in various forms. Thus, Ike Turner, who was soon to become another regular in the East St. Louis and St. Louis club circuit, used a slight variation of it as the basis for the 1951 number 1 R&B hit "Rocket 88," put out under Jackie Brenston's name, the vocalist and sax player for Ike Turner's Kings of Rhythm. It was old wine in new wineskins, but black audiences in East St. Louis and elsewhere found its up-tempo bouncing rhythm irresistible.

The Tommy Stevens Combo, meanwhile, mined a different musical vein. For the most part, they played the blues and black pop standards. "Muddy Waters, Elmore James, Big Joe Turner . . . Nat Cole . . . and Harry Belafonte . . . were the types of songs that made up our selections, along with the backbone of our program, which was always the blues," Berry remembered years later. But Berry brought something to the Tommy Stevens Combo it had not previously had, something that the Sir John's Trio sorely lacked: showmanship. It started one night when Berry, in the middle of a set, began to play a country-and-western tune. The effect of this audacious move on the all-black crowd was remarkable. "The people seemed to really get a kick out of it," recalled Johnnie Johnson, who checked out the rival band's show when he could. "They'd be hollerin' and dancin' havin' a good ol' time."

The reaction of the audience was not lost on Tommy Stevens; in fact, Berry recalls the bandleader encouraging him to go further. Toward the end of 1952, their act had become much more visual. "They were doing kind of a variety. . . . It was more of a clown act, really," Johnson remembered. "The saxophone player, you know, he had these phony eyes, you know, and he'd get to playing and he could do something . . . make his eyes come out. I don't know how. But more of a Spike Jones type of thing." Indeed, their repertoire was beginning to expand to include novelty and show numbers. Johnson recalled one, a country shuffle called "Mary Jo" that told of a woman who "was so hot, she went to Alaska to melt the snow." Another, called "The Buggy Ride," seemed to have been popular in East St. Louis among a number of acts; it was an improvisational piece in which Berry acted out his attempts to seduce a woman while taking a carriage ride with her.

Clearly, in a very short time, Chuck Berry had learned what it took to stand out in a competitive music scene, and Johnnie Johnson was quick to see Berry's potential. On New Year's Eve, 1952, Johnson placed a fateful call from East St. Louis to the Ville; Alvin Bennett, the saxophone player for the trio, had been taken ill, and Johnson felt Berry was just the man to replace him. New Year's Eve has always been the most important night of the year for entertainers; the music has to be of the highest quality to satisfy the large and boisterous crowds, and the money is usually double or triple that of a regular show. The arrangement, then, was beneficial to both parties. Berry could fill in for Bennett and provide the visual entertainment sorely missing in the Sir John's Trio and, in return, he could play in a larger club for more money and with a better band. As Johnson said later:

> Chuck brought something to the group that was missin' . . . that dancin' and playin' to the crowd. Ebby and me, Alvin, we was quiet, didn't none of us sing or dance around. We'd been playin' music for a long time and we were good at it. We played for the love of playin' and we figured our music would do the talkin'. That's the mistake that a lot of musicians make, and 'cause of that, a lot of the best ones never get out of the small clubs. It don't matter who's better at playin', although that matters some. It's who can hold the crowd. People want to be entertained.

And hold the crowd he did. That night, Johnny Johnson saw the full effect the charismatic Berry could have on an audience. When Berry broke into "Mary Jo," with Ebby Hardy banging out the insistent country backbeat on the drums, the crowd went wild. Although it was a "hillbilly" song, and the crowd at the Cosmo was predominantly a blues crowd, "The people loved him," Johnson remembered. "They just ate it up. And I felt really happy for Chuck, 'cause . . . that was real brave of him. I guess I should have known. The public was always lookin' for somethin' new, and a group of black men playing hillbilly songs was definitely new." It was a revelation that certainly was not lost on Joe Lewis, the Cosmopolitan's owner, who approached Johnson at the end of the night and immediately requested that the arrangement with Berry become permanent.

It would be easy to argue—as Johnson's biographer Travis Fitzpatrick, Rolling Stones' guitarist Keith Richards, and others have done—that the relationship between Berry and Johnson, both musical and personal, was one of opposites bringing to a partnership something that the other could not. Berry, they have argued, was simply a showman and not a musician; a singer of "hillbilly" songs and not of the blues; and, when the two later began to record, a lyricist providing words to Johnson's music. The world—in particular, the musical world—is too complex to support such binary oppositions, and this analysis ignores some fundamental facts about Berry's life. Berry brought to the relationship musical ability beyond the "hillbilly" songs of Huff's Garden and the Cosmo. The gospel songs of the Antioch Baptist church, the classical music of sister Lucy, the vocal harmony and jump blues of Po' Sam, and the influence of Tommy Stevens all formed part of the extensive musical knowledge Berry brought to the relationship. Johnson and Berry had not begun as equals, but as 1953 wore on and the engagements at the Cosmopolitan became steady, Berry's influence on the trio began to outstrip that of his counterpart. And Berry's ambition, fueled by the work ethic learned from his father, the Ville, and Booker T. Washington, inspired him to take the Sir John's Trio to bigger and better heights and paralleled Johnson's descent into alcoholism.

Unsurprisingly, then, the two were headed for an inevitable conflict. It was precipitated by Berry's clumsy and insensitive attempt to wrestle control of the band away from Johnson. After a show one night at the Cosmo, Berry pocketed the change the band had accumulated during the evening in their tip jar. On the ride back home, when it became apparent to Johnson that Berry was not going to divide the money equally, Johnson decided to bring matters to a head.

As Berry pulled the car over in front of Johnson's house, Johnson asked for his share:

He got this look on his face, cold as ice. "They came to see me, not you. Nobody cares 'bout you." I kept my cool and said, "Well, I know you're new to this scene, but we are a trio and we're gonna split the tips three ways." He just sat there tryin' to stare me down and I stared him right back. Next thing I know, Chuck jumps out the car and says, "You want the money, come and take it!"

The normally passive Johnson, bigger and stronger than Berry, decided not to back down; he jumped out of the car, ducked Berry's first punch, and slammed him against a nearby fence. "Give me my money," Johnson demanded. And Berry relented. "He gave me the money he owed me and Ebby," Johnson remembered, adding "that was the end of that, and Chuck never tried to threaten me again. That was the only problem we ever had. From then on, everything was cool."

But it was not. Although he had misjudged the situation, using the kind of strong-arm tactics more appropriate to dealing with bar owners than bandmates, the fact of the matter was that Berry's influence on the trio had surpassed that of his more laid-back partner. Johnson's drinking and laissez-faire attitude were getting in the way of Berry's ambitious plans. After a year of playing with the Sir John's Trio, a year of bars and clubs in seedy East St. Louis, Berry was ready to see if he could take his music to the next level. And if Johnson and Hardy were not prepared to go with him, he would do it on his own.

At some point in 1954, Tommy Stevens, Berry's old friend and bandleader from the Huff's Garden days, called him with an interesting business proposition. The Crank Club, located on Vanderventer about three blocks east of the Berry home on Whittier, was looking for a house band; they would pay almost twice what the Cosmo was paying. After a brief audition with Stevens's band, Berry got the job and immediately put together a band: Richard Culph on saxophone, Erskine Rogers on piano, and Bill Erskine on drums. Together, as the posters Berry had professionally printed, they would "crank it up at the Crank Club" every Monday, Wednesday, Friday, and Saturday.

It was a move that angered Joe Lewis; it was obvious to the patrons that Berry's departure from the Cosmo was a big loss. Although the Sir John's Trio was able to cover the loss of a guitar player instrumentally, vocally Johnny Johnson was not able to handle Berry's singing chores. And there was no focal point to the band, no one to entertain the crowd and give the band a visual presence. In a short time, Chuck Berry had created a space that was difficult to fill.

The new gig at the Crank Club occurred at the same time that a new and rather unexpected opportunity came along. At some point that summer, Berry was approached by Oscar Washington, owner of Ballad Records, a small, independent St. Louis label, about the possibility of playing on a recording Washington was going to record Joe Alexander, a largely unknown local singer who went by the popular nickname of Calypso Joe. A native of New Orleans, Alexander had moved to St. Louis as a child with his parents at some point in the 1940s, and had won the Ted Mack Amateur Show in 1947. After several years playing in St. Louis, mostly at the Casbah Lounge, Alexander was drafted for a two-year stint in the army; by August of 1954, however, Calypso Joe was ready to hit the big time with a song he and Washington had written called "Oh Maria."

On August 13, Washington, Alexander, bongo player Freddy Golden, and Berry, still going under the moniker of "Chuck Berryn," recorded four songs at Premier Studios in St. Louis. The two songs that were eventually released on Ballad were fairly unremarkable to the rest of the world, but to Chuck Berry they would have been an inspiration. "Oh Maria" was a Harry Belafonte-esque calypso about a man who caught a boat from Trinidad to America and was kicked out of his apartment by his girlfriend, "just because me I no work." The third verse, in particular, contained a number of elements that were to become Berry trademarks in the years to come. The narrator tells how he tried to impress his girlfriend by buying a fancy car ("a Dynaflow"), but this only gets him into trouble with the tax man, who pithily says "Pay the taxes without fail/And if I don't, I go to jail." The humor, the references to cars, and the narrative story in the lyrics were all elements Berry had incorporated into his act in the previous two years. As the musicians played through the songs in the dark studio, it must have occurred to Berry that Alexander was a man who was recording his song, making permanent what was always so transient on stage.

The B-side, "I Hope These Words Will Find You Well," was equally unremarkable save for another, albeit brief, taste of what was to come. After a nondescript, two-verse vocal over a Latin beat, a tentative guitar solo is heard. It is unclear whether it was Washington or Berry who took the solo that summer afternoon, but in the middle of the solo, the guitar player uses a reverse bend and a quick five-note arpeggio turnaround, reminiscent of T-Bone Walker, the Texas blues guitarist and singer whose music became incredibly influential in the late 1940s and early 1950s. Both were trademarks of Berry's guitar style during the latter part of the decade, and it is not too far-fetched to assume that Chuck Berry was making his first halting steps toward music history.

Both Berry and Johnson have denied that the session ever took place, but the evidence of the American Federation of Musicians' recording contract for the session is fairly conclusive. For Berry, the session must have been a revelation. His fascination with technology, already well-developed through his friendship with Harry Davis and the wire-recorder Berry had purchased four years earlier, must have been piqued by the experience.

Not long after, Johnnie Johnson and Joe Lewis called. Would Berry consider coming back to his old gig at the Cosmo, they asked? Berry considered the offer and made the first major deal of his fledgling musical career. He would come back, he told them, but only as bandleader and only with a contract. Johnson agreed, having no head for business and little ambition other than a regular-paying club gig. There was one other stipulation, he told Johnson: The combo was going to aggressively pursue a recording contract. On this, Johnson had little to say. "Nobody ever thought about making records," he was to recall years later. "But Chuck got hung up on the idea. I told him I didn't know nothin' 'bout the record business myself, but if he wanted to make a record I wouldn't stand in his way." The only problem was, how were they going to do that? Oscar Washington had made it clear to Berry that he was not interested in recording him at the time he recorded "Oh Maria" and, at the time, St. Louis had no other label, big or small, to record on. The answer would come to Berry several months later, after a chance encounter with his hero, blues great Muddy Waters, in Chicago, and a meeting with a 48-year-old Polish Jew named Leonard Chess. Together, Chess and Berry would change the lives of millions of white American teenagers and countless others all over the world.

3

Maybellene

"You could tell right away," says Phil [Chess], who doesn't bother a bit to conceal his admiration for Berry. "He had something special that—I don't know what you'd call it. But he had it."

—Peter Guralnick, *Feel Like Going Home*

There was little to distinguish 4750 South Cottage Grove from any of the other businesses on the street. A single-story, red-brick building on the corner of the block, it sat next door to Victory Stationary, a print shop owned by Russ Fratto, 4750's landlord. On the other side of the street were an auto-parts store, a tire company, and a carpet company, and up the block were a liquor store, a bank, and small restaurant. On a Monday morning, at some point in late April or early May 1955, Chuck Berry walked off the street and into the building's small reception area. To the right of the desk in front of him, he noticed a narrow hallway leading to an office and, behind that, out of sight, lay a larger room reserved for rehearsals and recording sessions. If he had been expecting Broadway, or Hollywood Boulevard, or even the Grand Avenue of his hometown, he was sadly mistaken. There was precious little show-business glamour to be found on the South Side of Chicago.

Several days earlier, Berry had driven to Chicago from St. Louis with an old friend from Sumner, Ralph Burris. Although he has always maintained that Chess Records was the first and only record company he visited, before or during the trip he may well have planned to visit all of the Chicago record companies; by the mid-1950s, Chicago boasted several. It is entirely possible—as Leonard Chess, the man he was visiting that May morning, maintained years later—that he began at Mercury, a major label headquartered among the high-rise buildings on upscale Wacker Drive in the Chicago Loop, the heart of Chicago's white business district. If he did, it would have been a very ambitious choice for a newcomer to the business.

By the early 1950s, the music business was dominated by a handful of major labels—Mercury, Decca, RCA-Victor, Columbia, Capitol, and MGM—most of whom concentrated on marketing pop music to the white population. Of the six majors, only Mercury and Decca had shown any real interest in the kind of R&B music that Berry and others were making at the time, but they stopped short of signing black artists in favor of having white acts cover rhythm and blues songs. If Berry did visit Mercury, his welcome uptown would have been very short indeed.

Berry and Burris then headed to Chicago's South Side, home to a different kind of record label that would have been a far more logical choice for Berry's rough-and-ready homemade recordings. A new breed of record company had sprung up to capitalize on the growing market for black artists and their music. Although the major labels had been interested in so-called race recordings since the 1920s, and some recordings, such as Bessie Smith's "Down Hearted Blues" on Columbia, had even sold well by pop standards (Smith's recording sold an estimated 750,000 copies when it was released in 1923), the audience for such records was small and hard to reach. It existed for the most part in the scattered and impoverished rural communities in the South. But the huge migration of blacks from the agricultural South to the industrial North, spurred by the growth of manufacturing industries during World War II, created concentrated black communities in the large Northern cities. By the late 1940s, they constituted a visible market for black music, about a million and a quarter strong in the North, or about 6 percent of the American record-buying market. Even so, sales of a hit blues record could only reach in the 50,000- to 80,000-copy range in the early 1950s, with a respectable R&B hit only managing perhaps four or five times that number—hardly enough to sustain the interest of the major labels. But they were numbers that attracted the attention of smaller businessmen, who seized on the opportunity to market music by black artists to the black population. Known as independents, or indies, they began springing up in large numbers (more than 100 were in business by 1952). Their names are synonymous with the rise of rhythm and blues and rock and roll in 1950s America: Atlantic and Savoy in New York; King in Cincinnati; Modern, Specialty, and Imperial in Los Angeles; Sun in Memphis; Duke/Peacock in Houston; and Chance, Vee Jay, and Chess in Chicago.

Berry's account of the visit to Chicago that May makes no mention of whether he visited Chance or Vee Jay, but Johnnie Johnson recalls that Berry did visit at least one independent label on the South Side. "First place he went was Vee Jay," Johnson maintained years later, "but they turned him down flat. Wasn't no surprise; they was strict blues." They were also a black-owned company and, at least at this point in their history, were more interested in producing regional R&B hits; as such, a singer like Berry with aspirations toward the white pop market would hardly have interested them.

Both Berry and Johnson agree, however, that at the end of the day Berry and Burris ended up at the Palladium, a South Side club where Muddy Waters happened to be playing. At the end of the night, Berry approached the blues singer and asked how he could go about making records. "See Leonard Chess," Waters replied. "Yeah, Chess Records on 47th and Cottage." And so, bright and early the following Monday morning, Chuck Berry found himself on Cottage Grove in the cramped quarters of Chess Records, face to face with the man who would change his life irrevocably.

On the surface at least, the two men were an odd combination. Nine years Chuck Berry's senior, Leonard Chess had emigrated to Chicago with his family from the Polish ghetto of Motele in 1928. He was, by all accounts, hardened by the experience of growing up on the tough streets of Chicago's South Side. For eight years, beginning in the early 1940s, he had been in the liquor business, first as the owner of two liquor stores (Cut-Rate Liquor and 708 Liquor), then as a bar owner (the Macomba Lounge). At Cut-Rate, he had witnessed a knifing, and his father had been beaten and robbed in the 708 store one Sunday morning. In the Macomba Lounge, bloody fights were commonplace; Leonard Chess's son Marshall, at the age of 5, remembered one fight when shots were fired. Anyone meeting Leonard Chess at the time immediately noted that his language mirrored the hardness of the South Side. The bar business was "a rough fuck," he used to say, and his son Marshall recalls musicians sending his father Mother's Day cards because he would call everyone a "motherfucker." For Chuck Berry, the immediate impression must have been that Leonard Chess had far more in common with East St. Louis than he did with the Ville.

But underneath, the two shared some strong common bonds. First, both had witnessed prejudice first hand, Berry as an African American during Jim Crow, and Chess as a Jewish immigrant. In *Spinning Blues into Gold*, her history of Chess Records, Nadine Cohodas described the relationship Chess later enjoyed with his black artists as "the convergence of outsiders," the shared experience of being excluded from mainstream American culture. Malcolm Chisholm, who engineered many of the great Chess recordings, agreed with this assessment. "They didn't come into the country with any prejudice about blacks one way or the other," he observed in a 1989 interview. Jewish immigrants were also "prejudiced against"; moreover, "having never seen blacks" in their home country, they were less likely, in Chisholm's eyes, to carry the cultural baggage of racism that many Americans bore at the time. The link between the two worlds also extended to music, the common language of Leonard Chess and all of the musicians who came in and out of 4750 South Cottage. Ralph Bass, a seasoned veteran of the music business who joined the Chess operation in 1960, once told journalist Peter Guralnick, "You gotta remember one thing, there's a close tie between the Negro and the Jewish people. . . . There's an affinity between blues and Hebrew music. I hear that blues in a minor key, and hey, baby, I'm back in synagogue."

But Chuck Berry, steeped in the philosophy of Booker T. Washington, found an even deeper connection with Leonard Chess. Aside from his business ventures in the world of alcohol, Leonard worked at various times as a milkman, shoe salesman, and a junk dealer in his father's business. An Irish immigrant in the early part of the century once commented that "A Jew would rather earn five dollars a week for himself than ten dollars a week for someone else." It is a comment that, racism aside, holds some truth: Blacks and Jews alike, especially those who had experienced the harsh realities of the Depression, realized that financial independence from the mainstream, white economy was necessary for their survival. Right from their first meeting, then, Chuck Berry realized that the two had a common, entrepreneurial background; in time, Berry came to trust Leonard Chess's advice in matters of music as well as business.

Not surprisingly, Marshall Chess later recalled,

> [My] father and [Berry] had a very close relationship, extremely close. Next to Muddy Waters, I think he was the artist he was the most friendly, or more friendly with. Chuck came to him, to my recollection, for a lot of advice, on a lot of different things. Chuck and he had a very good relationship. . . . It was a real symbiotic relationship.

And, as Berry noted some 30 years later, it was a relationship based not just on business but on mutual respect. Leonard Chess, he wrote in *The Autobiography*, would not use the language of the Chicago streets around him: "He never used profanity while doing business with me at any time in our affiliation." And Chuck Berry's respect for Leonard Chess would have been built on his admiration for a man who had achieved the kind of success he had only dreamed of.

Chess's success had been almost a decade in the making, beginning not long after Leonard opened the doors of the Macomba in 1947. When Leonard learned that one of the local singers performing at the club, Andrew Tibbs, was attracting some attention from record-company talent scouts, he decided to try his luck with a new venture. He booked time at a local studio and recorded Tibbs himself, then entered into an agreement with Evelyn and Charles Aron, fellow South Side Jews who had begun a fledgling indie label, Aristocrat. With the release of Tibbs's song, "Union Man Blues," on the Arons' label, Leonard Chess added a new occupation, record-company salesman, to his already extensive resume.

For a while, the relationship between the Arons and Leonard Chess seemed to benefit both immensely, especially when Leonard signed Muddy

Waters to the label and both Waters and Tibbs had a succession of modest regional hits. By the end of 1949, however, Evelyn Aron had decided to leave the company, leaving Aristocrat to Leonard Chess. When the Macomba burned down in the fall of 1950, Leonard and his brother Phil were free to concentrate solely on record production; at the suggestion of Aristocrat's Memphis distributor earlier in the year, they started a new label simply called Chess Records.

Almost immediately, the label achieved as much success as an indie label could reasonably expect, marketing as it did a rough and powerful electric urban blues. Like most independent labels, the small size of the Chess operation allowed the owners to take risks with both the choice of material and the means of recording it. From the first record released on the Chess label, Gene Ammons's "My Foolish Heart," the Chess brothers began to innovate, using arguably the first echo chamber on a record, a primitive affair consisting of a microphone and a speaker set up in a bathroom in Universal Studios in Chicago. The song was a hit, at least by independent standards, selling well in Chicago and other Northern industrial cities and helping Leonard Chess to set up a network of distributors for the label's releases, the lifeblood of any independent record company.

The second release on Chess was by Muddy Waters, who became synonymous with the label for the next 20 years. The song, "Rolling Stone," also was a modest hit, selling between 60,000 and 80,000 copies and giving Leonard Chess the impetus to begin setting up distributors in the South, which he did by driving 5,000 miles every three months for the next five years. With a solid market for its releases in the South and Midwest, Chess was able to release a number of significant recordings throughout the 1950s. Among them were Jackie Brenston's "Rocket 88" in 1951, recorded by Sam Phillips at Sun Studios in Memphis, licensed to Chess, and regarded by many as the first true rock and roll record; "Moanin' at Midnight" by Howlin' Wolf; Willie Mabon's "I Don't Know" and "I'm Mad"; and "Juke" by Muddy Waters's harmonica player, Little Walter.

"Juke," released on the newly formed Checker subsidiary label, was a good example of how the indies could take far greater risks than the majors. According to Marshall Chess, his father and uncle repeatedly said of unusual recordings, "That's different; it just might sell." Although previously they had never released a harmonica instrumental, let alone one drenched with their favored echo-effect, they knew their market well enough to take the chance. For the sake of venturing a few hundred dollars in recording, pressing, and promoting the disk—a fraction of the amount it would cost the majors to get the song to market—the Chesses had another hit on their hands.

By the time of "Juke's" release in 1952, Leonard and Phil Chess had demonstrated a consistent ability to read black musical tastes. The result was a string of hits, modest by major label standards, but big enough to help influence national trends. But company distribution had yet to really penetrate the lucrative Northeast market, although it was to do so in a large way a year after the release of "Juke," when the Chess brothers began their relationship with disc jockey Alan Freed.

By 1953, Alan Freed had become the most influential of a small band of white deejays who were beginning to play black records to a growing white audience across the country. In that year, *Variety* reported that more than 260 radio stations nationwide were programming R&B music. Freed's evening radio show on Cleveland's WJW, which was first broadcast in 1951, was beginning to attract a lot of attention. An R&B dance promoted by Freed in August 1953 and advertised exclusively on his show attracted not only 10,000 people from the Cleveland area but national attention in *Billboard*. And, by December, Freed's "Moondog House" show was being taped and rebroadcast on WNJR out of Newark, New Jersey, the first station to program black music exclusively to the metropolitan New York area. By the end of the year, Freed was well placed to have a significant influence on the burgeoning market for R&B music.

That same month, Freed booked Little Walter to appear at his Moondog Coronation Ball in Akron, Ohio, and, at around the same time, had sent to Chess a demo of a song called "Nadine" by an unknown vocal group named the Coronets. They were the second doo-wop group that Freed agreed to manage; the previous year, he had introduced a Cleveland group known as the Crazy Sounds, whom he had renamed the Moonglows (to tie in with his Moondog moniker) and placed with rival Chicago label Chance. "Nadine" was released by Chess in September 1953; it was a hit in the Midwest and was the first of several Chess releases to be falsely credited to Freed (the song was actually written by a member of the group).

Although a second Coronets single, released at the end of the year, flopped and the Chess brothers dropped the group from the label, the relationship with Freed continued. In September 1954, Freed left his disc jockey position at WJW in Cleveland for WINS in New York, a move that made him arguably the most influential deejay in the country. Now, through Freed, the Chess brothers gained a foothold in the extensive and lucrative New York market.

The following month, the relationship between Freed and the Chess brothers was cemented when Freed encouraged the label to sign the Moonglows. Their first release, "Sincerely," became the first Chess R&B number 1 of 1955, selling 300,000 copies. As had become the practice with the first two Moonglows releases on Chance, the song was credited to its writer, Harvey Fuqua, and Freed. Freed, of course, had not written a note, but he had contributed something arguably of greater value to the song's success: He had guaranteed, for a percentage of the song's royalties, airplay on his radio show. This business arrangement, which the press was later to dub payola, was illegal, because it clearly created a conflict of interest for a deejay. According to the government, Freed—or anyone else—could not simultaneously promote a song and have a financial interest in its success. But the system, prevalent in one form or another throughout the history of the music business, leveled the playing field for the indies in the 1950s, in competing against the vast distribution and promotion resources of the majors. More important, it ensured the rise of rock and roll.

The success of "Sincerely" early in 1955 resulted in the immediate release of a white cover of the song by the McGuire Sisters on Coral, a subsidiary of Decca, which sold more than a million copies. It was yet one more example that the major labels could not ignore the volume of sales R&B tunes were achieving. But it also showed that they were still unwilling to sell black music by black artists; the more lucrative white pop market, a reflection of the society that had produced it, was still not ready for that. And so the practice continued unabated. Atlantic saw its hits "Sh' Boom" by The Chords and "Tweedle Dee" by LaVern Baker covered by white artists The Crew Cuts and Georgia Gibbs, respectively, both for Mercury. But perhaps the most interesting example of this practice was another Atlantic song, Big Joe Turner's 1954 hit "Shake, Rattle, and Roll," which was immediately covered by Bill Haley on Decca. Haley's version of the song sanitized the lyrics for the white audience, however, with the opening lines from the Turner original, "Get out of that bed/And wash your face and hands," revised to the less controversial, "Get into that kitchen/And rattle those pots and pans."

But, for the Chess brothers, the success of "Sincerely" had demonstrated that one of their records could sell in major-label numbers. All of the elements were in place for something big, and they began to look for other acts that could achieve even greater success on the pop as well as the R&B chart. Once again, the brothers succeeded almost immediately. In February 1955, two struggling Chicago musicians, guitar player Ellas McDaniel and harp player Billy Boy Arnold, walked into the Chess offices with a demo disk of two songs, "I'm a Man" and "Uncle John." Phil was sufficiently impressed to ask them to return on the following day, when they played the songs again for Leonard Chess, Muddy Waters, and Little Walter. Responding to the different beat and unusual guitar sounds, Leonard took a chance on the new act and brought them into the studio to re-record the songs; on the suggestion of Billy Boy, Leonard renamed both the song "Uncle John" and the guitar player Bo Diddley. The subsequent release, in March, reached number 2 on the *Billboard* R&B chart and, although it did not appear on the pop chart,

Diddley's biographer, George White, maintains that the song eventually went on to sell more than a million copies. In May, Muddy Waters reworked Diddley's "I'm a Man," and the resulting new song, "Mannish Boy," provided Chess with another huge single, reaching number 9 on the R&B chart.

As successful as the first six months of 1955 had been for Chess, the releases had yet to "cross over" and achieve success on the white-dominated pop charts. All that was to change, however, with Chuck Berry's arrival on Cottage Grove. In their initial conversation, Berry impressed Leonard Chess with (in Berry's words) "the businesslike way I'd talked to him," and Chess agreed to hear some tapes Berry claimed he had made. Within a week, Berry had returned with a demo tape of some of the material he and Johnson had been playing at the Cosmo over the previous two years. The first, a piano-based blues titled "Wee Wee Hours," was unremarkable to Chess's ears; it was generic, a typical, run-of-the-mill blues number. Johnson, who had been playing the song's progression during breaks between sets at the Cosmo just to pass the time, realized as much years later when he described the song as being "nothing complicated," and "a regular old blues in G." Uninterested in the recording process and detached from the music business, Johnson felt that the song was their best shot at success. "I figured if they ever did end up makin' a record, then that would be the side people listened to, 'cause it was straight blues. 'Course," he added with hindsight, "I was wrong 'bout that."

However, another song on the tape, a more polished and complete performance of a song Berry had written, attracted Chess's attention. Almost immediately, recalled Phil Chess, they knew they had something. It was, in Phil's words,

> Different. Different from Bo, different from everybody. Like nothing we'd heard before. . . . We figured if we could get that sound down on record we'd have a hit. There was just something about the rhythm—the beat. The song had a whole new kind of feel to it. Leonard knew we had something.

And both Chess brothers were conscious of the fact that music was beginning to change, and the racial lines between popular music genres were beginning to blur. Phil said, "You could feel it. You could tell it was crossing over. We just didn't know how big it was going to be." And, added Leonard Chess, "The big beat, cars, and young love. It was a trend and we jumped on it."

The next person to hear the song was Willie Dixon, bassist, songwriter, arranger, and producer for Chess Records who was, in all likelihood, in the Cottage Grove offices at the time. His reaction was as immediate as Leonard and Phil's:

The first time Chuck Berry came there, we knew "Maybellene" could be a crack-shot hit. The minute I heard it, I knew it had that certain quality and feeling, a complete story with good understanding. The average youngster liked automobiles and racing, it had to go.

To Dixon's ears, though, Berry still had some work to do on the song. "Chuck had it sounding more like a country and western tune," he remembered, "but I always felt that some kind of bluesy idea or feeling that wasn't in there would make it a better song."

The song that had Cottage Grove buzzing that morning was "Ida Red," a breathless, two-minute burst of energy detailing the narrator's attempt to catch up to a girl named Ida Red, driving in her Cadillac Coup Deville while the song's protagonist pursued her in his V-8 Ford. In parts, the song owed small yet significant debts to other songs that shared the same name. "Ida Red" (or, as it was sometimes known, "Shootin' Creek") was a traditional dance-song that had been recorded in 1928 by Charlie Poole and the North Carolina Ramblers. Poole's original lyrics to the song were full of humorous exaggeration ("Ida Red she lives in town/Weighs three hundred and forty pounds," goes one verse, while a second tells that Ida "bit a hoecake half in two"). The versions Chuck Berry may well have been familiar with, however, were both recorded a little later. Bob Wills and His Texas Playboys recorded a version in 1938 whose only similarity with Berry's song and with the original folksong seems to have been the humor in the lyrics and the driving country 2/4 beat. Another version, recorded in 1952 by blues singer Amos Easton, recording under his usual pseudonym of Bumble Bee Slim, has a jazzier feel. Musically, Easton's and Berry's songs have little in common, although the double-string slurs in the guitar breaks in Easton's song are reminiscent of another one of Berry's admitted heroes, Carl Hogan of Louis Jordan's band. A third song, Bob Wills's sequel to his "Ida Red," called "Ida Red Likes the Boogie," may also have contributed musically to Berry's song. Recorded in 1949, its guitar parts featured a double-stopped bend that Chuck Berry would have first heard in the recordings of another one of his guitar heroes, T-Bone Walker.

But if the song the Chess brothers and Willie Dixon were listening to was an amalgam of other musical creations, lyrically the song was something entirely original. Fred Rothwell has made the case that the lyrics to the song were inspired by "Hot Rod Race," a song so popular in 1951 that four different artists had chart hits with it (Arkie Shibley, Ramblin' Jimmy Dolan, Red Foley, and Tiny Hill), inspiring Shibley to make four sequels that year with new lyrics over the old tune. In truth, however, the only thing the songs have in common is the idea of a car chase. The verbal play in Berry's song, like that in the original folksong, is full of tall-tale humor: Berry imagines that the "rain water blowin' all under my hood" was helping to cool his car's racing engine. Even the diction—Berry introduced the word "motorvating" to the English language—contributed to the overall effect and distinguished Berry's song as something very new.

Like all musicians taking their first tentative steps in their careers, Berry had woven existing genres and ideas together in "Ida Red" and given them his own twist. Perhaps "Ida Red" was not original in the sense that it was not solely the result of Berry's own creative abilities. But, as with all fledgling artists, the freshness, enthusiasm, and passion with which he approached the song gave it a new immediacy and vitality. It may not have been new, but in Chuck Berry's hands "Ida Red" sounded like it was.

On May 21, Berry wrote in *The Autobiography*, he, Johnnie Johnson, and drummer Ebby Hardy returned to Cottage Grove to record "Ida Red" for Chess. With the ubiquitous Willie Dixon on bass, the foursome set about capturing the excitement of performing "Ida Red" for a crowd at the Cosmo. It was to prove an ordeal; Berry recalled doing 35 takes of the song as Leonard and Phil Chess struggled to get the sound they wanted, improvising innovative recording techniques as they went. As Phil Chess later pointed out, the song was so new to them,

> we didn't have anything to compare it to. . . . We just kept playing with it, trying to get the sound down on the record that we heard in the studio. My brother came out with a phone book and a drumstick and started beating on it. We even had Chuck doing his vocals in the bathroom, so when his voice went through the pipes, we'd get an echo.

Johnson admitted his disinterest in the whole procedure; he "couldn't tell the difference between most of them [the takes]. . . . They just had us doin' it over and over and we was all gettin' tired."

At some point during the session, a dispute arose over the song's title. Those who were present agreed that it was Leonard Chess who pointed out to Berry that the title had already been taken and that, besides, it sounded too rural. But those present disagreed over exactly who came up with the new title and how. Johnnie Johnson remembered that the inspiration and eventual decision came from Leonard Chess:

> We started puttin' our heads together tryin' to come up with a title. See, it had to be something with the same number of syllables so Chuck could fit it into what he was already doin'. Well, we were sittin' there thinkin', when all of a sudden Leonard looked over in the corner and saw a bottle of Maybelline

mascara. Leonard got a big ol' smile on his face and said, "Why don't we call the damn thing 'Maybelline'?"

Significantly, in Johnson's version of the story, Chess's business savvy plays a small yet significant role. Johnson concluded his account by noting, "We had to change the spellin', 'cause Chess said he didn't want to get in trouble with the company, but that's where the name 'Maybellene' came from." It was a small but telling moment for Berry; years later, he was to adopt the same ploy in *The Autobiography*, as he changed the spellings of several people's names, presumably to avoid any legal problems with them. And, in a further attempt to hide "Maybellene's" origins, Berry also used *The Autobiography* to make a claim that he had originally named the song "Ida May," not "Ida Red," and that the song was named after a cow in a storybook he had read when he was 8.

The May 21 session concluded with the recording of the other song Berry had presented to Chess earlier that month. "Wee Wee Hours" had now been polished with Berry's words; "when Chess asked us for another song," Johnson recalled, "Chuck had me play that blues again and he started puttin' words to it. Wasn't but fifteen minutes later we had 'Wee Wee Hours.'" Then, late that night, Berry, Johnson, and Hardy packed up their equipment and made the 300-mile trip back to St. Louis. Typically for the day, all had been paid a flat fee—union scale of $42.50 for the session—though Berry as the bandleader was entitled to double.

Curiously, Chess did not release the song immediately, although he could easily have done so. At the time, the company was able to release songs rapidly after they were recorded because it owned a pressing plant, Midwest Record Pressing, in the building next door to the Cottage Grove offices. (Marshall Chess remembers, "We could cut a record—literally, I could record on a Wednesday and put a record on the radio on Thursday. Sell it Thursday, next day.") But for two months, they sat on the tune to let the success of "Bo Diddley" and "Mannish Boy" die down or, less likely, because they really did not feel it would be as big a hit as it eventually became. It took a meeting with old business associate Alan Freed during an already scheduled business trip through the Northeast to convince Leonard Chess that the time was right to release the song. "I was going to New York anyway," Leonard recalled shortly before his death, "and I took a dub to Alan and said, 'Play this.' The dub didn't have Chuck's name on it or nothing. By the time I got back to Chicago, Freed had called a dozen times, saying it was his biggest record ever." Indeed, so taken was Freed with the song that one night during that summer he played it for over two hours on his WINS show, now called the "Rock 'n' Roll Party."

By the time Leonard Chess returned to Chicago, the Chess Records distributor in New York had placed a number of orders for "Maybellene," and Chess lost no time in pressing huge quantities of the disk. "Chess would never get over 1,000 or 2,000 records on anybody," remembers Willie Dixon, "but when we first cut that Chuck Berry number, I think he put 10,000 on the floor at the first shot." What Freed and thousands of other record buyers, black and white, were hearing was something at once both old and new: a hybrid of country and blues, with the trademark Chess Records beat.

"Maybellene" is, indeed, a landmark in the history of popular music. Released in July 1955, the song, despite all of its influences, was brand new to the teenage audience, who immediately sent the song soaring up both *Billboard* charts. Significantly, with Freed's influence, the song caught on in the Northeast (on July 30, *Billboard* reported that it was selling well in Boston, New York, and Philadelphia, as well as in the well-established Chess markets in the South and Midwest). Eventually, the song peaked at number 1 on the R&B chart; most importantly, at least in terms of numbers of the records sold, the song had "crossed over" onto the pop chart where, on September 10, it peaked at number 5, spending a total of over 16 weeks on the chart.

What made the success of "Maybellene" all the more remarkable is that it was one of the first rock and roll songs sung by a black artist to outsell its white cover versions. *Billboard's* September 3 issue noted that the original version's sales were "way ahead of pop versions by Jim Lowe on Dot and Johnny Long on Coral." Both Long's version (on a subsidiary label of Decca) and another version by country singer Marty Robbins on Columbia had the weight of major labels behind them, yet they failed to connect with the record-buying public. In fact, "Maybellene" was so popular that the same *Billboard* article reported that "the tune has apparently brought back 'answer' songs"; a record called "Come Back, Maybellene" was released by John Greer (on Groove) and Mercy Dee (on Flair).

But it also engendered the first big controversy of Berry's career. Although the record of "Maybellene" lists Berry as the song's sole author, the copyright of the song listed two other coauthors, Alan Freed and Russ Fratto. In fact, the Library of Congress has two separate filing dates for the song. Originally, a song registered as "Maybelline" was copyrighted on July 5, 1955, a few weeks after the original recording session. Then, on August 2, days after *Billboard's* announcement of the song's initial success, the copyright was registered again. This time, the song was listed with its correct spelling and with Freed and Fratto as coauthors.

In *The Autobiography*, Berry maintained that this was done without his knowledge; he wrote, "I didn't have any idea that Alan Freed was being compensated for giving special attention to 'Maybellene' on his radio program by a gift from Leonard registering him part of the writer's credit to the song." But was this done without Berry's knowledge? Marshall Chess disagreed, maintaining that "it wasn't anything behind Chuck Berry's back, he was definitely a party to it." Indeed, it is highly unlikely that Berry would not have agreed to such a deal, given Freed's importance at the time and the phenomenal success of "Sincerely" just six months earlier. Leonard Chess would undoubtedly have convinced Berry that the move made a lot of business sense, which indeed it eventually did. As Marshall Chess was to say later, it was the "cost of doing business. A start-up cost" for the unproven Berry.

No one disagrees, however, that Freed was being compensated for playing the song, and perhaps even convincing Chess to release it. And at a time when deejays were taking payola from record companies for playing records, this was a semilegitimate way of rewarding Freed for his efforts. Later, Leonard Chess confided to Jack Hooke, Berry's first manger, that he felt "'terrible that I can't give Alan Freed any money for what he's done for me.' [Leonard] said, 'Jack, I used to come to Cleveland, I didn't have enough money for a hotel room. I used to sleep in the car. He played my records. He made me a millionaire. Are you gonna tell me I can't give him anything?' So, I think, this is the way Leonard Chess thought he was repaying Alan for all he did for him."

But the involvement of Russ Fratto in the scheme is less easily rationalized, and through the years Marshall Chess has offered two contradictory stories for why this occurred. In a 1982 interview, Marshall's explanation calls into question Chess's own business practices. Fratto, the Chess's landlord at 4750–2 Cottage Avenue as well as a partner in Midwest Record Pressing, "got interested" in the record business. "We didn't have much money in those days," recalled Leonard's son, "so he put up half the money, y'know, with my father and they started this Midwest record pressing." Fratto's name on the recording of "Maybellene," then, allowed Chess to clear some of his debt to Fratto. Although such a deal would help Berry in the long term by enabling the Chess empire to grow, it is hard to see how such a move would have been in his interests at the outset of his career in the way that the deal with Freed was.

But in a 1998 interview Marshall asserted that Berry may have struck a deal with Fratto himself, perhaps under the approving eye of his mentor Leonard Chess. "Russ probably paid Chuck money for that," Marshall speculated years later. "That's what my Uncle [Phil Chess] thinks. And he wasn't there when that went down. And believe me it wasn't because Russ knew that he was going to make him money on it. It was probably, they were gambling, you know, he was probably just like, 'This is his chance.' And Chuck, that day it was like Chuck could have easily grabbed it." In other words, Marshall feels that Berry could have opted for the certainty of a cash deal against future royalties that, at least at the time of the song's recording, would have been completely unpredictable.

In a mere three months, Chuck Berry had been plunged from the comparative safety of the Ville into the world of show business, where ambiguous music deals, which simultaneously benefited and cheated an artist, were the order of the day. He had been hardened by his days in East St. Louis, and had asserted his control over The Sir John's Trio—the recording of "Maybellene," perhaps on Leonard Chess's insistence but certainly with Berry's approval, was credited to the Chuck Berry Combo—but it was hardly an adequate preparation for what was to come. For a black man entering a white-dominated business in the segregated America of the 1950s, how could it be?

Breaking White

We used to say that if he would have been white, Chuck Berry would have really been much bigger, y'know. We had a lot of problems those days, y'know. The only reason he broke white so big was there were guys on white radio, like Alan Freed, who would play a black record. And there were very few that would play black music.

—Marshall Chess, 1982

In July 1955, around the time "Maybellene" began to be noticed by *Billboard*, a burly, gruffly spoken Brooklynite named Jack Hooke stepped out of a plane at Lambert Field in St. Louis and into the sweltering heat of a Midwest summer. Typical of the inhabitants of the music business's lower echelons and in many ways similar to Leonard Chess, Hooke was a hustler with many fingers in the musical pie. He was a talent scout, a music publisher, the co-owner of a small jazz label named Royal Roost, and an employee of the Gale Agency, one of New York's major booking agencies. He and his partner, Teddy Reig, had become friends with the Chess brothers and Alan Freed during their frequent song-plugging trips through the Midwest, and through them they had become acquainted with "Maybellene" and its singer, Chuck Berry. Like many in the business, they were becoming aware that the St. Louis singer was on his way to becoming a hot property. *Billboard* was reporting that interest in "Maybellene" "was unusually high," and that the song was "clicking as few records have this summer." So Hooke, at Reig's urging and with the blessing of the Gale Agency, had come to St. Louis with a contract in the hope that Chuck Berry would agree to let the agency handle his concert bookings exclusively.

Hooke professed ignorance as to what the contract contained; like Berry, he was new to the world of music. "I'd only been in the business since '54," he remembered, "and I had been in the music publishing end, so I really didn't know that much. I wasn't much concerned at what [the contract] contained or what it was all about, but I told Chuck 'the Gale Agency would be able to get you some work.'" What Hooke had, however, was a very lucrative offer, indeed. The average fee for a solo or small combo at that time ranged between $300 and $500 a night if, as Berry now had, the artist had a charted disc—and that was just the guarantee. Most venues offered a contract of around $3,000 a week with a percentage deal on top, so that if receipts at the door exceeded the guarantee, the artist would pocket a higher amount. In fact, Berry's claim that the contract offered $40,000 a year for three years, as high as it seems for the time, may well be low, considering the amount of work the Gale Agency could get for the Chuck Berry Combo. As a big agency, they could promise far more than the $30 or $40 a night the Sir John's Trio had been getting at the Cosmopolitan; they could also obtain work all over the country. Berry recalled a conversation with Tim Gale, the agency's head, shortly after he arrived in New York for the first time. "You can ride on this," he said, referring to "Maybellene," "for three years." Lured by such an enormous sum of money, Chuck Berry signed Hooke's contract on the spot.

"He was overjoyed, naturally," remembered Hooke, although he added that Berry was also very naïve, not just about the music business but about the world beyond the confines of the Ville. The lessons learned in the clubs of East St. Louis and in his early encounters with Leonard Chess had not fully prepared him for what was to come. The first series of bookings—engagements at the Royal Peacock Lounge in Atlanta, Gleason's in Cleveland on August 15, and the Copa Casino in Youngstown, Ohio—passed without incident. But on their way into New York for the next shows, a weeklong engagement at the Brooklyn Paramount, Johnnie Johnson remembered that a curious incident occurred. While driving through the Lincoln Tunnel, Berry, who was at the wheel at the time,

> was passing cars in the tunnel. But you couldn't pass nobody in the tunnel, so when we got to the end, there was about five or six police cars and we were stopped. On the front of his car, he had a California license plate, and on the back he had a St. Louis license plate. And in his drivers' license he was notified as an Indian. They didn't arrest him or nothing. They just told him to get them plates straight on that car and to get that California plate off.

The New York police were clearly unlike any the musicians had encountered in St. Louis; less than three years later, a minor traffic incident like this in St. Charles, Missouri, would lead to disastrous personal consequences for Berry. But this first encounter with police in the Northeast was easier than Berry would have dared expect and a foretaste of other freedoms to come. Indeed, as Berry was later to recall, he was truly surprised at how liberal and open the city of New York was compared to St. Louis. Playing at such a prestigious theater as the Paramount must have reminded him of the Fox Theater back home, and of the day when his family was refused admission there. Equally surprising to Berry was the fact that whites in New York were not ashamed to make eye contact with blacks, and that they were more inclined to use the word "black," rather than "Negro," "colored," or "nigger," when referring to African Americans.

But the story also suggested a racial ambivalence, at least at this point in Chuck Berry's life. The identification of "Indian" on his driver's license, for Johnnie Johnson, indicated that Berry was uncomfortable with the label "black." "He wanted to be everything but a St. Louisan, but an Afro-American I guess," Johnson concluded years after the event. It was the first indication that Chuck Berry felt the need to disguise his racial identity. Not long after this incident, he would make several other attempts to disguise his roots. Perhaps he felt it was the only way he could gain success and acceptance in a white-dominated society, something that his philosophy, guided by the ideas if not the actual teachings of Booker T. Washington, made it easy for him to do.

The Paramount show marked the first anniversary of Alan Freed's arrival in New York; the shows were to become legendary and a New York tradition. That previous April, the deejay had rented the theater for a week's run, putting on six or seven shows a day that featured a movie and eight or ten of the hottest acts. The event was so successful that he booked a second series of shows over the long, end-of-summer Labor Day weekend, and then repeated this formula three times a year for the next five years. But the Labor Day shows of 1955, perhaps more than any of the subsequent shows, provided a powerful symbol of the changing face of popular music.

Chuck Berry, of course, was not yet a star, and so was the first of the acts the audience saw at each of the shows. For seven precious minutes, seven or eight times a day for seven days, Berry, Johnnie Johnson, and Ebby Hardy were on stage chugging through both sides of their new hit record. They were followed by several of the most successful vocal groups of the day: the Harptones, the Cardinals, the Nutmegs, and, more importantly, Chess label mates the Flamingoes and the Moonglows. Lilian Briggs and Nappy Brown rounded out the rhythm and blues acts on the bill before the headliner appeared. On the first day, the Friday of the holiday weekend, that honor fell to Tony Bennett.

Although he was born in the same year as Chuck Berry, Bennett's music was by now old hat for the young record-buying public. Bennett had begun recording on Columbia, one of the biggest labels in the world, in 1950, and by the time of the Freed show he had produced a succession of pop hits including "Boulevard of Broken Dreams" in 1950, "Because of You" in 1951, and "Rags to Riches" in 1953. All featured a distinctive, gentle vocal style and smooth jazz instrumentation and arrangements, and they could not have been more different from the rough-and-ready rhythm and blues that was the trademark of artists like Berry and Nappy Brown.

By the end of the first day, Bennett complained of throat problems and left the show. Some, however, maintained that his departure had little to do with illness and everything to do with the reception he had been given by Freed's young, rock-and-roll–hungry fans. A life-size cardboard cutout of Bennett that had graced the Paramount's lobby was destroyed by the fans minutes after the doors had opened for the first show. And, according to Leroy Kirkland, musical director of the band Freed had assembled to provide backing for the musicians in the show, Bennett had been heckled by the audience every time he had appeared that day. If Alan Freed or Chuck Berry had wanted a demonstration of how significant a musical movement rock and roll was becoming, they could not have found a more powerful one than this. And as great a singer and entertainer as Bennett was and continued to be, he and the generation he represented were powerless to stop it.

The September 14 issue of *Variety* claimed that the Brooklyn Paramount shows grossed $154,000 for the 38-show, seven-day run. Opening on Wednesday morning, September 7, the run kicked off with six shows, with more than 2,000 people waiting on the Flatbush Avenue sidewalk for the 12:15 A.M. show to begin. The majority of the audience, about 80 percent (in the estimation of Gene Pleshette, the theater's managing director), were white and in their late teens and early twenties. In contrast to the image of rowdy, teenage rock-and-roll fans later painted by the media, they were very well-behaved. In the *Variety* piece, Pleshette was quoted as saying that the crowds were fanatical all day, "but," according to Pleshette, "it never took the shape of anything worse than they wanted to sit down front. They couldn't sit still, and were playing musical chairs as they constantly improved their vantage points, but otherwise no damage. And," he concluded, "I've never seen anything so exciting" in 26 years in show business. "I've gone through the Benny Goodman and Frank Sinatra fever at the Brooklyn Paramount and back to the old Rudy Vallee days, so I know!"

But attitudes in the black community were mixed about this new musical force. Buddy Franklin, writing in his weekly "Brooklyn After Dark" column in the *New York Age-Defender*, provided an early voice of concern. "We are not anti-Rock 'n Roll," he wrote in his review of the Freed show. "Some of the R. and R. music—a whole lot of it—is really good and quite entertaining." But although the recordings of the artists who graced the Paramount stage were acceptable to Franklin's ears, their performances were not. "They just didn't seem to click," he noted, adding, "At one point in the show we got the impression that we were witnessing one of those unrehearsed amateur shows."

Some of Franklin's criticism was, understandably, leveled at Freed himself, the white interloper from Cleveland who was in competition with black, native New Yorker Tommy "Dr. Jive" Smalls, a deejay who often presented shows at the Apollo in Harlem, and a frequent advertiser in the pages of the *Age*. But when Franklin turned his attention to the band Freed had assembled for the show and to the crowd Freed had attracted, the full force of his criticism took effect. "When the curtain went up and we saw the big band we felt kind of good," Franklin wrote. "We thought about our plaintive cry through the years for the return of the big bands." But no such nostalgic display of good and acceptable music reached Franklin's ears. "The band," he noted, "comprised of 15 pieces, could have left at least 10 of them home." He added, "when they began to play—Oh Brother, such confusion."

If the band was not capable of playing sophisticated music, the audience at the show was, in Franklin's eyes, a perfect match for them, because they were incapable of any kind of sophisticated response to the spectacle they were witnessing. "We got the biggest kick out of the audience," he wrote, pointing out later that it was difficult to understand them. "We couldn't figure out what they liked and what they didn't like. We finally discovered when they applauded that meant that they were glad the act was finished but when they screamed and shouted and stomped and yelled, so that the act could not be heard, they were showing their appreciation." For Franklin, there was no doubt that this unrefined music could only produce a mystifying, backward reaction in the teenage crowd. And in his review, he had perfectly captured the middle-class, black response to rock and roll music: It was not the corrupting force that the white middle class would soon make it out to be, but it had no value or substance, or anything to recommend it to an intelligent listenership.

But the Paramount shows were just the beginning of Chuck Berry's education in the world of show business. The Gale Agency had booked Berry, Hardy, and Johnson for a grueling, seven-week tour of one-nighters with Buddy Johnson, the Nutmegs, the Four Fellows, and several other top acts. Almost immediately, the tour encountered difficulties. Two days out of New York, the show at Pittsburgh's Soldier and Sailors Memorial Hall was canceled when building superintendent Gilbert C. Cloonan complained to the hall's managers about the advertisements that had been run for the show in the local Sunday paper. The advertisements featured one of the acts— Queenie Owens, "the queen of the quiver and shake"—shockingly clothed in two pieces of cloth. Immediately, Theodore Logan, the local promoter, scrambled to pull together another venue, finally settling on a much smaller movie theater, the Triangle, located in a local suburb. "Everything was against him," wrote *Variety* the following week as the rescheduled date suffered from the last-minute changes.

A few days later, enroute from a date in Houston to a show in Beaumont, Texas, 18 of the 20 members of Buddy Johnson's Orchestra were arrested on charges of marijuana possession. They were on board a private bus when, as they were being pulled over by the local police, one of the musicians threw a bag of pot out the window. A subsequent search of the bus found more marijuana in a trombone case. Eventually, all except two of Johnson's musicians, Julius D. Watson and Steve Pilliam, were released and rejoined the tour.

Eventually, the tour moved deep into the heart of the South. At the Southern shows, racism was inescapable, and it was here Berry witnessed the realities of segregation in full force. Until this time, Jim Crow in St. Louis had been a series of painful yet isolated incidents; now, it was a constant presence, necessitating caution at every turn. Johnnie Johnson recalled that conditions were incredibly hard on the black entertainers:

> A lot of times, we couldn't find no place to sleep or eat, 'cause most of the places down south didn't let no black people in the hotels and restaurants. We'd sleep in the bus a lot of times. When the bus stopped for dinner, we'd go round the back of the restaurants to get food from the black cooks, and sometimes they could get us in with some folks who would take us in for the night. They kept things separate down there.

The realities of Jim Crow did not escape the theaters where the musicians played. "A lot of times we had to play two shows for the price of one—one show for the blacks and one show for the whites," remembered Johnson. But at the shows, an interesting phenomenon was beginning to take place. At some places, the promoters were allowing mixed-race audiences to see the show, although some attempt was made to keep the races apart. At a date in Jacksonville, Florida, Berry recalls ropes being tied down the center aisle of the auditorium to separate the whites from the blacks in the audience, a practice common to many Southern shows at the time. The results were, perhaps, predictable: At some point during the evening, the rope would come down and both sides of the auditorium would come together and dance. H. B. Barnum, a saxophone player for Berry's contemporary, Little Richard, recalled that, "although they still had the audiences together in the building, they were *there* together. And most times, before the end of the night, they would all be mixed together." And although Richard's music, like much of Berry's, was apolitical and strictly, in Barnum's words, "fun," its existence was not. It "had a lot to say sociologically in our country and the world," Barnum quite rightly maintained. "The shot was fired here and heard all round the world."

During the tour, on October 15, the Chuck Berry Combo's second single was released, "Thirty Days," backed with "Together (We Will Always Be)."

The songs, recalled Johnson, had been written by Berry while on the road and hastily recorded in Chicago. "We knocked both these records off in no time flat," remembered Johnson, adding, "I don't think that it took more than an hour for each one." Clearly, the intention was to imitate the "Maybellene" formula: an uptempo A-side featuring Ebby Hardy playing the same 2/4 hillbilly rhythm as before, and a slow, bluesy B-side to appeal to the black audience. Indeed, the similarities between "Thirty Days" and "Maybellene" were striking; aside from the rhythm, Berry's guitar introduction was an almost note-for-note reversal of the first single's. But lyrically, Berry was again innovative, describing his escalating attempts to make his woman return home, threatening to go to a judge, then the FBI, and finally the United Nations if she refused to return. The lyrics, and Berry's fine rapid-fire mandolin-style strumming on the instrumental guitar break, made the song an adequate follow-up to "Maybellene," which was still at number 17 in the *Billboard Hot 100* on the day of the new single's release.

Significantly, Chess immediately began marketing the song to the pop market. The advertisement in *Billboard* for "Thirty Days" marked one of the first times that Chess advertised a song in the pop, not the R&B, section of the trade magazine. As far as the record-buying public was concerned, however, the follow-up was not as satisfying. The song did respectably on the R&B charts, making it as high as number 8, but it never entered the *Hot 100* at all. Once again, it was covered by a county act, Ernest Tubb, whose version on Decca did well on the country charts but also failed to cross over.

On Friday, November 18, the Chuck Berry Combo joined the Buddy Johnson Orchestra, Arthur Prysock, the Solitaires, the Valentines, and the Four Fellows for a week at the Apollo, the famous black Harlem nightspot. Here, the audience reacted far differently than the white New York teenagers the Chuck Berry Combo had encountered in Brooklyn over two months earlier. The crowd, more savvy about the music and less reticent about voicing a negative response to it, heckled Berry and his, to their mind at least, less-sophisticated hillbilly music. "Some of the hecklers at the Apollo did protest outright," Berry remembered many years after, "standing up during a soft ballad and yelling, 'Sing some 'um we know, fool! Don't nobody wanna hear that crap.'" Clearly, although the black audiences in East St. Louis had accepted Berry's music as a novelty, the Apollo audience positively rejected it.

Variety's review of Berry's engagement at the Apollo was also less than complementary. "There's no opportunity either to take rhythm & blues or leave it alone at this sesh at the Apollo," complained the reviewer. "Songsters are shuttled in an [sic] out during the close to 60-minute layout ... the r&b'ers come on for two 'live spins' and off." There was no let-up in the frenetic pace of the show, the reviewer lamented, but it was the simple lack of variety in the music presented that was especially singled out for criticism: "The style and the songs all get to sound alike . . . for the most part, the rest of the bill [with the exception of veteran singer Arthur Prysock] is cut-and-dried r&b with no shadings."

It must have been with mixed emotions, then, that the group headed home to St. Louis in Berry's station wagon for Thanksgiving. Berry, Johnson, and Hardy had been on the road since August 8. They had played at least one show a day, more often than not two or three, for nearly 15 consecutive weeks, "playing one song," as Johnnie Johnson remembered it, "for a hundred and one nights, over and over and over." They had toured to the point of exhaustion and been humiliated by Jim Crow. They had been received with wild abandon by white and black teenagers alike, the same group that had bought their first record and ignored their second. And they had been rejected by the Apollo audience, leaving Berry to ponder, not for the first time in his life, whether he and his music could be accepted in both white and black worlds.

As if the external pressure of segregation was not enough for Berry to deal with, the internal friction caused by the presence of manager Teddy Reig also was beginning to take its toll. Reig, like Jack Hooke, was a Brooklyn-born hustler, about ten years Berry's senior. Everyone who met him agreed on two things. The first was his size. "He weighed about 400 pounds," remembered Hooke; "he reminded you of a big old fat moose," laughed Johnnie Johnson. More significant, though, were his unethical business dealings. "He was a shyster," Johnson added, with "shifty eyes. He was a fast talker." Hooke was far less charitable than the genial piano player. "I hate to say it but I have to," Hooke said shortly before his death. "He was the greediest person in the world. Every nickel, dime he could skim or steal he was there."

Trouble with Reig had begun for Berry from the beginning. Some time after he returned from St. Louis with Berry's signature on the bottom of the Gale Agency contract, Jack Hooke began to get wind of Reig's practices. "Teddy was selling Chuck Berry to a promoter for $5,000," Hooke realized to his horror, "and having Chuck sign a contract that said he's getting $3,000. In other words, the promoter paid five, got a contract for three, and gave Teddy two in cash."

Hooke, to his dying day, denied any complicity in the scam. First, he maintained, Reig's actions demonstrated little honor among "thieves." "We were two street guys, we both came up from Brooklyn together," he argued. "The right thing, if I was agreeable to it, was for him to come to me and say, 'Hey, Jack, you went down, you signed him for me, I'm getting five, I'm only giving him three, so we'll split the two.' That guy never told me nothing. Just said to me, 'Look how great I'm doing for Chuck.'"

The second reason was Hooke's fierce loyalty to Leonard Chess: "Leonard was a dear friend of mine. He was great people—a beautiful person. He trusted me implicitly." In fact, it was that loyalty that enabled Hooke to realize very quickly that his partner was ripping off everyone concerned. The initial agreement between Chess, Hooke and Reig, and the Gale Agency called for Chess to split the standard 10 percent booking and management fees with the two in return for exclusive management of several Chess acts, including Berry and the Moonglows. As Hooke told the story:

> The first few jobs we had, I forget if it was the Moonglows or Chuck, I put the money in the desk drawer in our office—"our" meaning Teddy Reig and I—and I figured when I accumulate $500 or $1,000, I would send Leonard his half. But before I could even get up to $1,000, I came to the drawer one day—I went out of town on a disc jockey trip, promoting—and I come back to my office and I looked in my drawer and the money was gone. So I confronted Teddy, and I said "Teddy, what happened? I had about $6, 7, 800 here."

According to Hooke, Reig looked at him and said, barefaced, "That guy who works for us must have taken it."

It was the end of a very lucrative relationship for Hooke and Reig. "I called Leonard," remembered Hooke, and said, " 'Leonard, the money was here. It's gone. Somebody stole it.' So now I don't blame Leonard; he ceased to make the relationship, you know. He didn't want to know about it. In other words, he didn't want to send us any more acts."

Quite how soon Berry realized this was going on remains debatable. Berry himself maintained he was suspicious of Reig's practices almost from the start. "After a concert in Lynn, Massachusetts, in 1955," he wrote in his autobiography, "he handed me a hundred dollar bill.... That night," he continued, "the crowd had to number over twelve hundred and the admission was $1.50.... We should have earned near to $750 aside from our guarantee of $150, but I could not have proved it."

Johnnie Johnson maintained that Berry knew something was going on toward the end of that first tour. At some point, Reig talked Berry out of $400 and headed for the nearest airport. "After he found out that Teddy ripped him off with his money," Johnson said, "he went out to the airport to get on the plane that Teddy was on. Chuck tried to catch the plane as it was taking off; Chuck was trying to run out on the runway to stop it. It wasn't but $400, but $400 back then was a lot of money." Then, he added with a chuckle, "I think Chuck cried about that for four months!"

It was at this point, or shortly after, that Berry parted company with both Reig and Hooke; certainly, by the end of 1955, the unscrupulous pair had begun to devote more of their attention to their own record label, Royal

Roost, and Hooke himself was becoming more involved with Alan Freed's career. Instead of searching for another manager, however, Berry made the bold and unusual step of beginning to handle his own business arrangements. It was a decision directly influenced by Booker T. Washington and Leonard Chess's business philosophy; it was a decision, too, that was to be widely misunderstood and criticized by many who would have business dealings with Berry in the ensuing years.

A typical comment came from Red Holloway, Vee Jay session musician and band leader at the Stage Lounge, a Chicago club where Berry appeared at around this time. "Chuck Berry was at the Stage Lounge when he first came out with 'Maybellene,'" Holloway recalled in a 1976 interview. "And Chuck Berry was getting $3,000 a week. $3,000, man, that was a l-o-o-o-t of money.... Three grand a week!" But, added Holloway, "what was so funny about Chuck Berry that first year, Chuck Berry saved $100,000 the first year but he was sleepin' in his car, he was half eating, he wouldn't stay in hotels or nothing, he was just going the back route saving that money."

But Berry's actions were not mere frugality. In part, they were forged by the incidents of racism he had encountered in the South. Rather than having to suffer the indignities of buying meals from a restaurant kitchen or being refused a room in a segregated hotel, Berry opted to ignore white main-stream businesses and go it alone. Berry's contemporary and Chess labelmate Bo Diddley, commenting on the fact that Berry used to carry an electric hotplate with him to cook his own food on the road, perhaps put it best. "Here am I," he noted indignantly, "gotta go in some white dude's *back door*, an' I've got ten—maybe fifteen thousand dollars in my pocket! I'm gonna get a 95¢ hamburger 'cause I can't go in the front door."

In part, too, Berry's business practices were the result of Tim Gale's advice that the results of "Maybellene" would last only three years. While others around him immediately began to spend their royalties and appearance fees as soon as they came in, Berry ignored the trappings of show-business success in favor of long-term financial stability. Bo Diddley, like many other artists who found themselves going from poverty to riches in a matter of weeks, fell into the trap created by the instant wealth of music stardom. "I went through a spendthrift era," Diddley once said, "buying a lot of crap, like things I didn't have when I was a kid." Later in life, however, he was to realize the error of his ways and admire Berry's sharp business mind. "A lot of people will say—Chuck Berry this, Chuck Berry that," he told veteran rock journalist Robert Christgau during a 1979 radio show. "Chuck Berry is a businessman. I admire him for being a businessman. The name of the game is dollar bills."

The model of the Chess brothers must have also influenced Berry's down-to-earth attitude. To Leonard and Phil, the music business was just that: a business. Phil Chess, for example, when asked in the early 1970s by journalist Peter Guralnick whether he enjoyed the experience of building Chess Records, responded in disbelief. "'Enjoy it?'" Chess replied to Guralnick's question, staring at him "incredulously. 'Enjoy it? We worked our tails off. It was our job.'" And Marshall Chess, no doubt echoing his father's sentiments, has also pointed out that, for all the talk of glamour and artistic achievement that surrounds the music scene, the mundane realities of the profession are never far away. "You have to look at that '50s period," he once said, "when you had Muddy Waters, Howlin' Wolf, Sonny Boy, Little Walter, Chuck Berry, Moonglows, Flamingos. All that happening, hot. Those artists changed the sound of music, so that's the magic period. After that, it's just a fucking business."

Understandably, then, Chuck Berry spent little time mourning the loss of Hooke and Reig and immediately took the Chuck Berry Combo back out on the road. There were shows in Chicago at the Regal Theater with Clarence "Gatemouth" Brown, Nappy Brown, and Red Prysock on November 28, then shows on December 2 and 3 with the Moonglows in Detroit. Then, on December 21, it was back to the Cosmopolitan Club in East St. Louis. It was, as the *St. Louis Argus* billed it on December 16, "a pre-holiday treat." The local paper proudly noted that Berry had departed the club "a few months ago" and was now "being hailed as one of the nation's greatest recording artists in the rhythm and blues field."

A week later, the *Argus* summed up Berry's amazing year:

> "Maybelline" [sic] has skyrocketed St. Louis' own Chuck Berry, his guitar and trio to the position of one of the nation's greatest box-office attractions in the rhythm and blues field. This all happened within the last six months, Maestro Berry recalled. Last Christmas he was only a feature with the Johnny Johnson trio playing nightly at East St. Louis' Club Cosmopolitan.... TODAY ... IT'S A SUCCESS STORY.

For the *Argus*, as they were to show throughout the 1950s, the significance of Berry's music was not its quality but the financial success and nationwide reputation that it brought. The music itself was not sophisticated enough to be treated with any degree of depth; that was exclusively reserved for classical music and, to a lesser extent, for jazz. But the *Argus* was always willing to promote one of its own, especially when success could not be ignored.

The new year continued at the same frenetic pace. On January 3, the Chuck Berry Combo was booked for a weeklong engagement at Mandy's Lounge in Buffalo, New York; this was followed by a swing down the West Coast in February with a stop at the Savoy Ballroom in Los Angeles over the three-day holiday weekend on Lincoln's birthday. That weekend,

February 10–12, also saw the release of Berry's third single for Chess, the memorable "No Money Down." It was a song that immediately caused a minor controversy, because the lyrics mentioned by name the Ford and Cadillac car companies. It was enough to cause some radio stations not to play the song. *Billboard*, in proclaiming the song its "Buy of the Week," mentioned that, despite getting little airplay, "word about it has spread and it is as hot a novelty as has been seen for some time." *Billboard* noted that sales were strong in major markets—including Chicago, Detroit, St. Louis, Memphis, Nashville, Durham, Atlanta, Cleveland, and Philadelphia—but concluded that the other side of the disc, by virtue of its getting more radio exposure, was also fairing well.

"No Money Down" once again digs deep into Berry's descriptive skills. Its stop–start verses, developed from such songs as Muddy Waters's "Hoochie Coochie Man" and "Mannish Boy" and Bo Diddley's "I'm a Man," begin by describing the unscrupulous tactics of used car salesmen. The buyer, in the second and third verses, counters the salesman's pitch with a lengthy list of features that he wants in his Cadillac, including wire wheels and (humorously) a "full Murphy bed" installed in the back seat. Like so many Berry songs, it is this attention to detail and exaggerated humor that distinguishes the song.

The B-side, "Downbound Train," featured Berry playing over drummer Ebby Hardy's fast-paced shuffle imitation of a train. Melodically inspired by the 1950 country hit "Ghost Riders in the Sky," lyrically the song was a cautionary tale recounting the alcoholic hallucination of a drunkard who had passed out on the floor of a bar. In the dream, the drunk boards the train only to find a hellish scene: An imp using human bones to fuel the furnace, which "rang with a thousand moans," and the "devil himself" at the controls.

It was a hellfire and brimstone sermon right out of the Antioch Baptist Church, in all probability addressed to his bandmates whose drinking had become progressively worse since leaving St. Louis. They were, as Berry was to recall in *The Autobiography*, "showing increasing deficiencies in their performances due to their drinking," adding that "Johnnie would become quiet and clumsy while intoxicated, while Ebby would get loud and silly." Johnson himself admitted later that he was becoming a liability to all around him. On stage, the drinking was beginning to cause tension. "It got to where we didn't socialize much on stage," he recalled. "I always had my whiskey and Ebby liked his highballs. It got on Chuck's nerves because he never drank at all. Never."

Like "Thirty Days" before it, "No Money Down" faired well with the black record-buying public but failed to cross over to the mainstream audience. The week of the song's release, the *Billboard Hot 100* reflected the changing tastes of the American public; although the charts were still dominated by mainstream pop, rock and roll was beginning to make a real showing. Even though pop crooner Dean Martin's "Memories Are Made of This" topped the chart, and such white pop staples as Pat Boone, the Four Lads, the Crew Cuts, Frank Sinatra, and Dinah Shore all had multiple entries on the chart, Bill Haley had no fewer than three songs in the *Billboard Hot 100*. His "See You Later Alligator," "Burn That Candle," and "Rock a Beatin' Boogie" all occupied spots on the chart, as did songs by the Platters ("Great Pretender") and the Cadillacs ("Speedoo"). But the charts also showed white mainstream musicians continuing to appropriate R&B music; Little Richard's version of "Tutti Frutti" was being edged out by Pat Boone's insipid cover, while Kay Starr's oxymoronically titled "Rock and Roll Waltz" was at number three.

It was a strong enough showing, however, that by the spring of 1956 the impact of rock and roll on American culture could no longer be ignored. During the week of Chuck Berry's Thanksgiving performance at the Apollo, rock and roll took two giant steps toward greater visibility. On November 20, Tommy Smalls, the WWRL deejay whose shows at the Apollo competed with those of his crosstown rival Alan Freed, put together a segment featuring rock-and-roll artists for Ed Sullivan's Sunday night show. For a full 15 minutes, audiences across the country saw Lavern Baker, Bo Diddley, the Five Keys, and the Willis Jackson Orchestra and heard, many perhaps for the first time, rock and roll. Then, one day later, news came from Memphis that Elvis Presley had signed with RCA Victor records, leaving the small, indie label Sun Records and its owner, Sam Phillips, the unimaginable sum of $35,000 richer. Clearly, rock and roll was moving into the mainstream consciousness, and there was a lot of money to be made.

Following Elvis Presley's first national television appearance on the Dorsey Brothers "Stage Show" on February 4, interest in rock and roll approached fever pitch among teenage Americans; within the next two months, their parents would have all the evidence they needed that rock music was dangerous and a threat to society. Several so-called riots broke out at rock-and-roll shows in Boston and Hartford, Connecticut, that spring. The April release of the film *Rock Around the Clock*, starring Alan Freed, was also blamed for outbreaks of vandalism and rioting in both American and European theaters. Small wonder, then, that Berry's next single became more successful than the previous two. It captured lyrically the tension between highbrow and lowbrow culture, and between white and black culture, that was now beginning to play itself out in American society. On May 19, with exquisite timing, Chess released "Roll Over Beethoven," a song that perfectly illustrated the playful yet rebellious spirit of the new music.

Musically, the song was an extension of the boogie-woogie piano style that Johnnie Johnson had been playing when Berry first met him in 1952.

"When we started puttin' music together for 'Beethoven,'" remembered Johnson,

> the way he had written out them lyrics, it just had a boogie feel to me, so it was just natural for me to start that choppin' bass [the arpeggiated, eight-to-the-bar left-hand piano pattern]. Chuck knew that bass from when I'd play "Johnnie's Boogie" at the Cosmo, so when I started, he caught on to the rhythm right off. All we did was take the choppin' bass, the left hand from "Johnnie's Boogie" and speed it up a little bit so it had more of a drive to it instead of that bounce. Once you got that rhythm, then you on your way.

As they had done with "Maybellene," Johnson and Berry had taken a preexisting musical form and, filtering it through their own styles and abilities, begun to fashion something different and exciting to the music-buying public's ears.

The sheer energy and intensity of the music, which begins with a machine gun-like solo from Berry, was described perfectly by the lyrics. Berry's inventive and economical use of images in the contagious new music shows how teenagers were enraptured by rock and roll. "My temperature's risin'," Berry sings, adding that even the mechanical "jukebox [is] blowing a fuse." Suffering from this "rockin' pneumonia," Berry's only anecdote is "a shot of rhythm and blues." The cumulative effect of this feverish activity, of course, is to upset the old order and its values: "Roll Over Beethoven," Berry sings in the second verse and the song's chorus, "and tell Tchaikovsky the news." It is an explicit threat to high-brow culture, inspired in part by the rivalry between his sister Lucy's classical-music training and Berry's own self-taught, rough-and-ready music preference.

In case we miss the point, in the fourth verse Berry makes the threat more explicit, directly referring to Carl Perkins's "Blue Suede Shoes," two different versions of which were, on the day of "Roll Over Beethoven"'s release, on the *Billboard* charts. Indeed, there was plenty of evidence that the artistic revolution predicted by Berry's lyrics was already coming to pass. On that same day, Elvis Presley's "Heartbreak Hotel" had been at number 1 for three weeks. Two other Presley songs were on the charts that week, along with three Bill Haley songs, two Little Richard songs, two by Fats Domino, and a number of other rock and roll titles. There was no doubt that rock and roll had become a major force in popular music.

Public reaction to the growing rock-and-roll phenomenon was, predictably, mixed. In the "Vox Jox" column of May 19, *Billboard* writer June Bundy wrote of two polls of listeners conducted by radio stations. One, by WDOK in Alan Freed's old hometown of Cleveland, found that 78 percent of 2,532 listeners polled were against the new musical style. Some Pittsburgh residents, meanwhile, were overwhelmingly in favor of rock and roll: 625 out of a total of 639 callers phoned radio station WJAS to express their positive opinion of the music.

Meanwhile, in the South, more ominous reactions against rock-and-roll music were beginning to be voiced. Following the 1954 *Brown v. Board of Education* Supreme Court decision, and no doubt spurred on by the bus boycott that began in Montgomery, Alabama, in December of the previous year, "white citizens councils" began to appear throughout the South. In a piece entitled "The Up-Town Klans" in the April 20 edition of the *St. Louis Argus*, A. Scott Pride noted that, in the two years since the Supreme Court's decision, about 300 councils had sprung up in Mississippi, boasting about 30,000 members. In New Orleans, another 7,000 whites claimed membership in the citizen's council there, and Pride claimed that chapters also had appeared in Texas, Arkansas, Alabama, South Carolina, and Georgia.

Unlike the Ku Klux Klan, whose reputation for violent confrontation with blacks had long been established, the white citizens councils, composed mostly of middle-class whites, decided to apply economic pressure on supporters of the nascent civil rights movement. Blacks and sympathetic whites in the areas where the councils were strong could expect to find it next to impossible to find jobs, buy houses, or secure bank loans as council members, prominent in their communities, practiced what Pride labeled "manicured Kluxism."

One of the most prominent councils was headquartered in Birmingham, Alabama; its leader, Asa Carter, was a notorious racist who was one of the first to accuse rock and roll of being a vehicle for the National Association for the Advancement of Colored People (NAACP) and other pro-integration forces. At the end of March 1956, Carter spoke out against anyone who played the music, calling it immoral and threatening to publish the names of any jukebox operator, bar or restaurant owner, or radio station that dared to continue playing the music. Few in Birmingham took the threat seriously; none was directly contacted by the Alabama white citizens council anyway. But 20 days later, Carter's group got the attention of the whole nation through an incident that could not have escaped Chuck Berry's, or any other rock-and-roll fan's, attention.

On Tuesday night, April 10, one of Berry's musical heroes, Nat King Cole, appeared at the Birmingham Civic Auditorium. In the audience that night, several members of the Alabama white citizens council sat in their seats waiting for their moment. When Cole was just a few numbers into his show, they charged the stage, beating Cole in plain view of the entire audience. Although no one would suggest that Cole, with his smooth singing and jazzy songs, was in any way a rock-and-roll act, it was an indication of the social and cultural climate of the times. And it was a warning that all black acts, especially Chuck Berry, could not fail to note. Barely two weeks later, in response to the Montgomery bus boycott, the Supreme Court ruled that bus companies in the South could no longer force blacks to sit at the back of a bus. The strike in Alabama, however, was to continue until December; the racial temperature of the country was rising, and rock and roll was increasingly blamed as one of the symptoms.

Deliver Me
from the Days of Old

We've set up a twenty-man committee to do away with this vulgar, animalistic
Negro rock and roll bop. The obscenity and vulgarity of the rock and roll music
is obviously a means by which the white man and his children can be driven to
the level of the nigger.

—Asa Carter, c.1956

The summer of 1956 began with the flickering, black-and-white image of
Elvis Presley, swiveling his hips and singing "Hound Dog" in homes
throughout America. The reaction to Presley's appearance on Milton Berle's
June 5th show was immediate; now the voice of Southern bigot Asa Carter
was joined by critics throughout the nation. Their language was less blunt
than Carter's, to be sure, but the message was the same: One critic labeled
Presley's performance as "grunt and groin," and others categorized it as
"primitive," "suggestive and vulgar," "animalism," and an "aboriginal mating
dance." Rock and roll played into every stereotype white Americans had of
their black neighbors: It was the music of sexual abandon, base emotions,
and miscegenation.

Meanwhile, the media was reporting news of more "riots" breaking out at
rock-and-roll shows, although, as in the incidents reported in Boston and
Hartford earlier in the year, the reports tended to be sensational and exaggerated. In early June, *Variety* ran almost weekly reports of troubles at the
concerts. The "whisky 'flowed like water,'" it reported, at a Bill Haley show
at the Raleigh, North Carolina, Memorial Auditorium on May 23, leading to
the arrest of 17 people for public drunkenness at one performance and the
cancelation of another because of a bomb scare. A show at the National
Guard Armory in Washington, D.C., on June 3 was marred by disorders "at
and near" the armory in which four teenagers were hospitalized, and "stones
were thrown at windshield and taillights of automobiles passing the armory."
Another Haley show at Miami's Dinner Key Auditorium, although "rela-

tively orderly," attracted the ire of the local censorship board anyway. The show, which saw one arrest "despite a nonsegregation policy," was condemned by the board for producing dancing that was nothing more than "shoving boys and girls around" and "vile gyrations." The following month, rock-and-roll shows were banned in Jersey City and Asbury Park, New Jersey ("following a knock-down fight at Convention Hall on June 30 among 2,000 teenagers"); there was a riot in San Jose during a Fats Domino concert on July 7, and "a near riot" at a youth dance in Minneapolis. As they were so often to do, the media and local authorities were quick to blame any local incidents on the shows, regardless of whether there was a legitimate connection or not, and they always failed to point out that the great majority of audience members were peaceable and well-behaved.

Such was the backdrop for Chuck Berry's next tour, which was scheduled to begin on July 1. Elvis Presley's enormous success had overshadowed Berry's achievement with "Roll Over Beethoven"; it spent just two weeks on the *Billboard Hot 100* chart, entering at number 29 on June 30, only to drop to number 87 the following week before disappearing altogether. But it was enough to demonstrate to Berry and the Chess brothers that the cross-over promise Berry had shown with "Maybellene" was still very much alive. Irving Feld, one of the biggest promoters of rock-and-roll shows in the country, did not need to be convinced; he immediately snapped Berry up for a package tour to run through the summer. During July and August, Berry joined Carl Perkins, Al Hibbler, Illinois Jaquet and his orchestra, Frankie Lymon and the Teenagers, Bobby Charles, the Spaniels, and Shirley and Lee for a tour through the South, Texas, the Midwest, and Canada.

The tour was a phenomenal success, although it did not escape the problems that had confronted other rock-and-roll shows that summer. On July 14, the package, with Little Richard as an added attraction, drew 13,084 paying customers to the Maple Leaf Gardens in Toronto, the biggest crowd that facility had seen until that date. But two days later, during a stop at the Syria Mosque in Pittsburgh, several incidents took place. Eight teenagers were arrested outside of the auditorium, according to *Variety*, "when it looked as if a gang war might develop"; twin 18-year-olds were arrested for public drunkenness; and, after the show had concluded, four youths assaulted two 15-year-old girls. Once again, the incidents seem small and only loosely attached to the event itself, but they gave the media plenty of ammunition to fire at rock-and-roll music.

The tour moved on, seemingly unaffected by the incident. A day later, almost a third of the population of Canton, Ohio, nearly 4,000 people, packed into the sweaty Memorial Auditorium for the show; the local newspaper, the *Canton Repository*, commented on the "orderly, well-behaved crowd." But nothing could prepare the acts for the scene in Annapolis,

Maryland, on July 21. At Carr's Beach Amphitheater, 8,000 people crammed into the shows, with an estimated 50,000 to 70,000 others left waiting outside. According to reports, they "jammed approach roads for five miles on route 655 and blocked all entrances to the route. The Annapolis police reported that it wasn't until 3:30 A.M., approximately seven hours after the show began, that normalcy was restored."

A week later, the tour rolled into the Kiel Auditorium for a Saturday, St. Louis homecoming. *Variety* reported that the St. Louis shows were as successful as any on the tour, drawing 8,500 people and grossing $18,000. Even so, Chick Finney's review in the August 3 edition of the *St. Louis Argus* seemed to echo Buddy Franklin's *New York Age-Defender* review of Berry's Brooklyn Paramount debut from the year before. Little was said about the quality of the music, but the antics of the crowd seemed to be endlessly fascinating to both journalists, as did the prospect of rock and roll being a vehicle for black artists to achieve fame and fortune. "The terrific sounds of rhythm and blues," wrote Finney, "seem to usually move the large audience impressively," initially acknowledging the power of the music. But it was clearly the audience and not the music that attracted Finney's attention. "Audiences stealing the show from the 'Rock 'N' Roll' attraction seemed to provide the spectacular moments at the Kiel Auditorium," he noted, adding that, as the show began, "the jolly patrons took off in hilarious spirit, getting as much attention for their floor exhibit as the artists in the limelight."

Berry, of course, as a hometown hero, garnered some special attention in Finney's column. "The 'jump for joy' mood seemed to start in a big way," wrote Finney, "when Chuck Berry of 'Maybeline' [sic] and 'Roll Over Beethoven' fame appeared upon the scene." But, rather than discuss Berry's music, Finney was more interested in Berry's achievement in making the big time. "His success story was thoroughly discussed by many in the audience who remember Chuck during the period of his 'lean' days. Maestro Berry's first waxing of 'Maybeline' [sic] did the trick, and other records to follow are among the best sellers, especially his latest 'Roll Over Beethoven.'" The importance of Berry's story, Finney went on to note, had to do with the lessons to be learned from it, not from the musicianship it exhibited. "Don't laugh at a newcomer or professional struggling toward stardom," cautioned Finney, ever the booster of the local St. Louis music scene. "His 'SAD PERFORMANCE' made the hopeful both fame and fortune sooner than expected, says a jazz fan who's wild about the showing of both Chuck Berry and Elvis Presley," noted Finney, hinting at Berry's struggles in convincing the St. Louis crowd of the worth of his hillbilly music early in his career. But, added Finney on a hopeful note, encouraging his black readers to great heights of achievement, " 'IT CAN BE DONE.' "

But if Finney praised Chuck Berry and stopped short of criticizing the music, the crowd attending the show would have been well aware of another prominent St. Louis media figure, who expressed the more mainstream black opinion of rock and roll. Two weeks earlier, one of the fixtures of the local radio scene, Jesse Burks, better known by his on-air name of Spider, was fired from the disc jockey job he had occupied for nine years because he refused to play rock and roll. Burks, a jazz aficionado, lambasted the station on his dismissal. "They wanted me to play all 'gut-bucket' music. That's an ignorant type of music," Burks was quoted as saying in *Variety*.

In August, at the tour's conclusion, filming began on *Rock, Rock, Rock*, the third movie produced by and starring Alan Freed (although it was the second to be released). Like *Rock Around the Clock* before it, and *Don't Knock the Rock* after it, the movie was a thinly veiled excuse to cram as many musical performances as possible into a movie with a corny plot and vacuous dialogue. Rather than deal with a big studio like Columbia, which had produced *Don't Knock the Rock*, Freed opted to work with Distributor Corporation of America, a small movie studio that granted him total control over the musical content of the movie. Freed immediately booked artists represented by all his close business associates, among them the Johnny Burnette Trio and Jimmy Cavallo and the House Rockers, who recorded on Coral, the Decca subsidiary that also released Freed's own recordings; Cirino and the Bow Ties, who recorded for Jack Hooke and Teddy Reig's Royal Roost Records; Frankie Lymon and the Teenagers of Gee Records, owned by George Goldner and Morris Levy; and the Moonglows, the Flamingos, and Chuck Berry, represented by Chess Records.

For Berry, the venture was none-too-glamorous. Rather than the glitter of Hollywood, he encountered the sweltering heat of a huge New York studio where, dressed in a white suit, Berry duckwalked and lip-synched for two lone cameramen. The song he and Leonard Chess had chosen for inclusion in the movie is an interesting one in the Berry canon. "You Can't Catch Me," recorded the previous December, was undoubtedly written after Berry's first visit to New York, because it recalls Berry's run-in with the police in the Lincoln Tunnel. Musically, Berry repeats the 2/4 hillbilly backbeat of "Maybellene" and "Thirty Days." The lyrics also work familiar territory: As he did in "No Money Down," Berry describes a fantasy car, a custom-made Flight DeVille with "a powerful motor and some hideaway wings." In the second verse, the car and driver get involved in a chase with another car ("old flattop") reminiscent of "Maybellene." As the two race "in the wee, wee hours," Berry hears the "moanin' sirens" of the highway patrol. To elude arrest, he activates his car's hidden wings and takes flight.

The final verse has Berry and his girl flying off under a moonlit sky; more important, however, as he had done in "No Money Down" and would continue to do on a number of occasions later in his career, Berry included lyrics that referred to his previous work. He gives his girl the name "Maybellene," reminding the listener, as he had done in the second verse, of his very first single. And with the car "set on flight control," he tells us that the radio is "tuned to rock and roll."

But the story of Berry's involvement in the film is far more interesting than the song he contributed to it. When the movie was released, someone involved in the project, most likely Freed himself, came up with the audacious idea of releasing a soundtrack album. Until then, long-playing records were exclusively the domain of high-brow music: classical, jazz, and showtunes. An article in *Billboard* in January 1957, a month after the film's release, noted that up to the end of 1956, "the total number of rhythm and blues LPs available was estimated to be no more than 25." The indies, according to Gary Kramer's piece, had "viewed the LP medium with caution and, in some cases, outright skepticism"; Atlantic and Chess "had no significant r&b LPs in their catalogs."

But with so many artists, labels, and publishing companies represented in Freed's film, the issue of who would release the LP and who would publish the songs would have been open to question, even though the financial success of the venture into the LP format was uncertain. Eventually, Chess was given the rights to release the recording; the publishing, however, went to Snapper Music, a company formed by Alan Freed and, in quick succession, sold to Morris Levy and his partner Phil Kahl. Levy, owner of several New York nightclubs including the legendary Birdland jazz club, was a ruthless businessman and one of the first rock-and-roll entrepreneurs to fully understand the value of copyrights. After being introduced to Freed through their mutual friend Jack Hooke, Levy, Freed, and Freed's radio station had tried, unsuccessfully, to copyright the name "rock and roll." Undaunted, Levy made his fortune buying up the recording catalogs of bankrupt labels, especially those run by his partner, George Goldner, a cash-strapped compulsive gambler.

Once again, as had been the case with "Maybellene," Chuck Berry found himself forced into a business deal that both cheated and profited him. Although he never mentions "You Can't Catch Me" by name, Berry alludes to the deal in his autobiography, claiming that Leonard Chess had again cheated him out of publishing monies in a deal with Alan Freed. "Whenever he [Chess] was about to do something that was not in your favor, he would inevitably precede the scheme with an unexpected good deed," wrote Berry. In this case, the good deed was to give his star artist "a handsome royalty check as he shoved an unrelated songwriter's agreement toward me to sign quickly as he was leaving for an urgent appointment." The agreement was undoubtedly the one that gave the publishing rights to "You Can't Catch Me" to Snapper Music, as Berry was to note that "six months later I realized what took place at the signing which took me twenty-eight years to redeem." That would have been 1984, the year that the song was re-registered with the Library of Congress as a copyright administered by Isalee, Chuck Berry's own publishing company.

Had Chuck Berry been cheated out of his royalties by his employer and mentor, as he claims? Or had Chess and Berry realized that the deal would further Chuck Berry's career, and that for the sake of losing publishing rights he could gain tremendous exposure in a movie and on the soundtrack, a "legitimate" LP recording? Certainly, Berry and Chess would have been well aware that Elvis Presley had begun shooting his first picture, eventually to be called *Love Me Tender*, that month in Hollywood. While *Rock, Rock, Rock*, independently produced and cheaply filmed (the entire production took a mere two weeks), was hardly the vehicle for Chuck Berry that *Love Me Tender* was to become for Presley, the movie did, perhaps, represent legitimacy as well as money and visibility for Berry's career.

When Chuck Berry returned to St. Louis that September, it was not as a Hollywood movie star. And there were more problems to deal with at home. At some point that month, the original Chuck Berry Combo disbanded. Signs of unrest had been appearing since earlier that summer. Berry's appearance at the Club Riviera on June 29 and 30 that summer, for example, had been billed in the *Argus* as being with Jimmy Houston's 14-piece orchestra rather than the combo. Naturally, different accounts exist as to exactly what happened. Berry has always insisted that he let Ebby Hardy and Johnnie Johnson go because of their incessant drinking on the road; indeed, by that time Johnson was very much in the grips of his lifelong battle with alcoholism. And, mindful of the gospel of economic independence preached by Booker T. Washington and others, Berry realized how important it was to be his own operator. On the road, he could book himself into clubs and use local musicians for his backing band for one night, paying them union scale and pocketing the rest of the guarantee himself.

Johnson, however, maintained that the pace of the incessant touring was getting too much for both he and Hardy; additionally, Berry was starting to fly to shows, something that Johnson refused to do. "When he came back from his first trip, we hooked up together, and maybe four or five months we played," Johnson remembered. "And then he starts flying over, and I wasn't flying nowhere." So, in the September 28, 1956, edition of the *St. Louis Argus*, a small advertisement appeared announcing the appearance of "Johnnie (Sir John's) Johnson, His Piano and His Royal Knights," at the Moonlight Inn, a bar on Tudor in East St. Louis. At the bottom of the advertisement, Johnson is listed as having "formerly played with Buddy Johnson" and, in slightly bolder type, "Chuck Berry's Orch."

The loss of Hardy and Johnson was hardly a crushing blow for Berry.

That month saw the release, still under the name of the Chuck Berry Combo, of the next Chess single, containing two new Berry compositions titled "Too Much Monkey Business" and "Brown Eyed Handsome Man." The former once again revealed Berry's genius for detail, wordplay, and rhythmic structure in his lyrics, as the couplets in each verse describe the mundane routine of everyday occupations that only succeeds in exasperating the song's narrator.

But it is the other side of the single that makes the release truly significant among Berry songs. "Brown Eyed Handsome Man," written in 1956, boasts an extraordinary set of lyrics that, if not for the first time in a popular song, then certainly for the first time in a rock-and-roll song, expressed pride in being black. The title indicates brown eyes, and—but for the times—it could equally well have said "brown skinned," so overt was its message. The song's dramatic opening lyric describes an all-too-familiar situation that Berry and many blacks before and since have encountered: the constant harassment of the legal system. Berry's protagonist finds himself in the courtroom, having been "arrested on charges of unemployment," a wonderful phrase that in just five words manages to describe both the social and economic inequalities that were—and are even today—realities for many African Americans.

But Berry had an even more radical, even subversive message for his listeners: Many of the verses describe women of some social standing, presumably blue-eyed themselves, in pursuit of the brown-eyed man. In the first verse, it is the judge's wife who pleads for the man's release; in the fourth, a young girl deciding "between a doctor and a lawyer man" is told by her mother to "find yourself a brown-eyed handsome man." These were words that must have confirmed the worst fears of Asa Carter and Elvis Presley's critics from earlier that summer.

But the last two verses are pivotal and, although Berry encompasses their true meaning in humor, the point is taken. In the first, Berry introduces "Milo Venus," that epitome of European art who, like those who championed her artistic value, "had the world in the palm of her hand." "But," sings Berry, "she lost both her arms in a wrestling match/To get a brown-eyed handsome man." If, as critics like Fred Rothwell have argued, the song is thinly disguised autobiography and Berry is the song's brown-eyed handsome man, then beneath the playfulness of the words lies a deeper meaning: Rock and roll, in the guise of Berry, will triumph over high-brow culture in the artistic struggle of the modern world.

And the last verse, a scene that Berry described later as "a fictional condition always appreciated in a baseball game," takes on added meaning given the year and the race of the protagonist. It described a last-minute home run scored with "two, three the count with nobody on" by the brown-eyed handsome man. In 1956, audiences would have instantly recognized this as a reference to Jackie Robinson who, a decade earlier and at tremendous personal cost, had broken the color barrier in American professional sports by becoming the first black baseball player in the white major leagues. By 1956, he and a handful of other black baseball players were still the only blacks playing any of the professional sports in the country; Robinson, however, by virtue of his skill on the field and his eloquent defense of civil rights off it, had become a household name.

It could hardly have been a surprise, then, to Berry or the Chess brothers that the single did not have mass appeal. Both sides of the single charted on the *Billboard* R&B charts, with "Too Much Monkey Business" peaking at number 4 and "Brown Eyed Handsome Man" at number 5. But the single made no appearance on the *Hot 100*, suggesting that the song's appeal was predominantly to Berry's smaller black audience.

Meanwhile, on the road Chuck Berry became an unwitting witness to the racism that was escalating in the South that fall. The beginnings of school integration all over the country, following the *Brown v. Board of Education* decision in 1954, resulted in riots in Mansfield, Texas, Sturgis, Kentucky, and Clinton, Tennessee. At a show in Little Rock, Arkansas, Berry—along with bassist Little Aaron Mosby, pianist Dinky Lewis, and saxophone player Johnny Floyd Smith—was attacked by a group of whites. As Little Aaron remembered it,

> this club that we were playing in Little Rock; we went there and did this show. When we came out, Chuck's Cadillac—he had a red Cadillac with a spare on the back, beautiful Cadillac. So we went and got in the car. Chuck then come out— I guess he knew what was happening—and when we got in that car they was throwing bricks and bottles and trying to break the windows out.

Inside the club, some time after the performance had ended, members of the audience caught Berry in an embrace with a young white girl. The all-too-predictable response of some of the audience members led the band to rush out of the club and into Berry's car. "Later on Chuck run to the Cadillac," according to Mosby, "got in the Cadillac and scooted her over, vroom, and got away. I was sitting there, I was scared to death, man. I said, 'Lord, I'm gonna lose my life.'"

It was clearly a dangerous time for Berry to be touring, even beyond the racial climate of America in the late 1950s. Now that he was touring on his own, often playing with unfamiliar local pickup bands, he was vulnerable to all manner of rip-offs and deceptions. Richard Nader, a concert promoter whose own dealings with Berry created problems for both of them in the 1970s, recalls a story Berry once told him about a show he had played in Fayetteville, North Carolina. After agreeing on a fee of $750, Berry made the

800-mile trip from St. Louis only to find an audience of 20 teenagers in a seedy ice-cream parlor. Against his better judgment, Berry played the show, only to be handed at the end of the night a fee of $1.75 and a list of expenses. "She had everything down there," Nader recalled Berry saying, "down to the light bulbs." It was a lesson Chuck Berry would never forget, one that would shape his view of the music business from then on.

Berry also recalls being turned away from shows in the South when promoters learned that he was black. At a show in Knoxville, he was barred from the auditorium when the promoter told him, "It's a country dance and we had no idea that 'Maybellene' was recorded by a niggra man." Although Berry was able to recoup the deposit on the contract, such humiliations must have taken their toll, even though many of these incidents were of Berry's own making. Vocally, the recordings he had made gave little clue to the race of the singer. More important, the publicity shots he had furnished to the Gale Agency had been underexposed causing Berry's facial features to appear lighter than they actually were. In all probability, the shots, taken by his cousin Harry Davis and developed either in his or in Berry's own darkroom, had the effect of creating an ambiguous racial identity for the singer. Like the information Johnnie Johnson saw on Berry's driver's license during the traffic stop in the Lincoln Tunnel a year before, it was another example of Chuck Berry denying (or at least obfuscating) his race. It would be hard to conceive of a white performer attempting the same thing; Elvis Presley may have become successful—like other white performers, before and since—by imitating black performers, but never once would he have felt it necessary to change his appearance and pass for black. For Chuck Berry, however, such racial ambiguity was necessary if he, like Presley, was to cultivate a white audience.

The year 1956 ended in the same way that the previous year had. In November, Berry was back out on the road as one of several artists on another one of Irving Feld's package tours, the "Biggest Show of 1956." On Saturday, November 3, Berry, Bill Haley, the Platters, Frankie Lymon and the Teenagers, and several other acts (including the ubiquitous Buddy Johnson Orchestra), played two shows at the Missouri Theater. It must have been a sweet homecoming for Berry, because the theater was located on Grand Avenue, just a stone's throw from the Fox, now forever etched in his memory with the segregation of his childhood.

That December, the movie and companion soundtrack of *Go, Go, Go* finally were released. The movie itself was hardly a critical or artistic success, although Berry's commanding stage presence was singled out by Gary Kramer of *Billboard* as being the "most impressive act in the picture. He mimes the lyrics of the tune with his hands, feet, face and body movements, all but making a humorous ballet of it. His performance alone," concluded

Kramer, "is worth the price of admission." The single of "You Can't Catch Me" along with "Havana Moon" did not fare so well, however. Despite the obvious publicity boost given the former song by the film, and the calypso-flavored flip side, released at a time when Harry Belafonte had made such music popular (the week of the soundtrack album's release, Belafonte's "Jamaica, Farewell" and "Mary's Boy Child," along with a cover of his "Banana Boat Song" by the Tarriers were all in the *Billboard Top 100*), the single failed to enter any of the music charts, the first Chuck Berry single in his short career to date to do so.

Musically and personally, it had been a mixed year for Berry. He had achieved some success with "Roll Over Beethoven," only to see his first chart failure at the end of the year. His relationship with Johnnie Johnson had become tenuous at best, and the Chuck Berry Combo had fallen apart. Professionally, he had been forced into making yet another business deal that again had simultaneously worked for and against him; he had also, by choice and by necessity, presented himself ambiguously to the world.

So, between Chuck Berry and the Chess Brothers there must have been a sense that there was more to be achieved; 1956 was the year that rock and roll exploded into the American conscience, with Elvis Presley leading the pack. On October 24, just days after Chuck Berry's 30th birthday, *Variety's* front page announced that Presley had made his first million in less than a year; he had starred in the most-watched television appearance ever on the *Ed Sullivan Show* in September and would go on to rack up record sales of 7 million for the year. Of course, Presley was white; but Berry could not have been unaware that two of his black contemporaries had begun to achieve success on almost as great a scale. Little Richard had scored five entries on the *Billboard Hot 100* that year, including "Long Tall Sally" and "The Girl Can't Help It," which both cracked the Top 10 in April and December. And Fats Domino was already achieving unparalleled success for a black R&B artist. "I'm in Love Again," "My Blue Heaven," "When My Dreamboat Comes Home," "So Long," "Blueberry Hill," "What's the Reason I'm Not Pleasing You," and "Blue Monday" had all achieved extraordinary success on both the R&B and pop charts that year. Domino was well on the way to having 16 gold records, with certified sales of a million or more during the decade of 1948–1958, placing him second only to crooner Bing Crosby, who had 20 gold discs in his entire career to that point. Early in 1957, when Berry and Domino shared the bill on Irving Feld's "Greatest Show of 1957," Berry heard the rumor that Domino was earning $10,000 for one appearance. Chuck Berry knew that, with one big-selling single, a black entertainer could achieve that kind of success. In 1957, he was determined it would be his.

In January, Berry made his usual trek to Chicago for another recording session for the Chess brothers. With him was Johnnie Johnson; the two had recorded together briefly the previous month and their relationship, at least at this point, was not so badly strained as to hinder them from making music together in the studio. Significantly, the two were set to record a song they had worked up some point during the previous year, although the subsequent single, like the one before it, would not be issued under the name of the Chuck Berry Combo. Berry had contributed the words, a lyric deliberately pitched to the teenagers who had been the most visible faces at his shows since his debut at the Brooklyn Paramount nearly 16 months before. Rather than singing about cars or the problems of adult life, he would sing about school, something all of his audience could identify with.

The chords and rhythmic structure were based around the piano boogie Johnson had taken from Meade "Lux" Lewis's "Honky Tonk Train Blues" and renamed "Johnnie's Boogie." Because of the rhythm, the song needed an intro. Recalled Johnson:

> You just can't go right into a shuffle, it don't sound right. You need an intro. Chuck had that Carl Hogan intro he liked to use, but it didn't seem to fit what we was doin'. We played around and played around, finally I said since we were doin' it in G, we could use the intro to "Johnnie's Boogie," which I got from "Honky Tonk Train." That was supposed to sound like a train whistle. Well, when Chuck played it on the guitar we thought it sounded like a school bell ringin', and that was perfect for a song called "School Days" [sic].

Rhythmically, instead of the continuous train-like shuffle of "Johnnie's Boogie" or "Downbound Train," Berry decided on a more driving beat, almost a combination of a shuffle and the 2/4 beat of "Maybellene." For extra effect, drummer Fred Below was instructed to stop at the end of each verse; according to Berry, this was "to emphasize the jumps and changes I found in classes in high school compared to the one room and one teacher I had in elementary school." And over the chugging, incessant rhythm section of Fred Below on drums and Willie Dixon on bass, Berry's guitar mimics his vocal melody at the end of each line.

Lyrically, "School Day" may not have been Berry's best; some, including Fred Rothwell, have argued that it is too commercially calculated. Yet Berry was still able to build some narrative tension into the piece. The first two verses, for example, contain a litany of problems reminiscent of "Too Much Monkey Business" and "Brown Eyed Handsome Man," all written in the second person, "you," to enable the teenage audience to identify with the song. The first verse speaks of suffering through classes in "American history and practical math" while "the guy behind you won't leave you alone." The second verse continues in the same vein, complaining of being "lucky if you can find a seat" in the lunchroom, and being "fortunate if you have time to eat." Arriving back into class after recess, Berry sings a familiar complaint of all students of all ages: "Gee, but the teacher don't know how mean she looks."

The next two verses, however, follow the student out of school and into the "juke joint" for some dancing, with the rock-and-roll music giving him a feeling of liberation. At this point, the song takes off, with Berry's guitar providing the familiar, fluid two-string lead that by now had become his signature sound. After the break, the last verse is repeated before Berry breaks into the "Hail! Hail! Rock and Roll" refrain. "Deliver me from the days of old," Berry sings for his teenage fans, once again reminding them, as he did in "Roll Over Beethoven," how much of a break with the past rock and roll represented. Again, in Berry's lyric, high and low culture had been pitted against each other; in the very song itself the beat of Fred Below's "drums loud and bold" was delivering Berry's listeners from the old ways of school, of the establishment. In 2 minutes and 40 seconds, a 30-year-old man had distilled the essence of teenage existence and defiance: How could the song fail?

On March 16, the week of the single's release, *Billboard* correctly predicted that the song "can't miss." By the first week in April, the song had entered the *Billboard Hot 100* at number 78; a slow, steady climb up the charts brought it to number 11 by the end of the month. At that point, it became clear to Phil Chess that the song was going to be huge for the company; the song had become "the biggest thing we ever had: The tune has caught on locally like a house-a-fire," he noted, adding that the tune had already received orders of more than 100,000 "and the disk isn't even a month old."

Throughout May and the first three weeks in June, the song stayed in the Top 10, rising as high as number 5 on May 27. It would stay in the charts for a remarkable 24 weeks, to be joined by another song, "Oh Baby Doll," at the end of July; for 7 weeks at the end of the summer, Berry would have two songs in the charts simultaneously. Once again, though, Elvis Presley dominated the charts that spring and summer, with "All Shook Up" and "Teddy Bear" taking top honors in May and August, respectively.

The weeks leading up to the success of "School Day" were tremendously busy. On February 1, Berry returned to the Apollo for another week-long engagement with the Buddy Johnson Orchestra and two vocal groups, the Spaniels and the Cleftones. *Variety* apparently had forgotten all about Berry in the intervening months, because the review of his portion of the show was featured in its "New Acts" column. But Berry's act was singled out for praise by the trade paper. The writer described him as "an energetic guitar-strumming Negro singer" and "a natural for a rhythm and blues bill" and went on to note his lively performance. "He sparks his songstering with some frantic maneuvering in an acrobatic vein," the reviewer noted, referring to Berry's by-now trademark duckwalk and other, similar stage antics. But, the reviewer went on to say, "It's strictly in the r'n'r groove and in that idiom the frenetic and athletic delivery had appeal." Indeed, the review of the whole show took a similar tone; the acts, Berry included, were good at their genre—but the genre itself had some serious shortcomings. "Current Apollo bill is heavy on vocals, with a good portion of the lyrics indistinguishable," the opening paragraph began. "It's a generally noisy session. In their metier, the acts are okay, and that's about it."

Beginning on February 15, Chuck took part in yet another grueling package tour promoted by Irving Feld's Super Attractions agency. Featuring Berry, Fats Domino, LaVern Baker, Clyde McPhatter, Bill Doggett, and a number of vocal groups (including Chess labelmates the Moonglows), the tour was hugely successful: Two sold-out shows at Syria Mosque in Pittsburgh, the traditional opening location for all Feld's rock-and-roll shows, were followed by sell-outs in Detroit and Youngstown and near-capacity crowds in Toledo, Indianapolis, and Toronto.

On February 23, it was back to St. Louis for a show at the Kiel Auditorium. The following week, the *Argus*'s Buddy Lonesome described the scene in a piece headlined "3,500 Shriek for Fats Domino and other R&R Stars." Lonesome made much of the fact that "no one was injured" at the show, despite similar shows headlined by Domino at the Brooklyn Paramount and elsewhere being marred by "riots," a reference to the incidents from the previous year. The relative calm, Lonesome noted, was due to the "many local police in attendance." Interestingly, the only performer mentioned in the review was Atlanta-born Tommy Brown, the new lead singer for Bill Doggett's band, who was now based in St. Louis and heralded as "a local product." Conspicuous by his absence in Lonesome's review was the other local product on the bill that night: Chuck Berry.

Lonesome's review underscored the black middle-class community's discomfort with rock and roll in general and Berry in particular. As Chick Finney had done before, Lonesome made no comment on the music's merits except, perhaps, in the implied criticism of the column's headline that, once again, said more about the teenage audience's inability to behave in a respectable manner. Moreover, Lonesome had seen fit to comment on the dangers of the music, indicating that the black middle class, like its white counterpart, still viewed rock and roll as encouraging violence and antisocial behavior. And Berry had once again been shunned by the black press in his hometown, while Tommy Brown, striving for success in a more R&B-oriented outfit, was singled out for praise.

Shortly after the Kiel Show, Feld took the unusual step of chartering two Convair planes to fly the artists to dates in the West, including stops in Denver, Salt Lake City, Butte, Calgary, Edmonton, Spokane, Tacoma, Portland, Vancouver, and Seattle. In Portland at the Civic Auditorium on March 5, the tour grossed $39,000 over the course of three shows. After that, the tour began its long swing back East, hitting a number of auditoriums already played during the first half of the tour. So great was the drawing power of the acts that when the show returned to the Syria Mosque in Pittsburgh on April 10, it grossed $18,000 in two shows. On April 20, the ensemble made another stop in St. Louis for two more shows at the Kiel Auditorium. Once again, the *Argus* made little of Berry's appearance. In three similarly-worded articles written to promote the shows in the weeks leading up to them, the paper virtually ignored Berry, enticing its readers with the promise of another chance to see Fats Domino instead. It was yet another example of black St. Louis turning its back on its successful son.

On May 5, with "School Day" firmly entrenched in the *Billboard* Top 10, the tour concluded; the following day, without missing a beat, Berry was in Chicago for his next recording session with Chess. It was a tremendously productive session, with Berry laying down the next two singles, "Oh Baby Doll" and "Rock and Roll Music," as well as one minor gem, "Thirteen Question Method," his first experiment with formula lyrics that he was to perfect in "Reelin' and Rockin'" the following year. But the session was notable for another reason: This time, Lafayette Leake, a stalwart of the Chicago blues scene, had replaced Johnnie Johnson as Berry's pianist.

"Oh Baby Doll," the first release, was yet another variation on the 2/4 hillbilly backbeat rhythm, this time taken at breakneck speed. Lyrically, the song was deliberately calculated to follow up "School Day"; this time, however, Berry sings of a high-school romance that threatens to disrupt classes. Painting a typical scene of high-school mischief, Berry and his friends celebrate every time the teacher leaves the room; with a "portable radio" (a symbol of 1950s teen independence) providing the accompaniment, "we was ballin' the jack." But, "we'd be all back in order when the teacher got back."

"Rock and Roll Music" also does not represent a major departure lyrically; like "Roll Over Beethoven," it praises the merits of rock music while condemning the more high-brow music of the black middle class: jazz. Modern jazz, in Berry's opinion, has become as arty as a "symphony," changing the "beauty of the melody." But rock and roll—played in the black clubs "over cross the tracks" in the undesirable section of town—is the music Berry and his girl prefer, because it emphasizes a simple melody and beat. And it is rock's humble roots Berry celebrates in the song's third verse. Describing a down-home, hillbilly "jamboree," replete with moonshine and dancing, Berry notes that the music gets everyone "all shook up"—a direct reference to Elvis Presley and the criticism of his earthy, "hillbilly" style.

The summer continued at an unbelievably hectic pace. With "School Day" still in the *Billboard* charts, Berry played a number of shows on the East Coast, including shows at Carr's Beach in Maryland, and Schenectady, New York, before heading to New York City to film another short segment for an

Alan Freed movie. This time, the song to be lip-synched was "Oh Baby Doll" for *Mr. Rock and Roll*, a movie that was to follow the same formula as *Rock, Rock, Rock* and that, on its release the following October, would garner even less critical acclaim. The relationship with Freed, despite the deejay's growing alcoholism, was still strong that summer, and Berry was invited back to New York the following month to star in Freed's latest Broooklyn Paramount show. This time, however, the weeklong engagement at the Paramount seemed less successful than in the past, partly because Freed's New York teenage audience had abandoned the heat of the city for camp or vacation with their parents. Those who remained behind were once again singled out for heavy criticism by the established entertainment press. Commenting on the unruly behavior of some in the crowd, *Variety* expressed its displeasure that the front few rows tried to "virtually beseige" the stage and that the girls, in particular, were "constantly doing something to excite attention" from the performers. "The demonstration is noisy and much of it is exhibitionistic," the reviewer noted, declaring that "Behavior of that kind from the first few rows isn't normal from any seat in the house." The *New York Times*, however, under the headline "Rock 'n' Rollers Collect Calmly," noted that the crowds were very quiet, and that the barricades in the area around Flatbush Avenue were, after the opening day crowd had entered, completely superfluous.

Once again, Freed himself was singled out by *Variety* for some harsh criticism as they claimed he was failing to expand rock and roll's horizons. "His taste is limited and seemingly without the imagination to give it [rock and roll] a wider base." Rock and roll, the reviewer noted, needed a wider audience and "literate and understanding composers." But in a moment of conciliation, the reviewer singled out the "professionals" in the show for their "air of authority." LaVern Baker, Clyde McPhatter, Big Joe Turner, and most of all Chuck Berry were praised—especially Berry, for his "hearty tone that holds on to his audience despite the fact that the show is overlong at this point."

Back home in St. Louis, another violent incident marred a rock performance. At a show at the Kiel Auditorium on August 12, featuring Roy Hamilton, the Clovers, the Spaniels, Ella Johnson, and Screamin' Jay Hawkins, a member of the audience, Clyde Phelps, was shot to death in the balcony. The following week, the *St. Louis Argus* contained an editorial warning against accusing the music of lessening moral values. "You can't blame the rock 'n' roll artists that had come to entertain," the paper declared, adding, "Undoubtedly, however, that is where a lot of the blame will fall."

Gripping the attention of blacks and whites in St. Louis and the nation, however, was the growing issue of school integration. After the 1954 *Brown v. Board of Education* decision and the May 1955 admonition from the

Supreme Court that integration should take place "with all deliberate speed," many Southern and Midwestern states, including Missouri, had failed to follow the government's ruling. On July 5, concluding a series of articles on the issue, Buddy Lonesome offered a scathing attack in the pages of the *Argus* on his fellow blacks of St. Louis for dragging their heels on integration. "It seems as if the Negro parents in this city are either inescapably rooted in deep-seated lethargy—or they just don't really care," he wrote, adding that the local chapter of the NAACP was not helping any by focusing more on jobs than on segregation issues.

It was a timely wake-up call. Two months later, the nation watched as Arkansas state troopers barred nine black students from entering Central High in Little Rock. As the month of September wore on, the nation sat glued to their televisions and watched as government troops were sent in to ensure that the students could attend school and integration could continue throughout the country.

For Chuck Berry, however, it was business as usual. As the crowds surrounded Central High, Berry was at the Syria Mosque in Pittsburgh once more, kicking off yet another Irving Feld tour with Fats Domino, LaVern Baker, and Clyde McPhatter. With them this time was Frankie Lymon, now almost 17, without his group the Teenagers, and enjoying what would be the last major hit of his brief career, "Goody, Goody." The tour also featured some relative newcomers to the business. The Everly Brothers, riding the crest of their first hit single, "Bye Bye Love," had just released their second major release, "Wake Up Little Suzie." A 16-year-old from Ottawa, Paul Anka, was the youngest; his first single, "Diana," was at number 2 on the *Billboard* charts as the tour began. But the first artist Berry met and befriended was Buddy Holly, who would celebrate his 21st birthday two days after the tour began.

Berry initially met Holly and his band, the Crickets, in New York as they were finishing up a week's engagement at the Brooklyn Paramount with Alan Freed over the Labor Day holiday, and the two immediately struck up a friendship. The impressionable young Holly must have relished the opportunity to hang out with Berry; although Elvis Presley was his great idol, he would have been fascinated by Berry's abilities as a songwriter and his by now solid career in the music business. Indeed, "Brown Eyed Handsome Man" and "Roll Over Beethoven" were both featured songs in the Crickets' 10-minute section of the shows on that tour. In return, Berry was able to dispense a lot of the wisdom he had accumulated on the road, something that the Crickets and Holly must have valued, given their relatively newfound fame.

Initially, the two rode on one of the two Greyhound tour buses chartered for the tour; it is unlikely, however, that the frugal Berry ever shot craps with Holly at the back of the bus, as Holly's biographer, Ellis Amburn, has maintained. At some point in the tour, however, Berry bought a Cadillac; occasionally, he would take along Holly's bassist, Joe B. Mauldin, for company, but mostly the new transportation was more suited to the private Berry, who could now come and go before and after the shows as he pleased. In terms of its routing and its commercial success, the fall version of the "Biggest Show of Stars" was an almost carbon copy of its spring predecessor. 11 of the first 21 dates were sold out, according to *Variety*, with the remainder about 80 percent full; more important, however, the tour had been remarkably quiet despite the turmoil of the desegregation issues being played out in the South. But after the show in Raleigh, North Carolina, on September 19, the white acts, Buddy Holly and the Crickets, the Everly Brothers, and Paul Anka, all temporarily left the tour. It proved to be a shrewd move on Irving Feld's part, as he happily reported to *Variety* that there were " 'no incidents of any kind in the South,' " "although," continued *Variety*, "white persons made up a large part of the audience for the rock 'n' roller." Eventually, the Crickets and Paul Anka rejoined the tour when it arrived in safer territory in Tulsa on the 28th, with the Everly Brothers reuniting with the tour in California two weeks later.

After a relentless, month-long grind through Texas, California, the Pacific Northwest, and Canada, the tour then began to swing through the Midwest, where Berry encountered an unwelcome surprise in his hometown. At the November 6 show at the Kiel Auditorium, he was greeted backstage by local policemen with a warrant for his arrest. Stunned, Berry demanded to know what he was being arrested for; the detectives informed him that he was wanted in connection with an armed robbery of a white insurance man, Clarence Workes, at his home on Olive Street the previous June. They ordered him to appear at the St. Louis police headquarters the following day. Armed with a contract for the show at Carr's Beach as an alibi, Berry promptly arrived at the police station on the morning after the show; a statement by Workes also cleared Berry of the charges, and he promptly left the station, got in his Cadillac, and rejoined the tour in Indianapolis that night. But his teenage felony, and more significantly his growing fame and his race, were beginning to attract the attention of the St. Louis police.

The last three weeks of November the tour revisited the East Coast, with shows back at the Syria Mosque in Pittsburgh, Boston, and Hartford. The Boston show was to prove memorable as the only dates on the tour where any real trouble broke out. Though the Boston Garden was only a little over two-thirds full for the occasion, the tour still managed to draw 8,000 for one performance. But according to *Variety* a week later, "a 28-man police detail, assigned to keep order, made 12 arrests including a 40-year-old woman." *Variety* went on to report that "some two-dozen teenagers were put out when the beat made them 'too energetic.' "

The following day, Boston Municipal Court Chief Justice Elijah Adlow decided not to press charges of disturbing a public assembly on five of those arrested. Humorously, he decided that as the five had paid the exorbitant sum of $3 a piece for their tickets, they had already been punished enough. However, on a more serious and eerily prophetic note, the Judge called for local authorities to stop granting permits to promoters for rock and roll shows; they were, he declared, "a good thing for someone, but terrible for Boston."

On November 24, six days after a show in Ottawa where Paul Anka was greeted with hysteria as he returned home a hero, the tour concluded with a show at the Richmond Mosque in Virginia. Berry, along with the rest of the performers, was free to go home for the Thanksgiving holiday. In all, they had played 77 cities in 79 days, a punishing schedule that had seen them perform in over half the U.S. states and five Canadian provinces.

Looking back at the year in the Chess studios that December, Berry must have believed that success on the scale of Elvis Presley's was now his for the taking. "Rock and Roll Music" had become his second Top 10 hit of the year and was on its way to spending 18 weeks on the *Billboard* charts. Berry was in an expansive mood, even reconciling with Johnnie Johnson, who had accompanied him on the Irving Feld tour and to 2120 South Michigan Avenue for the recording date. Small wonder, then, that 1958 would become his *annus mirablis*, cementing his place once and for all in the pantheon of twentieth-century entertainers and musicians.

Windermere Place

Because my mouth
Is wide with laughter
And my throat
Is deep with song,
You do not think
I suffer after
I have held my pain
So long?
　　　　　—Langston Hughes, "Minstrel Man"

On July 15, 1958, Chuck Berry—accompanied by Themetta and their two daughters, 8-year-old Ingrid and 6-year-old Melody—got into the Cadillac and embarked on a short but enormously symbolic journey. In all likelihood, they left the house on Whittier and traveled southwest past the Homer G. Phillips Hospital, then right onto Easton Avenue, passing the offices of Chuck Berry Music that had opened six months earlier. They drove northwest a little over a mile, past the storefronts and the whitewashed façade of the small *St. Louis Argus* office, before turning southwest onto Kingshighway. Here, they made a quick right on Page and an equally quick left onto Union where, opposite Soldan High School—looking more like a medieval castle than a place of learning—they paused briefly to look at the two ornate pillars that stood guard over the homes of Windermere Place. All told, the trip was about three miles and had taken about ten minutes. But for Chuck Berry, it was a journey that had taken 32 years to complete.

Windermere Place is a cul-de-sac of 31 houses all built between 1896 and 1914, located just north of Forest Park, the scenic heart of St. Louis and home to the 1904 World's Fair. Most were built of red brick in the Colonial Revival style, two-story structures symmetrically built around a central door. Some had columned porches, others cupolas or dormer windows extending up from their roofs. Number 13, the house Chuck Berry had purchased four days earlier and that was the family's final destination that day, was no exception. The 11-room, two-story house boasted three large dormer windows rising up over the red-tiled roof and windows framed with stone blocks, an architectural feature known as a Gibbs surround. Six stone steps led visitors over a small, neatly groomed, sloping front lawn to an imposing front door flanked by two large bushes and two larger trees. It was quite a difference from the modest one-story, five-room brick cottage on Whittier, which lay the width of a sidewalk away from the road and four feet from the houses on either side.

Set back from the bustle of Union Avenue, the cumulative effect of the architecture and the silence transported the visitor back a century or more; Windermere Place was—and to this day still is—an elegant and exclusive St. Louis address. The Berrys' next door neighbors, the Williams, had moved there three years earlier from New Jersey so that the father, Paul, could take a position as a surgeon at Homer G. Phillips. Their daughter Paulette—who would later change her name to Ntozake Shange and become a well-known and respected African-American poet, playwright, and novelist—recalls jazz musicians Dizzy Gillespie and Miles Davis visiting the house; the black intellectual and philosopher W. E. B. Du Bois also frequented the home from time to time.

Clearly, the Berrys were now members of the black middle class. Like many of the Ville residents in the 1950s—indeed like many of the inhabitants of the city of St. Louis—they had moved west just in time to see the once-proud Ville neighborhood deteriorate; in the 20 years between 1950 and 1970, the Ville's population was almost halved as the families who could afford to moved away. Since the 1947 *Shelley v. Kraemer* ruling permitted blacks to own property anywhere in St. Louis, middle class blacks were now as free as their white counterparts to flee the inner city for more attractive suburban surroundings. In the 10 years between the passage of the ruling and the Berry family's move to Windermere Place, the areas immediately to the north and east of Forest Park had become about 30 percent black.

If the road to Windermere Place had been long and arduous, the last six months of the journey had been especially difficult. It had begun early in the New Year with a recording session at 2120 South Michigan Avenue; on January 6, Berry recorded seven new songs, two of which—"Sweet Little Sixteen" and "Reelin' and Rockin'"—were natural choices for the next single.

"Reelin' and Rockin'" was yet another example of Chuck Berry's ability to synthesize sources and create something that, if not new, was distinctively his own. The first and most obvious source for the song, as Johnnie Johnson has observed, is Bill Haley's "Rock Around the Clock"; Berry's lyrics adopt the same formulaic idea of starting a couplet with a time (such as "nine-twenty-one") and rhyming the second line ("having nothing but fun") with it. But other sources—including "Around the Clock Blues" recorded by both Wynonie Harris and Big Joe Turner, Jimmy McCraklin's "Rockin' All Day," and "Let 'Em Roll Blues," by King Perry—also contributed melodically and lyrically to Berry's updated version of the song.

Berry's version begins with his guitar playing several hesitant, slurred chords, perfectly matching the vocal line "Sometimes I will, then again I think I won't," sung before the whole band enters. Then, as if to punctuate the point, the band drops out, playing simple accents behind the humorous couplets of Berry's exposed vocal lines. At that point, the whole band jumps in with a straight-four rock rhythm over which Berry sings the chorus. Once again, as he had done with "Roll Over Beethoven" and "Rock and Roll Music" the previous year, Berry had used the lyric to extol the virtues of the new music. Here, though, for the first time, Berry also hinted at the sexual underpinnings of the music: "Well I looked at my watch and to my surprise/I was dancing with a woman who was twice my size," Berry sings toward the end of the song. In later years he was to change the lyrics and make them closer to the overt sexuality of Wynonie Harris's and Big Joe Turner's versions.

Instrumentally, however, the song features Johnnie Johnson's piano rather than Berry's guitar and provides another illustration of Leonard Chess's role in creating Chuck Berry's music. It was, as Johnson recalled, "the first song where Leonard had me rip the keys. What rippin' the keys meant was that you dragged your hands up the keys while you was playin' like Jerry Lee Lewis does." Chess, always aware of what was going on in the music business, obviously felt that the song needed the kind of energy Lewis had exhibited on his second single, "Great Balls of Fire," the previous November. When Johnson was reluctant to follow his instructions, however, Chess was more than willing to show Johnson what he wanted to hear. "I don't usually do that," Johnson explained,

> 'cause I felt it was all flash and no technique, but Leonard said it made the piano sound more excitin'. . . . While we was rehearsin', he'd come out of the booth and rip the keys himself while I was playin'. Then he'd give me this big ol' smile. It was kinda like he was sayin' 'That's right, I did it.' Leonard was a character, boy. Thing was, he was right most of the time, too. He knew what he was doin' when it came to makin' records.

Like "Reelin' and Rockin'," "Sweet Little Sixteen" was another showcase for Johnnie Johnson's piano. Leonard Chess again had Johnson ripping the keys to create a Jerry Lee Lewis excitement to the song. "I 'bout tore my thumbnail off," he recalls, "tryin' to get the piano part where Leonard Chess wanted it. He had me rippin' the keys up and down and up and down on the solo." Lyrically, as Berry himself has mentioned in *The Autobiography*, the song was inspired by an incident on the Irving Feld tour the previous November. The scene of a young fan, running frantically around backstage at the Ottawa Coliseum trying to gather as many autographs as she possibly could, provided the impetus. What makes the song interesting musically, though, is the tension created between the rhythm section and Berry's guitar. While the drums and bass play a swing shuffle, Berry's plays his trademark straight four on guitar. Additionally, for the first half of the first verse and for the whole of the second, the instruments drop out during the vocal line. The whole effect is to create a push-me-pull-you tension, perfectly capturing the girl's excitement.

The lyrics once again revealed Berry's ability to capture the teenage sensibility. The second verse, with its depiction of the "teenage blues," must have resonated loudly with its listeners, who would have been all too familiar with the girl's plight at having to abandon her "tight dresses and lipstick" the following day when she was "back in classes again."

But the lyrics also reveal another side of Berry's astute business mind, as the opening line of the chorus, "They're really rocking in Boston/Pittsburgh PA," is substituted in the two middle choruses for the line, "They'll be rocking on Bandstand/Philadelphia PA." The line, quite simply, was a blatant plug for *American Bandstand*, the Philadelphia-based television show hosted by Dick Clark, Alan Freed's rival in marketing youth culture to America in the late 1950s. It could not have escaped Berry that Clark had been able to do something that his long-time champion and business partner, despite his instinctive understanding of the teen market, had failed to do: translate his radio persona to the emerging medium of television. And Clark managed to do so with remarkable success: When *Bandstand* went to national syndication in August 1957, ABC estimated that his audience was around 20 million. Quite clearly, while still linked with Freed, Berry felt that this was a good time to begin courting Clark's goodwill.

But the line's promotion of Clark's show was fraught with meaning for black Americans, especially in St. Louis. Three days before the song was recorded, the *Argus* had published a letter claiming that Clark's program was being "Jim Crow" in showing only a "lily-white crowd" dancing to the music. The following week, the paper launched the first of a two-part attack on the racial policies on Clark's show. In conjunction with Art Peters of the black-owned *Philadelphia Tribune*, the *Argus* reporter accused the program of discriminating not only against participants, by turning away black teenagers at the door and featuring a predominantly white audience, but also against artists. Although Clark had always booked black acts on his show, they had never been allowed to dance with the audience like their white counterparts after their performances. Instead, they had been ushered to an "autograph table," where contact with the audience was limited to signing "books and scraps of paper" and participating with the crowd in a rating session for new record releases. Clark was well aware, of course, of the alleged reason for the cancelation of Alan Freed's short-lived television show in August 1957 after an appearance by Frankie Lymon. At the end of the show, Lymon was seen dancing with a young white girl, prompting Southern affiliates of ABC to pressure the network into removing Freed, a move that ultimately led to the first network airing of Clark's show from Philadelphia.

Perhaps Berry was unaware of the controversy surrounding Clark's show, and was simply trying to promote his career in his choice of lyric. But the possibility exists that once again, as he had done with "Brown Eyed Handsome Man" and was to do in his next single "Johnny B. Goode," Berry was faced with the awful reality of having to put aside issues of race in order to achieve success in the white-dominated society of the 1950s. If so, the subsequent success of "Sweet Little Sixteen" must have been bittersweet. On February 17, while "Rock and Roll Music" continued its 18-week stay on the *Billboard* pop charts, "Sweet Little Sixteen" entered the chart at number 46. Within three weeks, it reached number 2, and it spent the next 5 weeks either at the number 2 or the number 3 position, just failing to oust the Champs' instrumental "Tequila" from the number 1 spot. It was Berry's biggest selling single to date and became the second-biggest seller of his entire career.

Ironically, the song immediately became a source of contention between Berry and Clark. Not long after its release, Berry was invited to appear on *American Bandstand* for the first time to perform "Sweet Little Sixteen." Clark's version of the story is that Berry arrived 20 minutes before show time and immediately declared, "ain't going to do any dancing." Not only that, but he told Clark's producer, Tony Mamarella, that he would not lip-synch the song either. Clark immediately called Leonard Chess in Chicago, who in no uncertain terms told Berry to do exactly what Clark asked; Berry, mindful of his mentor's words, agreed to perform. Later, Clark noted that, after working with Berry on many other shows, "he's never gotten any easier to get along with; he's still an ornery son of a bitch, but I love him dearly."

It is unlikely, as Chuck Berry has maintained, that he was being asked to lip-synch for the very first time. With two movies for Alan Freed already under his belt, he would have been more than familiar with the process of miming to prerecorded music. Yet it is also unlikely, as Dick Clark has written, that the man who had promoted Clark's show on a million-selling single would simply refuse to perform on it. Instead, as happened so often in his career, this seems to be an incident in which Berry was confronted with a situation that had not been fully presented to him in advance, making him seem difficult to work with. Once Clark persuaded him to listen to Leonard Chess, the situation was diffused and he performed the song; immediately after the show was aired, however, Clark made the decision not to book Berry on *American Bandstand* again. Later, Clark would go back on his decision and the two worked together on other projects. At the time, though, Clark's growing influence in the rock-and-roll world must have ensured that word of Chuck's difficulty spread.

The visit to Clark's show was also eventful for another reason; on the show, Chuck Berry made the announcement that he now had a national fan club, headquartered at 4221 West Easton Drive, about a mile south of the house on Whittier. The announcement heralded a new phase in Berry's business life. As 1957 had progressed, Berry must have been feeling like his decision to manage his own business affairs was simply too much. He was just as vulnerable to ripoffs on the road as he had been when Teddy Reig had been his manager; meanwhile, off the road, he had quickly been taken to task by the IRS for irregular accounting procedures. After his appearance at the Stage Lounge in Chicago at the end of 1955, Red Holloway remembered that "Chuck Berry saved $100,000 the first year. . . . So the government asked him how much . . . they wanted the receipts and stuff for his expenses. So he told the taxman he ain't got none, he slept in his car and shit. So they charged him $48,000 tax!" Immediately, Berry hired Robert Goldenhersh of Rosenblum, Goldenhersh, and Silverstein to handle "his tax returns and corporate affairs," but it seemed clear that he would need someone else to take care of the day-to-day business of music.

That person was Francine Gillium, a 21-year-old blond white woman from a small town just outside of Pittsburgh. Berry's account of his meeting Francine contradicts the timeframe he establishes for the meeting in his autobiography. He maintained that they met in 1956, during a week of shows at the Rock and Roll Club in Pittsburgh. Although there is no doubt that he played those shows, the claim that they occurred after one of the Irving Feld tours with Fats Domino cannot be correct, because both of those tours occurred the following year. Berry has also disagreed with Gillium herself over how soon Gillium moved from Pennsylvania to take up residence in St. Louis. Berry maintained that the two became friends over the course of a year and that Gillium moved to Missouri on November 24, 1957—the day the second Show of Stars tour ended in Richmond, Virginia. Yet Gillium herself, only partly joking, recalled years later, "He needed a secretary and I needed a change. . . . So we went and saw Chuck Berry [at the show in Pittsburgh] and I left the next day."

Whether this uncertainty over the precise details of their meeting points to 30-year-old memory lapses or to a relationship deeper than the two are willing to admit remains the source of a great deal of speculation. However, the role of Francine Gillium as Chuck Berry's assistant has never been in dispute. It was a job with enormous responsibilities. "I was twenty-one," Gillium recalled, "and I was here a year and we had already established our offices, a night club . . . we were owning and operating two corporations." But one of her first tasks as Berry's new employee was to draft a press release detailing information about Berry's life and career to date. At her employer's dictate, Francine dutifully typed the fact that he had been born in San Jose in 1931. Berry, it should be said, was hardly the first show-business personality to shave several years off his age in an attempt to appeal to his young public. Yet, given his reluctance to admit being black and from the Ville, what has always been seen as a mere publicist's exaggeration takes on new meaning. The simple statement did not carry with it the implications that Berry's manipulation of his driver's license or his publicity photos did, but it once again reinforces the notion that Berry was uncomfortable with the facts of his early life and was anxious to hide them from curious onlookers.

Significantly, at the time Chess was preparing to release a second album of Chuck Berry's songs; for the album, Berry once again furnished one of Harry Davis's photographs, taken at the new offices of Chuck Berry Music and the Chuck Berry Fan Club on Easton Avenue. In the shot, Berry was crouching and cradling his blond Gibson guitar. He was wearing a blue Hawaiian shirt and his black hair had been heavily processed. He or Harry had underexposed the negative once again, so that his features appeared not black but tanned. Another, similar shot taken at the same time and used for the Fan Club, showed Berry sitting cross-legged on the floor playing guitar; this time, he was shirtless, in front of a fabric-textured wall and next to a tropical plant. The effect was certainly exotic, despite the mundane location for the picture.

Marshall Chess, who had turned 16 on March 13, was working in the back room of the Chess offices at 2120 South Michigan Avenue assembling albums for his father and uncle when the album, called *One Dozen Berries*, was being readied for shipping. He could not have failed to notice the photograph, now humorously superimposed on a photograph of ripe, red strawberries, as he stuffed the album into its sleeve. "He sort of had this persona of wanting to be Hawaiian," Chess remembered 40 years later, "the way his hair was, his shirts. He would say he was part Hawaiian, and in a way he could look Hawaiian." For Marshall Chess, just a teenager and free of the kind of prejudice that was now almost an everyday occurrence for Chuck Berry, the implication of the photograph would not have been immediately evident. With the passage of time, however, the reason became all too clear to the younger Chess: "I think that something with his being Hawaiian was knowing that he could be more successful if he maybe wasn't black. Being black, you can't get played. That's probably the reason." And, just to reinforce the message, one of the songs recorded in February, although released on a later album, featured Chuck Berry on a pedal steel guitar, a staple of Hawaiian music, plucking out a melody that would appear under the title "Blues for Hawaiians."

As the year progressed, so did Chuck Berry's problems. On March 7, Berry returned to the Apollo, this time as a headliner and to very lukewarm reviews. Referring to the other acts on the bill—the Heartbeats, the Shirelles, the Velvets, the Sarah McLawler Trio, the Sil Austin Band, and Big Maybelle— *Variety* commented that "some of 'em are good, one of 'em (Big Maybelle) great, but on the whole they are average." Berry, too, was damned with faint praise; "Chuck Berry, who concentrates much of the time on a style of talking rhythms," wrote the reviewer, "is okay as the closer."

Then, a little over a week after his return to St. Louis, Chuck Berry was involved in another incident that paralleled the controversy generated by *American Bandstand* earlier in the year. At the same time the *St. Louis Argus* was reporting the racial problems encountered on Dick Clark's nationally syndicated show in January, a local version of *Bandstand*, the *St. Louis Hop* aired by KSD-TV, also found itself accused of discrimination by the local black newspaper. The *Argus* reported that several black teenagers had gone to the St. Louis Arena hoping to get in to the show; then, "according to a deluge of *Argus* informants, only one of the Negro teenagers was admitted and she was promptly evicted for not having a ticket. The others reported that the doorman called them insulting names in refusing them admission."

It was a mark against the show that the black community would have been mindful of when, just two months later, a picture of Chuck Berry appeared in the *Argus* with the following caption:

SMILING CHUCK BERRY, rock and roll star who is currently riding at the top of the rock and roll parade with "Sweet Sixteen" [sic], was blasted by local deejay Rodney "Mad Lad" Jones when Chuck Berry ran out on a promised appearance at American Hall, Saturday. The same day Chuck Berry made a televised appearance at the "St. Louis Hop," Mad Lad told his audience.

No more information about the incident ever appeared in the newspaper, so it is impossible to know whether the slight to Jones was real or imaginary. But the newspaper's readers would have grasped the significance of the accusation: Once again, Chuck Berry had turned his back on the black community in favor of the exposure made possible by a white-owned and racially insensitive television show. But few white acts would be criticized so vehemently for the choice to perform on a television show and garner much greater exposure than any live performance could ever deliver. Like his choice to include *American Bandstand* in the lyrics of "Sweet Little Sixteen," Berry once again was faced with an enormously difficult choice and, for better or worse, he had chosen commercial success over fidelity to his roots.

But March also saw the release of "Johnny B. Goode," arguably Berry's greatest artistic triumph and one of the most widely known rock songs in the history of the genre. Vocally, the song is delivered with the same breathless urgency as "Maybellene," with Berry only pausing for breath at the end of each lengthy line. The song's three verses spin a thinly disguised autobiographical tale about a "country boy" from "close to New Orleans" who could "play a guitar like ringing a bell," itself perhaps a reference to the guitar introduction to "School Day," which was intended to mimic a school bell. According to Berry, the "'Johnny' in the song is more or less myself"; certainly, the third verse, inspired according to Berry by his own mother's prediction about his musical career, is Berry's story set to music. And, in case we miss the autobiographical point, Berry adds the extra "e" to the protagonist's name to remind his listeners of the street in St. Louis where he was born.

The song also had another meaning for Berry and Johnnie Johnson. Berry has admitted that the he "wrote it intending it to be a song for Johnnie Johnson," as the title, according to the pianist, came

> from when we used to tour. . . . A lot of times after we'd get finished with a show, I'd go out to the clubs and sit in with the local groups. . . . The problem was, we had a schedule to keep, and I'd get caught up playin' and drinkin'. By the time I finally dragged on in, the rest of the bands would be gone! A couple of times I had to call Chess and have them wire me some money so I could get on a bus and catch up with them. I'd get there just in time for the show and Chuck would be shakin' his head askin' me, "Why can't you just be good, Johnnie? Stay with us."

But there is a third and equally plausible explanation for the title of the song, one that adds a new dimension and depth to the story of the poor country boy whose "name would be in lights." In November 1942, the great black poet Langston Hughes began writing a column for the *Chicago Defender*, which was, in its day, one of the three most circulated black newspapers in the country. Early in the "Here to Yonder" column's history, Hughes came up with the novel idea of making the column an imaginary dialogue between two characters, "a man of the black masses with provincial concerns" and a "foil, an educated black man with a more global perspective." Between the two, Hughes could capture the gamut of black opinion on all the pressing social issues of the day. At first, the foil introduced his counterpart to the world as "My Simple Minded Friend," but as the column progressed, Hughes felt an increasing need to flesh out the character's biography and establish a more realistic identity for him. That would require, among other things, giving him a name.

At first, that was accomplished by giving the character a real first name, Jess, although that was used rather infrequently; later, Hughes would reduce the phrase "My Simple Minded Friend" to give the character a shorter nickname "Simple," by which the character would become widely known. But on the publication of *Simple Speaks His Mind* in April 1950, the first book of collected "Here to Yonder" columns, the character was given his full moniker: Jesse B. Simple, or Semple as it sometimes appeared.

The connections between the two fictional creations go beyond the names, however. Both are poor Southern country boys, and although Semple is originally from Virginia, he describes being a coach boy "on the L. & N. down to New Orleans," presumably traveling the same railway track Johnny B. Goode would sit next to strumming his guitar. And, as Hughes had done with Simple, Berry was trying—as he had done in "Brown Eyed Handsome Man," "Too Much Monkey Business," and "No Money Down"—to portray in the character of Johnny B. Goode the experiences of the average black man. One literary critic, Hans Ostrom, has argued that Hughes was "deconstructing other typical images of the African-American male" by creating the character of Simple. By "holding up the mirror to urban working-class African-American men," Ostrom explains, "he was also smashing the false images of 'the Negro' which white society had created." Similarly, Berry's creations are not black stereotypes, nor are they portrayals of great black leaders and thinkers. They are, quite simply, average people, with the same dreams and fears as their white counterparts, and in that realization so many racial divisions are broken down.

But like "Brown Eyed Handsome Man" and "Sweet Little Sixteen" before it, "Johnny B. Goode" showed how Berry was forced to compromise his racial identity to gain mass appeal. In the opening verse, Berry had originally written of "a colored boy named 'Johnny B. Goode.'" Later, in *The Autobiography*, he recounted how he thought "it would be biased to white fans to say 'colored boy' and changed it to 'country boy.'" The song then becomes, as so many incidents in Chuck Berry's life before and since, racially ambiguous, at once celebrating the achievement of the common black man and, at the same time, changing the racial identity of that man to gain mass acceptance from a white audience. But ambiguity need not be contradiction. In his Atlanta Compromise speech, Booker T. Washington had used the image of a hand to convey the notion that the black and white races could be as separate as fingers and simultaneously united "in all things essential to mutual progress." So, too, could Berry appeal to his white audience while positively portraying black success. In the end, though, Berry's instincts enabled the song to become successful. Initially, it stayed on the *Billboard* charts for 15 weeks and was a Top 10 hit on both the pop and R&B charts;

more important, however, it was to become one of the greatest standards in the rock-and-roll repertoire.

But no matter what our lyrical interpretation of "Johnny B. Goode" may be, musically this is Berry's signature tune. If "Sweet Little Sixteen" was a chance for Johnson to showcase his piano, then "Johnny B. Goode" is Berry's answer, from the blistering trademark double-string introduction, to the staccato licks that punctuate each line of the chorus, to the stuttering string bends of the solo. And, although Berry has always been the first to admit that his guitar parts were not original (many of the stopped string bends in "Johnny B. Goode," for example, were inspired by T-Bone Walker and Charlie Christian, Benny Goodman's guitar player), nowhere had they been used with such power and force as here.

On March 28, the same day that "Johnny B. Goode" entered the *Billboard* charts and Berry was blasted by the *St. Louis Argus* for his appearance on the *St. Louis Hop*, Berry arrived in New York for two nights at the Brooklyn Paramount, the opening shows of yet another long and exhausting package tour. In New York, he joined Alan Freed, Jack Hooke (who had split from Teddy Reig and the Gale Agency to become Freed's personal assistant), and Buddy Holly, his companion from the Irving Feld tour of the previous year. The major attraction for the tour was Jerry Lee Lewis who, at the tender age of 22, some 11 years Berry's junior, had been a star for almost a year. By the time of Freed's tour, he had released "Whole Lot of Shakin' Going On" in March 1957, "Great Balls of Fire" in November, and "Breathless" in February 1958. And Freed could hardly have forgotten the box-office receipts from Lewis's last appearance at the Paramount. The 12-day run over the previous Christmas holiday had broken the Paramount's records for single day and weekly grosses, eventually grossing over $300,000 overall, mostly from crowds anxious to see Lewis's dramatic stage show.

Some believe that this tour fueled an intense rivalry between Lewis and Berry; consequently, the opening night of the tour has been much mythologized, mostly through a number of unsubstantiated accounts. The story most often told is that Lewis, angry at Freed's decision to have him appear before Berry, set his piano on fire, then stomped backstage and yelled "beat that, nigger" to Berry as he waited in the wings. The account gained credibility when it was reenacted in the 1989 movie *Great Balls of Fire*, although the Lewis character, played by Dennis Quaid, calls Berry "killer" instead. And so the story has become a part of rock-and-roll lore.

But Jack Hooke, who would have been ideally placed in the Paramount's wings to have witnessed the incident, denies that anything like that could have happened, mostly because it was Lewis who finished nearly all the shows on the tour. In fact, Hooke recalled that the tour began quietly, and that there were no arguments about who was to headline. The top stars received festival, or equal billing, and the decision to have Lewis close the show was based on Berry's easy-going demeanor rather than Lewis's demands. As Hooke put it later, "When I would tell him [Berry] 'You're third on the show, you're fifth on the show,' he never would say 'Oh, I want to close the show.' No, I never knew him to be that way."

Variety's review of the two nights substantiates Hooke's recollection. No mention is made of Lewis's setting fire to the piano, surely something any reviewer would have taken note of, although the review did comment on Lewis's ability "even after the frantic acts that preceded him . . . to reach new heights of frenzy in his vocalizing and banging on the piano." Further, the review confirms that Lewis finished the show, with Ed Townsend and Jo Ann Campbell appearing between he and Berry.

But *Variety*, traditionally critical of Alan Freed's shows in New York, was especially critical this time around. Buddy Holly and Chuck Berry were singled out for praise (Berry was described as "a talented songwriter and singer with a regular, pronounced beat to which the audience can stomp and clap"), but the rest of the show was severely panned. "Unprecedented for a rock 'n' roll show," wrote the reviewer, "where the youngsters are usually so square that they will take anything just so long as it has the modern beat and sound, the kids booed some of the more pathetic combos." "The second half was a marked improvement," the review conceded, but "most of it hardly rated as professional entertainment."

Even so, the tour began prosperously, quickly grossing over $82,000 from shows at the Paramount; the State Theater in New Haven, Connecticut; Loews Paradise in the Bronx; Convention Hall, Philadelphia; and the New York Coliseum. There was little doubt that Lewis's stage antics played a major part in the box-office success. On April 6, in Cleveland, the local promoter attempted to turn a quiet Sunday evening into something far more memorable by supplying the tour with two grand pianos, hoping that the Killer would make one into firewood. Lewis duly obliged in the second show.

But trouble between the two stars was just around the corner. Two days later, they hit Columbus. Before the show, Hooke recalled, Chuck sat at the piano, "trying it out, and Jerry Lee comes over. So Jerry Lee says 'Hey man, the piano sounds good.'" And Berry, joking about the events from two nights previous, retorted "Yeah, it sounds good, and it'll be good, Jerry, if you don't put your feet on there and kick it." At that point, Hooke remembered, "the ugly words came out." Lewis "called him a nigger or a word to that effect and Chuck stood up to defend himself and said 'Don't you call me that.'" Then Lewis's father "came over with a big knife, and said things like 'Listen, nigger, don't you talk to my son like that.' So I had to get between them, and I separated them."

The fallout from the incident was immediate; all of the black musicians on the tour threatened to quit. Many came to Hooke and said, "We're not going to continue the show with that cracker." But Hooke, who had made friends with most as the tour progressed, went to each one and said, "Jeez, for my sake, continue the tour." To his credit, and theirs, the tour went on, although the atmosphere had changed considerably. According to Hooke, "things happened like we got to the next town, and Chuck had a car, and Jerry Lee knew it was Chuck's car and he would pull up right behind him. And Chuck would finish before Jerry Lee, which Jerry Lee knew, and wanted to get his car out and there's Jerry Lee's car blocking him in. That little eruption continued to the end of the tour."

Four days after the incident in Columbus, Berry was joined on tour by Joan Mathis, a pretty young white girl who, by some accounts, was between seventeen and eighteen at the time and who had begun an affair with Berry the previous Christmas after seeing him play in a St. Louis Club. After the show that Saturday night, they stayed at the Pick-Fort Meigs Hotel in Toledo; very probably, she accompanied him on the next few shows, traveling with him in his Cadillac until the tour hit St. Louis on the following Tuesday. In all respects, the relationship was unremarkable to Freed, Hooke, or any of the musicians traveling separately on the tour bus. It was to come back to haunt Berry not long after the tour's conclusion, however.

At any rate, there were more immediate concerns for Berry, Freed, and the rest of the Big Beat entourage. Competing with two other tours that spring, and economic and unemployment problems growing throughout the country, box office receipts began to dwindle. On the Monday following the Toledo show, Holly and Freed witnessed the smoldering remains of a helicopter as they flew into Cincinnati for the tour's next stop. The next day in St. Louis, Buddy Holly's guitar was stolen from the dressing room at the Kiel Auditorium. A week later, at Waterloo, Wisconsin, Jerry Lee failed to show, prompting "bouts of shoving and hair-pulling" in the audience. Only a performance in Minneapolis on April 25 produced any real cheer for the entourage, where the box office was so busy before the show that the show was delayed by 20 minutes. But the tour ground on throughout the Midwest, finally swinging back into the Northeast at the beginning of May.

On May 3, the tour played the Boston Arena. As Chuck Berry would have been only too aware from his experience at the Boston Garden the previous November, rock-and-roll shows had traditionally encountered problems in the conservative town, and this night was to be no exception. After an uneventful first half, the second half of the show had to be interrupted several times as the Boston police forced Freed to quiet down the audience. Then, as Jerry Lee Lewis began his set, much of the crowd rose and danced in the aisles; Freed and his entourage, seeing behavior that had been duplicated at many other towns before this, paid little attention. The Boston police, however, forced Freed to interrupt Lewis's set and quiet the audience; much to his chagrin, the Killer finished his set with the crowd squirming in their seats.

That night, Chuck Berry was scheduled to close the show, and as he hit the stage, the crowd once again rose and began to dance. Once again, the police forced Freed to quiet them down. Freed reluctantly obliged again; this time, though, one of the policemen refused to dim the houselights and allow the show to continue, prompting Freed to return to the microphone and accuse the Boston police of not letting the crowd have a good time. At that point, a faction of the audience, who could well have been rival gang members and not crowd members incited by Freed's comments, began throwing chairs and fighting. Berry must have realized that the situation was beginning to get out of control, because he quickly ran behind the drummer to get as far away from the front of the stage as possible. One eyewitness account later observed that some of the crowd thought that Berry was performing his trademark duckwalk, and that there was nothing to fear; they were "too far away to see the look of fear on Berry's face," however.

With the houselights up and Chuck sheltering behind the drummer, the crowd spilled out of the arena and onto the Boston streets; what happened then is a matter of dispute. The *New York Times* reported multiple stabbings, beatings, robberies, and rapes, with nine men and six women being hospitalized. Jack Hooke, however, maintained that nothing happened:

We finished the show; we felt bad that the kids had to see it in the bright lights. We went out the front, me, Alan, and his wife Jackie. I'll never forget, we walked out the front—nobody there. Nobody. So we left about a half-hour after the show. We went to the airport, played Montreal, and we hadda go to another city but stop off in Boston on the way back from Montreal. We stop off in Boston and passed a newspaper—"Riot in Boston: Alan Freed." So we said, "What riot?" you know. So what we finally assumed happened was that there was no riot, they were just so riled that Alan said, "I guess the police in Boston don't want you to have a good time." As I was told later by a lawyer, they took everything from the blotter in that precinct that happened that night and attributed it to Alan. . . . You know, this guy stabbed this guy, and this one shot this one, and these were people who were probably not even at the show.

The tour was effectively finished. Although a date at the Lewiston Armory in Maine attracted 2,500 and produced a heart-stopping moment when a young teenager jumped onto the stage, and a subsequent show in Hershey, Pennsylvania, went on without incident, scheduled shows in Troy, New York; New Haven, Connecticut; and Newark, New Jersey, were canceled. So, too, were all further Boston rock-and-roll shows by order of Mayor John B. Hynes. "These so-called music programs are a disgrace," *Variety* quoted the mayor as saying. "They must be stopped and they will be stopped here— effective at once. As far as the City of Boston is concerned . . . if the kids are hungry for this kind of music they'll starve for it—until they learn to behave like citizens instead of hooligans. Boston," declared Mayor Hynes, "will have no more rock and roll."

Publicly, Chuck Berry has never commented on this incident, or on his relationship with Jerry Lee Lewis which seems to have softened from this point on. Possibly, like Jack Hooke, he felt the incident was not as dramatic as the newspapers or Boston authorities made it out to be and thus was unworthy of comment. Possibly, too, he felt that incidents like this were damaging to rock and roll and, thus, to his own career. In this sense, it was perhaps better not to sanction the official public record and be silent. Whatever the case, as he was to do so often in his career, he returned to business as usual.

Over the Memorial Day weekend, Berry and Joan Mathis, accompanied by Berry's old friend Jim Williams, set out on a short tour of the Midwest. The three checked into the Rome Hotel in Omaha on Friday, May 30, and Berry played a show there at some point over the weekend. On June 2, they checked out of the hotel and made the three-hour trip south to Topeka, Kansas, for a Sunday night show. In the early hours of Monday, Berry and Mathis began the long trip across Missouri to St. Louis in Berry's 1958 pink Cadillac. At some point, it is unclear when, Williams left the couple, who made it as far as St. Charles before the car developed a flat in the rear driver's side tire.

Berry pulled the car off the new Interstate 70 and onto Highway 94, perhaps hoping to coast into St. Charles and find a repair shop or at least a quieter section of highway on which to change the tire. But the car could go no further than the 94 off-ramp, and it was there that Berry got out of the car and proceeded to change the tire. For a while, he struggled to open the continental kit on the car's trunk in order to get the spare out; in short order, Captain Andrew Pallardy of the St. Charles police drove to the scene and parked behind Berry's vehicle.

Why Berry attracted Pallardy's attention should be no mystery. Although Pallardy, in later testimony, said that he had driven to Berry's aid, fearing that Berry could possibly be injured trying to change a tire so close to a busy interchange, the real reason for his parking the patrol car behind the pink Cadillac was far more predictable. Judge Randolph Weber, on hearing Pallardy's testimony some two years after the event in a preliminary hearing to determine whether Berry should stand trial for the events that followed, summed up Pallardy's intentions far more precisely than Pallardy ever did.

"The officer," noted Weber, "went up to where the man was voluntarily stopped. He saw a situation which was suspicious, at least he says it was suspicious. The record might also show because it is a black and white record [i.e., a written report] it wouldn't reveal the fact that the court had seen the defendant. The defendant is a negro." And, to punctuate the point, Weber describes the situation once again. "There was a white girl in the car. . . . He was fumbling around over the back trying to get out a tire. He drove six or seven hundred feet on a flat tire in a pink Cadillac, a car with a New York license. That would arouse an officer's suspicions, I would think. I know it would arouse mine."

Because the car was parked about 50 feet outside the St. Charles city limits, the incident was outside of Pallardy's jurisdiction. He immediately called for back-up, and some 20 minutes later he was joined by Paul Neumann of the Missouri State Highway Patrol. Pallardy told Neumann that he suspected the car was stolen, and together the two walked to Berry's car. Neumann asked Berry for his license and registration; the license Berry produced had expired some two years earlier, and the vehicle was still registered in New York, leading Neumann to arrest him on the spot. Then, with Pallardy keeping a watchful eye on the couple, Neumann searched the car, where he found a model E MAP Brevete .25 caliber automatic pistol with a round in the chamber "ready to fire." At this point, Neumann handcuffed Berry and placed him in the back of his patrol car.

If the seriousness of the situation was not immediately apparent to Chuck Berry, it became so shortly after Officer Neumann took him to the St. Charles police station. After a round of questioning from Neumann and St. Charles Police Chief Earl Humphrey, Berry and Mathis appeared before Magistrate Webster Karrenbrock in the St. Charles Police Court. Immediately, Karrenbrock fined Berry $30 for having an expired driving license and improper registration of the Cadillac; the more important charge, of carrying a concealed weapon, was held over until June 20. Karrenbrock released Berry on a $1,000 bond; Joan Mathis, now a material witness in the alleged crime, was released on a $250 bond.

The Friday, June 6, edition of the *Argus* reported, with a degree of delight, that "the bail was no problem, however, for Chuck Berry peeled off $1,250 in cash from a roll that would choke a mule." It went on to reveal that Berry was carrying $1,000 in cash from the weekend shows in Omaha and Topeka, as well as an $800 royalty check. More intriguing, perhaps, was the *Argus*'s allegation, made public by Police Chief Humphrey, that Joan Mathis, the "pretty little secretary," was married.

Berry hired attorney Merle Silverstein, who realized the seriousness of the situation, to handle the case. Berry was in violation of a Missouri state law, which forbade convicted ex-felons to carry a firearm; worse, the presence of

FBI agent Tom Dempsey at Berry's questioning meant that the matter had become a concern of the federal government, because it involved the interstate transportation of a firearm. The federal charge alone was punishable by a fine of up to $2,000 and up to five years in prison, or both. Silverstein's response was to buy some time, and he successfully petitioned to have the court date moved to July 11.

But still more misfortune was to follow the couple. The night before Berry was due to appear in St. Charles to answer the weapons charge, the St. Louis police pulled them over. Just after midnight, the two were heading into St. Louis on Natural Bridge Road when Patrolman Philip St. Onge saw the Cadillac weaving between lanes. Berry was arrested on a second charge of improper registration and for "careless and imprudent driving"; he was released on bond and told to appear before Magistrate Leslie T. Lewis the following week. This time, the *Argus* was scooped by the *Globe-Democrat*, whose headline the following morning read, "Rock 'n' Roll Star's Pink Caddy Reels on Road and He's Roped."

Exhausted, Berry headed back up Natural Bridge Road for his hearing on the weapons charge in St. Charles the next morning. There, according to the *Globe-Democrat*, he arrived at the courthouse "dressed . . . in an eggshell-white suit with metallic silver threads, a white tie, black suede shoes and dark glasses." He was met by Merle Silverstein and, to Silverstein's amazement, a large group of Berry's fans. "I was not a rock and roll addict," Silverstein recalled, "I had never heard of him." But, at the courthouse Berry was confronted by "two hundred screaming girls around the building just fighting to touch him. One girl said, 'Sign my sleeve!' And another girl who didn't have any paper said, 'Sign my hand!' I heard her say, 'I'm never going to wash this hand again!' It was phenomenal. I couldn't believe it."

The scene inside the courtroom was more sedate, however. Silverstein filed a motion to have the charges thrown out on the grounds that the search of Berry's car was illegal; it was conducted, he argued, "without a warrant and was not incident to an arrest." Magistrate Karrenbrock ruled that the incident should be taken "under advisement," although eventually these state charges against Berry were dropped.

The following week, as the rest of the Berry family settled into the house on Windermere Place, Judge Lewis fined Chuck Berry a further $15 for the second set of traffic violations on Natural Bridge Road. But there were still the far more serious federal charges to be faced. A short time later, Merle Silverstein received a phone call from recently appointed Assistant U.S. Attorney Frederick Mayer. "I called Merle," remembered Mayer, "and told him what had been reported to us, and told him that I think it may be worthwhile if he and his client would come down to the U.S. Attorney's office and discuss the matter. At that point, I had not decided whether to charge Berry or not."

About a week after the call, Berry, Silverstein, and Silverstein's law partner, Bob Goldenhersh, made the trip to the federal office building in downtown St. Louis. At the meeting, Mayer "discussed the charges against him, and I told him that at this point I was not going to charge him with this offense. But if he had any future conduct of this type and the FBI had brought any charges to me, I would not only look at those charges but would possibly present the present case to the Grand Jury at that time."

It was, according to Merle Silverstein, a very strong warning. Mayer reminded them that there was a five-year statute of limitations, and that he could file the charge at any time during that period. Silverstein, according to Mayer, indicated that his client understood, and that he appreciated the consideration; as far as Berry was concerned, nothing like this would happen again. "And that," according to Frederick Mayer, "was basically the start of it and basically the end at that time."

Some confusion exists over whether there was mention at the meeting of invoking the Mann Act at this point; technically, Berry had transported a woman across state lines for, in the words of the act, "the intent of debauchery or any other immoral purpose." Both the *Argus* in its June 27 piece on the postponement of the St. Charles hearing, and Berry in *The Autobiography*, claim that the federal authorities had tried to accuse Berry of violating the act at the time. But, recalled Merle Silverstein, there was "absolutely" no mention of invoking the act during the meeting in the office, "because nobody even knew what she was doing with him, except that she was obviously very willing . . . even in love with him." And, although age is only one factor in so-called aggravated Mann Act cases (in which noncommercial, or cases not involving prostitution, are concerned), the fact that Joan Mathis was between 17 and 18 years old at the time indicated that there was no egregious violation of the law anyway, even by late 1950s standards.

For all intents and purposes, Berry had made it through the month-long ordeal with a handful of traffic tickets and a slap on the wrist from the district attorney. Certainly, he had been fortunate enough to escape the fate that had befallen Jerry Lee Lewis the previous month. On May 23, Lewis had begun a tour of England. When the British press got wind that the 13-year-old girl accompanying him was not only his cousin but also his wife, they began systematically attacking Lewis, resulting in the tour being canceled after just three shows in which Lewis was heckled and booed. Lewis's presence in London threatened to spark an international diplomatic incident; he returned to the United States, and within weeks was blacklisted by Dick Clark and, worse, by top-40 radio. After "High School Confidential," his hit at the time of the scandal, dropped off of the charts, Lewis was to wait three years for another record to enter the top 100; the successes of 1957 and the first half of 1958, however, were never to be repeated throughout the rest of his career.

In many ways, though, the St. Charles incident marked the zenith of Berry's career as well, just as mid-1958 marked the end of the first golden age of rock and roll. The July move to Windermere Place seemed to provide the only bright spot in Berry's personal life, while the string of controversies that dogged his musical career continued. The next was an ill-considered appearance at the Newport Jazz Festival, which, in Chuck Berry's defense, was not of his own doing. He had been booked—along with other nonjazz artists such as Big Maybelle, Ray Charles, and Big Joe Turner—to appear on Saturday evening, July 5, by John Hammond, the legendary jazz impresario, in order, according to Hammond, "to demonstrate the links among jazz, blues, and rock." But Hammond's plan backfired the minute Berry walked on stage. Backed by Jack Teagarden's 10-piece jazz band, Berry's duckwalking, energetic performance seemed out of synch with the band and incongruous in the refined surroundings of Freebody Park. By all accounts, Berry's performance drove the younger section of the audience into a frenzy; "the bleacher brigade," as *Variety* dubbed the teenagers there, "went wild as Berry tore into his 'Schooldays' [sic] and followed it with two other Berry originals, 'No Money Down' and 'Sweet Sixteen' [sic]." But, the *Variety* reviewer pointed out, "some of the jazz fans were appalled." *Billboard* reported the same reaction. "Chuck Berry received the biggest response from the crowd, the younger set especially," the trade paper observed, adding, "But he also received the worst response from the older set, the critics and the introspective jazz fans."

As the low-brow rock music reached the ears of the high-brow members of the audience, the crowd began to grow restless. "There was nearly a riot and the police were called," remembered John Hammond; *Variety* reported that "fights broke out and the local gendarmes had their hands full controlling the mob. Several fans," *Variety* noted, "were hauled away to the Newport lock up" as Berry concluded his show with a spirited "Johnny B. Goode."

The month ended on an equally disappointing musical note with the release of his next single, "Vacation Time"/"Beautiful Delilah." Interestingly, although Chess picked "Vacation Time" as the A-side of the single, it was the flip side that charted, a ragged, out-of-tune performance with uninspired lyrics such as "Beautiful Delilah, sweet as apple pie/Always gets a second look from the fellows passing by." Only the biblical references in the song's chorus—with Berry humorously observing that his girlfriend, Rebecca, will not allow him to fool around with Delilah—save the song from mediocrity.

The song remained on the charts for a mere two weeks, only reaching as high as number 81 on the *Billboard Hot 100*. It marked the end of a remarkable 39-week run of charted songs; nonetheless, with "Johnny B. Goode" still in the charts, this was the second time that year that Berry had two songs on the *Billboard* chart simultaneously. But the musical world was changing again; on June 2, the day of Berry's arrest in St. Charles, the *Billboard* chart began to document a shift away from rock and roll. To be sure, it was still represented well: "Johnny B. Goode" was at number 10, and "Sweet Little Sixteen" was still hanging on in the bottom end of the charts. Elvis Presley, meanwhile, who had been inducted into the Army four days before the Big Beat tour began in March, was at number 3 with the rockabilly rave-up "Wear Your Ring Around My Neck." Jerry Lee Lewis's latest single, "High School Confidential," had just joined his previous single, "Breathless," on the chart; Buddy Holly's driving rocker "Rave On" was in its second week; and even Bill Haley was represented by "Skinny Minny."

But public taste was beginning to change, and rock and roll was giving way to the novelty song. That week, David Seville's "Witch Doctor" and Sheb Wooley's "Purple People Eater" were both in the Top 10. Also in the chart that week were the Chordettes with "Lollipop," the Coasters with their brand new "Yakety Yak," Dickie Doo and the Don'ts with "Nee Nee Na Na Na Na Nu Nu," and the Pets with "Cha Hua Hua." Before the end of the month, they were joined by Bobby Darin's "Splish Splash."

It was the beginning of the end of rock and roll's golden age. In less than a year, the public taste would change again, and the charts would be dominated by young, white teenage idols; as Jerry Lee Lewis wryly observed many years later, "All you could hear was Bobby—Bobby Vee, Bobby Vinton, Bobbie Denton, Bobby Rydell, Bobby Darin. There was nothing but Bobbies on the radio." Berry's sweet little sixteen was beginning to fill her wallet with pictures of singers like Paul Anka, Ricky Nelson, and Frankie Avalon, all of whom were seeing their careers take off in 1958.

Club Bandstand

THAT'S GOOD NEWS shouted the enthusiastic music lover. Chuck Berry Club Bandstand (formerly the old Latin Quarters) 814 N. Grand, featuring big time entertainment nightly, should bring great distinction to both the owner and St. Louis.

—Chuck Finney, *St. Louis Argus*, March 27, 1959

The frenetic pace of Chuck Berry's career continued unabated into the autumn of 1958. "Carol," released in August 1958, provided him with his fourth major hit of the year, entering the *Billboard Hot 100* on August 25, four days before his appearance at the Brooklyn Fabian Fox Theater for another of Alan Freed's ubiquitous New York shows. Lyrically, the song is hardly one of Berry's best, which is not surprising considering it was probably hastily written and recorded the day after Berry's court appearance in St. Charles that June. Even so, the teenage theme and driving rhythm were enough to keep the song on the *Billboard Hot 100* for ten weeks, reaching as high as number 18 in the last week of September.

From the stage at the Brooklyn Fox Theater that Labor Day weekend, however, Berry would have been hard pressed to see the excitement the song was generating in his teenage audience. Following the incident in Boston three months earlier, the New York police were determined to keep a close eye on the proceedings. *Variety* noted that the audience's "enthusiastic response was nipped somewhat . . . by the 16 special patrolmen on detail throughout the house. In fact, the boys in blue rate a nod for keeping the kiddies under control without raising their ire. They moved quickly to halt any terping exhibition in the aisles and subdued the yowls and shrieks by panning their flashlights over the noisy areas of the darkened house."

Variety's reviewer made the usual complaints about the inexperienced performers on the bill. "Unlike the show biz era in the past," lamented the reviewer, "where youngsters broke in on the 'live' circuit after being 'born in a trunk,' the current crop was 'born in a recording studio' and have demonstrated in the four year history of Freed's 'Big Beat Show' that they seldom develop as show biz entities and are headed for oblivion as soon as their disk gets off the charts and off the deejays' spinning table." The bill reflected the growing change in popular music taste. Chuck Berry, Bill Haley, the Cleftones, and Bo Diddley were the only representatives from past Freed shows. They were joined by several of the new teenage idols: Frankie Avalon, Teddy Randazzo, and Jimmy Clanton. But only Haley and Berry garnered praise from the reviewer, Berry being described as a "standout . . . who breaks it up [with] 'Carol,' 'Schooldays' [sic], and 'Go, Johnny, Go' [sic]." For the rest of the bill, however, the reviewer listed only their names and their songs before offering the comment that "the aforementioned reads like a jukebox and that's what it sounds like."

In the last two months of 1958, Chess attempted to further capitalize on Berry's success by taking the unusual step of releasing two singles, "Sweet Little Rock and Roller"/"Jo Jo Gunne" and "Merry Christmas Baby"/"Run, Rudolph, Run" within a month of each other. It was indicative of the way the Chess brothers had stepped up Berry's career in 1958. They had released a total of six singles—double the usual three per year of the previous three years—and had Berry record as many songs that year (24) as he had recorded in the previous three years combined. But as Chuck Berry himself was to admit years later, the quality of the songs was beginning to suffer. The Chess brothers' business interests were keeping them out of the studio for longer and longer periods of time. In 1958, not only were the Chess labels expanding to include jazz on the Argo subsidiary label formed two years earlier, but the brothers had set up their own record pressing plant in Chicago, and their new company, L&P Broadcasting, was actively pursuing the purchase of a radio station in Flint, Michigan.

Chuck Berry's business interests, too, were beginning to branch out. The purchase and development of land in Wentzville, then an isolated rural community 30 miles west of St. Louis, the beginnings of a new venture, a nightclub, not to mention his close control of the business end of his musical career with Francine Gillium were all taking his attention away from creative matters. "At this time," he wrote in *The Autobiography*, "I let many distractions hinder me from really writing as I had in the beginning of my career." In the sessions in late 1958, he, Johnnie Johnson, and Jasper Thomas recorded songs that Berry admitted were "scribbled on the long Show of Stars tours. . . . Leonard and I both knew the recording session was inferior to the past ones."

Even so, both singles managed to hit the charts because they were deliberately geared toward the Christmas market. The first, the up-tempo "Sweet Little Rock and Roller," describes a young rock fan—just 9 years old—"all dressed up like a downtown Christmas tree." The song describes the rock and roller's attendance at a holiday show, similar to the ones Berry played for Alan Freed in New York. Lyrically, however, like "Carol" before it, the song is a disappointment. It mines territory already covered by songs like "Sweet Little Sixteen," without any of its memorable details. But also, like "Carol," the song's infectious and insistent rhythm and musicianship—Johnson's wonderful background piano fills and Berry's melodic guitar lead—gave the song enough momentum to stay on the *Billboard* chart for 9 weeks over the Christmas period, although its highest position, number 47, suggested that Berry's audience was also noting the decline in his creative powers.

The choice of the B-side for the single, however, is curious and worthy of comment. "Jo Jo Gunne" is not one of the most significant songs in the Berry canon, but it is important to understanding some crucial aspects of Berry's life. Lyrically, perhaps even more than songs like "Brown Eyed Handsome Man," "Too Much Monkey Business," or "Johnny B. Goode," the song draws on Berry's African-American roots. It is an adaptation of the story of the Signifying Monkey, a character from African-American folklore derived from the Yoruba figure of Esu, the trickster archetype found in many folk traditions.

Berry claims that he first heard "Signifying Monkey" in Algoa prison, which suggests that he would probably have heard, either directly or via one of his fellow inmates, one of the versions recorded by the Big Three Trio, Willie Dixon's first band, in 1946 and 1947. He also may have heard jazz musician Cab Calloway's version, renamed "The Jungle King," in 1947, and would have been familiar with another, far tamer version recorded by his long-time hero Nat "King" Cole in 1943 under the title "Straighten Up and Fly Right."

The story is a central part of black culture. Henry Louis Gates, the renowned scholar of African-American literature, notes that even though there have been literally hundreds of versions of the song recorded, the basic elements of the story are fairly universal. "The Signifying Monkey," Gates writes, "invariably repeats to his friend, the Lion, some insult purportedly generated by their mutual friend, the Elephant. . . . The Lion, indignant and outraged, demands an apology of the Elephant, who refuses and then trounces the Lion. The Lion, realizing his mistake was to take the Monkey literally, returns to trounce the Monkey." The Monkey's lying, the disrespect and insults, and the manipulation of language into parody are all key elements of the story and of "signifying."

Berry's version of the story follows the traditional format closely, although the Monkey avoids punishment by the Lion at the story's conclusion through one final deceit and lives to trick another day. Challenging the Lion to a boxing match, Jo Jo waits until the Lion gets ready to fight and then, before the match can begin, he "took a leap and jumped out of sight."

But the ending was not the only significant variation in the story. First, there are Berry's own typically detailed observations that flesh out the narrative beautifully. Berry has a number of curious animals come to witness the fight between the lion and the elephant, including a crocodile who "phoned and reversed the charge/comin' all the way from Egypt on a local barge" and a gorilla who takes Jo Jo's $3 bet on the elephant. Further, Berry's lyric captures the essence of the black tradition of signifying as he has Jo Jo yell to the lion, "Go on, knock him down/he don't outweigh you but a thousand pounds." Henry Louis Gates's definition of signifying, borrowing as it does from a number of sources, describes it as a "language of implication. . . . the language of trickery." It is also the language of reversal, where "complimentary remarks may be delivered in a left-hand fashion" and where "a particular utterance may be an insult in one context and not another." Clearly, by having Jo Jo engage in verbal play with the lion about the elephant's size, Berry is remaining faithful to the spirit of the original story.

But Berry departs from the tradition in one very significant way. One variation of the story, collected by Roger D. Abrahams in Philadelphia not long after Berry's version was recorded, and published in his seminal study of African-American folklore, *Deep Down in the Jungle*, begins:

> Deep down in the jungle so they say
> There's a signifying motherfucker down the way
> There hadn't been no disturbin' in the jungle for quite a bit,
> For up jumped the monkey in the tree one day and laughed,
> "I guess I'll start some shit."

The more subdued language in Berry's version was certainly deliberate; the original, Berry admits, was "naughty . . . and funnier," but as he had done in the past, Berry's ear for commerciality prevented him from delivering the song even close to its unadulterated form.

Despite the toned-down yet still humorous lyrics and the fact that a number of the verses are humorously punctuated by lines from popular songs played on guitar (Berry quotes "Merrily We Roll Along," "There's No Business Like Show Business," and even a contemporary commercial for Gillette razors), the song itself was a failure, lacking the musical hooks of much of Berry's better work. There is no chorus, and the song is delivered without any of the dynamics that made "Sweet Little Sixteen" or "School Day" so distinctive. Why, then, was the song released as a single? Perhaps Berry and the Chess brothers felt that the song did have commercial potential; the song, after all, did chart briefly on its own in *Billboard* early in December 1958, suggesting that Berry had once again found cross-over appeal for an overt statement of black culture.

But a more plausible explanation could be Berry's own fascination with signifying itself. The idea of the kind of verbal interplay the story represents would have fascinated a man for whom poetry and language were so central to life. Tall tales of the type told by the monkey are typical of Berry's lyrics; much of the humor of "You Can't Catch Me" and "Brown Eyed Handsome Man," in particular, depend on their willful exaggeration. But, as Gates points out, signifying occupies a place in black culture that goes beyond mere aesthetics. The art of signifying is important as it "is often a part of [black] adolescent education." Further, signifying belongs to the African, and African-American, oral tradition; as such, it stands in opposition to the white, European literary tradition; in Gates's argument, it is a way for blacks to "move freely between two discursive universes ... [between] the white linguistic realm and the black." Consequently, it mirrors not only the low-brow/high-brow debate that is at the heart of many of Berry's works but also the struggle of a black writer to negotiate the linguistic rules of the dominant, white culture. For the act of signifying is an attempt to reclaim language. A dominant power or culture controls language to maintain its power, and any attempts to wrestle control of the language back from that power must revolve around changing the meaning of the words it uses—in other words, signifying. In lying, deception, and subverting meaning, those oppressed by language become liberated; as in the case of the Signifying Monkey, they gain control over other, more powerful creatures. Chuck Berry's fascination with the protean nature of the Signifying Monkey, and the creation of "Jo Jo Gunne" that resulted from it, perhaps indicate his growing attempts to gain control over the ever-present threat posed by white society by using language that is both deceptive and manipulative.

With "Jo Jo Gunne," "Sweet Little Rock and Roller," and "Merry Christmas, Baby" all occupying chart positions that December, the year that at one point looked as though it was going to end in disaster finished triumphantly. Appropriately enough, it was capped with an 11-day stand at the Manhattan Loews State Theater in Alan Freed's "Christmas Jubilee of Stars." It was a show, oddly enough, headlined by Johnnie Ray, now past his prime but riding a recent hit, "Up Until Now." The singer, known for his emotional, sobbing singing style, was out of place on the bill; although *Variety* praised his performance ("In the midst of the unsubtle, heart-pounding and walloping singing," the reviewer wrote, "Ray comes over like an oasis of taste and talent."), *Billboard* noted that "the teenagers didn't dig him" and that he was "out of his element."

There were other problems. On the day of *Variety's* review, December 31, Freed himself was mysteriously absent; the MC duties were taken over by an Earl Warren ("who is no improvement over Alan Freed," according to *Variety*). Indeed, Freed's career had been in a downward spiral since the

Boston show that May. WINS had fired him in the wake of the Boston incident and, although he was immediately signed by rival radio station WABC, he was already embroiled in a dispute with that station over the promotion of his live shows. The shows that December and January were to be the last that Chuck Berry would ever do with the man who had propelled him to stardom, ending a lucrative, four-year relationship.

Freed and Berry, however, had one more project to complete before their careers took them in separate and, ultimately, downward directions. While on the bill in New York, Berry began the New Year working on Freed's fifth movie, *Go, Johnny, Go*; unlike the two previous movies he had worked on with his old friend and business partner, this time his contribution was far greater than just a musical one. The process began in New York during the shows at the Loews State, when Jack Hooke—who was the movie's associate producer as well as appearing as a policeman in the movie's conclusion—rounded up the musical talent to record their numbers with a small crew from the Hal Roach studios in New York, just as they had done before. Then, the principal actors—Jimmy Clanton (who played Johnny Melody), Sandy Stewart (who played his girlfriend Julie), Freed, and Berry—were flown out to the Hal Roach studios in Culver City, California, to complete the filming.

It was an intimidating experience for the seasoned performer, who had no knowledge of the ways movies were made other than his limited experience lip-synching on a sound stage. As soon as Berry arrived at the studio, he remembered, "they threw a script at me and we started shooting the next day. The next day I came and I think I had read the script . . . and I didn't remember any of it." On that first day, recalled Jack Hooke, "I have to assume that Chuck got frightened. He couldn't read the parts, he couldn't memorize too much—nobody could—you know, being an amateur, not an actor, there's only a certain amount you can memorize. Same with Alan. So, in the middle of the day, he says to me, calls me aside, he says, 'I'm going home.'"

Once again, as he had been in Cleveland a year earlier, Hooke was the voice of reason. He asked Berry what was wrong, and reminded him that "they've got that whole script, they've got a whole plan here to do a movie." To save face, Berry made up a story that executive producer Hal Roach had reneged on his promise to send him a first-class ticket. "They're going, they're coming," he told Hooke, "they gave me some flimsy excuse, and the ticket wasn't right, so I don't care, I'm going home."

Hooke sensed immediately what was wrong. "I took him, I said, 'Chuck, you don't have to read these lines all the way through.' But I convinced him that it'll be done a minute or two minutes at a time, and 'Be cool! Nobody's gonna overtax you. Alan don't know any more than you do, so just go along with it.' And I convinced him to stay."

In fact, Berry fares well in the film, appearing comfortable and natural in the strange environment, despite negotiating a typically thin plot and even weaker dialogue. In the movie, he plays a Hollywood screenwriter's version of Chuck Berry, complete with hip, 1950s slang. Early in the movie, Berry laments, "That Johnny Melody, he can really put over a Chuck Berry number. That's for the orioles!" And when Freed asks, "The orioles?" Berry draws an imaginary square in the air and declares, "Da boids!"

Berry's role in the movie is as a sort of musical assistant to Freed, championing various acts, including a new singer named Johnny Melody, representative of the innocuous white singers like Frankie Avalon and Fabian the record industry was now busy manufacturing for the teenage market. He talks Freed into managing the boy, who has won a talent contest sponsored by Freed and who then disappears before anyone knows what he looks like. This produces the story's most ironic and unfortunate moment, when Freed describes how he imagines Melody looks. "He's gotta be six-feet tall," says Freed, "with blond wavy hair, apple cheeks." To which Berry, who had been fidgeting with a match book during Freed's speech, cuts Freed off, blowing his cue, and sputters, "You know, we dig him the same way. As a matter of fact, with that voice he's got to look exactly like that!" It was a moment of great contradiction. Chuck Berry was appearing in a Hollywood movie, at the height of his success, but he was forced to say that a teenage idol had to be white. The fact that singers like Johnny Melody were, at that moment, starting to replace singers like Chuck Berry in the pop charts must have made the humiliation doubly painful.

Like all Freed movies, however, it was the music that had the most to offer, and for Chuck Berry, that was especially true. The movie featured appearances by a number of stars, including Berry's old Chess labelmate and long-time Freed associate Harvey Fuqua of the Moonglows, Jackie Wilson, Eddie Cochran, and Richie Valens—filmed literally days before his death in a plane crash in an Iowa wheatfield and singing, "Oooh, My Head." Berry, however, has the honor of having three songs featured: "Johnny B. Goode," which plays over the opening and closing sequences; "Little Queenie," in which he is joined, improbably, by Freed, who badly mimes drums in a supposed after-hours jam session; and one of his greatest songs, "Memphis, Tennessee."

Both new songs had been recorded prior to the movie. "Little Queenie," recorded in November at the same session as "Merry Christmas Baby" and "Run, Rudolph, Run," was another of Berry's observations of teenage life. As he had done in the opening lines of "Reelin' and Rockin'," Berry sings of the hesitancy and uncertainty of adolescent romance, producing a handful of memorable lines. But the song suffers from the self-admitted lack of creativity that pervaded much of Berry's output at the time, the uninspired chorus of "Go, go, go, Little Queenie" and the stale imagery (Queenie is described as "looking like a model on the cover of a magazine"). But, like "Carol" and "Sweet Little Sixteen" before it, the infectious, driving rhythm more than compensates for the lyrics' lack of originality.

In contrast, "Memphis, Tennessee," recorded some six months earlier, is a masterpiece of storytelling, simple and yet full of detail. It is also, quite possibly, one of the earliest pop songs ever to deal with the effects of divorce and child custody, certainly one of the first to deal with it from a male point of view. The song features a slurred, swooping bass line (some have credited Willie Dixon, although Berry maintains that he played the bass part himself) and chopping, up-stroke guitar chords; the drummer (again, some have credited Chess session ace Fred Below, and Berry has said that he was responsible) avoids the snare drum and the obvious hillbilly back beat entirely for a soft, subtle shuffle pattern played on the tom-toms. The whole effect is a quiet yet bouncy, reggae-like rhythm that offsets the sadness of the lyrics.

At the beginning, the song appears to be telling an ordinary tale of a broken love affair. But from the outset, Berry makes the story unusual, first by framing it in the form of a conversation with a telephone operator, through which he provides finely observed details that propel the narrative. Berry is apparently anxious to contact his ex-wife, who "did not leave her number" when she called to speak to him. He knows that she called, "'Cause my uncle took the message and he wrote it on the wall." The image of the last line, in one short, economical phrase, illustrates the singer's condition: He is living in poverty, perhaps forced there by his separation, in a place where phone numbers are written on walls. In the next stanza, this state is wonderfully contrasted by his former partner's home "high upon a ridge/Just a half a mile from the Mississippi Bridge."

After a subdued guitar break, the third stanza builds the tension of the piece, with Berry singing that the pair "were torn apart because her mom did not agree." Then finally, the last verse turns the lyric around, and we learn that the Marie of the story is not his wife or lover but his six-year-old daughter. And, in a lovely finishing touch, Berry writes of the "hurry home-drops" on Marie's cheek "that trickle from her eye." In a two-minute pop song, Chuck Berry captured the frustrations and sadness of a divorced father, a rare adult theme in the disposable world of 1950s teenage rock and roll.

Nonetheless, Berry returned to teenaged concerns in his following releases, "Anthony Boy" and "Almost Grown." Both singles, released in February and March, respectively, seemed to show that Chuck Berry was now a follower rather than a leader in pop music trends. "Anthony Boy" was a deliberate attempt to cash in on an already passe Italian song trend begun the previous year with releases of "Torero" by Renato Carosone and Julius LaRosa and "Volare (Nel Blu Dipinto Di Blu)" by Dominico Modugno and, more famously, Dean Martin and the McGuire Sisters in August. The song was recorded in September of 1958 at Phil Chess's insistence, and had it been released then it might have succeeded. As it was, the song, with its jaunty 6/8 rhythm and the by-now formula school-room lyrics, seemed just a little too contrived. After five weeks in the *Billboard Hot 100*, where it reached only number 60, "Anthony Boy" disappeared to be almost immediately replaced with "Almost Grown" the last week of March.

This time, Leonard Chess supervised the session, and the difference was dramatic. In an attempt to break the formula, Chess hit upon the idea of having the Moonglows, by then Chess Records' best-selling doo-wop group, contribute their vocals to the song. "I remember that session pretty well," Johnnie Johnson recalled years later, "'cause that was the first time we ever had a backup group singin' behind us. . . . I thought it was a good idea. We had been using the same music so long that I was gettin' tired of it. At least when they came in we had something new." But even so, Berry and Johnson did not stray far from the successful formula that previously had worked so well. Johnson recalls playing "the little rip up and down the keys on the solo for Leonard Chess, without him even having to ask. Just to keep him happy." Meanwhile, Berry's lyrics again looked to teenage life for inspiration, although the rhyming couplets seem forced: "Yeah I'm doin' all right in school," Berry sings, "They ain't said I've broke no rules," as the Moonglows and Etta James chant "waah-do-day" in the background.

But it was enough for the insatiable teen market. For 13 weeks "Almost Grown" stayed on the *Billboard* pop charts, the fourth consecutive Berry single released in six months to do so. But Johnnie Johnson realized that the formula was wearing thin; as different as the song was, the pianist felt "it just wasn't much different from what we had been doin'. I got to admit," Johnson confessed, "I was gettin' tired of rock and roll."

Meanwhile, back in St. Louis, Chuck Berry was expanding his business empire. He had long planned to open a nightclub, and his dreams were finally seeing fruition. The first announcement of the club's opening was in the January 9, 1959, edition of the *St. Louis Argus*; naturally, the news was broken in Chick Finney's long-standing "Blue Note" entertainment column. "CHUCK BERRY NITE CLUB on Grand Boulevard [sic]," read the article, "may add laurels to our town entertainment front." And, added Finney, "when the bossman, musician Berry is not on out of town engagements, he will be performing at his own club." The as-yet-to-be-named club was to be located in the old Latin Quarters nightclub, below Broadway and Emma's Chuck Wagon Diner, at 814 North Grand Avenue between Delmar and Enright in one of St. Louis's most vibrant and culturally rich areas.

With Chuck Berry out of town, first for the filming of *Go, Johnny, Go* and then for a short tour of Australia, work on redecorating the interior of the club was delayed until March. The next mention of the club's impending opening appeared in the *Argus* two months later, when Berry and Francine Gillium took out a series of advertisements for the club that now bore the name Club Bandstand. "'THIS IS IT!' CHUCK BERRY CLUB BAND-STAND," proudly proclaimed the first advertisement, adding that admission would be free for anyone with a paid Chuck Berry Fan Club card. The following week, on March 20, a second advertisement announced a Gala Floor Show beginning at 8:00. The advertisement also contained the words "EVERYBODY WELCOME," pointing to the club's interracial policy, an ironic statement considering few blacks would have been members of the fan club, and no whites would have read the *Argus*.

Although Bandstand was not St. Louis's first integrated nightclub (the same September 28, 1956, edition of the *Argus* that carried the advertisement announcing Johnnie Johnson's departure from Chuck Berry's band also carried an ad for Johnny's Interracial Bar on 814 N. Kingshighway), from the outset Chuck Berry was aware that opening an interracial club was bound to bring extra scrutiny from the white establishment. Unsurprisingly, then, Berry and Gillium took great pains to make sure that everything about the club was above reproach. "He was trying to get a carbon copy of Dick Clark's thing," Johnnie Johnson remembered, pointing out that Berry was trading on the squeaky-clean image of Clark's show in the club's name. "He had it decorated real good. It was down in the basement and he had carpets put down there and mirrors all around the wall, and he did it up real nice."

In an attempt to show the club's respectability, at the time of Bandstand's opening Francine Gillium wrote a curious piece for the first edition of the *Monthly Journal*, a business and professional magazine published locally in St. Louis. Titled "I Like Rock and Roll," it was an attempt to show just how harmless the music (and, by implication, nightclubs that feature it) really was. Club Bandstand is never mentioned by name in the piece, but its intent is unmistakable. Rock and roll, according to Gillium,

> is an expression that is a part of nature and should be given its freedom. Rock and Roll is a healthy, normal part of a teenager that should be encouraged in our attempt to create mature adults. I say this because I can picture a group of teenagers hanging around a jukebox, gathered on a dance floor, drinking coke after coke in a small dimly lit dance area; and at the same time I see them in the future—these very same teenagers walking beside me to the voting polls, buying groceries for their teenagers and taking their place in the community as mature, well-rounded citizens.

Gillium and Chuck Berry, especially as a lifelong St. Louis resident, may well have felt such propaganda was necessary. After all, the club was located in the area around Grand Avenue that, during Berry's childhood, would have been synonymous with white prestige and segregation. First, of course, were the theaters such as the Fox and the St. Louis (located three blocks and one block south of Bandstand, respectively), both of which had remained segregated during most of Berry's life. There were also the formidable buildings of conservative fraternal organizations, the Scottish Rite and the Masonic Temple, past the Fox and west around the corner on Lindell. And Berry would doubtless have known that during the 1920s and 1930s the Midtown area surrounding Grand Avenue was home to countless professional offices and deluxe auto showrooms.

Years later, Berry explained his concern about the club's location to *Los Angeles Times* journalist Robert Hilburn:

> I had a nightclub in St. Louis that was predominantly catered to by the white populace of St. Louis. . . . Now here you've got what they call a mixed racial club that was catered to by whites . . . and here down the street we are just trying to see what it is like to let blacks into the Fox. . . . I wasn't wanted on Grand Avenue. . . . I was the instigator.

But times had changed significantly since the Berry family had been humiliated at the Fox box office. By the end of the 1950s, the Fox Theater was desegregated; the first St. Louis showing, in 1959, of the black-themed movie *St. Louis Blues*, a biography of blues singer W. C. Handy, even attracted its star, Nat King Cole, along with black singer Pearl Bailey for a live appearance. The effort to desegregate the area had been led by the Third Baptist Church, located just a block south of the St. Louis Theater, and the gradually expanding St. Louis University. The school had desegregated in 1947 and was instrumental in leading the St. Louis Catholic diocese high schools toward integration in the late 1940s, several years before *Brown vs. Board of Education*. Several other black nightclubs and businesses dotted the area as well, including Club Plantation, at various times located on Vanderventer and Delmar, and the Sun Theater, across the street from the St. Louis Theater in Grandel Square, which was, in its current incarnation, a movie house catering to a predominantly black clientele. It was an area that, by the late 1950s, had become so diverse that a black-owned nightclub, even one catering to whites, would hardly have raised eyebrows. Even so, memories of his childhood and his recent difficulties would have been fresh in Chuck Berry's mind as the club opened its doors that March.

Within the black community, however, the opening of Club Bandstand had completely the opposite effect from that which Chuck Berry feared might come from the whites of St. Louis. In the pages of the *Argus*, Chuck Berry enjoyed the best publicity that paper had ever given him. In the last week of January, Chick Finney, writing in his weekly *Argus* column, had nothing but high praise for Berry's career, although as he had done so many times before he used Berry as an example of black achievement and enterprise rather than as an example of artistic creativity or intellectual endeavor. Looking back over Berry's career to date, Finney noted that in May 1955, "he was just another member of the Musician's Local 197, struggling along singing his songs with a beat up guitar. No . . Chuck didn't give up—he kept striving with hopes . . . I'm sure you know the rest of the history." But by 1959, even jazz aficionados like Finney had to admit Chuck Berry was "one of the greatest finds from St. Louis, Missouri."

Then, on the same date that the first advertisement for Club Bandstand appeared in the paper, Finney portrayed Berry as a true benefactor of the St. Louis music scene. Under the byline "Chance for Newcomers Now!— Chuck Berry," Finney announced in his column that Berry had taken on a protégé, sax player and jazz combo leader Chuck Tillman. Tillman, Finney wrote, "is set for the bigtime via recordings under the personal supervision of Chuck Berry." Berry, the column went on, "who skyrocketed to fame and still possesses a nation-wide box office appeal . . . believes Tillman will do the same." And, to show that Chuck Berry was intent on giving back to the community that gave him his first chance, Finney added that he would "be discovering and developing new hopefuls toward stardom." It was high praise and can hardly be attributed to his patronage of the paper; after all, Berry and Francine Gillium had only advertised the club twice during the year. Further, the issue of the *Argus* published during the week of the club's opening gave much greater space to the opening of another club, the El Capitan Lounge, which featured the more respectable sounds of jazz.

The relationship with Chuck Tillman resulted in a recording session at the Chess studios in Chicago and the release of a single, "I Would Holler (But the Room's Too Small)" on an obscure St. Louis label, Carter Records. The B-side, however, is of special interest as the song, "Pretty Blue Eyed Baby," featured a young, white teenage guitarist named Billy Peek. Not long after the single's release, Tillman and Peek were invited to appear on the *St. Louis Hop*'s first anniversary show alongside Chuck Berry. For Billy Peek this was a chance of a lifetime; not only would he be appearing on television for the first time, he would be doing so with his idol. Years later, Peek remembered, "when Russ Carter, the MC of the show, told me that Chuck Berry was gonna appear, I almost fainted because I had been listening to Chuck's records and I had never met him. So I was shook up about the whole thing but it was still something I really wanted to do. So I did that, and then that night I kinda like met Chuck and asked him for his autograph; I was really in awe of the guy." From such an inauspicious beginning, a lifelong friendship would emerge.

The period of time around the opening of Club Bandstand seems to be one of great satisfaction and happiness for Chuck Berry. At 13 Windemere Place, Themetta was expecting their third child, who would be born in November of that year, while out in Wentzville work continued on the land he had purchased some two years earlier. And around St. Louis, Chuck Berry seemed to be finding more acceptance than at any time in his career. The *Argus* continued to report a number of local appearances, including two large-scale shows, one at the Union Theater in July and the other on November 8 at the Kiel Auditorium. But nothing could compare to the kind of homecoming Chuck Berry must have received when a local organization known as the Frontiers of America asked him to appear at a star-studded fundraiser in the auditorium of Sumner High School on May 16. That Saturday afternoon would have been one of the most memorable in the illustrious history of the school as, one by one, George Hudson's orchestra accompanied Little Milton, Ike Turner, Jackie Wilson (in town to play shows at the Club Riviera), and Chuck Berry as they raised funds for Little League baseball at a mere 90 cents a ticket.

There seemed to be much to be thankful for at that time, which accounts for the upbeat lyrics of his next single, "Back in the U.S.A." Written on Berry's return to the country after his short tour of Australia that January, the song seems to be the heartfelt expression of someone who had finally achieved success beyond his expectations. The song's chorus, "Well, I'm so glad I'm livin' in the U.S.A.," seems to be anything but ironic. And, as a special tribute to the city that now seemed to give him the respect that was his due, Berry includes in the litany of American towns in the second verse "my home back in ol' St. Lou."

The single was another success—seven weeks on the *Billboard* chart during June and July—but the choice of B-side seemed to indicate that the Chess brothers had abandoned their old philosophy. Where once they had said "that's different, it just might sell," the coupling of "Back in the U.S.A.," with its by-now predictable introduction and rhythm, with the far more unusual "Memphis, Tennessee" indicated that they were becoming less enthusiastic with anything that didn't fit the formula. The fact that they had waited several months after the release of *Go, Johnny, Go*, the movie in which "Memphis, Tennessee" had been featured and, worse, that they had waited nearly a year to release the song, suggested that they and Berry had, by this stage, become unwilling to upset the status quo.

Almost a month to the day after "Back in the U.S.A." left the *Billboard* charts, the busy but satisfying days of 1959 came to a crashing halt for Chuck Berry. The first problem occurred five days into what should have been a routine five-week tour of small clubs and dances. On August 27, he had been

booked into the Key Field Officer's Club in Meridian, Mississippi, to entertain the Theta Kappa Omega fraternity of the local high school. What
happened that night was eerily reminiscent of the incident in Little Rock
three years earlier. Berry remembered that, toward the end of the dance,
"one of the girls threw her arms around me and hung a soul-searching kiss
that I let hang a second too long." At that point, according to *The
Autobiography*, Berry was surrounded by a group of dancers, one of whom
exclaimed to the excited crowd that "this nigger asked my sister for a date!"
Immediately, the mob began to turn on Berry, who managed to escape out a
side door and hide in a nearby building. Here one of the fraternity brothers,
along with a member of the local police force who had by now arrived at the
scene, escorted him away from the dance and into the local jail.

Berry's account of the incident then downplays its seriousness with
deadpan humor: "The sergeant," he wrote, "suggested that the entire seven
hundred dollars they had relieved me of would cover the fine for peace disturbance that I was being charged for." Further, he notes ironically, "they
decided I should stay there through the night" because a number of fraternity boys had made their way to the jail at that point.

The local newspaper's account of the evening's events corroborates Berry's
version in many ways; stripped of Berry's humor, however, it makes for
chilling reading. *The Meridian Star*, claiming to present "conflicting
accounts" of what happened, left no doubt about the local interpretation of
the incident. First, the *Star* took great pains to announce Berry's race in the
headline as well as in the first paragraph of its article; the racial identity of the
unnamed girl also was firmly established. Additionally, the paper carried
details of Berry's marriage, his children, and Themetta's pregnancy, clearly
painting a stereotype of Chuck Berry as a black, amoral, sexual predator.
The centerpiece of the newspaper story, however, is the girl's testimony to the
county attorney, Paul Busby. The girl, the *Star* declared in no uncertain
terms, "was on the verge of hysteria" as she recounted her story. "A white
youth," the article said, "told her that Berry wanted to see her. She claimed
she went to see the Negro and he asked her for a date. The girl then reported
the incident to others at the dance," and, apparently, then ran to report the
incident to the city police.

Berry, the *Star* reported, told Paul Busby, the County Attorney, "that he
never asked the girl for a date." According to Berry, the *Star*'s account went
on, "the girl and the boy came over of their own accord and asked for an
autograph." Interestingly, however, the *Star* also maintained Berry's incarceration after the event was for his own safety. Lending credence to this is the
information that Berry was moved at some point that night; the *Star* reported
that he "was first taken to the police station, but later lodged in the county
jail that night for his own safety." No mention, of course, was ever made of

the money that Berry supposedly paid as a fine; the morning that the paper ran the story, Berry was still in jail, and he was not allowed to go free on bond "until the investigation was completed."

In a sign of the times, the story made national news; even the *New York Times* ran the UPI story on the very back page of its Saturday, August 29, issue. But worse was to follow. Just three months later, Chuck, Johnnie Johnson, Leroy Davis, and Jasper Thomas embarked on another tour of one-nighters, which was to swing through Texas and the Southwest. The tour began in Albuquerque before heading into Texas with dates in San Antonio, San Angelo, and Buddy Holly's hometown of Lubbock. On the morning of December 1, while they made their way along the west Texas highways from Lubbock to El Paso in Chuck's new red Cadillac, a young Apache Indian girl named Janice Norine Escalanti was waking up in an El Paso jail cell. She had been held for 25 days on a charge of public drunkenness and was quite familiar with her surroundings; since she had arrived at her cousin Mary's house that March, she had been arrested by the El Paso police twice before, for vagrancy and prostitution. On her release, she made her way over the Rio Grande Bridge to Juarez, Mexico, where she spent that afternoon drinking at the Savoy, avoiding her waitressing job at the Deluxe Club across the border, just as she was avoiding high school back in Mescalero, New Mexico. She was 14, and ready for adventure.

She must have recognized Chuck Berry the minute he walked through the door of the Savoy. She had seen him, larger than life, in the movies, and now here he was, in Juarez, on a Tuesday afternoon. For a while, she sat and watched as Berry and another fellow (a bandmate, she guessed) talked to a man she later identified only as "Venchi," who was an acquaintance of hers from the Savoy; then, to her surprise, the three walked over to her. "Venchi" introduced Chuck Berry and the other man, Johnnie Johnson, to her, and explained that they had some time to kill before their show at the Coliseum Club in El Paso that night. They wanted to see the town, and Janice quickly agreed to take them.

They made their way to the red Cadillac, where she was introduced to Jasper Thomas and Leroy Davis, Berry's drummer and sax player, and together the five set off for a short tour of Juarez. After about an hour and a half, they stopped for dinner, where Berry gave her a fan card, explaining that this made her a member of the Chuck Berry Fan Club, entitled to a discount on a ticket for that night's show.

Eventually, they made their way over the bridge and back into the U.S.; Chuck Berry drove the band back to the Coliseum and dropped them off, then returned to Janice, who was waiting in the car. She confided in Berry that, even with the fan card discount, she wouldn't have enough money to go to that night's show. Quickly, he saw an opportunity that would benefit them both; what if Janice were to sell publicity photos for him in the club? She immediately agreed, and then directed Berry to drive her over to the Black and Tan, another club, where she had arranged to meet her girlfriend, who would let her into her apartment to change clothes.

While they were waiting in the Cadillac outside the Black and Tan, Berry began to ask Janice a little about herself. His first question was an obvious one, and Janice replied without even thinking: Yes, she said, of course she was 21. Her long, black hair and the broad, dark features of her face made her look anywhere from a teenager through to her early 20s; her worldly demeanor, however, made it easy to believe she was older than she actually was. The talk then turned to Janice's employment, and Janice was forced to confess that she had been turning tricks for the last year. But, she added, she wanted to stop. Immediately, as they had done with the photographs, Chuck Berry's opportunist instincts saw a mutually beneficial solution. He was looking for someone to work at his club back in St. Louis, as a hat-checker, perhaps, or on the door. Was that something she would be interested in, something that would help put her back on the straight-and-narrow path? Janice was hesitant; she would have to think about it.

Later, at the Coliseum, with the band playing those familiar songs that before she had only heard on the radio, she made up her mind. It was fun selling the photographs and meeting other Chuck Berry fans. And now she had the opportunity to travel with the band and to work and be close to him. At the end of the night, as the band piled their equipment in the Cadillac's trunk, Janice approached Berry and told him she would go with them. Then, the two dropped the rest of the band off in Juarez for a late supper and went back to Janice's apartment to fetch her clothes. The excitement of being on the road with a real star of radio, television, and the movies must finally have gripped her; this was the adventure she had been looking for.

The next show was in Tucson, and Berry and Johnnie Johnson drove through the night, making it to the Sands Hotel a little after 9:00 the following morning. What happened next is unclear; both Chuck Berry and Janice Escalanti checked into room 257 at around 9:30 that morning; they ordered room service at around 7:00 that evening before leaving for the show at the Casino Bar. Later, Janice recalled that they stayed in the room and slept for the remainder of the day; after eating, and before the show, she also posed for photographs, although, by her own account, she was fully clothed. Chuck Berry, however, remembered that the day was filled with the mundane and practical details of life on the road: visiting a one-hour cleaners and an auto repair station (to fix a turn signal on the Cadillac), going shopping (to buy shoes, a skirt, and a sweater for Janice), stopping at the barber (for Chuck to get his hair processed), and finally back to the motel to get ready for the show.

After the show at the Casino, they returned to the Sands at around 3:00 the following morning. Escalanti later recalled that Chuck Berry was accompanied by two female fans, and after spending time alone with one of them, he and Janice went for something to eat. When they finally retired, they stayed in the hotel room for the remainder of the day until checking out and heading to the next show in Phoenix.

The gig in Phoenix at the Marador Ballroom on December 3 followed the same pattern that the El Paso and Tucson dates had established, with Janice selling photographs while the band played their regular four-hour show. Afterward, when the instruments were packed in the car, the five set out for the next show, in Santa Fe, New Mexico. Chuck Berry drove the first shift, as was his custom, with the others sleeping as best they could; when tiredness set in, Berry switched places with Johnnie Johnson, sitting in the back seat with Janice and his guitar. In all, the trip took a grueling 12 hours, and on arrival in Santa Fe, they took in a movie before playing the show in order to unwind.

At the Santa Fe show, Berry first saw in Janice Escalanti the behavior that he later claimed led to her termination from his employment. He observed her less-than-enthusiastic attempts at selling photos that night; as he later recounted, "I asked her to sort of push the pictures. She was just sitting, waiting for people to ask for them." But in every other respect, the show went off normally, and the band immediately set off for the next show in Denver.

After another 12 hours on the road, the thought of checking in to the Drexel Hotel that afternoon must have given them great relief. As usual, it was Chuck Berry who registered the party into two doubles and a single; this time, however, one of the doubles, Room 334, was to be occupied by a "Mr. and Mrs. Janet Johnson." Whether by choice or because of her poor sales ability, Escalanti remained in the room for the whole evening while the band played the Denver gig.

Initially, the Saturday night show at the Rainbow Club was to have been the last of the tour, but at some point during the previous week the tour's promoter, Leroy Smith, added on a Sunday night date in Pueblo. In all respects, this show was as unremarkable as the rest of the dates on the tour had been, with the band leaving Denver at 3:00 in the afternoon, playing the show (which Janice Escalanti attended, although she did not sell the publicity photos), and then leaving in the early hours of the morning for the 860-mile trip back to St. Louis.

By the time the five reached Kansas City, Chuck Berry was completely exhausted, having driven most of the way through Colorado and Kansas on his own. Rather than endure the final 250-mile journey across Missouri, he opted to fly the rest of the way, making it to Lambert Field at around 5:00

that Monday afternoon. About four and a half hours later, Johnnie Johnson and Janice Escalanti arrived in the car at the house on Windemere Place; briefly, Berry took the girl to meet Francine Gillium across town at Club Bandstand. Then, all three went over to Berry's old house on Whittier, which was now occupied by Gillium and would also function as Janice Escalanti's home for the rest of her ill-fated stay in St. Louis.

Problems with Escalanti began almost immediately upon her arrival at Club Bandstand. While showing her around the club that first night, Francine Gillium asked the girl for her Social Security number and birth certificate so that she could put Janice on the payroll. She could not provide either, and never did during her entire stay. Then, on the second night, as Escalanti started her job in the hat-check room, she was reprimanded by both Berry and Gillium for leaving her station and wandering around the club, talking to the patrons. This scene was repeated several times during the first week of her employment, finally leading to Berry and Gillium changing her duties to working the door. But the temptations of nightclub life proved too strong for the young girl, and again she was scolded for leaving the money box open and unattended.

Finally, matters came to a head. Early in the afternoon of Thursday, December 17, Chuck Berry drove over to the house on Whittier and fired Janice Escalanti for not performing her duties at the club. She was going home, he told her, and she should pack immediately. A few minutes later, with all of her belongings in a big shopping bag in the back of the Cadillac, the two set out down Easton Avenue for the Greyhound Station. Berry purchased a one-way ticket to El Paso and, after placing some money in her hand, he left, leaving Janice to decide the course of her own future.

Once again, Janice Escalanti's impulses got the better of her. The El Paso bus was due to leave in an hour and a half, but in a short time she struck up a conversation with a stranger who took her to a nearby bar. She stayed there for the rest of the afternoon and into the evening, getting more and more drunk, before finally making up her mind to return to Club Bandstand. There, she struck up a conversation with one of the Ecuadors, another Chess Records act with whom Berry had accompanied on their single "Say You'll Be Mine" a month earlier. Perhaps she was trying to make Berry jealous; whatever her reasons, she stayed for the rest of the night until Berry, incensed by her behavior, walked over to the booth she was sitting in and took the ticket and the money from her purse. She could have both back when she was ready to leave for El Paso, he told her, before handing the ticket to Francine Gillium for safe-keeping.

After closing time, Jasper Thomas and Leroy Davis took Janice to the Deluxe, a "colored" hotel on Walton, about six blocks west of Club Bandstand. When she awoke on the following afternoon, she began to fume over the events of the previous evening. She tried to call Chuck Berry all afternoon and evening, but could not get past Francine Gillium, who usually took care of answering the phones at the club; Gillium kept telling her to call back, because Berry was busy getting ready to perform at the club that night.

It wasn't until the following afternoon that Janice finally managed to speak to Chuck Berry, and then only briefly. He told her she could have the ticket, but only if she agreed to let him put her on the bus; how could he trust her not to cash the ticket in and continue to stay in St. Louis? From then on, every time she called the club, Francine Gillium told her to stay away. That response only fueled Janice Escalanti's anger, and for the next three nights, Escalanti returned to prostitution to support herself.

Finally, on Monday night, December 21, Janice wandered over to Club Bandstand but, fearing reprisals from Berry and Gillium, she stopped short of going in; instead she went to the Chuck Wagon, the restaurant above the club, and considered her options. She was ready to leave, but the question was how to go about doing it. She could go back to El Paso, but that just meant a return to prostitution. And returning to Mescalero meant family and high school. In the end, she decided to call the police in Yuma, Arizona, perhaps hoping to stay with relatives or a friend who would not question her about her life over the last year. But the Yuma police could not help; instead, they told her to sit tight and wait for an officer from the St. Louis Police Department to come and get her. Not long after, she was arrested and taken to the Ninth District Police Station, where she was questioned by Detective Roland Norton and his partner, Jim Buford. A little after midnight, the two took Janice Escalanti to the club, where they waited for Chuck Berry to finish up his last set. As he walked off-stage, still sweating, Charles Edward Anderson Berry was arrested and charged with violating the Mann Act.

Sumner High School, St. Louis, with Tandy Park in the foreground. Courtesy St. Louis Public Schools Records Center/Archives.

Antioch Baptist Church, corner of West North Market Street and Goode Avenue (Annie Malone Drive). Photo by David Schultz, courtesy of the Missouri Historical Society.

4319 Labadie Avenue, St. Louis. The Berry family moved here in the mid-1930s; by the time this photograph was taken in 1997, the property had been abandoned for some time. Photo by the author.

Themetta Suggs Berry (left) and Charles Berry (right) in the late 1940s. Harry Davis Collection.

Henry Berry's van. Harry Davis Collection.

A young Charles
Berry in the late
1930s. Harry Davis
Collection.

The Sir John's Trio, c. 1953. From left, Ebby Hardy, Chuck Berry, Johnnie Johnson.
Harry Davis Collection.

The Cosmopolitan Club, 17th and Bond Street, East St. Louis, as it appeared in 1990.
Photo by Bill Greensmith.

Performing at the Cosmopolitan Club, East St. Louis, c. 1953. Harry Davis Collection.

Movie poster for *Go, Johnny, Go*, the 1959 Alan Freed movie which featured Chuck Berry in his first acting role. Johnny Melody, the white teen idol played by Jimmy Clanton, is pictured top, center. Courtesy Bill Greensmith collection.

Movie still of Alan Freed and Chuck Berry from *Go, Johnny, Go*. Courtesy Bill Greensmith collection.

The Chess family, shortly before Leonard's death, in 1969. From left: Leonard, Marshall, and Phil Chess. Copyright © 1969, Chicago Tribune Co.

Jack Hooke, Chuck Berry's
first manager, in 1997.
Photo by the author.

The brown-eyed
handsome man
himself. An unused
publicity shot taken in
the late 1950s. Harry
Davis Collection.

Chuck Berry in the offices of Chuck Berry Music, Easton Avenue, St. Louis, late 1950s. Harry Davis Collection.

Club Bandstand, 814 N. Grand Avenue, St. Louis, 1959. Francine Gillium stands behind the bar with Chuck Berry standing on the far right. Harry Davis Collection.

Master and student.
Chuck Berry with
Billy Peek (above)
as a young admirer
c. 1958–59 and
(below) as a band
member c. 1969–70.
Photos courtesy
Billy Peek.

13 Windermere Place, St. Louis. The house was purchased by Chuck Berry in 1958. Photo by Bill Greensmith.

Merle Silverstein, Chuck Berry's attorney during the Mann Act trials. Photo courtesy of Merle Silverstein.

Frederick Mayer, Assistant U.S. Attorney, Eastern District of Missouri, 1958–1964, and prosecuting attorney in the Mann Act trials. Photo courtesy of Frederick Mayer.

On stage during one of Richard Nader's Rock and Roll Revivals, Nassau Colliseum, Uniondale NY, May 1972. Courtesy Blues Unlimited.

Chuck Berry with Bo Diddley, backstage at Wembley Stadium, England, August 5, 1972. Photo by Bill Greensmith.

Chuck Berry performing his trademark duckwalk during the filming of *American Hot Wax* in 1977. Courtesy Mike Rowe.

Richard Schwartz,
Berry's attorney
during the video-
taping lawsuits
of the early 1990s.
Photo courtesy of
Richard Schwartz.

The Southern Air in Wentzville, 1997. Photo by the author.

Sharing a rare light-hearted moment with Keith Richards during the 60th birthday concert, filmed for the movie *Chuck Berry: Hail! Hail! Rock 'n' Roll*. Fox Theater, St. Louis, October 16, 1986. Copyright © Corbis.

Better days: Chuck Berry (left) and Johnnie Johnson (right) in 1995 before Johnson's copyright lawsuit. With them is Joe Edwards, owner of the St. Louis restaurant Blueberry Hill, where Berry has regularly performed since 1996. Photo by Bill Greensmith.

Being presented with a Kennedy Center Honor by President Bill Clinton, December 3, 2000. Copyright © Reuters New Media Inc./Corbis. Photograph by Phil Pott.

The Mask

8

We wear the mask that grins and lies,
It hides our cheeks and shades our eyes—
This debt we pay to human guile;
With torn and bleeding hearts we smile,
And mouth with myriad subtleties.

Why should the world be over-wise,
In counting all our tears and sighs?
Nay, let them only see us, while
We wear the mask.
>   —Paul Laurence Dunbar, "We Wear the Mask"

In the early morning hours of December 22, 1959, Chuck Berry was questioned by the St. Louis police; the report of the incident, written by district commander Captain Walter Eitzman, states that, in the upstairs restaurant, Escalanti had told officers Buford and Norton:

> that she had been transported to this City from Texas by a Negro known as Chuck Berry, who at the present time was in the basement of the above restaurant, the officers then proceeded to the basement which is known as Chuck Beery [sic] Band Stand Club, where the above subject pointed out a Negro, who she stated was the man who brought her to this City From Texas, this Negro was placed under arrest and identified himself as Berry, Charles.

The report's racial references went beyond the mere purpose of identifying him physically as a suspect in the incident. Immediately, the stereotypical sexual image of a black male with a nonblack female became an issue in the case.

Janice Escalanti's initial phone call to the police in Yuma, Arizona, coupled with the circumstances of the interstate journey she had described in her statement, put the incident outside the jurisdiction of the St. Louis Police. Accordingly, two FBI agents, Paul Stombaugh and Edward Moreland, were dispatched to the Ninth District station. The two questioned Berry and Escalanti, and their report found its way onto Frederick Mayer's desk later that day. True to his word from 18 months before, Mayer wasted no time in issuing an arrest warrant, and Berry was formally charged with violating the Mann Act.

By the time of Berry's arrest, the Mann Act had become an anachronism. Passed in 1910, it was a response to hysteria about "white slavery," the kidnapping of young girls who were forced to become prostitutes, that was perhaps more imagined than real. The legislation was part of the so-called Progressive Movement, a legislative program to rid society of a number of social problems; within that decade, the Harrison Narcotic Drug Act of 1914 and the Prohibition Amendment of 1919 were also passed. From its inception, the Mann Act was deeply flawed. Its ambiguous wording immediately enabled the Supreme Court to provide interpretations that widened its scope away from its original intention of prosecuting coerced prostitution to punishing any form of "immoral" activity. Section 2 of the Act states that

> any person who shall knowingly transport or cause to be transported, or aid or assist in obtaining transportation for, or in transporting, in interstate or foreign commerce, or in any Territory or in the District of Columbia, any woman or girl for the purpose of prostitution or debauchery, *or for any other immoral purpose* [my italics], or with *the intent* [my italics] and purpose to induce, entice, or compel such woman or girl to become a prostitute or give herself up to debauchery, or to engage *in any other immoral practice* [my italics]. . . . shall be deemed guilty of a felony, and upon consideration thereof shall be punished by a fine not exceeding five thousand dollars, or by imprisonment of not more than five years, or by both such fine and imprisonment, in the discretion of the court.

Two early trials lay the basis for a broad reading of the act. The first, *Wilson v. United States* in 1914, helped shape the idea that intent, and not evidence of the sexual act itself, was sufficient for the court to convict. In other words, evidence of sexual activity between the parties was not necessary for a conviction; all that was needed was evidence of a pattern of behavior from which an intention of sexual conduct could be derived. The verdict in the second, *Caminetti v. United States*, also in 1914, seemed to be a response to public opinion of the day, particularly as voiced by church assemblies and reform groups. It paved the way for noncommercial prosecutions—or prosecutions, in the words of the act, for "any other immoral purpose." Quite simply, the act could be used to entrap any citizen of the United States who traveled from one state to another with a member of the opposite sex.

By the 1920s, the morals crusade that produced the act ended, and the U.S. attorneys began declining to prosecute noncommercial prosecutions where no aggravating circumstances existed. By the time of Berry's arrest, such factors as age, adultery, and abandonment of minors could be considered in these cases, although there is evidence that by the late 1950s many such aggravated cases were not even brought to trial. Mann Act prosecutions seemed to be very much at the discretion of the local federal prosecutors and the FBI.

Clearly, Frederick Mayer felt that after the incident in St. Charles there were enough reasons for the charge. "Basically," he recalled, "with the Indian girl it was age. And the girl in St. Louis was either seventeen or eighteen, and I believe there was some information that Berry had done this on other occasions, which of course I took into consideration but I did not charge him with any of that. But I felt the fact that he was warned earlier about this and the age of the young girls was sufficient to go ahead and prosecute him."

Events that January unfolded rapidly. After obtaining the Grand Jury indictment for the first Mann Act charge on January 7, 1960, Frederick Mayer moved ahead with new charges stemming from Berry's involvement with Joan Mathis and, on January 25, Berry was arrested again. This time, he faced two new counts of violating the Mann Act, one for Mathis's trip to Toledo in April 1958 and another for the Omaha trip the following month. Berry also was charged with felony interstate transportation of a firearm from the St. Charles arrest. Because of his 1944 felony conviction, that indictment carried a punishment of a fine of not more than $2,000 as well as a prison term of not more than five years, or both. Coupled with the three counts of violating the Mann Act, Berry was looking at a total of 20 years in prison and up to $17,000 in fines. Quite clearly, Frederick Mayer was making good on his 1958 promise in a big way.

With the first Mann Act trial little more than a month away, Berry's attorney, Merle Silverstein, attempted to dimiss both of the new indictments. On February 10, he entered a motion that the gun charges and the earlier two counts of violating the Mann Act be dismissed on the grounds that "the defendant has been denied the right to a speedy trial and due process of law, which denials directly violate Amendments VI and V of the United States Consitution, and prevent defendant from obtaining a fair trial at this late date." Eventually the motion was overruled by Judge Randolph Weber on March 4, which coincidentally happened to be the last day of the first Mann Act trial. Weber set the second trial date for Monday, April 4, giving Silverstein only a month between trials to prepare.

During this flurry of legal activity, Berry's musical fortunes fluctuated wildly. Although Berry writes that "there were only three [live] jobs that February. . . . There were none in March," both sides of his current single, "Let It Rock" and "Too Pooped to Pop" managed to stay on the *Billboard Hot 100* chart throughout February and March. Despite some sterling piano work by Johnnie Johnson on the former song, the success was short-lived, as this was Berry's last pop chart success until March 1964, though five other singles were released during the following three years.

As events moved inexorably toward the February trial, a backdrop of two major political and social developments began to unfold across the country. On February 1, the same day "Let It Rock" entered the *Billboard Hot 100*, four black students from North Carolina A&T—Franklin McCain, David Richmond, Joseph McNeil, and Ezell Blair, Jr.—entered the Woolworth's in Greensboro, North Carolina, and asked to be served at the segregated lunch counter there. Although the four were denied the coffee and donuts they asked for on that day, within two weeks the Greensboro sit-in had sparked similar sit-ins in a number of North Carolina cities.

Meanwhile, Berry's old friend and business associate Alan Freed was being engulfed in the extensive payola probe that had begun the previous October with hearings before the House Subcommittee on Legislative Oversight; the probe had spawned, within a month, a number of investigations conducted by the FBI, the Federal Trade Commission, and the district attorneys of both New York and Philadelphia. On February 25, four days before the first of Chuck Berry's Mann Act trials, New York Assistant District Attorney Joseph Stone indicted Freed on a charge of commercial bribery, the first solid result of the New York investigation. Clearly, with the nation's consciousness turned toward matters of race and the evils of rock-and-roll music, the trial's timing could not have been more inopportune for Chuck Berry.

Leap Day 1960 dawned fair and cold when the first of the trials finally began. The St. Louis courthouse that day was a study in contrasts, with the dynamic, forceful personality of Frederick Mayer, a wily New Yorker, pitted against the soft-spoken, understated Merle Silverstein, a native St. Louisan. In many respects, however, despite their different styles, the two were equally matched: Both graduated from the respected Washington University Law School in St. Louis in 1951 and both had quickly risen to become two of the most respected lawyers practicing in St. Louis at the time. Between them on the bench sat Judge George H. Moore. Born in the small northeast Missouri town of La Grange in 1878, Moore was certainly old-school; when he died in 1962, his obituary described him as "a stickler for decorum in his courtroom." Publicly, at least, he seemed committed to fairness and equality. In 1955, he had ruled in favor of desegregating the St. Louis Housing Authority, finding that the Authority's "management in accordance with a policy of racial segregation is a violation of the Constitution and laws of the United States." Earlier still, in 1924 during his first and only run for office, he was the only one of four Democratic nominees for the governorship of Missouri willing to denounce the Ku Klux Klan.

But an enlightened public persona can hide dark personal prejudice. In the late 1940s, for example, Moore had turned down an invitation to speak at the law school of the recently desegregated St. Louis University on the grounds that they "had that 'nigra' out there." The "nigra," as it turned out, happened to be Theodore McMillian, a student who became the first black circuit court judge in Missouri history. Merle Silverstein vividly recalls Moore's prejudice. "One day," he remembered, "Moore was having criminal arraignments, and there were about four or five defendants to be arraigned, and they were all black. And they all had a court-appointed lawyer who was also black. They were all standing in front of the judge, and I think that there was no assistant U.S. Attorney there to conduct the arraignment, so he said, 'Somebody get the United States Attorney's office down here.' After three or four minutes, in walks the assistant United States Attorney; I don't know who it was, but he was white, of course. Judge Moore looks at him and says, 'Ah, Dr. Livingstone I presume.'" In Merle Silverstein's estimation, the judge was, quite simply, "one of the greatest bigots of all time."

Chuck Berry, on the surface at least, appeared unconcerned by Moore or the entire proceedings. Like his wife Themetta, who, according to the *Argus*, "sat calm throughout the entire trial in which adultery was alleged time and time again," Berry too "seemed unpurturbed [sic] by the serious charges resting against him." The *Argus* added, "From time to time he removed a copy of *Time* magazine from his pocket and thumbed through it lightly." But that afternoon, the spotlight was on a quiet, homely young girl from New Mexico whose plainly spoken testimony would, over the course of the next two days, spell out in lurid detail the events of the previous December.

Initially, Janice Escalanti appeared nervous at all the attention. As her testimony began, Frederick Mayer reminded her to speak up, and on several occasions Judge Moore asked her to repeat her answers to Mayer's questions. But her retelling of the events, in short, three- or four-word sentences, was clear and detailed; as Frederick Mayer was to recall later, "I felt she was telling the truth . . . if she was lying on this thing, she wouldn't have had all this information and knowledge."

Her testimony, though, never made it past the first meeting with Berry in the Savoy bar in El Paso when the first major incident of the trial took place. She was describing Venchi, the man who had introduced her to Berry, when Judge Moore suddenly broke in and asked Janice to clarify Venchi's race. "Is he a white man or a Negro?" he asked her, then straight after her reply, he asked again, "Is he a Negro?" To some, perhaps, this would have been innocuous enough—just a judge asking a point of clarification. Yet in front of an all-white jury, such a racial identification would have had the effect of further underscoring the role of race in the proceedings. Venchi's racial identity had no bearing on the case, and Moore's comments can only be seen as inflammatory.

Less than a minute later, as Escalanti described meeting the rest of Berry's bandmates, Moore interrupted again: "Who was Johnny [sic] Johnson?" he asked her. "Is he a white man or Negro?" Quite simply, Merle Silverstein maintains, with these outbursts Moore "made a mockery of Chuck's race. Every witness that got on the stand, when they identified somebody, the judge would interrupt and say, 'Was that a white man or a black man?'" attempting to remind the jury at every turn that they needed to view the events through the lens of race. Worse, according to Silverstein, "Several times, I think he used the word 'nigger.'" Later, Silverstein noticed that "It came out as a 'negro' in the court transcripts. I questioned the court reporter at the time, he said, 'Well, he has a southern accent, and he says "nigra" and it sounds like "nigger."' But I thought that was a lot of crap." So convinced was Silverstein that Moore had uttered the word that he had colleagues ready and willing to swear to the fact.

At this point, perhaps, Merle Silverstein should have attacked Moore for such out-and-out racism; Chuck Berry himself has voiced this opinion. Certainly, in *The Autobiography*, Berry typically absolves himself from any guilt in the incident and singles out Merle Silverstein for criticism, especially for his "mild voice" and "weakly sounded objections." "I had but little faith in my attorney," he wrote some quarter of a century later, "seeing many opportunities in the course of the trials where he had missed a point in rebuttal or could have intervened with a pertinent point."

But despite his low-key profile, Silverstein knew that this was not the moment to challenge Moore. As he later explained, "To confront him and say, 'You can't do this in front of a jury, Judge. I object to your constant interjection of race into the case.' Now that would have really gotten him pissed off at me." Silverstein also had to take into account his credibility in the eyes of the jury. In St. Louis at the time, juries were handpicked by the trial judge and often served for several months on a number of cases in that judge's courtroom. "If this was a fresh jury," Silverstein recalled, "I might have taken a different posture. This jury . . . had been in three or four or five or six cases in front of him. So they knew him very well, and he probably was a big hero to them."

In fact, Merle Silverstein was faced with the most difficult decision a "trial lawyer faces during the trial: when you have an antagonistic judge, do you confront him and keep this up during the trial, or do you try to subdue it, pretend like nothing bad is happening? And I made the decision; I saw what was happening, that confrontation—actually conducting and going to war with the judge—was not going to help." And if Berry was to second-guess his attorney's decision after the trial, Merle Silverstein's opponent would not. "In my opinion," Frederick Mayer would later say, "Merle . . . did everything in the world to represent [Berry] in a proper way."

Janice Escalanti's testimony continued unwaveringly. She described the events of the show in El Paso and the overnight trip to the Sands Hotel in Tucson, where, she maintained, she and Berry had sex for the first time. This led to a somewhat ironic interchange when Mayer, attempting to improve Escalanti's image with the jury and deflect the attack on her character that he knew Merle Silverstein would initiate later, asked the self-confessed, twice-convicted prostitute if she understood what he meant when he spoke of "sexual intercourse."

At this point, Mayer began the process of corroborating Janice's testimony by having her point out Ronald Kurn, a bellhop who had delivered food to Berry's room at the Sands and who had seen her, partially clothed, in bed at the time. The circumstantial evidence of the scene in the Sands must have been pretty powerful in the jury's minds. So, too, would Janice's ensuing description of a second act of intercourse in the hotel room prior to their departure for the show in Phoenix and of a photo session she engaged in for Berry right after (albeit one in which, she admitted, she was fully clothed).

Piece by piece, Fred Mayer was building his case, and the evidence of Berry's intent was beginning to mount. During the grueling trip from Phoenix to Santa Fe, Janice Escalanti recalled "another sexual relationship" in the back of Berry's Cadillac and again in the back seat after the Santa Fe show on the way to Denver. At the Drexel Hotel, she recalled another sexual encounter between the two. And, during the two weeks in St. Louis, Escalanti recalled having sex with Berry "just about every night" in the house on Whittier Street that she shared with Francine Gillium. For Mayer, the incidents in the car and in St. Louis would have been difficult to substantiate; if there were witnesses, they would be Berry's friends and business associates. But Mayer knew that he did not need to corroborate Janice Escalanti's allegations that she and Berry had sexual relations. With the ambiguously written law in his favor, all he needed was to convince the jury of Chuck Berry's intent.

Mayer's other tactic was to shoot holes in the idea that Berry had offered Janice Escalanti legitimate employment on the road and in St. Louis. Here, however, he was less successful, because Escalanti's own circumstances were wide open to interpretation. She testified that she received no money for selling Berry's publicity photographs at the shows in El Paso, Tucson, or Phoenix, and that she had not been asked to sell photographs at all in Denver, raising the question in the jury's mind about her purpose on the trip. Mayer's questioning in the initial direct examination also left the jury with the impression that Berry had deliberately not paid Janice for the two weeks she had worked for him as a hat-checker at Club Bandstand. No mention was made at that point that Berry had provided her with spending money during the tour for selling the publicity photographs or that Francine Gillium had made a concerted attempt to pay Janice for her work at Club Bandstand but could not because Janice could not furnish a birth certificate or Social Security card.

All that was left for Mayer in his direct was to show that Berry had essentially abandoned Janice Escalanti, that he had used her and tossed her aside; with his flair for the dramatic, this was a comparatively easy thing for him to do. First, he made sure that the jury knew that Berry had given her the bus ticket and a mere five dollars when she had been fired, and that he had taken both back when Janice had reappeared at the club. Then, he ended his questioning leaving the jury with a picture of a destitute Janice turning tricks in the Deluxe Hotel, but not before he pointed out to them that the hotel catered to colored clients. Once again, the message to the all-white jury was clear: Janice Escalanti had been made to sink so low that she had not only had to resort to prostitution, but she had to cater to black patrons. Perhaps Mayer's words could be excused in his zeal to obtain a prosecution; indeed, Merle Silverstein would later dismiss any allegations that Mayer was a racist. But whatever Mayer's motivation for the comment, the effect was to inject once again the issue of race into the trial.

Silverstein, who had quietly bided his time, now began to methodically make his case. First, he asked Judge Moore in a sidebar conference for copies of the statements Janice had made to the FBI and the Grand Jury, knowing that in them there were bound to be a number of inconsistencies. In those days, however, full-disclosure of evidence before a trial had yet to be mandated; Silverstein was not entitled to see copies of the statements, a fact that Judge Moore let him know in no uncertain terms. Taking that defeat in stride, he immediately grilled Janice Escalanti for the rest of the afternoon with the aim of casting doubt on her character and her motivations for causing Berry to come to trial. More important, he had to weaken the prosecution's premise that this was an aggravated Mann Act case; he needed to show that Janice entered into an arrangement of employment with Berry, and that the employment was legitimate.

Silverstein quickly painted a picture of Escalanti that was far from the naïve innocent Mayer would have had the jury see. First, he established that Janice had lied to both Berry and Francine Gillium about her age and about her Social Security card. Then he had her admit to an erratic employment history in El Paso, to drinking, to an arrest on a charge of public intoxication, and ultimately to being a prostitute; in short, she was unreliable as a worker and, presumably, as a witness.

Quickly, Silverstein's questions moved toward the purpose of Janice Escalanti's trip to St. Louis, a move that immediately incurred Judge Moore's wrath. After ascertaining that she had told Berry she had been a prostitute, Silverstein suggested that Berry's offer of jobs on the road and in St. Louis was an attempt to help her straighten herself out. She accepted Silverstein's description of Berry's motivation, leading Silverstein to ask whether employment was the sole purpose of her trip; quickly, Judge Moore jumped in to remind her just to repeat, word-for-word, the conversations she and Berry had engaged in. He cautioned Silverstein that if he would confine his questions to matters concerning "conversations between her and this Negro we will do a good deal better." Once again, the jury was pointedly reminded of Berry's race for no good reason; worse, they could not have ignored the vehemence of Moore's tone.

Moore then took over the questioning for several moments, asking the girl to recount the conversation in which Berry offered her employment to deliver her from her life in prostitution; it was the first exchange in a pattern of interrupting the flow of Silverstein's cross-examination that he continued for the rest of the day. For a while, Silverstein shrewdly sidestepped Moore, however, and attempted to pick holes in Escalanti's account of the Tucson engagement, showing that her version of the story differed quite radically from the one Berry would give later. At one point, Janice even doubts her own recollection, leading to her immature and ungrammatical statement that "I'm sure that it was on the second day, but not unless I'm mixed up it isn't." For the time being, at least, Silverstein was beginning to win the delicate battle of cross-examining a sympathetic witness, although the points he was scoring from Janice's testimony were not significant ones.

Silverstein's line of questioning then moved on to the other events of the tour, and several times he was again interrupted by Judge Moore. The first occurred when he attempted to show that Janice Escalanti's actions were voluntary and not coerced. Moore again interrupted and admonished Silverstein for this line of questioning. "There is no question involved about persuasion in this case," asserted the judge. "Save the time of the Court and jury." On this ruling, Judge Moore was entirely correct. In Mann Act cases, the willingness of the victim is not at issue.

The next, and potentially more damaging, interruption occurred when Janice recounted her arrival at Berry's home on Windermere Place. Here, the judge questioned Janice about the appearance of the house, making sure the jury heard that it had "big entrance gates" and that it was "a fine looking place." It gave one indication as to the kind of prejudice he harbored against Berry: Clearly, he resented the fact that a black man could be successful enough to own such a house.

Then, after Silverstein had spent some time attempting to establish the problems Janice Escalanti had caused during her employment, trying to show that Berry had good reason to fire her from the legitimate employment he had provided her, Moore interrupted again. This time, as she recounted her encounter in the Greyhound bus station with a man who invited her to drink with him, Moore asked the girl if the man was black or white. Although this time the character was white, Moore's comment again focused the jury on issues of race where those issues clearly had no bearing on the matter in hand.

But it was Moore's final interruption, coming right at the end of the first day of the trial, which may have done the most damage to Berry's defense in the jury's eyes. For some time, Silverstein's questions had gone unchallenged by Judge Moore as the lawyer systematically yet gently tried to illustrate for the jury the flaws in Janice's character. Eventually, he steered the questions to the issue of Janice's feelings for Berry; this immediately prompted an objection from Frederick Mayer. As Janice attempted to answer Silverstein's question, Moore jumped in, sustaining Mayer's objection and admonishing the witness not to answer the question. After a short side-bar conference, in which Silverstein offered his reasons for asking the question, Judge Moore decided to call a recess until the following day; it was the image of Merle Silverstein being reprimanded by the judge that would have stayed with the jury as they filtered out of the courtroom on that gray Monday afternoon.

The trial resumed the following morning with Janice again on the stand. It began uneventfully, with Merle Silverstein leading her through an account of her last few days in St. Louis before Berry's arrest. Rather than focusing on her character, and possibly risking alienating the jury even more, Silverstein's tactics were, at least at first, gentler than the previous day's. He trod lightly around the issue of her feelings for Berry as he introduced a letter she had written to him on the night of the arrest. He also introduced the notion of Janice's initiating her own departure by raising the issue of a letter she had written to a friend named Clarence in New Orleans. It was yet one more moment for Judge Moore to interject the issue of race into the proceedings, as he jumped in again to ascertain Clarence's race.

Silverstein had one more card to play, however, and that was the issue of Escalanti's contradictory testimony. Confronting her with the statement she had made to the FBI, he asked why she had not told them about the alleged sexual acts in the back of Berry's Cadillac. Then, in an unusually dramatic gesture for him, he ended his cross-examination abruptly without giving her a chance to fully explain, hoping to plant the seeds of doubt in the jury's mind.

At this point, Frederick Mayer kept his witness on the stand to answer several questions intended to clear up some of the inconsistencies in her previous testimony. One of them, directed at the day before the show in

Tucson, was a question about Berry's visit to the hairdresser. Mayer, however, went to great pains to make sure that the jury knew that Berry was having his hair processed, a procedure unique to nonwhites and which immediately aroused Judge Moore's curiosity. Perhaps the question had the intention of showing that Janice's recollections were vivid enough to be accurate and reliable. Consciously or unconsciously, however, Mayer had re-opened the issue of Chuck Berry's race for the jury and Judge Moore.

Judge Moore also had another occasion to turn the jury's attention back to racial matters when the next witness, Ronald Kurn, the bellhop from the Sands Hotel, took the stand. Kurn began by describing a phone call he had taken at the hotel desk for room service; when Mayer asked him to clarify what was on the room service order, Judge Moore immediately interjected, "By Mr. Berry, do you mean this Negro, the defendant?" Again, the identification of Berry here was gratuitous, while the use of the pronoun "this," like Moore's earlier reference to Berry during Janice Escalanti's testimony on the first day of the trial, made Moore's words highly pejorative.

Although it did not provide absolute proof of Berry's affair with Janice Escalanti, Kurn's testimony was pretty damning; it went a long way toward corroborating Escalanti's own testimony and circumstantially establishing intent. He recalled seeing a woman in Berry's room "in the bed closest to the door" and with "the covers up to her neck," although he was unable to precisely identify the woman in Room 257 as the woman who sat in front of him in the court that day. "I would have a pretty good guess it was her," he told Frederick Mayer during his direct examination, adding that the girl he had seen on the stand that morning "very much" resembled the girl he had seen that previous December.

Then, saxophone player Leroy Davis was called. His testimony—unsurprisingly given his status as one of the band—was not terribly helpful to the prosecution. Much of Davis's testimony covered the same territory already fully established, leaving Judge Moore irritated and impatient. But the cross-examination did yield one moment of levity, when Davis described how difficult it would have been for Berry and Escalanti to have engaged in any kind of sexual activity in the back seat of the Cadillac because there would have been no room, with Berry's guitar and the band's overcoats taking up too much space.

After the lunch recess, Silverstein concluded his cross-examination of Davis, and George Dixon, the clerk at the Drexel Hotel in Denver, took the stand. His testimony produced high drama at the end of the day's session, and once again Judge Moore was at its center. After Dixon had described, during direct examination, how Berry and Escalanti, registering under the names of "Mr. and Mrs. Janice Johnson," shared a room with only one bed, Silverstein began his cross-examination. He had begun to ask Dixon about the band's arrival at the hotel when Moore, out of nowhere, asked the clerk "Is that hotel patronized by the white?"

Dixon seemed puzzled by the question, and responded by saying, "Is it what?" Moore then repeated the question, "Is it patronized by white people?" Again, the clerk seemed confused by the judge's train of thought, and responded by saying, "All white people." Moore, beginning to be frustrated by the clerk's response, indicated to the band and angrily asked, "Do you call these people white?"At this point, Dixon seemed to understand what Judge Moore was driving at, and began to explain. "Well," he began, "up in Colorado we have a law. . . ." Angrily, Moore cut him off before he could offer any lengthy explanation of Colorado's laws against segregation. "I am not arguing," he responded. "I am just asking for the facts. Proceed."

Just moments later, heightening the drama, Judge Moore called an end to the day's proceedings at the end of Dixon's cross-examination. "I dislike very much to inconvenience anybody else," he announced to the court. "I am suffering terrific pain. Will anybody be greatly inconvenienced if we adjourn at this time?" And so, barely 40 minutes into the afternoon session, the trial was adjourned until Wednesday morning.

That night, St. Louis was hit with a late winter storm; nearly 10 inches of snow fell on the city and caused havoc with commuter traffic and public transportation for the next two days. Nonetheless, the trial continued the next morning, with Judge Moore apparently fully recovered from his mysterious "illness" of the day before. The day's proceedings bagan with Frederick Mayer calling Drexel Hotel night clerk Oliver Brown, who had originally met Berry when the musician visited Denver in October 1959. This first visit would prove to have an important bearing on the trial's outcome, but for the time being Mayer simply established that Brown had first met Berry in October and that Berry was traveling at that time with a woman who would later turn out to be Francine Gillium. Silverstein objected to the introduction of this previous meeting as "irrelevant," but the judge overruled him. However, under Merle Silverstein's cross-examination, Brown could not place Berry and Escalanti together in the hotel during their December visit. He was able to corroborate George Dixon's testimony, though, that they had registered under the names of "Mr. and Mrs. Johnson," and that Berry had asked about the woman's whereabouts on returning from the show in the early hours of the morning.

The final witness for the prosecution that morning was Johnnie Johnson, whose testimony corroborated two small but significant parts of the prosecution's case: that Berry and Escalanti had shared a room in Tucson and that he had driven Janice to the house on Windermere. Under cross-examination, Johnson's testimony was almost a replication of Leroy Davis's previous statements that Berry and Escalanti had nothing but a "businesslike" relationship.

Further, Johnson also insisted that the two could not have had sex in the back seat of the Cadillac because there was no room and Berry would have been too tired. In all, Johnson's testimony was to have been expected, as he was still loyal to Berry. It was a weak note on which to end the prosecution's case, but on these points, Frederick Mayer rested.

After a statement by Merle Silverstein to the jury followed by a lunch recess, the defense began by putting Berry on the stand. What followed that Wednesday afternoon was a perfect illustration of Berry's public persona in action: He was evasive, deceptive, and unwilling to admit anything to anyone in the St. Louis courtroom or beyond. At no time during his testimony did Judge Moore, the jury, or even his own attorney get to see the inner man— the thoughtful, compassionate Berry whom only those closest to him would ever know. And that, coupled with the racial currents swirling around America at this time, provides perhaps the best explanation for the jury's eventual verdict in the trial.

Throughout his testimony, Berry emphatically denied that anything improper had taken place between him and Janice Escalanti. It was a position he was to maintain up to and beyond the publication of his autobiography 25 years later, in which he was more than candid about many of the other sexual relationships he had engaged in throughout his life. As one would expect, his attorney believed him. "She was a very homely person," Merle Silverstein was to recall of Janice some 40 years later. "She was *not* very pretty at all. And that's why I believe Chuck. Because the women he went around with and cheated with were very pretty women. So I just couldn't picture him having a romantic or sexual relationship with this very, very homely woman."

Indeed, at least in this one respect, Chuck Berry remained consistent during his time on the stand. He testified that he and Escalanti had slept in separate beds in Tucson; in Denver, where there was only one bed in the room, he told the jury he slept on the floor. As for the sex in the car and later in St. Louis, he maintained that it never happened. But if Berry was consistent in his testimony about not having had sexual relations with Janice Escalanti, the sheer variety of reasons he provided to explain why he invited the girl to travel with him on the tour and later to come to St. Louis must have seemed to the jury to be dissemblance. He offered several reasons for inviting the girl to travel with him: He wanted her to refrain from prostitution; he felt sorry for her; he needed to fill a vacancy in the club for a hat-check girl; and he wanted to learn Spanish "so very much," as "I have written and published some songs in Spanish, and the general trend now in recordings is to sing in native tongues." All were plausible enough when taken on their own, even the explanation of wanting to write songs in Spanish. Berry had released a song in 1957 called "La Juanda," the lyrics of which, part English and part Spanish, describe a meeting between a boy who speaks only English and a girl who speaks only Español. Further, two Spanish-language songs—"Donde Esta Santa Claus?" by Augie Rios and "La Bamba" by Richie Valens—had charted with Berry's "Run, Rudolph, Run" in December 1958. Certainly, Berry could not have ignored the phenomenal yet brief career of Valens, with whom he had starred in Alan Freed's *Go, Johnny, Go*.

But if the number of explanations seemed implausible to the jury, Berry's inability or unwillingness to state facts must have made the testimony even less believable. The first to caution Berry about this, naturally enough, was Judge Moore. As Berry was describing a conversation with Janice Escalanti about her wanting to attend the show in El Paso, Moore interrupted by asking Berry not to "tell us what she wanted. Tell us what she said." Later, as Berry described the preparations for the Denver show, he recalled that he "must have dressed" for the show right after arriving at the hotel and eating a meal. Moore retorted, "Don't tell us what you must have done, tell us what you did." This initiated a brief and acrimonious exchange between the two, as Berry reminded Moore how hard it was to recall exactly what he did for one show when he performed "200 one-nighters a year." To this, Moore curtly responded, "Well, when you don't know say you don't know; there is no use taking up the time of this court and jury saying what you must have done."

Even Merle Silverstein was forced, at several times during the afternoon's proceedings, to caution his client to stick with the facts. The first such moment arose during Berry's recounting of registering at the Sands Hotel in Tucson. He stated that Jasper and Leroy usually roomed together, to which Silverstein responded "No. Don't tell me usually; how did they on this occasion, that is all." A little later, when the questions turned to the incidents at the Drexel Hotel in Denver, Berry was asked to recall what he discovered in the room. "I discovered that I had asked for a double bed," he replied, to which Silverstein responded, "No. What did you discover, not what you had asked for. Listen to my question. When you went into the room, what did you discover?" And again, when Silverstein asked Berry to remember the exact time Johnnie Johnson drove up to the driveway of the house on Windermere, Berry could only guess that it "had to be between ... " to which Silverstein replied, "No. Now don't tell us what it had to be. You either remember or you don't."

Worse, perhaps, were Berry's attempts to embellish his version of his encounter with Janice. In describing the stay at the Sands Hotel, for example, in responding to Silverstein's question about whether Janice had made any advances to him, Berry chose not to answer with a definitive "yes" or "no." Instead, he went on at length to explain that there was "none, other than if—I mean, I don't know whether this is an advance or not, but she could not sit up in bed with her slip on. I know now that this might have been the start. . . ." Small wonder that Frederick Mayer immediately objected; even less wonder that Judge Moore upheld the objection.

By the time Judge Moore called a recess a little after 4:00 on that gray Missouri afternoon, Berry's position in the eyes of the jury must have been precarious. His testimony would have seemed too facile and evasive to be believable. Perhaps, as Merle Silverstein and Frederick Mayer were both to argue many years later, if Berry had come out from behind his mask and shown the jury a more contrite, personal face, they might have found his testimony more credible. Merle Silverstein has speculated that Berry might have faired better had he said to them, " 'Yes, you know, we had a romantic attachment to each other. I slept with her. There was no force, there was nothing like that, no intimidation, it was voluntary on both sides. And that's the way it was. Not proud of it, but that was it.' " Perhaps then, Silverstein has argued, "He would have had a better chance." Frederick Mayer concurred. "I think if he had taken that position," he maintained, "he'd have had a better shot at being acquitted." Quite simply, in presenting to the jury his public face, Mayer believed that "Berry did not make the greatest witness in either trial. I think he was evasive."

The trial did not resume until 2:00 on Thursday afternoon. Ironically, that morning, the newspapers contained a small piece on Elvis Presley's discharge from the U.S. Army that previous afternoon, while Berry was on the stand. With his future still in the balance while his old rival was free to resume his musical career, Berry continued his testimony. He had spoken for less than a minute when Judge Moore cautioned him again to relate what Janice said or did, "not what she seemed to do." But for a while, at least, Moore remained silent as Berry recalled the two weeks Janice lived and worked in St. Louis. On this day, Berry's testimony was far more direct, delivered in short, crisp responses to Merle Silverstein's carefully chosen questions. Only at the end of Berry's testimony did anything approaching the problems of the previous day surface; Mayer objected, and then withdrew his objection, to Silverstein's question to Berry about his feelings for the girl. But it was a question that once again evoked the litany of reasons he had provided earlier for befriending her.

It was at this point that Mayer began his cross-examination, which immediately yielded one of the odder moments in the proceedings. It occurred when Mayer accused Berry of telling the mysterious Venchi he would like to "meet some girls," effectively accusing Berry of soliciting prostitutes. As Silverstein objected, Mayer apparently walked over to the bench and handed Judge Moore a piece of paper, which Silverstein argued must have looked to the jury like some sort of evidence that the conversation took place. What Mayer handed to the judge is unknown, as were his motives for the act.

Silverstein, clearly agitated, immediately requested that Judge Moore declare a mistrial, that was, not surprisingly, denied.

But it was Berry, and not Mayer, who seemed to create the most problems for his defense, as once again he hid behind his mask. Grilling Berry about the stay at the Sands Hotel in Tucson, Mayer asked whether the two occupied the same room; without hesitation, Berry replied, "No sir." Immediately, the jury must have thought that Berry was going to deny what he had already admitted under direct examination. Mayer pressed on, seizing his advantage and asking again if they had occupied the same room. But Berry's answer was even more evasive, as he retorted, "Sir, I understand occupied to mean within. We were not within the hotel room during the thirty hours."

This could not have sat well with the white jury members and the bigoted Judge Moore. To see a black man haranguing a prosecuting attorney and haggling over minute issues of language must have seemed, at best irritating, and at worst provocative.

But if Berry was digging his own grave, the interchange that immediately followed only made it deeper. Again, his detailed response to a question that could have been answered with a simple "no" led him into hot water. Mayer asked whether Janice had made any advances toward him; Berry replied, "She made this advancement, sir, if you call it an advancement, of sitting up in her slip. I didn't think this was unusual for her to do this, being what she said she was, because in show business the girls run across the hall sometimes in what would be ridiculous to the ordinary person."

"Then that didn't bother you, did it?" asked the wily prosecuting attorney, sensing Berry was about to miscalculate his audience.

"I am used to seeing these sorts of things," came the singer's reply, "even in hotel rooms."

"With other women?" asked Mayer, seeing that the witness had taken the bait.

"You were talking about women, sir," replied Berry, "talking about show girls." But it was too late. From the overly detailed initial answer, to the revelation that he was used to seeing seminaked show girls in hotel rooms, to his final attempt to turn the prosecuting attorney's statement around, this interchange must have appeared provocative to both judge and jury, especially while the civil rights movement and a payola scandal were playing out to a national audience.

Berry's inconsistent testimony must have been glaring to the observers in the courtroom. As the cross-examination continued, perhaps the greatest of those inconsistencies became apparent to the jury. Mayer asked Berry to recount Janice's first experience as Berry's employee, selling photographs of Berry while the band was on stage. It was, as Berry's own testimony would have it, a job she performed so badly that she was asked not to do it for the last two dates of the tour. Having established that Berry only hired people he could trust with handling the money to sell the pictures at his shows, the canny Mayer then asked if Berry felt he could trust Escalanti. Berry's response was ambiguous: "It didn't matter too much whether I could trust her," he replied to the Assistant District Attorney. "There were other reasons I wanted her."

"In other words," asked Mayer "this was an exception to your general. . . ."

Before he could finish his statement, Berry emphatically replied, "Absolutely."

Berry's answers could only point to two possible conclusions: either his hiring of Janice was ill-conceived, or his answer, that "there were other reasons I wanted her," had the sinister connotation that Mayer had been fishing for. Without doubt, Berry's vacillating on the issue of trust was disconcerting.

But such inconsistencies were not Mayer's main concern; the main thrust of his argument came on the last afternoon of testimony during Berry's cross-examination and again at the very end of the trial, when he returned to question Chuck Berry over the stay in the Drexel Hotel. It was the issue of the hotel registration cards that proved to be Mayer's biggest triumph and the pivotal moment of the trial, for, although not catching Berry in an out-and-out lie, the inconsistencies in his story, coupled with Mayer's evidence, must have given the jury pause for thought.

Mayer first went over territory that Silverstein had already covered, asking why Berry used pseudonyms when he registered in hotels. Berry answered that he did not want to be disturbed by fans in towns where he was popular. At this, Mayer seized on the registration card for the Sands Hotel. He first had Berry establish that he had played Tucson several times before and that "to some people" he was a favorite there. Then Mayer asked Berry to confirm that, in his own handwriting, he had registered at the Sands in his own name. Without pausing, he moved on to the registration at the Drexel, where Berry explained that his registration as "Mr. and Mrs. Janet Johnson" was due to his large popularity in Denver. Then, with as much theatricality as he could muster, the flamboyant Mayer produced a new exhibit: Slowly, painfully, he had Berry spell out the facts to the jury.

"Mr. Berry, I am going to show you now what is marked as Government's Exhibit No. 7," Mayer began. Then he asked with just a hint of sarcasm, "Can you tell me what that is, sir?"

Berry replied that it was a registration card from the Brown Palace in Denver, Colorado.

"Is there a date on that card, sir?" Mayer continued.

Berry established that it was October 23, 1959. Then, asked Mayer, "Is that your handwriting, sir?" to which Berry facetiously replied, "No. This is print."

Undaunted, Mayer moved on, "I mean the name on the card?" To which Berry finally had to admit that he had registered as "Chuck Berry."

Berry's retort to Mayer's question about the handwriting cannot have endeared him to the jury, although he went on to provide another legitimate reason for doing what he did. Berry stated, "In a big hotel [like the Brown Palace] you can stop the phone calls. In a small hotel you can't . . . half the time [at] this Drexel Hotel the manager is not even at the desk." There is no doubt that most entertainers are worried about these kind of security and privacy issues on the road, but even so Berry's account of the pattern of registering was again so inconsistent as to raise even more questions in the jury's minds.

Mayer's examination over the Brown Palace registration card must have had them wondering even more, as he had Berry read off the card the names "Mr. and Mrs. Chuck Berry." Although Berry denied that he had written that, and that he was in fact on his own during that previous stay in Denver, Mayer kept hammering home the issue, having Berry again read off the card the room rate, which indicated that there were two in the room. At this point, Merle Silverstein jumped into the fray, although Judge Moore overruled his objection that the line of questioning was improper. The damage was already done, of course; Mayer had set the goundwork for the trial's denouement.

Silverstein then called to the stand his next two witnesses, Francine Gillium and Berry's wife Themetta, to establish that they saw nothing improper in the relationship. For Gillium, the affair was simply that of an employer dealing with a bad employee. Escalanti "didn't seem to pay attention very well" and, on at least one occasion she became insolent when told to do her duties; when Escalanti was asked to remain in the vicinity of the checkroom, Gillium overheard her say, "What am I supposed to do, just stay in there all night?" As far as any kind of personal relationship, Gillium neither saw anything improper nor heard Escalanti or Berry discuss anything about any relationship they might have had. In fact, she testified that at no time, at least during the first five days of Janice's stay, was Janice out of Francine's sight for longer than a half-hour. It was testimony that was hardly surprising, given Gillium's position in Berry's life.

Mayer's cross-examination zeroed in on the tour in October 1959, when Berry previously had played in Denver. His questioning revealed that it was Gillium who had accompanied Berry, although she denied staying with him at the Brown Palace. Immediately, as he had done when Oliver Brown was being questioned, Silverstein objected that the line of inquiry by the federal prosecutor was irrelevant to the case at hand; once again, he was overruled by Judge Moore.

Themetta Berry's time on the stand, although brief, was potentially more dramatic. Her testimony, lasting less than a minute, revealed that she knew her husband "met a Spanish-speaking Indian girl that he was bringing back to the club," suggesting that she, at least, felt there was nothing improper about her husband's actions. Given that half of the jury were women, five of whom were married, this must have had some resonance, although one can only assume that the events that followed must have outweighed their feelings for Berry's wife.

The final witness for the defense was Roland Norton, the St. Louis Police Department officer who, along with his partner Jim Buford, had arrested Berry on December 22. Norton testified that, at the time of Berry's arrest, Escalanti "had been angry with him for trying to send her home," which supported Silverstein's contention that the whole affair was the result of Escalanti's anger and did not reflect any wrong-doing on Berry's part. On this note, waiving his right to examine Jim Buford, Silverstein rested the case for the defense.

But the afternoon's events were far from over: In a moment of pure drama, Frederick Mayer reintroduced Oliver Brown, the Drexel Hotel night clerk, and asked him once more about Berry's October 1959 visit to Denver. Although Chuck Berry had stayed at the Brown Palace that October, Berry, along with Francine Gillium, apparently had visited the night clerk at the Drexel Hotel during that trip.

The renewed questions relating to this first visit to Denver inspired multiple objections from Silverstein. The first objection came as soon as Mayer asked Brown, "Had you seen the defendant on any prior occasion?" As he had done during Brown's previous examination, Silverstein argued that the line of questioning "is most prejudicial to the defendant, is completely irrelevant, [and] does not tend to prove or disprove any issue in the case." But Mayer argued that he wanted to demonstrate that Francine Gillium's testimony had been biased in the case, and that he wanted to test Gillium's credibility. After all, he reasoned, at the time of the October visit to the Drexel, Berry had introduced Gillium as his wife. Judge Moore, as he has done so often in the case, was persuaded by Mayer's reasoning, despite Silverstein's declaration that his "objection will run the entire line of this testimony."

With deliberate calculation, Mayer rose from his desk and walked across the courtroom toward Oliver Brown. He had finally caught Berry in a lie, and Judge Moore had cleared the way for him to expose it. It was high courtroom drama, and with an actor's timing he slowly revealed the truth to the jury.

"And was Mr. Berry staying at the Drexel Hotel in October?" he asked Oliver Brown.

"No sir," replied the clerk.

"Do you know of your own knowledge whether the woman that was with him was staying at the Drexel Hotel?" asked Mayer, turning the screw.

"No sir, she was not," came the response.

"Now," continued Mayer, "do you see that woman that was with him at the Drexel Hotel in the courtroom today, Mr. Brown?"

"Yes sir," said Brown, "I do."

And, turning to the jury, Mayer asked, "Will you point her out please?"

Pointing to Francine Gillium, Brown stated simply, "She is the lady in the third row, the blonde-headed lady."

At this, Mayer pounced. "Did you," he said directly to Oliver Brown, "hear Mr. Berry refer to that woman in your presence at all at the Drexel Hotel?"

"Yes," Brown quickly replied, "he said, 'My wife and I are staying at the Brown Palace.'"

"Did he refer to this woman, Francine Gillium," Mayer asked, "as his wife in your presence?"

At this, Merle Silverstein jumped up from his desk, and objected to Mayer's leading of the witness; Judge Moore, in an unusual move, sustained Silverstein's objection, although he encouraged Mayer to rephrase the question, clearly understanding Mayer's tactics and tacitly wishing him to succeed.

"Is there any doubt in your mind," Mayer continued relentlessly, "that the woman you saw at the Drexel Hotel is the woman you pointed to in the courtroom?"

"None," came Oliver Brown's reply.

Up jumped Merle Silverstein once again. "Wait a minute!" Berry's attorney cried. "I object to the form of the question, Your Honor. It is certainly leading and suggestive and repetitious."

Once again, Judge Moore took the unusual stance of siding with the defense, and the objection was sustained.

Now allowed to question the witness himself, Silverstein simply asked, "The words that you can remember him saying are, 'My wife and I are staying at the Brown Hotel'?"

"That is correct," replied the clerk.

Although Silverstein did not make the connection, he was implying that Berry simply made a statement that his wife and he were staying at the Brown Palace, and that did not necessarily mean he was referring to Gillium as his wife. With that, perhaps sensing that his old classmate from Washington University had won both the battle and the war, Merle Silverstein ended his questioning.

But Mayer was not finished. Was the woman who was with Berry introduced by the defendant as his wife, he asked Oliver Brown.

"I used the statement referred to as my wife and I are staying at the Brown Palace Hotel," was the witness's response.

"And where was this woman standing when he made that statement?" asked Mayer.

"Right alongside of him," replied Oliver Brown.

At this, Merle Silverstein launched into his most spirited challenge of the whole trial, figuring he had nothing left to lose. He demanded of Judge Moore that "this witness's entire rebuttal testimony be stricken, the jury instructed to disregard it, and a mistrial declared," on the grounds that "the witness did not testify that she was referred to as his wife, introduced as his wife. The only thing he said, 'My wife and I are staying at the Brown Palace Hotel.' The entire line of testimony is irrelevant, immaterial, highly prejudicial." Judge Moore was persuaded at least on two of the points; the testimony was stricken and the jury instructed to disregard it. But, after a short recess, Judge Moore overruled the mistrial motion and ended the proceedings for the day. Once again, the closing moments of the day's proceedings had ended with fireworks, none of which provided any positive illumination for the defendant.

At two o'clock precisely on Friday afternoon, March 4, 1960, Frederick Mayer stood before the courtroom and delivered his closing comments. Stressing Janice's age and the fact that her unwavering testimony was corroborated at every turn, Mayer painted the picture of a cold, unfeeling Berry for the attentive jury members.

"When he got to St. Louis," Mayer recalled for the court, "he didn't want any part of her any more, he was tired of her. She had served his purpose. Yet what does he do? He transports her to a bus station, gives her a ticket, and he says, 'So long, Janice'." And, he reminded them, this was "a girl who he states he was afraid to leave in a hotel room at Denver, Colorado, but he was not afraid to leave her in a bus station down in St. Louis. This," he let them know in no uncertain terms, "was a beautiful way of kissing the girl off."

He reminded the jury about the two different ways Berry had registered in Denver hotels, and of the inconsistency over Janice's poor work ethic on the road and Berry's insistence on hiring her for work at his Club Bandstand. And, lest they miss the point, he reminded them, "Here is a famous performer, a TV and record idol, a rock and roll singer of national fame whose concerts and entertainment is pointed for one group of people, teenage children."

It was almost certainly a deliberate ploy to sway the jury; Mayer was to confess some 40 years later, "I can't remember the make-up of the jury exactly," but, "if it was an older group on the jury, I probably did." Considering all of the negative publicity about rock and roll being generated by the payola trials, Mayer's comments as much as any made that day would have registered deeply with the twelve men and women sitting before him. They also had a more sinister connotation, as he suggested that Berry, as a performer with a predominantly teenage audience, could well have done this thing before and could, if not convicted, do it again.

After a brief statement by Merle Silverstein, some final, closing comments by the federal prosecutor, and a lengthy set of instructions to the jury from Judge Moore, the jury retired. For 2 hours and 20 minutes, they deliberated the case, returning to the courtroom at a little after 6:00 that evening. What followed must have made Chuck Berry's heart sink. Although the foreman announced that the jury had yet to reach a verdict, both judge and jury expressed their desire to be done with the proceedings as soon as they possibly could. First, Moore reminded them of the bad weather St. Louis had been experiencing that week. "This is a terribly bad evening," he told them, "It is terribly bad weather. I dislike very much to have to lock this jury up and keep you all night. I don't want to have to stay down here myself."

Then, an unknown jury member revealed that he would not be available to stay the following morning because of a business appointment at ten o'clock. No one in the courtroom, it seemed, wanted to put Chuck Berry's future above their own interests. At this point, according to Merle Silverstein, everyone on the jury "glared at one specific guy." After Judge Moore cautioned them that they might have to stay overnight, the foreman, Silverstein remembers, said "just give us another half an hour or two. I think we could reach a verdict." Moore granted them the extra time, and they retired again.

It took a mere 15 minutes for them to take their seats once more in the courtroom. Although the *Argus* the following week described the rest of the courtroom as being "stunned at the rushed verdict," and Themetta Berry's breaking into tears as the jury foreman pronounced the results of their findings, the verdict must have surprised no one. Chuck Berry had been found guilty of violating the Mann Act, and was led away to the St. Louis municipal jail to await his sentence.

St. Louis Blues

I got the St. Louis blues just as blue as I can be
He's got a heart like a rock cast in the sea,
Or else he wouldn't have gone so far from me
—W. C. Handy, "St. Louis Blues"

Exactly one week later, Chuck Berry found himself back in the St. Louis courthouse to be sentenced for violating the Mann Act. Once again, the black rock-and-roll singer found himself staring into the cold eyes of an 82-year-old white judge from rural Missouri who was in no mood for niceties. After a minute or two of preliminaries, Judge Moore, careful not to make the kind of overtly racist statements he had made a week earlier, tore into the defendant.

"It is a shameful story that was unfolded," he began, as he related Janice's circumstances to the assembled crowd. Then, turning to Berry, Moore fixed him in the eye and said, "But you are not a very wholesome citizen, and there is nothing about your situation to arouse much sympathy." He accused Berry several times of lying before the jury, contrasting Janice Escalanti's honesty with his evasiveness: "Her story," Moore declared at one point, "to me indicated her to be frank and candid, and I was impressed by her candor. I was equally impressed by your deliberate and willful—according to my impression—perjured statements."

But there was more. "You came into this courtroom," Moore continued, "with a flimsy story, and I can't believe that anybody that sat in this courtroom and heard your testimony believed you when you talked about trying to reform her. You took her on this trip," he went on, "for the purpose of trying to reform her and get her out of a career in prostitution, and then used her for your own vile purposes."

It was here that Moore arrived at the heart of his feelings for the defendant, as he recounted Berry's achievements to the court. Clearly, he was incensed at the thought of a successful black businessman appearing before him, and with his racism bubbling just below the surface, he went on:

> According to your own testimony, you have been very successful. I have forgotten how many hundreds of records you sold. You testified from the stand that at least four records maybe had sold each over a million copies, and you made for several years a very large income from the sale of records. You must be a man of some ability and some intelligence; and you have three daughters yourself, and you were taking this young 14-year-old girl, pretending that you were. . . .

At this mention of his family, Chuck Berry finally broke down. Moore had penetrated Berry's mask and produced the musician's first and only genuine show of emotion during the entire trial. To those around him, those who knew the private man, this was a moment of very real pain and anguish. "He was very upset," recalls Merle Silverstein. "He always thought he was innocent. . . . I don't think he could believe this was happening to him. I guess he was just upset because it was obvious he was going to go to prison."

Judge Moore, of course, felt that this was more of Berry's dissembling. "Stand up," he boomed, "Don't go through any of that maudlin exhibition in my presence. I am not impressed by it. I have seen your kind before." And, without pausing, Moore continued his tirade. Referring to Berry's first prison term in 1944, Moore commented that he regretted not being able to give Berry a sentence that was as long as or longer than the ten-year sentence he was given then, and that the maximum five-year sentence was not enough. "There is no sentence," he intoned gravely, "that I could impose upon you, a man of your years, a man of your intelligence, a man who has met with your financial success, trying to help further degrade and lead this young girl into a life of debauchery." Then, after giving Berry the maximum punishment allowable, a five-year prison sentence and a $5,000 fine, Moore concluded with one final shot. "There will be no bail set by this Court," he declared:

> If the Court of Appeals thinks this man should be admitted to bail they may do it, and they may have it on their consciences. I would not turn this man loose to go out and prey on a lot of ignorant Indian girls and colored girls, and white girls, if any. I would not have that on my soul. That man would be out committing offenses while his case is on appeal, if this court is any judge. I have sat here for a quarter of a century. I have never sentenced a more vicious character than that kind, I don't believe. He will not be admitted to any bail by this court, unless it is under the order, coming down from the Court of Appeals or the Supreme Court of the United States; and society is well off with him incarcerated.

The racial slur, making reference to the stereotype of the black male as sexual predator, was all too clear; in Merle Silverstein's mind, the comments were, quite simply, "atrocious." They revealed the depth of hatred Moore had for Berry, a position so intractable that even the threat of the Supreme Court overturning his ruling on Berry's bail could not change it. But, given the context of the trial as a whole, Moore's comments provided an apt conclusion to the case of the *United States v. Charles Edward Anderson Berry.*

Neither Chuck Berry nor Merle Silverstein had much time to lick their wounds, however. Not only did the verdict have to be appealed, but preparations had to be made for the ensuing trial on the other Mann Act indictments and the gun charges. On the Monday morning following the sentencing, Silverstein confidently submitted the appeal; it was a document he had begun working on from the first day of the trial. "The case was so infiltrated with prejudice at points," he felt, "that I said, 'If I don't get this case reheard, I'm going to jump out of the window.'" No matter what the long-term success of the appeal, however, Merle Silverstein was able to score one victory that day. By filing the appeal, he was able to overturn Judge Moore's vindictive ruling that Chuck Berry should not be granted bail. For however long it would take for the appeals court to hear and rule on Silverstein's argument, Chuck Berry would be a free man.

Now Silverstein's attentions turned to the other charges, stemming from the incident in St. Charles in 1958. On the last day of the first trial, March 4, Silverstein had received notice that the second trial date had been set for April 4, giving him exactly one month to prepare his case. Clearly, the first order of business was to try and postpone the trial and buy some time; so, on March 26, Merle Silverstein petitioned Judge Randolph Weber for a continuance. Two days later, Weber granted the request and set the trial date for May 31. Silverstein now had the breathing room he needed, and he began preparing for the next trial.

At the end of March, in what must have been a difficult and uncertain time, Berry traveled to Chicago for the first of two lengthy sessions for Chess Records. Realizing there was a real possibility that they could lose their franchise for a very long time, Leonard and Phil Chess booked sessions for March 29 and again two weeks later in an attempt to stockpile as much new material as they could. The sessions, given Berry's frame of mind and the pressure of writing on demand, produced twenty songs of, not surprisingly, varying quality.

A single, "Bye, Bye, Johnny" coupled with the aptly titled "Worried Life Blues," was the first to see the light of day; released in April, the A-side proved to be the best of the entire bunch. Lyrically, it was a sequel to "Johnny B. Goode," in which Johnny's mother puts "her little boy aboard a Greyhound Bus" so that he can "make some motion pictures out in Hollywood." What makes the song memorable, however, is the tension created between Berry's guitar, playing the by-now-familiar chopping rhythm, and the drums, credited variously to Ebby Hardy or Jasper Thomas, playing a slow chugging shuffle in imitation of the trains traveling past Johnny as he played his guitar. The two seem at odds with each other throughout the song, creating a kind of push-and-pull rhythm that seems to fight hard to restrain itself. Whether intentional or not, it was a perfect musical illustration of Berry's life at the time.

Meanwhile, as the second trial neared, Janice Escalanti, almost unnoticed, left St. Louis. By order of Judge Moore, on May 8 she was escorted by a U.S. Marshal to Albuquerque, New Mexico, where, 10 days later, she took up residence in the Children's Welfare Home, left to piece together a new life and never dreaming that she would see Chuck Berry again.

On Tuesday, May 31, 1960, the second Mann Act trial finally began. The first morning was taken up with jury selection; initially, perhaps aware of the proceedings three months earlier, Judge Weber believed it might be a protracted trial and ordered that an alternate juror be sworn in, in case anything happened. But this was to be a much different affair. That afternoon, Frederick Mayer began making his case by first bringing in Joan Mathis Bates (who, by now, had taken the married name of Rolf). She was described in a small piece in the *St. Louis Post-Dispatch* following the trial as being 18 years old—making her 16 and, like Janice Escalanti before her, underaged, when the events happened. But almost immediately, unlike Janice Escalanti, Mathis proved to be hostile to Mayer's questions. "On the stand," recalled Merle Silverstein, she "said she was not forced, she was in love with Chuck. Yes, she had intercourse with him, and she would voluntarily have sex with him."

Berry, too, recalls having her cooperate in his defense. "Joan answered slowly and deliberately," he recalled in *The Autobiography* "and, as questioning progressed, the prosecutor began to fall behind in his attempt to prove me guilty of intent. The last point-blank question by the district attorney was, 'Well, are you in love with him?' The answer Joan gave was, 'Well . . . yes I am.' And at that instant the prosecuting attorney tossed his yellow tablet on the lawyer's table and retired his argument."

One can, perhaps, forgive Berry's dramatic license here; it is unlikely that a prosecutor as tenacious as Frederick Mayer would have given up so easily. In fact, Mayer did not give up at all, and continued on with his case. After Mathis had left the stand, he called Ward Straker, manager of the Pick-Fort Meigs Hotel in Toledo, Ohio; Bonnie Hopkins Anton of the Rome Hotel in Nebraska; and James Williams, Berry's childhood friend, who had accompanied the pair on the trip to Nebraska. History, sadly, does not record their testimony, as the trial transcript was later destroyed.

At 10:00 exactly the following morning the trial resumed, and Merle Silverstein began his defense. The only witness he called was the defendant; the only record of his testimony comes from the same *Post-Dispatch* article that mentioned Joan Mathis's age. In it, Berry is described as having "denied an intent to violate the law, testifying he and the young woman were in love." We can only speculate that he had learned his lesson from the first trial and had decided to present a more honest and personal face to the judge and jury. Noticeable by their absences in this trial, either for the prosecution or for the defense, were Officer Andrew Pallardy and Trooper Paul Neumann, who could perhaps have addressed the second count of the indictment.

At the conclusion of closing arguments, the jury retired to consider the verdict on the two counts. Unlike the jury members in the first trial, who seemed pressured to end their deliberations because of the impending weekend, this jury seemed unconcerned about time restraints and began a fairly lengthy period of deliberation. From 4 P.M. until 7, and again from 8:30 to 10:30, the jury pondered Berry's fate.

Unfortunately, we have no record of how the jury arrived at its decision, although it is possible to speculate that the deliberations, as those of Mann Act juries before and since must have done, centered around the ambiguous terms "intent" and "immorality." At various points during the hours the jurists were sequestered, they pondered, or were asked to ponder, the meaning of the phrase "knowingly persuade, induce and entice" and the question of intent the phrase implies, and the equally important phrase "debauchery and other immoral practices."

In several notes to the jury, Weber explained the legal definitions of the phrases. "Intent," he wrote in one, with handwritten amendments in italics

> is a state of mind, and it is not possible to look into a man's mind to see what went on, the only way you have of arriving at the intent in this case is to take into consideration all of the facts and circumstances shown by the evidence, *the acts of the parties involved, their statements at the time, their conduct, in other words, all the acts and circumstances attending and surrounding the occasion in question, and, from all the evidence it is your duty to determine* what the intent of the defendant *was* at the time, *and times,* in question.

In another handwritten note, Judge Weber defined "debauchery and other immoral practices." Like American courts before and since, he found the definition slippery at best; to him, the terms meant "acts of sexual intercourse . . . which tended ultimately to lead to that form of debauchery or immoral conduct which consisted in sexual actions." "The frequency, or other occurrences thereof" he continued, " do not keep the act from being immoral, if they are actually immoral or debauched. The marital status of one, or both, of the participants may be considered in determining if the act was immoral or debasing, if all the other elements thereof are present." But, he concluded, "whether the act or acts constitute a crime against the government . . . depends upon the transportation, inducement, intent and purpose as previously instructed."

Working through the circular, legalistic prose, two things become clear: in Judge Weber's opinion, it was only when the immoral acts were taken together with the intent of the defendant and the fact of transportation that they constituted a violation of the Mann Act. From these directives, then, the jury's decision seems to have been made. That Berry and Joan Mathis had been lovers seemed not to be in dispute; neither was the fact that the two had traveled across state lines together. It seems likely, then, that the jury decided on the evidence presented to them that there had been a relationship between Berry and Mathis, and that the purpose of their trip was not immoral, despite Berry's marital status—lending credence to Berry's account in *The Autobiography* that Mathis's declaration of love might have been the key to the jury's decision. Whatever the case, at 10:30 P.M. on June 1, 1960, Chuck Berry was found not guilty of both charges.

As the summer of 1960 wore on, Chuck Berry had further cause to be cautiously optimistic. On August 16, a letter from Judge Weber arrived at Merle Silverstein's office; in it was the half-expected decision to acquit Berry on the gun charges. Silverstein's hunch that previous winter had been proved correct, and all that was left was to await the appeal on the first Mann Act trial. Also that month, the next single from the marathon sessions at Chess was released. Although "Got to Find My Baby," like "Bye, Bye, Johnny" before it, failed to chart—leaving Berry with his longest string of chart failures since his recording career had begun—his music was still being made available to rock fans all over the country. And the following month, Berry began a Thursday night residency at the Moonlight Bar, just a few blocks south of his childhood home on Goode Avenue. His choice to play a small corner bar could hardly have been motivated by money. Instead, Berry's decision would have been based more on his love for playing to a live audience, or to sharpen his guitar playing or stage act with the hope he would soon be in demand again as a performer. Whatever the case, it must have felt as if he was starting his career all over again, but at least he was still free.

Then, just 12 days after his 34th birthday, the optimism turned to a guarded joy, as the Eighth Circuit Court of Appeals released its verdict. So stunning was their decision that both the *St. Louis Post-Dispatch*, on the same day as the verdict, and the *St. Louis Argus*, a week later (due to its Friday publication schedule), ran the story on their respective front pages.

Merle Silverstein's appeal had attacked Judge Moore's decision on two grounds: that to make Berry's transportation of Escalanti a criminal offense, the judge "erred in certain rulings on evidence and in his instructions to the jury"; and "the hostile and prejudicial conduct and remarks of the trial court" had prevented Berry from receiving a fair trial. Citing Moore's comments at various points in the trial, Silverstein had written that the events in the St. Louis courthouse that March had been "conducted in an atmosphere of complete hostility created primarily by prejudicial interjections by the trial court." Judge Moore, he went on, had repeatedly made comments "to emphasize the racial aspects of the case" and had disparaged Berry "because he was a Negro associating with a woman outside his race."

The first part of the appeal was rejected by the upper court. "There was ample circumstantial evidence of his intent," Judges Sanborn, Woodrough, and Matthes wrote, "to make the issue of his guilt one for the jury." As for Judge Moore's rulings on evidence, denying Silverstein from seeing Escalanti's statements to the FBI and her grand jury testimony, the panel doubted "that any of them affected the defendant's substantial rights."

However, "what has given us concern," the judges went on to say, is "the attitude, conduct and remarks of the trial judge." The judges, defending their own, tried to minimize the impact of Moore's comments; "many of them," they argued, "would probably not rise to the dignity of reversible error." And they went to great lengths to provide excuses for Moore's conduct: "Much occurred to try his patience," they pointed out. "The record shows that he had difficulty hearing witnesses; that he was apparently in physical discomfort much of the time; that the trial dragged," and that Berry's treatment of Escalanti was "inexcusable" and his testimony "had its irritating aspects."

Nevertheless, the three-judge panel agreed that "a trial judge who, in the presence of the jury, makes remarks reflecting upon a defendant's race or from which an implication can be drawn that racial considerations may have some bearing on the issue of guilt or innocence has rendered the trial unfair."

"Reluctantly," they decided "that the trial accorded Berry was unfair because of the attitude of the trial judge toward him, as evidenced by the remarks made by the course of the trial."

But because of the ample evidence against him, "Berry was not entitled to a direct verdict of aquittal," they decided; instead, they vacated the judgment and remanded the case "to the District court for a new trial."

By the end of 1960, Chuck Berry's life was in limbo. He had been acquitted on three felony charges but had a fourth charge sent back to court. Musically, he was still in the public eye; his last single—"Jaguar and Thunderbird," released in October—had achieved modest success, just failing to enter the *Billboard Hot 100*. But it was a song that showed his career had stalled. Not only had he not recorded since the sessions earlier in the year, but musically the song demonstrated little growth. From the insistent 2/4 rhythm to the fast-paced, eight-syllable lines and melody of the verses to the story line of a race between two cars, the song bore a superficial resemblance to "Maybellene." It was only Berry's inventiveness in the song's catchy chorus ("Slow down, little Jaguar/Keep cool, little Thunderbird Ford") and the story of the racing "sky blue 'bird" and Jaguar that made the song memorable. Once again, Berry's genius for lyric detail shone through. The story takes place outside of the mythic village of Dudenville, Indiana (actually, a village in Missouri), with a population of "102 and nine acres of ground," and it features a sheriff who "laid low half hid in the weeds/And parked for eight days" waiting to catch the speeding cars before they made the county line. With some sterling right-hand triplets from Johnnie Johnson on piano filling out the background, the song, like "Bye, Bye, Johnny" before it, was certainly a worthy effort, especially given those trying times.

But if Berry was stuck legally and musically, one area of his life was moving forward, sometimes which would provide him with the peace and stability that he found so elusive in his public life and in the city of St. Louis. With no shows or recordings that summer, and with plenty of time on his hands, Berry had labored all summer to finish building on the property in Wentzville. By the end of the year, the project had advanced far enough that Francine Gillium could leave the house on Whittier and the offices on Easton and transfer them all to new offices in Berry Park, nestled among the farms and rolling green countryside of Buckner Road. In good times and in bad, this was to become Berry's refuge, the only place in his life where he was free to live the way that he saw fit, to be the private Charles and not the public Chuck Berry.

The third and final Mann Act trial began on March 13, 1961, before Judge Roy Harper. Born in the Missouri bootheel town of Gibson in 1905 and raised on a small cotton farm in nearby Steele, Harper had gained a reputation in his 13 years on the bench as a no-nonsense judge. In Merle Silverstein's estimation, Harper was "tough"; he was also a participant rather than a silent observer in a case. "He stuck his nose in in order to get the truth out," recalled Berry's lawyer. "He'd interrupt the case and point out something. He would ask the witness, 'Do you mean to say that you were 80 feet away and you could see the color of his eyes? You expect the jury to believe that?'"

In fact, Silverstein had every reason to be optimistic about the trial's outcome as it began that Monday. Although Harper had a reputation for not letting past friendships enter into his courtroom, Silverstein's stint as Harper's clerk 10 years earlier was certainly a propitious sign. And then there was the fact that Silverstein knew exactly how Janice Escalanti and Frederick Mayer would conduct themselves in the courtroom—no small matter considering these were still the days before full disclosure.

The morning was spent swearing in the jury; once again, they were all white, although this time they were mostly middle-class professionals. And, as in the second trial that previous May, they all were male. After Frederick Mayer had laid out the case and after a lunch recess, Janice Escalanti took the stand. Getting Escalanti back to testify was no small task for Frederick Mayer's office. "We had one heck of a time finding Janice," Mayer recalled. And, after they had located her, she proved none too cooperative. "Once we found her and brought her back," he remembered.

> I had to put her somewhere. And she wasn't real happy about coming back, but if I lost control of the witness or couldn't find her, the case was out the window. So I got one of the Catholic convents here in St. Louis to put her up, and they would keep her until the time of the trial. And I remember the Mother Superior called me and said, "You better get this case over with in a hurry" because she seemed to be driving them crazy over at the convent!

But despite her difficult nature outside of the courtroom, inside the court Escalanti made as compelling a witness as she had during the previous trial. Her testimony under direct examination was once again straightforward and detailed; in only one or two minor details did it waver from the testimony she had given before. Twice, Merle Silverstein had objected to points Frederick Mayer raised in his questioning; once, Judge Harper ruled in his favor, and once Silverstein was overruled. In all, Harper had been very quiet on the bench, and the trial up to that point had been free of his remarks, racial or otherwise.

At the end of Escalanti's testimony, Merle Silverstein again demanded to see the statements she had made to the FBI and to the Grand Jury, in order to show discrepancies in her story. Unlike Judge Moore, who had ruled that Silverstein had no right the see them, Harper ruled that he could at least see the FBI testimony. It was an encouraging sign for Silverstein as he began his cross-examination of the witness; although Harper had not ruled in his favor every time so far, he had at least not been as dismissive as Judge Moore.

Armed with the FBI statements and with the knowledge that "the second time I knew what she [Escalanti] was going to say," Silverstein began his cross-examination. But, as he had done in the previous trial, Silverstein was mindful of arousing the jury's sympathies for the witness; rather than immediately confronting her, he preferred to have her recount the events of her initial meeting with Berry and details of the financial relationship between the two. Finally, about halfway through the questioning, Silverstein asked her about the alleged incidents of sexual intercourse in the back seat of Berry's Cadillac between Phoenix and Santa Fe. She had, Silverstein pointed out, not mentioned them in her initial statement to the FBI; she also had forgotten to mention the other alleged incidents in the car, between Santa Fe and Denver. In her initial statement to the St. Louis police as well, Silverstein reminded her, she was inconsistent in alleging that Berry had made sexual advances toward her at Francine Gillium's house. And, to punctuate this flurry of questions, he elicited her confession that she also had sex with Jasper Thomas during her time in St. Louis. More, Silverstein had her declare to the jury that she had not been coerced, persuaded, or induced into any of the events in which she had participated.

It was enough to break down the usually implacable Janice. Her testimony about Berry's criticisms of her job performance at Club Bandstand became fuzzy and unclear; she didn't remember when he reprimanded her for not performing her duties, nor could she remember how many times he had done so. "I can't remember no four or five times," she answered Silverstein at one point, "I only remember once." At this point, Silverstein reached over his desk, picked up the hefty, 400-page transcript from the first trial, and began to read from it; it was the litany of transgressions Janice had committed while working at the club, told in her own words.

Finally, Silverstein looked up from the pages and fixed her with his eyes. "You remember those questions and answers being asked you in regard to this incident?" he asked.

"No," she replied.

"Would you say," he went on, "that those answers that I've read to you, to those questions, are not true?"

"I don't remember him getting," Escalanti began, and then, after some thought, she added "now, I don't remember him getting after me more than once."

"Did you give those answers, then, last year?" Silverstein asked.

"I don't remember giving them," came the reply. "If they're there, I guess I did."

Quite why Janice Escalanti's memory was askew is a unclear. Perhaps, at this point, she was fed up with the proceedings and the entire Chuck Berry affair, and felt that her testimony didn't matter much anymore. Or perhaps, as Silverstein had suspected, Berry's criticism of her employment at the club was the real reason for her eventual departure from St. Louis—that it was she, and not Berry, who had made the decision to leave, because she had become disenchanted with the whole business at that point. It was an important fact for the jury to hear, because it reinforced the notion that the trip and its termination were both her idea. Berry had neither forced her to come nor cast her aside after she had served her purpose.

Further, it set up the scenario that Escalanti had framed Berry, and that she had called the police with the intent of having him arrested. She admitted to calling Club Bandstand a number of times after Berry had taken back the bus ticket to El Paso, and that she had spoken with Francine Gillium; now, Silverstein wanted to know, "Didn't you make a statement to her, 'Somebody is going to pay for this'? Didn't you make that statement to Francine Gillum [sic] on the telephone?"

Escalanti flatly denied that she was exacting revenge on Berry, but Silverstein pressed on. Once again, he reached for the transcript of the previous year's trial and read back her words to her, how she had made the veiled threat that if Berry was "going to act dirty then I might as well act dirty too." Now Escalanti became confused about the number of times she had called Berry, but that was not what Silverstein was aiming for. What, he asked her on a number of occasions, did she mean by acting "dirty"?

Finally, after avoiding the question several times, she responded, "I meant like that when he acts like he don't care whether I have the ticket or not, I can always work for my own way."

To this, Merle Silverstein asked, "Is this what you mean by acting dirty, going back to prostitution?"

"In a way," she responded, "yes."

"Didn't you mean," he asked again, "that you were going to do something dirty to him?"

Again, Escalanti flatly denied this was the case.

Silverstein was unwilling to take that for an answer. Reading once again from the transcript, he asked what Janice had meant a year ago when she had said, "Well, if he is going to be stuck up and treat people mean, I might as well be the same way he is." Again, Silverstein asked, what did she mean by "mean"?

Janice Escalanti's response was evasive. "If he thought," she replied, "I was going to reform and all that and waste all my time and come up here and try and reform, and not even . . . " (and here she paused for thought) "not even have me do me any good for coming up here."

"So, in other words," Silverstein summarized for the court, "you thought Mr. Berry was treating you dirty, and you were going to get even with him simply by going back to the life of prostitution that he was trying to reform you from?" Quietly, she agreed.

Now Silverstein sensed he had the advantage. He asked the question that he had asked of Joan Mathis nine months before, the question that Judge Moore had enjoined her from answering: Was she in love with Mr. Berry? Her expected denial was met with Defendant's Exhibit A, the letter she had written to Berry between being fired and calling the police. Now, free of Judge Moore's interference, Silverstein read it to the courtroom, although he only needed the opening line to prove his point: "Dear Chuck," he read aloud, "like I said before, I love you."

But getting Janice Escalanti to admit to writing the letter was the easy part; as Silverstein continued with his questioning, she stubbornly refused to admit to the emotion behind it. She was not in love with Berry, she maintained, and her actions were not inspired by the anger of being jilted. Instead, she insisted, the only anger she felt was over Berry's refusal to hand over the bus ticket, even though she was forced to agree with Silverstein that she was not promised the ticket and did not need it, as one was being sent, at her own request, by her friend Clarence in New Orleans. It was an argumentative point, one that the unusually quiet Frederick Mayer was forced to challenge. Yet even though Judge Harper sustained Mayer's objection, Silverstein's point had been made. Janice had appeared evasive in the jury's eyes, and he now had grounds to show that the relationship between Berry and Escalanti was consensual.

After several more minutes of questioning about the trip from the bus station to Berry's club, Escalanti's testimony was interrupted by a juror who needed to be excused. Judge Harper called a ten-minute recess, during which he decided, for whatever reason, that Escalanti had had enough for one day. At this point, Mayer—perhaps relieved that his main witness had survived the defense attorney's grilling bloodied rather than broken—introduced the exhibits from the Sands Motel in Tucson and called bellhop Ronald Kurn to the stand.

Once again, Kurn described delivering room service. He recalled the order in detail—"two pork chops . . . a milkshake, some coffee, and strawberry shortcake"—and this time he was also far more certain in his identification of Janice Escalanti; she had been the woman he had seen in Room 257, he said with more confidence than he had a year earlier. After a brief cross-examination, Kurn was excused and Judge Harper called a recess to the first day's proceedings—but not before he sounded a note of caution to the jury: "During the night recess, gentlemen of the jury," he warned, "do not discuss the case among yourselves." Most important, however, he insisted that they remember "the admonition that I've given you with respect to the press, radio, and television." As that turned out, it was to be a significant directive, because the following morning, the *St. Louis Globe-Democrat* published a short piece on the trial, tucked away on page 15. It contained mostly information about the preceding trials under the sensational headline, "Berry Lured Her to St. Louis, Girl, 14, Says."

The next morning, Silverstein returned to cross-examining Janice Escalanti. He started out gently, going back over the same territory he had been exploring the previous day, hoping to pick away at the inconsistencies in her story. But the next half-hour proved to be frustrating and, ultimately, inconsequential. Silverstein was unable to establish any important contradictions, and Mayer, in his final questioning of the witness, reestablished the basic facts that Escalanti and Berry had shared a bed in the Tucson hotel, and that it was Berry who had originally approached Escalanti about making the trip.

As he had done a year earlier, Mayer next called saxophone player Leroy Davis. The intervening year had done nothing to change his testimony, except for the revelation that he was the person who had taken Escalanti to the Deluxe Hotel in St. Louis, and it was there that the two of them had had sex together. Silverstein's cross-examination, too, yielded nothing of consequence, and at its conclusion, Judge Harper asked the jury to file out. In conference, Silverstein once again requested to see Escalanti's grand jury testimony; once again, Harper refused. In his statements to Silverstein, Harper summed up the state of the trial at this point. "In my opinion," Harper stated, "I thought she told a pretty straight story.... This woman was on the stand for the equivalent of over half a day, and over and over, and repeated over and over, the same thing. Of course, I'm sure on any witness you're going to find some minor differences.... She told you her memory wasn't as good now as it was a year ago. That's logical, isn't it?" Then, asking the jury to enter back into the courtroom, he asked them if they had seen the *Globe-Democrat* article that morning. None had, and the trial began again.

Johnnie Johnson then took the stand. Suffering from an excruciating toothache, he became confused and could not remember the sequence of shows on the tour. By the time Merle Silverstein began his cross-examination, Johnson seemed a little more lucid and was able to help Berry's attorney corroborate the theories advanced in the first trial: that Berry would have been too tired to have intercourse with Escalanti during the tour, and that there was a possibility both beds had been slept in in the Sands Motel.

In quick succession, George Dixon and Oliver Brown testified about Berry's stay at the Drexel Hotel; then, before the lunch recess, Merle Silverstein laid out the case for the defense. After lunch on that Tuesday afternoon, Silverstein, perhaps with his eye on a possible appeal should the trial not go as planned, immediately requested that a copy of the *Globe-Democrat* article be placed as evidence in the trial's record. With the jury already having admitted that they hadn't seen the piece, and with Judge Harper safe in the knowledge that they were following the admonition he had given them earlier, the act had little bearing on the trial's eventual outcome. But with the morning's proceedings having not gone his way, it was a small piece of insurance Silverstein badly needed at that point.

Now Berry himself took the stand. Initially, at least, he made a much better witness than at the first trial. His answers, short and direct, pieced together a much more believable account of the events than had been presented a year earlier. He painted a much more coherent picture, although one thing still remained from the original trial: Berry insisted that not once, during the time they were together, did he and Janice Escalanti ever have sex. At the close of his direct questioning, as proof of Berry's honorable intentions, Silverstein introduced as evidence the bus ticket from St. Louis to El Paso.

Frederick Mayer's cross-examination was far less dramatic than the one he had performed in the original trial, and free of Judge Moore's constant interference and confrontations with the prosecuting attorney, Berry's performance on the stand was credible, to say the least. Only once, when Mayer asked why Berry did not wait for the El Paso bus with Escalanti at the Greyhound terminal, did Berry come close to creating a problem for himself. He answered Mayer's question by saying he had left because he was "disgusted" with Escalanti. When pressed, though, Berry explained that the two had created a scene at the bus station. "She started an argument about wanting to go to Yuma, Arizona, instead of El Paso," he said in response to Mayer's asking him to clarify why he was disgusted, "after as many times as I told her if things didn't work out I would send her back to El Paso, and she spoke loud in the bus station and after I put the money in the envelope I walked away." Besides, explained Berry, he had to be elsewhere at a business appointment at 3:00 that afternoon.

After another brief appearance by Themetta Berry, Francine Gillium and then Roland Norton took the stand, as they had done in the original trial. Little had changed in their testimonies since that time, but Norton's testimony occasioned a last-minute flurry of objections from Merle Silverstein. As Frederick Mayer was wrapping up his cross-examination of Officer Norton, he asked Norton if Escalanti's statement to him had indicated that Berry "had picked her up in El Paso and had brought her by various routes to St. Louis." Then, he asked Norton if the FBI had been called, again indicating that a federal offense had been committed. These were both attempts by the crafty prosecutor to slip in questions that were tantamount to conclusions for the jury. But, despite Silverstein's objections, Judge Harper decided that they were legitimate questions to ask and be answered. One would imagine, however, that at this point in the trial, they would have had little effect on the outcome.

After Norton's questioning, Judge Harper decided to halt the proceedings for the day; recess was called until 10:00 the following Wednesday morning, when both Silverstein and Mayer were allowed exactly 40 minutes to conclude their cases for the jury. Frederick Mayer did not need that much time. Pointing to Escalanti's age and the corroborating evidence of both interested and disinterested parties to her testimony, he dismissed as insignificant any inconsistencies in Escalanti's testimony.

Merle Silverstein, on the other hand, used his time to deliver a strong summation in his usual understated way. One of his first points provided a fitting conclusion to the entire 16-month ordeal that Berry had been through, which had brought him to the St. Louis courthouse, to that moment. In reminding the jury that the government had the burden of proof, he also reminded them why: that the name of the case they were hearing was "the

United States of America versus Charles Edward Anderson Berry. Those," he mused, "are pretty long odds. The United States of America with its staff of district attorneys," he said, gesturing toward Frederick Mayer, "with its Federal Bureau of Investigation, with its unlimited resources and facilities, is the plaintiff in this case, and one individual, Charles Edward Anderson Berry, is the defendant." Indeed, whether one believed that Berry was guilty or innocent, he had been placed in the mechanism of the American justice system, a system that threw its whole energies behind laws such as the Mann Act that so easily lent themselves to racist and personally invasive interpretations. This second trial lacked a clear villain in the order of Judge Moore. But the judicial process itself, set in motion through the impetus of archaic and flawed legislation, rendered such a villain unnecessary.

This thought led Merle Silverstein to a meditation on the Mann Act. "If you believe," he argued to the jury, "that Charles Berry took this girl from Texas to Missouri for the purpose and with the intent of inducing, compelling and enticing her into committing immoral practices, then you should find him guilty." But, he went on, "the mere fact that there may have been some immoral conduct or evidence of immoral conduct, or there may have been some acts of intercourse on this trip, do not make the defendant guilty."

"The crux, that is the main, that is virtually the only issue," he went on, was this: "If this trip from Texas to St. Louis was to give this girl employment, then there has been no violation of the act." For Merle Silverstein, the case could be boiled down to three questions: Did the two have a sexual relationship? What was the purpose of the trip? And did Berry "induce, compel, and entice this girl to do anything?"

But Merle Silverstein could not rely on the jury sharing this interpretation of the 50-year-old statute, and time was quickly running out. In desperation, he reminded the jury of Janice's character and the inconsistencies in her testimony; this time, however, he fed into their prejudices. "This girl is not so dumb," he told them. Whenever he had pointed out some problem with her testimony, "she was quick to answer, every time, do you remember that? She is not so dumb, or as they say, 'Dumb like a fox.' Everything that we have heard about Indians being cunning is true."

It was not Merle Silverstein's finest moment, but the comment, coming as it did at the end of the trial when fatigue and the pressures of winning the case were beginning to mount, was, perhaps, forgivable—especially in light of his next move.

Immediately, he set about tearing apart the myth of the black sexual predator, the stereotype that could well have been in the minds of some in the white, male jury. It was, he argued, a "preposterous story" that Berry was "going to spend virtually every waking moment of intercourse with this girl." That Berry would do this on tour in such close proximity to bandmates who knew his wife, in full view of his secretary every night, and that "he can't even miss a night, so he has to have intercourse with her in an automobile going sixty or seventy miles down the highway with three men in the front seat" all seemed beyond the realms of credulity to Merle Silverstein. To illustrate his point, he traced the two different accounts of the two days in Tucson to show that, following Escalanti's version, the shopping expedition must have happened on the first day, which would not have left any time for sex. If the second bed was not slept in, he argued—while marveling at the "fantastic" memories of the government's witnesses for recalling such a minor visual detail—it was simply because the maid had come in around noon to make it up.

At this point, Silverstein looked at the 12 men in front of him. He had one more important card to play. Recounting the changes in Escalanti's testimony once more, he then reminded them that this testimony could ruin a man's life. "Why," he asked, "is this girl doing this? There is a saying as old as the world, 'Hell hath no fury like a woman scorned,' and this is exactly what you have got in this case. . . . Chuck Berry is not on trial because he had immoral relations with the girl," he continued. "He's on trial here now because she did not have them, and because she got good and mad and stayed good and mad." Again, as he had a few minutes before, Silverstein was close to crossing the line with these comments, but with time running out and an all-male jury for an audience, it was a gamble he had to take.

Finishing with the issue of why Escalanti was never paid for her work for Chuck Berry, in order to show conclusively that this was her fault and hence that the reason for her coming to St. Louis was legitimate, Silverstein rested the defense's case. But it was Frederick Mayer who had the last words, and they were difficult ones to argue against. "This defendant's actions," he twice maintained during his summation, "speak louder than any words he might have said."

Casting doubt on Francine Gillium's testimony because of her status as Berry's employee, Mayer also fed into the jury's prejudices. "Remember," he told them, "this is Charles Berry, Chuck Berry, an entertainer." Then, relying on them feeling the same way as so many older whites across the country, he reminded them, just as he had done to the jury a year before, of the kind of entertainment in which Berry was engaged. "His music and entertainment is directed to who? The teen-agers of the country." Equating Berry's actions with the corrupting influence many attributed to rock and roll at that time immediately incurred Merle Silverstein's wrath, but, although his objection was sustained, it was enough that Frederick Mayer had planted the seeds of the idea in the jury's minds.

After a lengthy set of instructions from Judge Harper, and several objections from Merle Silverstein as to the wording of the charges, the jury retired to consider their verdict. Unlike the first trial, there is no record of how long they deliberated; and we do not know how they arrived at their conclusion. We do know that, as in the first trial, they were persuaded by Escalanti's testimony and Berry's actions, as the verdict remained the same as it had been twelve months earlier. Charles Berry was once again found guilty of violating the Mann Act.

A month later, on April 14, Berry found himself back in front of Judge Harper for sentencing. Before the formal sentence was pronounced, Harper called Silverstein and Mayer into his chambers and pronounced an informal sentence of his own. "I learned an old rule when I was young," he said to the two lawyers, referring to his southeast Missouri childhood. "If you're going to fuck a whore, you've got to pay 'em!" And with that, he sentenced Berry to three years' imprisonment and a $5,000 fine, shaving two years off Judge Moore's original sentence and doing so without the prejudicial comments his predecessor had so loudly pronounced.

It was a bitter blow, not just because the second trial had gone so much better than the first. In less than a year, both the Department of Justice and the FBI were to hand down instructions to local prosecutors forbidding them to prosecute Mann Act violations unless they involved "organized commercial prosecution." Quite simply, had the whole affair happened two years, or even a year after it did, Chuck Berry would not even have had charges pressed against him. Now, however, he was convicted, waiting for his appeal to be heard again, although this time with very little faith that the upper court would overturn the decision.

"Never Saw a Man So Changed"

Repeatedly some writers claim that I have a bitter attitude about this or that, but mainly toward the circumstances and verdict of the Indian girl case. The conclusion is drawn that my state of mind is uncontrollable.

—Chuck Berry, *The Autobiography*

On February 19, 1962, Chuck Berry entered the Federal Prison in Terre Haute, Indiana, and began serving a sentence "for what," he wrote later, "I was convicted of just having the intention of doing." While he could have been forgiven for biding his time during the intervening months, waiting as the appeals process once again moved slowly through the Eighth Circuit Court of Appeals, Berry, true to his character, remained busy on all fronts, personal and public.

Work on the property in Wentzville continued, absorbing much of his time and energy and fulfilling the ambition thwarted by the closing of Club Bandstand the year before: to provide a place where all people could enjoy themselves free of the racial barriers that were still so prominent in American society at the time. By the summer of 1961, Berry Park was opened to the public; the first public announcement occurred on June 16, 1961, when the *St. Louis Argus* ran an advertisement for a Father's Day Picnic. Sponsored by the Southern Kitchen, a St. Louis restaurant with two locations on Franklin and Delmar, the picnic featured free swimming and music by the Caravans, featuring Austin Wright, all for 1 dollar. For an extra 75 cents, patrons could ride in an air-conditioned bus from the Delmar restaurant to Berry Park.

On the surface, Wentzville made an odd location for a black-owned enterprise, and Buckner Road even more so. Home to some 3,000 predominantly white residents of German ancestry, Wentzville was and still is a typical Missouri rural town. The most prominent features in the town's center are the train tracks, running between the two- and three-story brick buildings on Main Street to the South and the small wooden houses and businesses on Allen Street to the north. At the side of the tracks, the Wentville Exchange, with its brightly painted white corrugated metal walls and tall grain elevator, is the town's literal and symbolic center, one more stop for the cattle cars on the Union Pacific between the East St. Louis and Kansas City stockyards. Directly south of the Exchange is Church Street; so rural is this part of the state that, at the city line, about half a mile from the tracks near the on-ramp to Interstate 70, the road has no need for a name and becomes Avenue Z. Buckner Road itself lies another two and a half miles south; Berry Park, however, lies almost a mile and half west of the junction, down a roughly surfaced, gently undulating country road flanked by hedgerows, trees, fields, and the occasional house. It was, in the early 1960s, over an hour's drive from Windermere Place and the city of St. Louis.

The choice of Buckner Road for Berry Park becomes evident just a few yards further on from the main park entrance. There, a sign for the Kingsmen Club reveals the presence of another black-owned country club also providing swimming, games, food, and music. A third black country club also existed on Buckner Road at the time of Berry Park's opening; the Double H's Labor Day celebration in 1960 boasted music from Albert King on the weekend and Ike Turner on Monday afternoon. Berry's ambition clearly was to rival both, and in only four short years between the purchase of the land in 1957 and the park's opening in 1961, Chuck Berry's dream had come a long way toward being realized. After completing work on a lake, Berry's next project was a guitar-shaped, 180,000-gallon swimming pool. At its deepest, the guitar body was 12-feet deep; the neck was a walkway leading to a clubhouse, which was the next structure to be completed. By the early 1960s, this contained a fully functioning nightclub with a stage, spacious dance floor, bar, restaurant, and game room.

Musically, however, little had happened since he had spent all those hours in the Chess studios during February and March of 1960. Only two sessions, yielding a total of 10 songs, were held in 1961. The first, in January, produced a single, "I'm Talking About You," a mid-tempo rock song that was lacking in almost every department. Lyrically, the song was a fairly generic love song, missing the telling detail of Berry's best work; even Berry's guitar work, featuring the by-now familiar double-string leads, was tentative and, in the introduction, out of tune. The second, in late July, was memorable for a number of reasons. Accompanying Berry and Johnnie Johnson on the trip from St. Louis to Chicago was Berry's younger sister, Martha, who added her voice to the session's stand-out cut, "Come On." The song begins in a similar lyrical vein to "Too Much Monkey Business," with Berry outlining a catalog of problems over a bouncing rhythm.

The B-side of the single, "Go, Go, Go" also was memorable, as the lyrics continue the "Johnny B. Goode" saga. Johnny, this time, is playing at the "weekly record hop" where, like his creator, he is "duckwalking on his knees" and "pecking like a hen." Curiously, though, the man who once extolled the virtues of rock-and-roll music over modern jazz has Johnny being backed by a band featuring Ahmad Jamal, Erroll Garner, and Stan Kenton.

As interesting as the continuation of the Johnny B. Goode saga may be, the song is important for another reason. Like "You Can't Catch Me" before it, the song makes reference to "Maybellene," as well as "Johnny B. Goode" and "Sweet Little Sixteen" in an attempt, perhaps, to remind listeners of its author's glory days—which, by then, must have seemed a lifetime past. But it was not enough to persuade the teenagers who had bought those songs to buy this one; like "I'm Talking About You" before it, the single failed to chart.

Certainly, the Mann Act conviction had its part to play in the decline of Chuck Berry's career at this time. Although neither trial garnered a large amount of press either in St. Louis or in other parts of the country, Berry's concert bookings had declined significantly during that time. But tastes in music, too, had changed; 1961 saw a revival of interest in doo-wop singing, and the twist dance craze was at its peak, with Chubby Checker's "The Twist" and "Let's Twist Again" and Joey Dee and the Starlighters "Peppermint Twist" all big hits during the year. It was a time of lightweight pop songs, and Berry's energetic guitar-driven music was, at least temporarily, out of favor with the teenage record-buying public.

Finally, on January 8, 1962, the United States Eighth Circuit Court of Appeals released its opinion regarding the second trial of *United States of America v. Charles Edward Anderson Berry*. The appeal lodged by Merle Silverstein rested on Silverstein's allegations that Judge Harper had erred in the trial both by giving misleading instructions to the jury and by not letting Silverstein examine the grand jury testimony for inconsistencies. On both counts, the three-judge panel agreed, Judge Harper had behaved correctly; the written opinion, in fact, curtly dismissed Silverstein's first charge with little explanation except to say that Judge Harper's instructions in the trial were "adequate, fair, and accurate." Of the second charge, Judges Sanborn, Matthes, and Ridge had more to say. Their opinion, citing Supreme Court rulings on several trials, sided with the "long established policy that maintains the secrecy of the grand jury proceedings in the federal courts." In short, the appeals court affirmed the verdict handed down by Judge Harper in the second trial; on January 16, the Eighth Circuit Court opinion was filed, giving Chuck Berry thirty days to surrender to the custody of the U.S. Marshal.

Berry's twenty-month incarceration occurred at a pivotal and volatile time in the struggle for civil rights in America. From February 19, 1962, to his 37th birthday on October 18, 1963, while Berry served his time—first in Terre Haute, Indiana, then at Leavenworth Federal Prison in Kansas, and finally at the Federal Medical Center in Springfield, Missouri—American society was being forced to come to terms with the realities of racism and segregation. In September 1962, the admission of James Meredith, the first black student at the University of Mississippi, sparked riots on the campus. In April and May of 1963, protest marches in Birmingham, Alabama, also triggered riots; the televised pictures of police using dogs and water canons on the demonstrators did much to sway public opinion toward supporting the civil rights movement. In June, further rioting across the South followed the assassination of civil rights leader Medgar Evers. The summer culminated in the massive peaceful demonstration on the Washington Mall in August, where Dr. Martin Luther King, Jr., delivered his "I Have A Dream" speech, perhaps the defining moment of the movement toward racial equality in the twentieth century. Almost a month before Berry's release, however, the fight for desegregation in Alabama led to the terrorist bombing of the 16th Street Baptist Church in Birmingham, resulting in the deaths of four young black girls.

The struggle for civil rights also found its way to St. Louis at that time. In the same week that Dr. King spoke to the massive crowd on the Washington Mall, the St. Louis Committee on Racial Equality began a protest of the Jefferson Bank and Trust, a downtown bank on the corner of Jefferson Avenue and Washington Boulevard. The bank, which catered to a largely black clientele, refused to hire black employees; for seven months, CORE peacefully demonstrated and disrupted the bank's activities. Finally, in March 1964, the action resulted in the Jefferson Bank agreeing to hire blacks, marking a small yet significant gain for the black population of St. Louis.

Just as the fortunes of black America seemed delicately balanced in October 1963, so did Berry's own career. Musically, the world had changed, too; the protest songs of Bob Dylan and Joan Baez, so prominently featured in the Washington demonstration, were part of a folk music revival in America. But Berry's legacy still lived on, even though he had not had a hit single since March 1960. Three years after "Let It Rock" and "Too Pooped to Pop" had graced the middle and lower reaches of the *Billboard* charts, the Beach Boys had released their second single, "Surfin' U.S.A." It was an almost note-for-note cover of Berry's "Sweet Little Sixteen," with a new set of lyrics more suitable to the California lifestyle the group represented.

Still incarcerated in the Federal Medical Center in Springfield, Missouri, Chuck Berry was unaware of the song's release that March. But the Chess Brothers were not; as "Sweet Little Sixteen's" copyright was administered by ARC Music, their publishing company, they immediately accused Beach Boys songwriter Brian Wilson of copyright infringement. So blatant was the plagiarism that the accusation never even made it to court. "It never went to a lawsuit," Marshall Chess recalled, "it was a total infringement. Had Brian Wilson's lawyers come to Chuck and said, 'We're doing this with our lyrics, let's go 50/50 on the copyright,' it probably wouldn't have happened. But Brian Wilson tried to steal the song, so it became a copyright infringement." As questionable as some of their actions may have been in the past, this time the Chess Brothers were adamant in representing the interests of their friend and star performer. "Chuck," Marshal Chess declared, "became the full writer."

Meanwhile, across the Atlantic, interest in rock and roll, and in Chuck Berry's music in particular, had never gone away. Throughout the summer of 1963, teenagers in Britain could hear the Beatles, now beginning to become a household name, play a variety of Berry songs on BBC radio. The group's appearances on *Saturday Club* on Saturday mornings and on *Pop Go the Beatles* on Tuesday evenings that summer featured Berry songs such as "Too Much Monkey Business," "Carol," "Johnny B. Goode," "Sweet Little Sixteen," "Rock and Roll Music," "Roll Over Beethoven," "I Got to Find My Baby," and "Memphis, Tennessee" (a Little Walter song they would have heard from Berry's recording), one of the 15 songs they had played on their first record label audition for Decca nearly 18 months earlier. Then, on June 7, the Rolling Stones released their first single, a cover of Berry's "Come On"; within a year, they would also release covers of "Carol" and "Around and Around" along with "Route 66" and "Confessin' the Blues," which they had learned from Berry's versions.

Not wanting to miss out on a good thing, Pye International, the British label licensed to release Chess recordings in the United Kingdom, quickly released the "Come On"/"Go Go Go" single in July; it was swiftly followed up by re-releases of "Memphis, Tennessee" with "Let It Rock" in September and "Run, Rudolph, Run" with "Johnny B. Goode" in time for the Christmas market in December. All three records did well for Berry, and prompted Leonard Chess to send his son Marshall, now out of college and working for the label full-time, to Europe to renegotiate old deals and set up new ones. That winter, Marshall and Chess partner Gene Goodman traveled to London, Paris, Cologne, and Milan to lay the groundwork for future deals that would make Chess records, and especially Chuck Berry's recordings, widely available outside of the United States.

"I made this deal with Pye Records," Marshall Chess recalled, "and we did a mid-priced and we launched Chuck big. And then Eddie Barclay in France. That's very important to his career, his worldwide career, his internationalness. He was the key person I was trying to spread when I did that European thing." Indeed, within the next year the label was to become, through Marshall's intervention, much bigger in Europe than a small, independent U.S. label could have the right to expect. Three years earlier, Berry's album *One Dozen Berries* had only been available to European R&B fans by placing an order directly with the company in Chicago. It was seeing a copy of the rare album, obtained by mail order by an enterprising young Mick

Jagger, that first caught the attention of future fellow Rolling Stone Keith Richards when the two happened to meet on a train platform in London. Now, early in 1964, the stage was set for distribution throughout Europe.

Not surprisingly, then, both Berry and the Chess brothers were anxious to get back to business following his release from prison, which they did with a recording session and another hectic round of live dates barely a month after Berry's release. "We began all over again," remembered Marshall Chess. "When he got out of prison, he and us wanted to immediately get going. My dad said, 'Chuck's coming in this week. He's getting out; he's coming right here. There is a tour of one-nighters being set up and you're going to go with Chuck.' So I had this experience traveling across America, it was just Chuck and me with pick-up bands."

As he had done before, Berry resumed his practice of traveling with just a guitar, working with local musicians at each show. Marshall gave Berry's reasoning for touring without a regular band, "His side of it related to the financial aspect, but I always told him it definitely doesn't make the music work good, you know, to do it that way. He doesn't get it about the outcome it had. But he didn't care, he didn't care. I guess if he cared he would do it." On the occasions that Berry was matched with a competent backing band, however, the results could be breathtaking. "The first job," Chess remembered, "was in Flint, Michigan. It was the Motown rhythm section backing him up. That was, like, a classic thing." Chess recalls that the show was recorded, but the tapes remained unreleased, due to a royalty dispute with Motown Records boss Berry Gordy. "Too bad," Chess mused some 40 years later, "it would've been an amazing thing."

But Berry's fierce independence, forced on him by the harsh realities of life on the road in the 1950s and his term in jail, had led him to carry on as he had before. Like Bo Diddley, Marshall Chess also noted that he "carried a little electric plate in his suitcase. He'd buy like canned beans and he'd cook it." More important, however, according to Chess, Berry's personality remained the same as it had been before the jail term. If he had changed, Chess maintained, it was "nothing that I recognized."

Not long after the Flint show, Berry arrived in Chicago for a crucial recording session that would determine whether the past scandal would slow his career to a crawl—as had happened to Jerry Lee Lewis six years earlier— or whether he would survive and continue on. What happened that November on Michigan Avenue was nothing more or less than Berry had done for years before. Perhaps because he knew music was not the only way he could make a living, Berry approached the session in a typical workman-like way, laying down 10 songs in a two-day stint. Several of them, like the unissued remakes of blues standards "Mean Old World" and "Dust My Broom," were less than inspired. But Berry had stockpiled several gems in jail, and two songs, "Nadine" and "You Never Can Tell," emerged as strong candidates for single releases.

In an interview with the British music newspaper *Melody Maker* the following year, Berry was very open about "Nadine's" origins. "I took the top hits of my past and reshaped them," he told journalist Max Jones. "I took 'Maybellene' and from it got 'Nadine.'" Indeed the rhythm, a little slower than its predecessor, and lyrical content, about a chase for a girl, this time on foot and by taxi through city streets rather than by car on the open road, are strikingly similar. But like the best of all Berry lyrics, "Nadine" is packed with finely observed visual detail. Many have pointed out the song's striking phrases, especially the "coffee-colored cadillac" in the evocative second verse. When Berry spots his girl on the crowded street, he calls out to her "campaign shoutin' like a Southern diplomat." In all probability, again in order not to offend anyone and to increase the marketability of the song, Berry changed the last line from "Democrat" to "diplomat"; certainly, the Southern Democrats (such as George Wallace) were known for their fiery oratory, though Wallace's racist speech and actions would also have led Berry away from using the party designation.

The other single recorded at the session was "You Never Can Tell." Although the release of the song was delayed until midway through the following year, it again showed Berry's lyrical command of detail and was full of memorable images. In telling the story of Pierre and his mademoiselle getting married in "a teenage wedding," Berry describes their first dwelling and its contents. "They furnished off an apartment with a two room Roebuck sale," sings Berry in a marvelously compact phrase alluding to the giant Sears and Roebuck department store, then adding, "The coolerator was crammed with T.V. dinners and ginger ale." In the third verse, as in "Sweet Little Sixteen," the young couple are portrayed as avid music fans, with a "hi-fi phono" and "seven hundred little records/All rock rhythm and jazz." And, like all Berry teenagers, their lives were not complete until they bought a car, the vividly described "souped-up Jitney, 'twas a cherry-red fifty-nine."

Shortly after the session, Marshall Chess remembers that the tour of one-nighters finished at the Cow Palace in San Francisco. Although the nation had been plunged into mourning by President Kennedy's assassination, the cultural scene at the end of 1963 in San Francisco was beginning to become even more bohemian than it had been during the time of the beats in the late 1950s. One chronicler of the nascent hippie movement, Hank Harrison, noticed that after Kennedy's death, "the city took on a new mood, a mood which was a bit nasty and yet zany." Harrison observed that "people tried to outdo each other to see who could do the weirdest stuff, be the most outrageous. People started to wear different clothes, got busted for going skinny dippin', or saying 'fuck' in public." In *The Autobiography*, Berry maintains that he had seen such activity on his first trip to San Francisco in 1956; however, this is unlikely, as his recollection has him playing at the Fillmore Auditorium, which did not become a venue for rock music until November 6, 1965. It is entirely likely, then, that Berry's vision of stoned concert goers and open love-making stems from this appearance at the Cow Palace; it was a vision that to him represented not drug-induced excess but individual expression, especially sexual expression. Within years it was this scene, and not the more militant forms of black political agitation, that Berry was to identify with.

For many Americans, the beginning of 1964 was synonymous with one thing: the arrival of the Beatles in the United States. On the evening of February 9, an estimated 70 million people, nearly two-thirds of the total television viewing population that Sunday, watched them perform on the *Ed Sullivan Show*; that and their subsequent grip on the radio and music charts that year could easily have overshadowed Berry's comeback. But their old idol had more to offer that winter, as he once again came out of the cold of Michigan Avenue to heat up the Chess studios. On February 20, two days before the Beatles left America in triumph, and again on March 26, Berry took up where he had left off with "You Never Can Tell" that previous November.

The February session is significant as it was described in full by Guy Stevens, owner of the British Sue label, for *Jazzbeat*, a British jazz magazine. As was the custom at 2120 South Michigan Avenue, the session began in the rehearsal room on the second floor of the building. Berry, unlike many of the Chess blues acts, preferred daytime or early evening sessions; so he, Willie Dixon, whose huge frame must have almost filled the tiny room, pianist Lafayette Leake, and drummer Odie Payne began running through the songs at about 6:00 in the afternoon.

Once Berry, who, Stevens noted, was supervising the session with Phil Chess at the controls, was happy with the way the songs were going, the musicians moved into the larger room, where after an hour and a half, the first song was in the can. The song, "Promised Land" was lyrically so amusing that Stevens observed the studio engineers, and especially Phil Chess, "frequently grinned and laughed during the recording." (It was, perhaps, the thought of the notoriously frugal Berry flying first class and "Workin' on a T-bone steak a la carte/ Flying over to the Golden State" that tickled Chess's funny bone as the session progressed.) Equally amused, apparently, was Chuck Berry himself, who can be seen laughing in the two photographs accompanying Stevens's piece.

The lyrics are a natural variant of the rags-to-riches stories found in songs like "Johnny B. Goode" and "Bye Bye Johnny," with the poor protagonist traveling across the country all the way from Norfolk, Virginia, to the Golden

State of California in search of the Promised Land. Like the previous songs, there are some interesting elements in the words, with Berry singing of "motor trouble" which "left us all stranded/In downtown Birmingham." The lines should not, perhaps, be strictly interpreted as a commentary on the other, more overt racial struggles that Berry and the rest of the country had witnessed in that town and state. But it is hard not to relate the lines to the freedom rides of three years earlier—where blacks and whites, especially in Alabama, rode buses in a direct challenge to Southern policies of segregation—given the specificity of the reference.

It is tempting, too, to identify the references in the fifth and sixth verses as being directed toward one of Berry's numerous lovers. At the end of summer 1960, Berry met Candace Mossler, with whom he would have a long-standing affair until her death in 1976. Some 12 years Berry's senior, the small, vivacious blond was born a farmer's daughter in the small town of Buchanan, Georgia. In 1947, after her first marriage ended in divorce, she married Jacques Mossler, a banker and financier. Together they lived in a 62-room mansion in Houston along with Candace's two children from her first marriage. "We've been friends for eighteen years," she told *Esquire* magazine of her relationship with Berry in 1976, a few months before her death. "Chuck came to the house once when I was married to Mr. Mossler. Chuck said to Mr. Mossler, 'If you leave us alone for fifteen or twenty minutes, Candace and I can get this song done.' So we sat and wrote "Memphis, Tennessee," right at that piano there."

Although her memory is a little different from Berry's (Berry recalls that he first wrote the song in St. Louis, and that the two met three years after the song had been written and recorded), clearly the two shared some intimate moments at the time. So it is entirely possible that when Berry sings, "Just help me get to Houston town/There's people there who care a little 'bout me/And they won't let the poor boy down" it is Mossler whom he has in mind. And he continues with an unmistakable reference to the wealth of the Houston millionairess by telling his audience that "They bought me a silk suit/Put luggage in my hands" before he finds himself "On a jet to the promised land."

The session then continued on briskly, according to Stevens, with the band quickly moving on to the next song, "Brenda Lee." Although Stevens and Phil Chess expressed their pleasure with the song, which was recorded even more quickly than its predecessor, Stevens noted that Berry himself was dissatisfied with the work. Then, just as quickly, it was on to some improvisation, an unrehearsed jam that Berry did "for about ten minutes with the other musicians running through various familiar tunes on his guitar to the jovial amusement of Willie Dixon, who later told me [Stevens] that he was remembering the original recording sessions when such classics as

'Maybellene,' 'School Days' and 'Sweet Little Sixteen' had been recorded."

Almost two weeks later, and four years after Berry's last chart success, "Nadine" entered the *Billboard* charts in the U.S. On March 14, the song was joined by the Beatles' cover of "Roll Over Beethoven," the same week that the Beatles occupied the top three positions in the *Billboard Hot 100*. Although Berry could now hardly compete for the teenage market with his young protegees, "Nadine" fared extremely well, staying on the chart for 10 weeks and rising as high as number 23. It was a sign that he was to be more than just an influence on popular music during this time of dynamic change; he was to be an active participant as well.

Another session at the Chess studios on South Michigan Avenue followed rapidly, this time yielding the follow-up single to "Nadine." "No Particular Place to Go," as Berry candidly explained, was, like "Nadine," a remake of an older song. This time, the chord and rhythm structures were almost identical to "School Day," with the only change being that the band cut out behind the vocal lines, giving an even more stop–start feel to the piece than that achieved by its predecessor. But Berry used the technique to great effect yet again. In "School Day," Berry had attempted to mimic the halting progress of a typical school day, moving from class to class, stopping and going from room to room. In "No Particular Place to Go," however, the stops in the music more humorously represent the state of the narrator's sexual passion, as he attempts to make out with his girlfriend only to be denied not by the girl but by "the safety belt that wouldn't budge." The song is a wonderful evocation of late 1950s and early 1960s teenage sensibility by the 37-year-old Berry, with the song's opening verse perfectly capturing the sense of freedom and sexual exploration of the times. By the end of May, it too had entered the *Billboard* chart, rising as high as number ten by the middle of July.

In an ironic answer to the Beatles's February conquest of the United States, Berry's next career move during this remarkable comeback was to tour England. On May 9, at the Finsbury Park Astoria in London, the opening night of his British tour was a resounding success. On stage, he "came through with all the strength of his recorded work," according to Chris Roberts of *Melody Maker*. Berry played "memorable guitar" and performed "his famous duck walk and Russian dance steps."

As always, Berry's backup band became an issue. For the tour, the promoters had chosen Kingsize Taylor and the Dominoes to accompany Berry; veterans, along with the Beatles and the Searchers, of the Liverpool music scene during its heyday, the band certainly had the pedigree to do the job. Eric Burdon, lead singer of the Animals, who accompanied Berry on the tour, recalls that Berry and his British band had at least managed to rehearse before the opening night, although the rehearsals did not go smoothly. At one point during a run-through of "Reelin' and Rockin'," Berry stopped the song abruptly and turned around to stare accusingly at the Dominoes drummer. "Hey, listen, man," Burdon recalls Berry screaming, "when I stomp this foot, the whole *world* stops turnin.' Now let's try it again."

At the Astoria, a number of problems between Berry and the band surfaced. In his *Melody Maker* piece, Chris Roberts commented that "Chuck was a little unsure of his backing band," and that the pacing of Berry's set coupled with the extended and unrehearsed solos detracted from the overall performance. But two days later, when Berry and the band found their way to the BBC Playhouse Theater to record a session for *Saturday Club*, the Saturday morning radio show so instrumental in introducing the Beatles to the British public the previous year, the problems were beginning to work themselves out. Although the endings of the songs were still ragged (Chuck, according to Ted "Kingsize" Taylor, tried to fool the drummer whenever he had the chance), the arrangements were tighter and more precise.

Off stage, Berry's personality seemed to fluctuate wildly. During the interview with *Melody Maker* after the Astoria show, Berry was "posing pleasantly for a knot of photographers." Chris Roberts observed that Berry was "smiling to order . . . laughing infectiously as something about the scene tickled him," adding that "his mood varied between solemn-faced discussion and bubbling wisecracks with anyone, over anything."

But it was at this show, and later in the tour, that Berry chose to snub his other British protegees, the Rolling Stones. Former bass player Bill Wyman recalled going backstage at the Astoria to meet Berry. "Although we passed messages to him," Wyman remembered, "he refused to come out and see us." Eventually, however, Berry relented and briefly met the band in his dressing room. Like Bo Diddley and Marshall Chess before them, they found him "cooking his dinner in there on a portable stove. His attitude toward us was weird, uncommunicative." Later in the tour, Mick Jagger and Charlie Watts were again snubbed, this time in much less intimidating circumstances. The two Rolling Stones "were in a hotel elevator," according to Wyman, when "the door opened and there stood Chuck Berry. He stepped in, saw the two Stones, turned his back and, when the doors opened again walked out without saying a word."

Wyman and the Stones were not the only ones to witness Berry's mood swings. The tour promoters, Don Arden and Peter Grant, who had acquired a reputation for less-than-scrupulous business tactics, also found themselves on the receiving end of Berry's anger. At one show on the tour, according to Eric Burdon, Berry refused to go on stage. The two impresarios were "on their knees peeling off single pound notes and pushing them under the door of Chuck Berry's dressing room" in their attempt to get Berry to perform.

But the tour finished on the highest possible note. On the final night in London, Teddy Boys—who favored 1950s-style hairdos and dress along with basic rock and roll, but who were already an anachronism in 1964—turned out to see their idol in full force. As Berry was finishing his set, the crowd, whipped into a frenzy, began to jump onto the stage with him. Then, according to Burdon, the singer duckwalked to the side of the stage where Arden and Grant were standing. "Did you get the money yet?" Berry asked Peter Grant, to which the 6' 5" former wrestler shook his head. At this, Berry went back into the now riotous throng, threatening to whip them into an even greater frenzy and cause more damage to the theater that the promoters would have to pay for. A short while later, Berry duckwalked back to the apprehensive pair, asking the same question as before. When Grant finally replied in the affirmative, Berry finally decided to end the performance. "Chuck just kept duckwalking," remembered Burdon. He "unplugged his Gibson guitar and duckwalked all the way off the stage, down the stairs, and into a waiting limousine."

Writing for the *Record Mirror* a year later in anticipation of Berry's next tour of Britain, journalist James Craig summed up the events at the Astoria on the tour's opening night. To him, Berry's behavior could be attributed to preperformance nerves. He "was usually alone before a show," wrote Craig. "He'd sit quietly … apparently in a state of intense concentration which was not to be disturbed by anyone. Then his name would be announced and, as if a switch had been flicked, there would be an instantaneous change to the familiar broad grin of the cool, confident professional Chuck Berry." To Craig, there were clearly two Chuck Berrys, the "wild, duck walking, zoot suit clad rock and roller" onstage, and the professional business man who "carries himself with the polite air of a visiting diplomat, right down to the sober cut of his black, city-styled suit." "People meeting him for the first time," Craig continued, "think he is uncommunicative because he does not gush in the usual show business manner.… He speaks with complete conciseness on any matter, conveying his message without one word too many.… Relaxed and away from the crowds, a droll brand of humour appears."

But to those who really knew Chuck Berry, a profound change had come over him since his conviction. Johnnie Johnson, for example, noticed a big difference in Berry's demeanor. "Chuck changed," Johnson recalled in 1999:

> He wasn't too much different with me, we always got along good. But I could see
> him, how he acted with other people, and I knew he had a chip on his shoulder.
> He was angry at how the law had treated him and he thought that everyone
> wanted to cheat him. He calmed down a little bit over the next couple of years,
> but he was definitely a different person after he got out of prison.

Carl Perkins, a veteran of tours with Berry in the late 1950s, also saw a changed man. He recalled years later about the 1964 tour of Britain:

> Never saw a man so changed. He had been an easy going guy before, the kinda guy who'd jam in dressing rooms, sit and swap licks and jokes. In England he was cold, real distant and bitter. It wasn't just jail, it was those years of one nighters, grinding it out like that can kill a man, but I figure it was mostly jail.

Along with speculation about Chuck Berry's personality change at the time, considerable speculation has surrounded the effect of the Mann Act conviction on Berry's marriage to Themetta. Some, such as veteran music journalist Robert Christgau, have claimed that the incident resulted in the breakup of the relationship, and there is no doubt that the two began living separately at some point after Berry's incarceration. In a 1983 interview with Kim Plummer of the *St. Louis Globe Democrat*, Ingrid Berry revealed that her parents had lived apart for some time, with Themetta leaving the home on Windermere Place for a house in suburban Richmond Heights and Berry preferring the seclusion of Berry Park and Wentzville. Even so, Ingrid Berry was quick to point out that the family was still "very close," coming together for holidays and family occasions. Indeed, in 1998, the couple celebrated their golden wedding anniversary, renewing their wedding vows in front of Berry's older brother Henry, now an ordained minister, their four children, and a number of their grandchildren and great grand-children.

Following the tour of England, one of Berry's first stops in the U.S. was the Chess studios in Chicago on June 10. Although there is no record of his having recorded there at that time, Bill Wyman recalled him attending a Rolling Stones session at 2120 South Michigan on that day. For the Stones, recording at the legendary studio was a dream fulfilled, and they used the time quite naturally paying homage to their heroes who had recorded there. Among the songs they recorded during their two-day stay were Berry's "Around and Around," along with "Confessin' the Blues" and "Down the Road Apiece," both of which they had learned from Berry's records. At one point during the session, according to Wyman "Berry himself walked in and stayed a long while chatting about amps and things." " 'Swing on, gentlemen!' he told us. 'You are sounding most well, if I may say so.' " For Wyman, this was a welcome change from the encounter he had witnessed a month earlier. "This was the nicest I can remember him ever being," he wrote in his 1991 autobiography *Stone Alone*. "But then," he added, "we were making money for him!" But it must have been a wonderful moment for the members of the band, now starting to generate a lot of attention in the United States, when, between takes of "Down the Road Apiece," Berry declared, "Wow, you guys are really getting it on!"

During the summer of 1964, Berry's comeback had reached its height. At the time of his encounter with the Rolling Stones, "No Particular Place to Go" was in the middle of its 11-week run on the charts; it was joined on June 6 by Johnny Rivers's uptempo, driving version of "Memphis, Tennessee" that would go as far as number 2 in the first two weeks of July, eclipsing Berry's original and more subtle version. Then, in August, a remarkable event took place. As Berry's next single, "You Never Can Tell" entered the chart, Johnny Rivers prepared to release another cover of a Berry song, his version of Berry's first hit "Maybellene." This was followed by Dion DiMucci's version of "Johnny B. Goode" later in the month, a remarkable string of successes, especially considering that the pop scene was, at this point, dominated by the Beatles's own version of Berry's music.

Meanwhile, Berry himself was busy in St. Louis, welcoming his old idol Muddy Waters to Berry Park for a show on July 12. Typically, in the St. Louis area, little mention was made of Berry's recent good fortune; the *Argus* contained no pieces on Berry that summer. Later, in October, the paper carried a story about the Supremes' first visit to Britain, ignoring that Berry had already triumphed in Europe and was currently negotiating a follow-up tour for early in the New Year.

That summer also provided more indications that racial tension in the country was growing. Two days before the Muddy Waters show at Berry Park, a "full-scale riot" took place in St. Louis not far from the notorious Pruitt-Igoe housing development. Police dispersed a mob of between 500 and 750 teenagers with tear gas, with injuries resulting to just two rioters and fifteen police. It was a portent of things to come, as the following month riots broke out in Harlem and then in Brooklyn and Rochester, New York, and in several New Jersey cities. Although much had changed since the days of Berry's first success, much still remained the same.

As the summer wound down, Berry recorded his next single, "Little Marie." Inspired, perhaps, by Johnny Rivers's success with "Memphis, Tennessee," and continuing Berry's philosophy of remaking his old songs, lyrically the song was a sequel to "Memphis," even down to its opening line that reprises, *in media res*, the telephone call at the center of the original song. "Yes, oh yes long distance, I'll accept the charge, I'll pay," sang Berry over a straight four beat that owes more to Rivers's remake than the original, before continuing recounting Marie's mother's pleas for the narrator to "come back and see Marie." The dramatic tension and subtlety of the original—in which the identity of the girl the caller is trying to reach is not revealed to be his daughter Marie until the penultimate line—is replaced with sentimentality. The detail of the original lyrics also is missing. But such was Berry's appeal late in 1964 that the song spent six weeks in the *Hot 100* in October and November, albeit in the lower half of the chart.

That December, Chess released "Promised Land" which, despite its obvious superiority to "Little Marie," fared about the same in the *Hot 100*. But it marked the end of an astounding year for Berry, who had kept a remarkable five songs on the charts for a total of 38 weeks, and had seen five more of his compositions appear on the charts as well. It was the beginning of the end of his triumphant comeback, however, as 1965 would see the decline of Berry's powers as a songwriter. Over the next five years, the pop music world changed dramatically, and Berry's rugged individualism would prevent him from keeping pace with the artistic changes occurring around him.

In January 1965, Berry traveled back to Great Britain for another month-long tour, hoping perhaps to recapture the magic of his triumphant comeback of the previous year. But the opening night, at the Lewisham Odeon, garnered mixed reviews from the British music press. As was by now his practice, Berry showed up for the show minutes before he was due to go on, inducing panic backstage. Jet lagged, Berry managed to kick into an energetic "No Particular Place to Go" to start the show, but the rest of the performance "fell flat" according to one reviewer, with "Let it Rock" sounding "stereotyped" and "Sweet Little Sixteen" showing Berry losing his way. "One couldn't help but get the feeling," Rod Harrod of *Disc* commented, "that he was just playing the same notes that he has been striking for the last 10 years."

Berry's live performance that night was erratic at best. A comedy routine inspired hecklers, which in turn inspired Berry to snap back, "If everything you had was as big as your mouth, you wouldn't have to work" to one and "You had better shut your mouth" to another. Then, according to Chick Kattenhorn, drummer for the Five Dimensions who were to back Berry on the tour, Berry started to get moody and "change keys in the middle of songs." Finally, just as Berry was building up a head of steam during the closing medley of "Johnny B. Goode" and "Bye Bye Johnny," he decided to close the show, taking the stage hands by surprise and causing them to miss their cue to drop the curtain. Claiming that he had signaled them four times and bowed to the crowd twice, he tore into them as they finally lowered the stage curtain. "What do you have to do to get the curtain lowered around here?" he angrily shouted, before slamming his guitar into its case and striding to the dressing room. "They were late closing the curtain," Kattenhorn told *Melody Maker* a month later; "He went mad!"

Several other dates on the tour were equally eventful. One night, Kattenhorn remembered, Berry decided to eschew playing his hits in favor of an all-blues set; when he sensed the crowd beginning to get a little restless, he turned to the drummer and said "'Oh well, I suppose we'll have to do some commercial things,' and launched without warning into 'Memphis, Tennessee.'" Then, at a show in Cardiff, the Five Dimensions came in for some criticism when they kept playing during an audience invasion of the stage. "Why didn't you stop?" Berry asked them in a scene reminiscent of the first show of the tour.

Rightly or wrongly, this and all of the other incidents during the 1964 and 1965 British tours had begun to give Chuck Berry a professional reputation for volatility and eccentricity that would precede him from that point on. The existence of a well-developed music press in Britain meant that Berry's behavior at shows was being reported in great detail, ensuring that insiders in the music business would be very aware that Chuck Berry could be difficult and unpredictable. At the same time, Berry added to his reputation by developing a strict contract for his live performances. Based in part on the lessons learned during the 1950s, and fueled by the anger and resentment of the Mann Act imprisonment, Berry used the fine print of his contracts to maintain strict control over concert promoters when he was at his most vulnerable—playing live. Cub Koda, a respected musician and music journalist who appeared on the bill of numerous Berry shows in the 1960s and 1970s, understood Berry's philosophy well. In addition to stipulating a 55-minute performance with no encore, Koda remembered,

> The usual Berry contract called for two Fender Dual Showman amps, a backup band that knew all his tunes and his money in front. When a promoter reneged on any of these crucial elements or tried to "help" him by altering the arrangements in the contract, Berry could immediately turn into the most difficult performer in the world to deal with.

In a sense, the contract became another of Chuck Berry's masks, something to shield and protect him from the rest of the world. He had been burned too many times by promoters, unscrupulous managers and businessmen, and the American legal system. Now, he had a deliberately cultivated reputation for unpredictability and a strictly enforced business contract behind which he could safely hide and live his private life.

Mercury Falling

When I left to go to Mercury . . . he [Leonard Chess] said, "Go and I'll see you in three years," which was my term with Mercury. Since I have been with Mercury, things haven't been going too well . . . I have kept in constant touch with Chess Records. I like little companies because there's a warmer relationship between the artist and the executive.

—Chuck Berry, 1969

On August 6, 1966, a small, three-paragraph article, tucked away on page 52, appeared in *Billboard*; a little over a week later, a smaller, similarly worded piece appeared in *Variety*. With very little fanfare, Mercury Records announced that they had signed the composer of "'Maybelline' [sic], 'Roll Over Beethoven,' and 'Johnny B. Goode.'" For the first time in his professional career, Chuck Berry agreed to work for a major record label, severing his ties with Chess Records and, most important, with Leonard and Phil Chess.

The eleven-year relationship had ended positively. Early in 1967, Berry told Norman Jopling of *Record Mirror*, that "there were no bad feelings. We just shook hands and they [Chess] wished me good luck. The change over was just a business deal." Marshall Chess, too, recalls that "it was actually a very amicable thing." Earlier in the year, Chess remembered, as he had done so many times in the past, Berry "came to my dad to discuss it. My dad advised him to, because they gave him the money. They gave him some giant advance. We couldn't pay him that much, it didn't make sense at that point of his career and where we were at. It was some amazing amount of money. And my dad said, 'Take it and run, baby!'"

On the surface, in fact, the deal made perfect sense for both Berry and Mercury. *Billboard*'s article noted that the move was a key component in Mercury's "drive to become a major factor in r&b." In the previous months, they noted, "Mercury has signed r&b artists Jerry Butler and Junior Parker as well as Berry. The firm also has appointed Norm Rubin as full-time promotional director of r&b product." And for Berry, not surprisingly, the money was the major factor, although the actual figure has always been in doubt. In a 1969 interview with *Rolling Stone*, Berry himself disclosed that the advance was $150,000 ("I might as well," he told Greil Marcus, referring to his unusual candor in talking about money matters, "because it's spent now."); by 1986, Berry had revised the figure down to $60,000. Whichever figure is correct, the amount was still an impressive figure for 1966, although as Berry would learn quickly, the money could never replace the loss of Leonard Chess and the intimacy of the Chess company.

A month after the announcement, Berry rounded up the old Chuck Berry Combo, supplemented them with several other St. Louis musicians, and made the short trip from Wentzville to Clayton to begin recording songs for his new company. If he was hoping that the reunion with Johnnie Johnson and Ebby Hardy was going to rekindle the magic of the old Chess days in Chicago, he was sadly mistaken. In particular, during the two, two-day sessions in September and October of that year, Johnson hardly came close to producing the kind of memorable contributions he had made to Berry's music in the 1950s. Now heavily in the grip of alcoholism, and playing electric rather than acoustic piano, an unfamiliar instrument to him but heavily featured in the pop music of the day, Johnson stumbled through the sessions. On some of the tunes, "Promised Land" and "Carol" for example, Johnson played an adequate yet uninspired role; the remake of "Thirty Days," however, was a flurry of missed notes and botched chords.

Ebby Hardy, too, was struggling, clashing horribly with bassist Forrest Frierson, a virtual unknown on the St. Louis scene. On "Maybellene" and "Johnny B. Goode," Freirson's walking lines worked at cross-purposes to Hardy's attempts to add jazz swing to straightforward 2/4 and 4/4 rhythms. Occasionally—on "School Day," "Roll Over Beethoven," and "Carol," for example—the two found their groove, mostly because Frierson opted to play more simple, rhythmic lines and Hardy's meter was much straighter. But Berry, who was quite clearly in control of these first sessions, must take the lion's share of the blame. Twice, on "Maybellene" and "Rock and Roll Music," he ended his performance without adequately signaling the band, catching them off-guard. He had done this, and continued to do this, with underrehearsed bands on stage for years. But here, in a studio setting, such sloppiness was easily correctable; Berry had eschewed studio craft in favor of more spontaneous performances, disregarding the trend in modern pop and rock recording. Whereas musicians like the Beatles and Brian Wilson of the Beach Boys were now spending months perfecting their material in the studio before releasing it, Berry still felt that the studio environment should match the live one.

In March 1967, the first fruits of the deal with Mercury appeared in the form of an album, *Chuck Berry's Golden Hits*. The liner notes—taken from an article written by Jim Delehant, the editor of *Hit Parader*, and which appeared in the March edition of the magazine—said it all. "I have witnessed many recording sessions that went into as many as 30 takes for one song," wrote Delehant, "But Chuck did everything here in three takes." What was a virtue in the 1950s was now a liability; the record was met with complete apathy from the record-buying public, who had no time for this old-fashioned music.

Meanwhile, Chuck Berry's main nonmusical venture, Berry Park, was thriving, and became the backdrop to a developing relationship with a young guitar player who would see a very different side of the entertainer. Since his first encounter with Chuck Berry as a star-struck teenager in 1959, Billy Peek had encountered his idol on several other occasions. In between the Mann Act trials, Berry began to catch some of Peek's shows in a south St. Louis club called the Sundown. It was there that Chuck Berry showed the more generous side of his personality; Berry posed for a picture with Peek, and later agreed to do an impromptu show at the club. "That was what was so great about Chuck," Peek recalled many years later, "he would do those kinds of things, even being the star he was, he'd come in and just do a show in town."

While Berry was imprisoned, Billy Peek began honing his guitar craft on Berry's material; "by that time," the guitarist remembered, "I had gotten a little bit of a reputation in St. Louis playing around." One night, late in 1963, Peek was playing at the Terrace Lounge on the DeBaliviere strip. After playing a set featuring a number of Chuck Berry's songs, the guitar player walked off stage only to find himself face-to-face with the songs' author himself. "I was scared to death," Peek remembered, especially as the majority of his repertoire at the time consisted of Berry covers, and he had little option but to continue playing his regular show that night in front of his mentor. Berry, however, was flattered by the imitation; according to Peek, "he started coming in and hanging around again." But, the guitar player remembered, "for the longest time he came in and just looked at me, which always intimidated me because he would just sit there and look at me."

The young musician remained undaunted by the attention, and his persistence was finally rewarded. "Finally after coming in there for quite a few times," Peek recalled, "he told the waitress to have me come to his table and then he asked me if I would be interested in playing in Wentzville in his park." Peek naturally jumped at the chance, and periodically throughout the mid-1960s he and his band made the hour-long trip to the Wentzville countryside to play on Sunday afternoons.

By this time, Chuck Berry had added significantly to the facilities at the park; a new ten-bedroom lodge had sprung up, along with a four-bedroom guest house. Around the pool, bathing huts and a concession stand also had been added, all designed and built by Berry himself. On warm summer Sunday afternoons, Billy Peek would regularly play for crowds of 200 to 300. "It was a great place to be," remembers Peek, "kinda like stuck out in the middle of nowhere but then when you got there it was like a picnic park. That's the only way I can describe it. He had tennis courts out there, he had the whole schmeer. Anything you needed he had it out there. It was a fun place; it was a lot of fun out there."

And, at the center of it all, whenever he wasn't on the road, Chuck Berry would remain in control of the festivities, making sure that the party did not get out of hand. "I seen him pick a guy up one time out there in Wentzville," Billy Peek recalled. "This guy had gotten drunk or something and there was a fence about as high as a bar. And Chuck just grabbed him and picked him up like this and just threw him right over the fence and that was the end of that!"

But for Peek, the true highlight of his time at Berry Park was his growing relationship with Chuck Berry, a relationship he firmly believes was based on the older musician's generosity. "When I was in Wentzville," Peek recalled, "and playing at the park and he would sit in and I would see him do a lick and I'd go, 'Man!' you know. And he'd take the time, he'd say 'Here, Billy,' he'd come over and show me the lick and say, 'Here's what you do.' So I'd learn a lick from him, and over a period of time I'm learning a lot of licks! And before you know it, I'm getting all the licks!" Far from seeing his young protégé as a threat, Chuck Berry was more than happy to share his time and musical knowledge, belying the reputation he was garnering in the music world outside of Missouri.

Another visitor to Wentzville at that time was Bill Graham, the San Francisco rock promoter and manager of the legendary Fillmore West. By now, Berry's distrust of rock-music entrepreneurs had become so great that Graham had to fly out to St. Louis to make the deal. "Chuck wouldn't even come out to the airport to meet me," Graham recalled in his autobiography, published posthumously in 1992. "I had to rent a car and drive out to his farm." Even then, all Graham witnessed was Berry's mask. "'I don't bring no band,'" Graham recalled Berry saying, "'You supply the band. You supply the Dual Showman Amp. You supply me a Cadillac at the airport.'" And Graham had to wait until his return to San Francisco to finalize the deal. Berry demanded "eight hundred dollars for two sets a night, three nights in March," Graham remembered.

That March, Berry was scheduled to play on a bill with Johnny Talbot and Da Thangs and the Grateful Dead; there were to be two shows at the Winterland on March 17 and 18, with a Sunday afternoon show at the Fillmore. On the Friday night, minutes before Berry was due on stage,

Graham found himself on the phone calling the airport to find out whether Berry's flight had been delayed when Berry himself knocked on Graham's office door. It was St. Louis all over again; Berry immediately dispensed with the pleasantries and wanted to get down to business. "He didn't move or speak," wrote Graham years later. "He set his guitar case down on the floor and stood there staring at me."

Graham didn't have to guess what Berry wanted. "'You want cash or a check?'" he asked. "The look he gave me was, 'Are you out of your mind? Why do you ask such a stupid question? I won't even honor it with an answer.'" Graham wrote out a check and pushed it across the desk for Berry to endorse it and get the cash. It was an act that was more reminiscent of combat than business. "He signed the check on the back," Graham continued,

> then he moved it halfway over toward me. Like into the medium, *neutral* zone of the desk. He still hadn't said a word. I pushed eight hundred dollars in cash over to his side of the desk. He counted it out in front of me. He took the money in one hand, slid the check all the way over to me, and put out his other hand for me to shake. "Mellow," he said.

But the mask was far from being lifted. First, Graham was surprised to find Berry heading straight for the stage rather than the dressing room. "He said, 'Let's go.' It was like, 'You want me to fight ten rounds?'" Graham recalled, once again using the language of aggression to describe Berry's demeanor. "'I'll fight ten.'" Then, there was the matter of getting acquainted with his backing band; after Graham had offered to introduce them, all Berry could do was to greet each with a curt "Hello" and continue his walk to the stage.

It was, in Graham's estimation, a memorable performance, with Berry delighting the crowd for 45 minutes. Then, as he had done to Peter Grant and Don Arden on the last night of his triumphant 1964 tour of England, he began to taunt Graham. Having whipped the crowd into a frenzy, Berry walked to the side of the stage and began to put his guitar back into its case. "'Chuck, listen to that applause," Graham recalls saying, to which Berry responded, "'I don't hear it. I don't hear it. They don't want me." Finally, Graham saw what was happening. "I knew it was a number," he remembered. "But I figured I had to get into it or else." So, with two other shows to go and the possibility of a longer business relationship with the music legend on the line, Graham found himself becoming Berry's stooge. As Berry snapped the guitar case shut and began to head for the back stage exit, Graham played his part in the routine. "'They *want* you, Chuck,' I told him. 'You can't leave. They *love* you.'" The wily promoter guessed his role correctly and Berry played his part to the hilt. In mock disbelief, he turned to Graham and asked, "They *love* me? They *want* me? I'm goin' out there." And he returned to the microphone to give the crowd what they wanted.

"That short thirty seconds was pure genius theater of the very first order," Graham wrote later. "What he was really saying to me was, 'They want me, they love me, but *you're* not paying me enough money. . . . Next time, *you're* gonna pay me more, right?' And," Graham admitted, "I was saying, '*Right.*'"

Graham's instincts, from booking Berry in the first place to knowing how to handle the star, were, as they were in so many things, absolutely correct. Before the end of the year, Berry made the trip from St. Louis to San Francisco four more times, playing seventeen shows in all at Winterland or the Fillmore; before Graham closed the legendary venue in July 1971, Berry had returned to play another thirty-two shows. And every time, as former Fillmore manager Paul Baratta recalled, the same backstage performance that Berry and Graham had begun at the original show was reenacted. "It's a ritual every time Chuck plays here," Baretta told journalist Michael Lydon:

> Chuck breezes into the office about five minutes before showtime the first night and says, "Let's do our thing." I give him a check, he endorses it. I count out the money, give it to him, then *he* counts it, pockets it, and gives me back the check as a receipt. He says, "Mellow," then goes on stage and knocks 'em out. We've done it so often now, maybe he'll wink at me, but it's still a ritual.

With the failure of *Golden Hits*, Mercury decided to capitalize on Berry's strengths as a live performer and his newfound relationship with the fans at the Fillmore by putting out a live album, recorded at the second set of shows Berry played for Bill Graham in June of 1967. This time, he was fortunate to be backed by a very competent band, the locally based Steve Miller Band. Its rhythm section, with Tim Davis on drums and Lonnie Turner on bass, was able to read Berry's guitar lines well and anticipate most of the songs' arrangements. When it came out later that year, however, the album featured a predominance of slow blues selections, an unusual ploy for a Chuck Berry album. Willie Dixon's "Hoochie Coochie Man," Tampa Red's "It Hurts Me Too," Big Joe Turner's "Wee Baby Blues," Charles Brown's "Drifting Blues," and a slow, syncopated version of the standard "C. C. Rider," all enabled Berry to stretch vocally and instrumentally. The rest of the album also was unusual because it was composed chiefly of instrumental jams. A mid-tempo funky "Feeling It," featuring some fine traded lines between Berry and organ player Jim Peterman; "Fillmore Blues"; and two swinging, jazz-like improvisations— the opening "Rockin at the Fillmore" and Benny Goodman and Lionel Hampton's "Flying Home"—all highlighted Berry improvising at his best. Oddly, the only Berry original composition to be featured, the ubiquitous "Johnny B. Goode," was a disappointment, because Davis and Turner lagged behind the beat. To add insult to injury, an unknown studio engineer at Mercury cropped the song immediately after Berry's solo, omitting the final verse and going straight to the familiar guitar figure that ends the song, making the song an anticlimatic ending to an otherwise different and adventurous collection.

In retrospect, the album was to prove the highlight of Berry's tenure with Mercury Records, although a contemporary review in *Rolling Stone* felt that it merely illustrated the ever-widening gulf between Berry and the music of the day. The reviewer took great pains to point out the irony that, at the Fillmore, Berry's talents were now being surpassed by those whom he had once taught. The Steve Miller Band, the reviewer notes, were "musicians who learned from him, grown up and migrated to San Francisco to breathe new life into what Berry and all of them laid down so many years ago." And, the reviewer goes on to point out, "What he [Berry] did was great, but since that time the generation that he raised has learned well and, as he would no doubt applaud, moved far ahead."

Certainly, that reverence is echoed by Bill Graham's spoken introduction to the album, although Graham cannot help but infuse his opening words with irony, born of his trip to St. Louis earlier that year. "You meet him as a person and you don't forget him," Graham begins, before adding, "as a performer, the big, big, daddy of them all, Mr. Chuck Berry!"

Altogether, from the release of *Golden Hits* at the beginning of 1967 through the middle of 1969, Mercury released five Chuck Berry albums; the remaining three, like *Golden Hits*, were erratic, with only the occasional hint of the inspiration of Berry's former years. *Chuck Berry in Memphis*, released in September of 1967, was a smoother, slicker package than the previous two, with ace session musicians and the Memphis Horns providing the accompaniment. On "Back to Memphis," for example, the warm humor of Chuck Berry's early lyrics made a welcome return. In a beautifully syncopated vocal line, Berry sings, "I wish I was in Memphis back home there with my mama / The only clothes I got left that ain't rags is my pajamas" in the first verse. Then, in the second, his mama, in an effort to make him return, reminds him that the city is so free and easy that "You can walk down Beale Street, honey, wearing your pajamas." And musically, too, the horn section added significantly to a number of songs; the long, slow horn lines behind the verse of "Goodnight, It's Time to Go" loosely based on the Spaniels' "Goodnight, Sweetheart, Goodnight," and the funky licks around the chorus of the remake of "Oh Baby Doll," so reminiscent of James Brown, are tremendously effective. But "Oh Baby Doll" and the other remake featured, "Sweet Little Rock and Roller," were both played a little too stiff and straight compared to the originals. Despite the swooping trumpet lines embellishing the second verse when Berry sings, "You should have seen her eyes when the band began to play," the latter certainly lacks the intensity of the Chess recording.

In fact, the major criticism of the album was that the recording was too studied and mannered to be effective. Berry's vocals, for example, were way too smooth for a blues song like "It Hurts Me Too," and his attempts to embellish the end of each line on "Ramblin' Rose," the old Nat King Cole standard, lead to the vocals wavering and falling flat. And the guitar tone, flat and thin throughout, detracted from the otherwise fine, trademark solos that punctuated each song.

It is hard to provide any one explanation for the failure of *Chuck Berry in Memphis*. Certainly, as *Golden Hits* illustrated, Chuck Berry was less than comfortable in the new studio environment of the mid-1960s. The eleven songs for the album, plus one which would be released later, were all recorded in a three-day period in Memphis early in March 1967, four songs a day just like many of the early Chess sessions. But there was another, related reason for Berry's erratic inspiration at the time: his increasing isolation from the rest of the world.

The isolation extended throughout all facets of Berry's life. Tensions between Francine Gillium and he had been building for some time; Berry's need for female companionship at the Park had been a constant source of arguments between the two. Eventually, Berry recalls, he "suggested she leave rather than tolerate what she saw as my freedom." Berry believes, too, that his relationship with Gillium was strained by the racial prejudice of a number of Wentzville residents; at some point during that time, a brick was thrown through a window of an office she had been using in town. The town residents, Berry argued, believing the two were married, were all-too-quick to jump to conclusions about their relationship; they "were unable to cope with the thought of a black man, right there in their country town, having a Caucasian wife." In January 1969, the two temporarily parted ways, though so strong was their relationship that the two reunited a year later.

Musically, too, Berry was isolated from contemporary trends. For example, in 1965 he told Peter Meadon of *Record Mirror* that he rarely bought records himself. "I go to a record store once a year to get a record I have in mind," he told the journalist, adding that "Sometimes I don't get it." And although musicians like Billy Peek were constant visitors to Berry Park, others were conspicuous by their absence. After the sessions for *Golden Hits*, the original Chuck Berry Combo had been dissolved; there would be other attempts to get the threesome back together, but never on a permanent basis. By 1968, Berry and Johnson in particular had little or no contact at all. "Chuck was off in his own world. . . . I never saw him, never heard from him. That was perfectly OK with me," Johnson noted, as "I had my own life to lead," having just been remarried and being busy caring for his invalid mother.

Wentzville, and Berry Park in particular, had become Berry's refuge, his sanctuary from the outside forces exerted on him from all his dealings, public and private. Two years later, he was to tell a group of students in Berkeley that "Berry Park captivates quite a bit of my time. I'm heavy into property, in property management. And the other portion of the time, which is about 30 percent of the week, I go out to play music." Billy Peek, now a regular at the park, agreed; speaking of the early 1970s, when Berry had purchased another home outside of Los Angeles, Peek believed that Berry Park "has been his favorite place" of all the property he owned. According to Peek, Berry had a "beautiful place in LA in the Hollywood Hills . . . nice pool and a tennis court as well and four-car garage, you know, big house and the whole nine yards. But he favors staying in Wentzville."

Chuck Berry's isolation in Wentzville was also symbolic of his increasing isolation from the political and racial issues of the day. Whereas in the 1950s he had flirted with statements of black pride in songs like "Brown Eyed Handsome Man" and "Johnny B. Goode," only to back away from race issues in his own public persona, the 1960s found him not even ambiguous about his race but simply silent musically and personally. At the same time, other black artists were able to be more openly vocal about race and politics in their music, with increasing commercial success. At first the sentiments were couched in metaphor, but they quickly became more overtly political; Martha Reeves and the Vandellas, 1964 hit "Dancing in the Street," for example, talked about racial harmony using the image of the whole world dancing together. Three years later, however, Aretha Franklin's version of the song "Respect" could more easily carry the double meaning of respect for a woman from her man and respect for blacks from the rest of the world. And by 1968, James Brown not only could record a song called "Say It Loud—I'm Black and I'm Proud," a far more literal celebration of race pride, he also found enough support among the general record-buying public to take the song to number 10 on the *Billboard* pop charts.

Chuck Berry's album *From St. Louie to Frisco*—released just two months after James Brown's revolutionary single in November 1968, and in the aftermath of Martin Luther King's assassination earlier in the year and the racial turmoil that followed—contained no such sentiments. Even the title, with its reference to the birthplace of the hippie movement, carried with it the suggestion that Berry found more inspiration in a white social movement than in a black political one. The album contained a number of successful moments: the gorgeous Mexican-styled ballad "Song of My Love," a remake of a song recorded in 1964, this time with immaculate harmonies sung by Berry's daughter Ingrid; the chugging rocker "Misery," with its rhythmic roots in songs like "Bye, Bye, Johnny"; and "Mum's the Word," with its humorous tale of rumor and intrigue between members of a family—all suggested that Chuck Berry's inspiration had not completely abandoned him. But they sat side-by-side with songs like "The Love I Lost," with its out-of-tune guitar parts, and "I Love Her, I Love Her" with its chorus repeating the song's title over and over, lessening the overall impact of the collection.

But the album has become known for one particular track that was to become of great interest again in just a few short years. "My Tambourine" was, on the surface, a minor song in the Berry catalog, a schoolyard ditty filled with sexual innuendo that bore a striking resemblance to several songs composed by New Orleans musician and songwriter Dave Bartholomew in the early 1950s. Bartholomew had recorded the first two versions of the song—"My Ding-a-Ling" on King Records and "Little Girl Sing Ding-a-Ling" on Imperial in 1952—under his own name; they were followed by a third version of the song, also on Imperial but renamed "Toy Bell," by a vocal group named the Bees in 1954.

The song's lyric, set to a childlike melody and interspersed with a "shave-and-a-haircut" riff, were full of sexual innuendo; in the original, for example, the ding-a-ling is not described but the simple, repetitive chorus, extolling the virtues of playing with it makes the meaning apparent. By the Bees version, however, the ding-a-ling has become the toy bell of the song's title, creating the double entendre that Berry's song was to take for its inspiration. So, in one verse, the Bees sing of being in church; "when the choir stood up to sing," they continue, "I was playing with my ding-a-ling."

By the time Chuck Berry got around to recording it some twelve years later, he had changed the song's lyric considerably. The bell was now, perhaps less humorously, a tambourine, "a drum with jingles in between," but the intent of the new verses was the same, as was the melody. So, Berry sings, when he was "in grammar school ... talking to a girl in the vestibule" he "showed her how to shake my tambourine." It is unlikely, though, that Dave Bartholomew would have heard this version of the song, at least at this point in its incarnation. *From St. Louie to Frisco*, like the other albums Chuck Berry recorded for Mercury, did little for him in terms of his exposure as a recording artist.

In the meantime, Berry was still in great demand as a live performer, playing hundreds of dates a year and garnering little or no media coverage for the work. Bob Baldori, piano player for the Lansing, Michigan-based band the Woolies, recalls how little exposure Berry was attracting at the time. One night in the late 1960s, Baldori met Berry at the opening night of a week-long engagement at a Lansing roadhouse named the Dells. The bar's owner, Joe Oade, had booked a back-up band just as Chuck Berry's contract had stipulated, but they were completely unsuited to Berry's style of music. "I have no idea how they got them there," Baldori remembered, "but they were like a precursor to heavy metal or something like that. It didn't work out—the first night was a disaster—and Joe Oade, who was an old friend of mine, saw me in the audience and he grabbed me and he said, 'Boy, I need someone for the rest of the week. Will you do it?' And 'Sure!'" For the next decade, Berry and the Woolies played, in Baldori's estimation, "hundreds of dates together. I mean there was just a constant stream of them, all over the country." But they were dates that were, in Baldori's words "invisible; we were playing to sold-out houses week after week after week and Chuck's walking home with $30,000 in cash in a briefcase, but we're not above the radar."

The information that survives from the time shows just how much the musician based his career around live performances. Although perhaps not on the exhausting scale of the Irving Feld and Alan Freed tours of a decade earlier, the demands of life on the road were still great, and required Berry to constantly shift from playing small clubs to auditoriums to large festival crowds. After an appearance at the Miami Pop Festival in late December 1968, for example, the New Year began with another series of dates at the Fillmore West with white blues musician Mike Bloomfield at the end of January. Then, in a perfect illustration of his mobility as a performer, Berry picked up at a moment's notice a week later and flew out to the Fillmore East, opened by Bill Graham the year before in New York's Greenwich Village, for the first of three appearances that year. The second, that June on a bill with Albert King and the Who, was one of Berry's few shows to be reviewed by any of the major media. Berry, according to *Billboard's* reviewer Ed Ochs, "incited fans to riots of ecstasy with . . . a classic romp through the rock and roll graveyard." Berry, wrote Ochs, "reeled . . . tough and tender anecdotes . . . off his slick guitar in bursts of jazz and swing" which were "delicious, flirting fantasies that jumped though the audience like hot potatoes."

The following month, however, the metaphorical riot described by Ochs turned into a real one as Berry, once again sharing a bill with the Who, was again in the middle of a situation that the media exaggerated. In an episode reminiscent of the so-called Boston riot ten years earlier, Berry had the misfortune to be the entertainer on stage at London's Royal Albert Hall when the audience, in the words of *Melody Maker,* "stormed the stage." The hall's manager at the time, Frank Mundy, unlike his Boston predecessors, was quick not to blame Chuck Berry or rock and roll in general. Although banning "Chuck Berry and other rock-and-roll acts" from the hall, Mundy explained, "it's not the artists we object to but the hoodlums they attract." It was a sentiment echoed by show promoter Roy Guest, who was to back out of promoting a subsequent tour with Berry and the Everly Brothers because "Chuck Berry attracts a minority fringe who have to wreck it for everyone else." Although establishment attitudes about rock and roll had changed somewhat, the thought that the 41-year-old entertainer could still whip a crowd into a frenzy was all the proof they needed that the music still had power and danger.

August found Berry back in San Francisco for another three-day engagement at Bill Graham's Fillmore West before another, prestigious festival show in Toronto on September 13. The show, which began life as a "rock-and-roll revival" featuring Little Richard, Jerry Lee Lewis, Bo Diddley, and Gene Vincent, suddenly became a major concert event with the addition of contemporary acts like the Doors and Alice Cooper. The show—filmed by D. A. Pennebaker, director of the Bob Dylan tour documentary *Don't Look Back*—shows Chuck Berry in an energetic, animated performance that is at times electrifying and at others, as in the case of his leading his Toronto-based backing band through the opening to "Wee Wee Hours," ragged and undisciplined. It stands as a suitable example of Berry's performances at the time—although Berry's performance, like all of the others on the bill, was overshadowed by John Lennon, making his first public appearance ever without the Beatles, with the Plastic Ono Band (featuring Eric Clapton).

By the time of the Toronto Pop Festival, the last album of Chuck Berry's tenure with Mercury Records had been available for several months; like the others on the label before it, it made no impact on the music scene of the day. The trouble with the label, which Berry hinted at in the May 1969 *Rolling Stone* interview, led him to record the album *Concerto in B. Goode* at his own studio in Berry Park, with Billy Peek's band for his accompaniment. The retreat to his Wentzville sanctuary, however, resulted in an album that can best be described as a product of its times. From the cover, a photograph of a duck-walking Chuck Berry wearing a flowered jacket, to the idea of an extended instrumental with a title suggestive of classical-music pretensions, everything about the album indicated that it was created at the height of the flower-power era. The first side, comprised of four somewhat undistinguished new songs—two slow blues, a mid-tempo funk, and a typical Berry rocker—was flawed by Berry's production. "Good Looking Woman," for example, featured three guitar tracks all competing with each other in the mix, one of which was so drenched with reverb that it succeeded only in muddying the sound; and the vocal track in "It's Too Dark in There" disconcertingly jumped in the stereo mix from one speaker to another. Still, there were some pleasures to be found; Billy Peek, for example, contributed some unexpectedly nice harmonica playing on several tracks.

But it was the second side of the album that was its main problem, an ill-conceived instrumental jam built around a repetitive bass figure. In this so-called Concerto, guitars came and went, dropping in and out of the mix for no apparent reason, while the same heavy reverb effects that plagued the first side reappeared. The entire piece ended in the same place it began 18 minutes and 40 seconds earlier, without any real sense of composition or progression.

On its release, the album garnered a positive review from legendary music journalist Lester Bangs; it was, in the critic's estimation, "a record worthy of his reputation." Rightly singling out the trademark Berry humor in the lyrics of "It's Too Dark in There," Bangs had high praise for the Concerto. "For all the thematic and improvisatory repetition," the review read, "you can't help but dig it, because it's so happy, driving and exuberant, overflowing with the spirit of life joyously lived." Indeed, there were sections of the piece that were interesting and infectious, although they were few and far between. In the end, Billy Peek's own review of the album, that it was simply "a terrible record," was perhaps the most accurate way to sum up Berry's last offering for the Mercury label.

By the time of *Concerto in B. Goode's* release in June, Berry was already contemplating a move back to his old label. In the *Rolling Stone* interview on May 9, Berry declared, "I shall be going back, soon, to Chess." What Berry did not know, however, isolated as he was from the music community and all its gossip, was that the Chess Records he was contemplating returning to was not the same family operation that shipped records out of the back of the two-story house on Chicago's South Michigan Avenue. The rumors that the Chess brothers had decided to sell their business had begun with the November 2, 1968, issue of *Billboard*, whose front page carried the simple headline "Chess to Be Sold to GRT," the giant California tape manufacturer. By January of 1969, the rumors had become reality and, although the Chess brothers along with their two sons, Marshall and Terry, still remained active in the music-production side of the business, the entire operation was undergoing a drastic change by the time Berry's announcement hit the pages of *Rolling Stone*. If Chuck Berry knew of the sale, and the increasing corporate nature of the once proud indie label at that time, he could at least console himself with the knowledge that his old mentor and business partner, Leonard Chess, was still involved in the company.

But that, too, was to come to a sad end just two days before Chuck Berry's 42nd birthday. As Leonard Chess was driving to a business appointment in Chicago, his already suspect heart finally gave way; he suffered a massive coronary while behind the wheel of his car and crashed into some parked cars. Dead at the age of 52, Leonard Chess would no longer be available to counsel and advise his most successful artist. Chuck Berry had come back home to the record label that had made him an international star, but it was a home he would no longer recognize.

Back Home

Late in 1969, Chuck Berry returned to Chicago to cut his first session for Chess Records in over three years. This time, however, everything was different. There was no Ebby Hardy, Johnnie Johnson, Willie Dixon—and especially, no Leonard Chess. Even the studio had changed, the claustrophobic confines of 2120 South Michigan Avenue had been replaced by a spacious new studio at 320 East 21st Street, still a part of the same South Side neighborhood but seven times the size of 2120. Officially, he had not yet signed with Chess—that was to come five months later, on May 9, 1970—but, after the experience of five failed albums with Mercury, the chance to work in familiar, albeit changed, surroundings must have been appealing.

There was another familiar face waiting for Chuck Berry at the new Chess studios. Assigned to the project was producer Esmond Edwards, back at Chess for a second term after having left in 1967. Edwards's experience was mostly in jazz, having recorded acts like Eric Dolphy, Coleman Hawkins, and Eddie "Lockjaw" Davis for Prestige, an independent New York jazz label, between 1958 and 1962, and Ramsey Lewis and Yusef Lateef for Chess during his first stay with the company, from 1962 to 1967. After the GRT acquisition of Chess, Edwards was brought in to produce a number of rock and blues projects, including Chuck Berry, and the *London Sessions* series, albums featuring Muddy Waters, Howlin' Wolf, Bo Diddley, and Berry himself, accompanied by young lions of the British electric-blues scene.

Chuck Berry's recollection of Edwards from their first stints with Chess in the early 1960s was not a favorable one. During an interview with William Patrick Salvo in December 1972, Berry recalled that his earliest impression of his new producer was that he was prejudiced against rock musicians. "At that time," he told Salvo,

> anybody that played rock and roll was like scum. . . . When I would pass by Esmond's office, you know, Esmond doesn't laugh too much anyway, he doesn't go around grinning.
>
> And I would look in on him and he would look up and say "hi," and I'd say to myself, "you bastard, that's all right I'm playing what I like. . . . "
>
> So I figured that we were enemies, unknown enemies for a long while 'cause he didn't like what I was into. But, now I know different because he understands and appreciates my music.

But, at the time of this first session, the tension between the two was still palpable. To piano player Bob Baldori, who had been invited to play at the session, things "were a mess." He immediately sensed that the artist and producer were completely mismatched; Edwards, he felt, "had a real patronizing attitude about Chuck's music." He recalled "sitting in the control room when Chuck's out there overdubbing or doing something and Esmond Edwards is saying to me that 'it's just the same thing over and over again, just like James Brown,' as if that sums it up. I'm thinking, 'What are you doing here, man, if that's the way you're hearing this?'"

For Baldori, in the presence of heroes like Lafayette Leake and Phil Upchurch, the experience was a painful disappointment. "It was surprising to me," he remembered, "and I think Chuck got the picture right away. Chuck's attitude to these sessions was, he cuts the master, he does the best he can, you know, brings what he does to the session, he gets his money—and he always had, you know, the cash deal—and then he leaves. And that's what he did on that session."

In fairness, Esmond Edwards had no such recollection of the session; some 30 years later he even doubted his own presence in the studio. "I don't recall it at all," Edwards has maintained about the session, although he has also observed that

> everyone has tension with Chuck. So, if I was there I wouldn't deny that, but I don't recall having any problems with it in terms of recording. You don't have problems with Chuck because he does what he wants to do. So, when you acknowledge that, there's no reason to have a problem. If I was involved with that, then maybe I hadn't learned to deal with him at the time. But I have no recollection of that at all.

But with or without tension or Esmond Edwards's presence, the session yielded one more masterpiece in the Berry canon: "Tulane." Musically, the song underscored Edwards's accusation that Berry was simply playing the same thing over and over: The introduction, rhythm, and three-verse structure adhered to the formula Berry had developed over a decade earlier. But the lyrics, a tale of a couple running "a novelty shop" that sold not novelties but "the cream of the crop" from beneath the counter, were some of Berry's best in years. The second and third verses recounted Johnny's advice to his partner Tulane as she fled from the impending drug bust. It was a song every bit as relevant to its time as "School Day" was to 1957; as Marshall Chess observed not long after hearing the song for the first time, "Chuck has got the fucking art . . . of always keeping up with the times."

The *Back Home* album, which was eventually released in August 1970, was by no means the disaster it could have been. In Edwards's defense, the rest of the material is not Berry's strongest. However, the slow blues of "Have Mercy Judge" (which extends the story of Tulane and Johnny begun in "Tulane"), the straight-ahead rock of "I'm a Rocker" (although it borrows the "Reelin' and Rockin'" formula), and the gentle funk of "Some People" certainly counter his opinion that this was just "the same old thing." But the experience with Mercury and now with Edwards in Chicago led Berry to do with his recording career what he had done with his performing and publishing: He took control of it himself.

Bob Baldori recalls receiving a phone call not long after the release of *Back Home*:

> He called me up and said "I'll come up, we'll cut an album," and, you know, it was Chuck Berry and I'm thinking, "Is he really going to do this?" And I scheduled the band and I said, "Yeah, Chuck's coming in to record an album," and everyone went, like, "Sure!," and, you know, comes the time, he comes pulling up, pulling into the studio with his guitar.

From such a casual beginning came the next Chess album, *San Francisco Dues*. Recorded in January 1971 in Baldori's studio in Lansing, Michigan, with the Woolies, the album was a reflection of Berry's *modus operandi* while on the road. Baldori remembered, "He spent a week [in the studio], and he was focused. He was writing lyrics and songs while we were in there and we didn't stop for five days straight and he packed up, took the masters and left."

In the Woolies, Berry had found a tight and sympathetic backing band; unfortunately, the material did not approach *Back Home*'s standards, and only the rocking "Festival" really stood out. When Esmond Edwards received the masters from Berry, he immediately felt that the album was "a marginal effort" and that it was "abominable." At this point, Baldori recalled, "there was all these politics involved with it—and I think Esmond Edwards or somebody got their hands on it after a certain point and remixed and remastered some of it." Two cuts—the previously unreleased "Viva, Viva, Rock and Roll" and "Lonely School Days," the B-side of the 1966 single "Ramona Say Yes"—were added to the album that was finally released in September 1971. But even Edwards's decision to add these extra cuts could not help the work; Chess had so little confidence in the new release that they refused to release a single from the album, and it quickly disappeared from view.

In the meantime, Chuck Berry was still playing hundreds of live dates; now he had several stable bands to back him, including the Woolies and Billy Peek's band, who had made their official debut backing their mentor at the Mississippi River Festival at Southern Illinois University, Edwardsville, in August 1970. Berry's approach to promoters was now becoming even more aggressive; he had developed a system of fines for unscrupulous promoters who failed to live up to their side of the contract. Bob Baldori recalls one such incident that illustrated perfectly the method behind Berry's so-called difficult nature. "We go to a gig in Indianapolis," the pianist recalls,

> and the amps aren't there, or one of the amps isn't there. Well, you can make do, but the promoter has breached the contract, and Chuck says, "You've breached the contract, I want another $2,000, 'cause I'm going to have to go up there." Well, the guy on the other end of the deal says, "You're screwing with me here; you're ripping me off"; he goes and gets the cash, Chuck takes it and goes on. And the other guy walks away telling people, "Chuck Berry's temperamental, hard to work with, and he fucked me on this deal," and Chuck just looks at him and says, "I'm not screwing you." And he's not! But, you know, the guy's going to go away and tell people whatever he's going to tell 'em. But if I'm on Chuck's side of the table, I want him to go away and do that so the next guy knows better.

Clearly, in Baldori's mind, this was not Berry being difficult to work with. Instead, it was a deliberately calculated move to warn other promoters not to breach contracts and to provide Berry with some much-needed protection as he traveled alone from show to show.

Another promoter who had seen Berry at his most combative was Richard Nader. In 1969, figuring there might be a market for nostalgia for old rock-and-roll music, Nader had hit upon the idea of reviving the old Irving Feld and Alan Freed package tours from the 1950s. So on October 18, 1969, Nader rounded up Chuck Berry, Bill Haley and His Comets, the Platters, the Coasters, the Shirelles, Jimmy Clanton, and Sha Na Na (a contemporary group whose act drew heavily on the music and dress of the 1950s), and rented Madison Square Garden for two shows. Nader's instincts paid off handsomely; both shows sold out and, according to *Rolling Stone*, more than 1,000 people tried unsuccessfully to get into the second. The audience was part curious teenagers ("1969's own dear trendies," wrote *Rolling Stone* writer

Jan Hodenfield, "out to goof on it") and part older rock and rollers ("In the last few years of rock concerts," wrote Mike Jahn of the *New York Times*, "never has so little hair been seen in one place at one time").

For Bill Haley, the show was a resounding success; his last New York appearance had been in 1961 and he was determined to make the most of it. Nader commented that Haley was "glad to get the money," and the reviews of Haley's performance were universally positive. Mike Jahn commented that his group sounded "as exciting as almost anything heard lately"; Jan Hodenfield, commenting on the eight-minute long standing ovation given the group by the 4,500-person crowd, noted that although the band resembled "a winning bowling team: paunchy, perspiring in their watered silk jackets but . . . in shape . . . it was a thrilling comeback."

For Chuck Berry, however, the story was different. Even getting him there had been a struggle, with Nader having to convince Berry and his agent, Dick Alen, that he had money to pay for Berry's appearance before the show. When Nader failed to provide adequate proof of his financial stability for Berry, Alen promptly booked Berry into a show in New Hampshire, forcing Nader to pay off the agent to reschedule the New Hampshire show. On his arrival at the Madison Square Garden show, Nader recalled, Berry was upset about the arrangements; he was not happy at the thought of playing two shows and at the thought of not only sharing the bill with the Platters but having to go on before them. It is unclear whether these details had been ironed out in the contract beforehand, but the resulting bitterness, according to *Rolling Stone*, surfaced in Berry's performance. Comparing his show to one played in New York two years earlier, Jan Hodenfield wrote that "tired then, [Berry] is exhausted now. The eyes are dead. But, like a jiggling puppet with bills to pay, he gives what he has left." The anger with Richard Nader finally spilled out onto the stage; during the second show, Berry "interpreted a signal from the wings . . . as a sign he was being hooked from the stage." Although the audience persuaded him to come back for another song, and veteran New York deejay Murray the K. tried to smooth over the situation, "sourness was in the air."

In the next three years, Richard Nader staged more than 125 of these "Rock-and-Roll Revivals" all over the country; many of them, like the Mississippi River Festival show in August 1970, featured Chuck Berry. It was the beginning of a long and difficult relationship for the pair, one that was both financially rewarding and troubling. Later, Nader maintained that he was paying Berry under the table for many of the shows. Berry was paid sometimes as low as $280 a night in the written contract for the shows, when Berry's guarantee was said to be around $2,000. Nader also alleged that Berry would show up at shows and demand more cash than was stipulated in the contract, although this again may have been Berry fining the promoter for some real or perceived breach of their agreement. At a show in Pittsburgh, Nader recalled, Berry reacted angrily to Nader's refusal to meet his demands and tuned up for three-quarters of his contracted set. At that point, the musician demanded the promoter's presence on stage to explain to the crowd why he had refused to pay him; from the wings Nader shouted to Berry, "Just fucking *play*, Chuck." Amid boos and catcalls, Chuck Berry reluctantly complied.

In February 1972, Berry and Esmond Edwards flew to London to begin work on the next Chess album. Initially, the plan seems to have been to produce a live album; Berry was booked for a single show at the Locarno in Coventry, part of an arts festival bill that included upcoming British band Slade, Billy Preston, the Roy Young band (who were to provide Berry's backing for the evening), and, in a second, later show, Pink Floyd. The fact that this was a one-off show suggested that the strategy to record it would have been made known to Chuck Berry at the time; oddly, however, he said later that the recording made that night was done without his knowledge. "I can't deny that it [the subsequent *London Chuck Berry Sessions* album that contained the recording] turned out okay," he wrote in *The Autobiography*, "but it would have been better for the band and myself to know if and when the recording was being made."

The performance in Coventry garnered mixed critical reviews; veteran music journalist Charles Shaar Murray was unreservedly enthusiastic about the show. "Chuck Berry is no battered old relic being trotted out for a rerun," he wrote in *Cream* magazine the following month. "He's a living master of rock and roll. . . . Chuck Berry was, is, and ever shall be." Tony Stewart, of Britain's *New Musical Express*, however, while agreeing that Berry was "the highlight of the first house," felt that he was just going through the motions: "He'd play the first bars of any of his famous numbers, do a little on vocals, and leave the rest to the audience." For Stewart, it was an exercise in nostalgia; "he's no ace on guitar, and his voice has a hollow quality. . . . He ain't got that much music ability, but he's got feel."

But the audience proved to be the ultimate judge of the show. Murray noted that, right from the opening number, "Reelin' and Rockin'," the crowd began "to bounce in perfect time and they yelled the words right back at him." Berry, according to Murray, could not believe the audience's reaction; "he kept looking over at the side of the stage and pointing out over the audience grinning in ecstatic disbelief." That set the tone for the whole evening, inspiring Berry, despite his reputation for playing short shows, to play past his allotted time. When a concert organizer came on to ask him to quit, Berry responded with a 12-minute call-and-response version of "My Ding-a-Ling" and a blistering rendition of "Johnny B. Goode"; so worked up was Berry at this point that he began with a first verse mistakenly taken from

"Bye Bye Johnny" instead. Tony Stewart, as critical as he was of Chuck Berry's performance that night, had to admit that it had been a remarkable show: "The way the audience reacted, with incessant calls for more and Berry's delight in continuing to perform, it was amazing that he ever left the stage. It took a handful of organizers . . . to stop him from reappearing."

Given that kind of atmosphere, the show promised to yield a tremendous live recording for Chess to release, but technical problems may have rendered some of the recording unusable. Four numbers into the set, Berry's microphone blew, suggesting that at least the first part of the show would not be of sufficient quality to make the transition to an album. Consequently, Esmond Edwards hastily arranged studio time in London two days later, a brief five-hour session with veteran British rockers Kenny Jones and Ian McLachan of the Faces and Rick Grech, former bassist with Family and Blind Faith. In an interview conducted later that year with freelance journalist William Patrick Salvo, Berry confirmed the arrangements, again suggesting that he was fully aware of the recording made two days before. "We really didn't have enough adequate or audible material from Coventry for an album," he told Salvo, "so that's why, on the spur of the moment we got the London thing together."

Despite the adverse circumstances of the recording, the five-hour session produced some worthwhile material; an inspired reading of former Chess labelmate Little Walter's "Mean Old World," the driving instrumental "London Berry Blues," and even the oddly metered "Let's Boogie" were solid Berry material. But when the album was finally released in April 1972, it was the usable live material from Coventry that attracted all the attention. The performance captured on side two of the album begins with "Reelin' and Rockin'," with lyrics suitably rewritten to reflect the sexual attitudes of the times. Then, the recording captured the show's climax, the lengthy "My Ding-a-Ling," the raucous "Johnny B. Goode," and the dramatic appeals of the management for the audience to leave the building. "Listen, please! Please! He's overrun 15 minutes," the exasperated MC yelled into the microphone, quickly adding, "Look! There's about 2,000 people outside waiting for another concert. I'm sure lots more of you are going to come back in to see the Pink Floyd. We don't have a Pink Floyd concert if we don't clear the place!" But his appeals initially go unheeded, drowned out by the applause and the chants of "We want Chuck! We want Chuck!"

What happened next was one of those unusual moments in an artist's career when the whims of public taste and some careful management combine to create a remarkable if unrepresentative commercial achievement. According to Esmond Edwards, "what happened was that some DJs latched on to 'My Ding-a-Ling' and started to play it." Consequently, the *London Chuck Berry Sessions* entered the *Billboard* album charts in June. The deejays,

Edwards recalled, then pressured the company to put the song out as a single and, at first, Chess was hesitant to do so. "We were rather reluctant to put it out," remembers the veteran producer, "because it was more than a double entendre. We expected trouble with it." But, Edwards believed, the record company finally gave in to the DJs's pressure. "They had insisted on it being released, so we put it out as a single. I spent hours editing that thing down to four minutes or whatever to get airplay."

On August 5, the edited version of "My Ding-a-Ling" entered the *Billboard* pop charts. Slowly, the song rose up the chart; by September 30, it reached the number 13 spot and was certified by the music industry magazine as a million-seller. Ironically, it was Richard Nader who, ten days later, made the presentation of the ceremonial gold disc to Chuck Berry onstage at another of his Rock-and-Roll Revivals at Madison Square Garden. But in perhaps the most delicious irony of all, "My Ding-a-Ling" rose to number 1 for the last two weeks of October, holding Elvis Presley's "Burning Love" to the number 2 spot during the most successful year of Presley's career since his discharge from the army in 1960.

The success of the single also sparked interest across the Atlantic, leading to the song's eventual release in Britain. On November 4, the song entered the British pop charts, where it stayed for a seventeen-week run, also eventually reaching number 1. But the triumph was tainted by the song's being banned from airplay on the BBC; the song's lyrics, tame even by the standards of the day, reached the ears of Mary Whitehouse, a moral watchdog and conservative media critic who successfully argued for its removal from the BBC's airwaves. "My Ding-a-Ling" was consequently awarded the dubious honor of being the first number-1 song not to be performed live on the BBC One's chart show "Top of the Pops." Instead, viewers were treated to children's TV host, entertainer, and quick-draw artist Rolf Harris's cartoon renditions of the song's verses, with Harris literally interpreting the song through drawings of various people holding two small spheres hanging on a string.

But the controversy surrounding the song did not end there. Later, music critics began to notice the similarities between Chuck Berry's and Dave Bartholomew's songs, and accusations of plagiarism began to surface. Indeed, a comparison of the Dave Bartholomew and Chuck Berry versions of "My Ding-a-Ling" reveals both significant similarities and differences. The choruses, for example, vary both in syncopation and in melody on the second and, in the case of "Toy Bell," the fourth lines; lyrically, however, they are very close. But it is in the verses that the greatest similarities and also the greatest differences occur. Berry's version on the *London Chuck Berry Sessions* is substantially longer, consisting of eight verses, compared to "Toy Bell's" four and the original's three. The verses all share the same melody line;

further, both "Toy Bell" and Berry's version of the song have a verse in common, about playing with the ding-a-ling in Sunday school. But the major difference between the songs is Berry's inventiveness both in quantity and, arguably, in detail.

The second major difference between the songs lies in the performance. Esmond Edwards maintains that the song's greatest appeal lies in the live recording and in the interplay between Berry and his audience; "the thing that sold," according to the song's producer, "was the spontaneity and the audience response on the English live session." Indeed, without the energy of the Coventry crowd's singing and laughing to Berry's improvised humor, the song, whether it be Berry's or Bartholomew's, as Fred Rothwell quite rightly points out, "comes across as what it essentially is: a silly little ditty." The fact that Bartholomew's versions, and Berry's earliest attempt at covering them, "My Tambourine," went largely ignored by the record-buying public is proof that Edwards's and Rothwell's assertions are correct.

Clearly, though, the similarities between the songs are so great as to constitute plagiarism, and whether Dave Bartholomew has ever sued Chuck Berry remains a matter of significant conjecture. Recorded versions of Chuck Berry's "My Ding-a-Ling" have always listed Berry as the author and Isalee Music, Berry's publishing company, as the publisher. Indeed, Broadcast Music International (BMI), the performing rights organization responsible for collecting fees from institutions who use music performances in all their various formats, lists Chuck Berry and Isalee as the owners of one song with that title, and Dave Bartholomew and Sam Rhodes and their respective publishers (Fort Knox Music and Trio Music) as the owners of a separate and distinct song with the same title. But a search of the copyright records reveals that Bartholomew and Rhodes are the sole owners of the copyright on a song called "My Ding-a-Ling." The copyright, originally registered on June 27, 1952, was renewed on May 8, 1980, several years after Berry's hit. A search of the copyright records for "My Ding-A-Ling" does yield five copyrights for the song under Berry's name, but they are sound-recording copyrights, copyrights for specific recorded versions of the song, not for the song itself.

Esmond Edwards, for one, believes that there may have been a lawsuit filed against Berry for the song; "I had heard that there was a suit brought against Chuck for plagiarizing that tune," he recalled in 1998. "I had heard that he had lost the case and it [the song's copyright] had been awarded to someone else. But looking at the recent label copy, it's still credited to Chuck Berry. He's the only one that's credited for it." And, Edwards notes with some bitterness, Dave Bartholomew was not the only person slighted by the song's success. Edwards's role in the song's success, editing it down to a commercially viable single suitable for radio airplay, also was never fully acknowledged. "I understand that he doesn't mention my name in his auto-biography, which again is Chuck," said Edwards. "I know one thing: that recording brought him from about $1,000 a night to $10,000 a night. And, you know, I certainly feel that I was instrumental in that."

Ultimately, questions of the song's authorship and credit for the song's success are secondary to the fact that Chuck Berry's performance on a cold English February evening in 1972, his ability to capture an audience with his words, delivery, and timing, made possible "My Ding-a-Ling's" trans-formation from an obscure R&B song to a number-1 song on both sides of the Atlantic. Whatever critical and legal wrangling the song engendered also should not be obscured by the knowledge that the hit in many ways compen-sated Chuck Berry for the loss of royalties on songs far more deserving of critical and financial success. The $250,000 royalty check Berry claims he received from the song could in many ways be seen as payment on a career that, by that point, was about seventeen years old. Seen in that way, Chuck Berry is and probably should be regarded as the song's author, in spirit if not in fact.

The immediate effect of "My Ding-a-Ling's" success was to create an enormous demand for live appearances by Berry, and Billy Peek recalled the whirlwind of activity that occurred during the next few years. At the time, Peek was playing a regular weekly show at a club called the Rainbow on St. Charles Rock Road in St. Louis; knowing that he wanted Peek and his band for the upcoming tours, Chuck Berry quickly made a deal with the club owners for Peek's services. According to Billy, Berry was insistent that Peek and his band should not lose their residency at the club, so Berry agreed to play shows for the owners at a greatly reduced fee as compensation. "What he was doing," Peek felt, "was saying, 'Look, I'll do a show here for you, but I want to be able to take Billy out on some shows with me, and you've gotta guarantee that he's got his job when he comes back.' It worked out beautiful for everybody and it almost became a legendary thing in St. Louis at the Rainbow."

One of the first big shows the band played at that time was at the Las Vegas Hilton; it was a memorable occasion for a number of reasons. First, there was yet another issue with a breach of Berry's performing contract, once again over the stipulated Fender Dual Showman amplifiers. "We came in the afternoon for rehearsal," remembered Billy Peek, "and Chuck looks around and he sees, I think they were Twin Reverbs. 'Alright,' he says, 'Where's the Dual Showman?' And the hotel entertainment director says, 'Oh, Chuck, we've got that coming up from LA, it'll be here tomorrow.' So Chuck says, 'Fine, but you know what you're going to have to do.'"

The director's negligence precipitated a heated argument. He began screaming at Berry, "You're never gonna work in Vegas, you're never gonna do this, you're never gonna do that." Berry, meanwhile, was angrily shouting back, "You don't get a Dual Showman up here, I ain't even gonna play. Forget about the rider, the money or anything else, I just ain't gonna play if I ain't got a Dual Showman." The two were almost ready to come to blows when they were separated by an agent who calmed things down temporarily. Peek remembered that Chuck Berry walked over to the band at that point and assured them that everything was going to be all right. "You're gonna get paid," he told Peek, "don't worry about it. I'm gonna take care of you, you will be paid no matter what happens. Why don't you guys go on back to the rooms and just go out and enjoy yourself. Go out and have a good time tonight."

So the band did just that; they left the hotel, spent the evening sampling the city's nightlife, and returned some time in the early hours of the morning. "I'm just about to go to sleep," Peek recalled, and the phone rang. "This is Chuck, man," announced the voice on the other end of the phone "Is everybody back at the hotel? Can you get 'em together, man? Get over here, we're going to do the three o'clock show."

"Yeah," Billy Peek said, "We can get over there. How soon do you need us?" "About an hour ago!" came the reply, and Peek immediately rounded up the rest of the band and went down to the casino lounge. And as he walked out onstage, Peek witnessed a sight that still brings a smile to his face: "Chuck's out there all by himself," the guitarist recalled, "he's got his guitar on and he's talking to the audience, he's telling jokes and he's putting on a little show all by himself. And we just kind of sneaked in behind him . . . and Chuck, he hears us and he turns around and when he sees us he goes, 'OK, and now I guess we'll open our show!'"

The hostilities of the previous afternoon had, at least in Peek's estimation, paid off. "I don't know what went down, but that entertainment director was really nice to Chuck from then on. Something must have went down 'cause he treated Chuck with a lot of respect after that."

During the run at the Hilton, the band was paid a visit by another entertainer who happened to be playing the casino's main room. In the middle of a show, Billy Peek remembered, he caught a glimpse of Elvis Presley in the wings; "he was dressed to the nines, he had the cape, he had the whole nine yards. He was with his wife at the time, Priscilla Presley; then he comes back the following night with his wife and he's got Sammy Davis, Jr., with him. So he came two nights to watch Chuck Berry play." It was, in Peek's estimation, "a pretty big nod to Chuck. I mean you could tell he was enjoying it." The possibility of an impromptu and historic collaboration, however, never materialized. "Chuck was trying to get him to come up and sing one," Peek recalled, "but he wouldn't do it. But that was one of the big highlights at the time."

But difficulties with promoters continued to overshadow the music. In Scotland, a promoter who failed to read a contract correctly nearly caused a riot. At a club called Green's in Glasgow, Peek remembered, the promoter ignored a stipulation that Berry be paid in American dollars, leaving him with the unenviable task of trying to find and exchange thousands of pounds into dollars after the Glasgow banks had all closed. Peek recalled,

> The guy just lost it, you know and during the period of time that he was trying to get the money, get it in American money and all of that, they damn near tore that auditorium apart. I mean the kids were just agitated, because the show kept getting delayed and delayed. We finally went on and played the show and then everything was cool, you know.

Reflecting on the incident years later, Peek was adamant that his former employer was right in taking such a hard stance. Promoters, maintained Peek,

> blame it on Chuck, that he's difficult and this and that, but the promoters don't abide by the contracts that he sends them. And I guess that just aggravates them, you know. I mean, he's thinking, "Can't these people read? You know, it says it right there in black and white so when I get here that's all done, it's not a problem."

As an example of how unscrupulous promoters can be, Billy Peek recalled another incident that year in which he became the unwitting victim of a promoter's attempt to get around Berry after an alleged breach of contract. "Chuck," Peek recalled, "was having a problem with a contract again or something and he was trying to sort it out with the guy in the hotel lobby. And Chuck told me, he says, 'You guys go back to your room and don't come down till I call you.'" So the band, as they had done in Las Vegas, left and waited for the negotiation to be concluded. Not long after he got back to his hotel room, Peek received a phone call. "But it ain't Chuck," he remembered, "it's the agent. And he says, 'Billy, Chuck told me to call you. He wants you guys to come on down to the lobby, we're just about getting ready to leave to go to the gig.'"

As the band reassembled and walked through the lobby, Billy got the sense that something was wrong. "I thought Chuck looked at me funny, like 'What are you doing down here?'" the guitar played recalled, but at the time nothing was said. When they got to the show, however, Berry called Peek into his dressing room. "He kinda reads me the riot act," Peek remembered. "He says, 'Billy, why did you come down to the lobby like you did?' And I says, 'Well, the promoter called and told me everything was cool.' 'Oh, I see,' he says." Then, Berry added, " 'I felt like a fool, man.' And I said, 'Why?' And he says, 'I hadn't straightened nothing out with those guys.' "

All of a sudden, the two realized what had happened. A suitably chastened Peek apologized to Berry; "I said, 'Well, I've been had.' And Chuck said, 'See how people are. From now on, whenever I tell you that I'll call you, if it ain't me, don't do anything. If someone gets on the phone and says something to you, just always remember: 'I have to talk to Chuck.' " Clearly, Peek maintained, "he did that to protect himself," adding that he "really felt bad, because I don't think Chuck and I ever had a rub—the whole relationship we've never had a rub. And I felt bad because I wasn't smart enough to see through that."

But Peek also witnessed another side to Chuck Berry's public persona, one that few people in the music business have ever seen. Backstage at a show at Will Rogers Stadium in Oklahoma City, Berry and the band were greeted by a visibly upset promoter; very calmly, according to Peek, the promoter explained that he had only been able to sell 400 hundred tickets for a show in a 12,000-seat venue. "The promotion was horrible," the promoter offered by way of explanation. " 'It's because of us. None of this has to do with you, it's not your fault. So here's your money. We really appreciate your coming down here, but we don't want a man of your stature to have to come in to a room and play for 400 people."

"I've never seen Chuck do this much," Peek remembered years later, "but he gave that guy the money back. He gave it back to them and he says, 'Look, I don't want to take your money, you're a nice guy, we'll try it again some other time.' " It was a very generous offer that the promoter gratefully accepted, a rare gesture from a hard-nosed businessman. "He won't do that often," Billy admitted, "but that guy, I guess he just said the right things, and he said them the right way."

Clearly, both Billy Peek and Jim Marsala, who joined Peek's band in 1973 and who has played bass for Chuck Berry on a regular basis ever since, do not share the widespread opinion of Berry's difficult and hostile persona. "He's pretty loyal," Jim Marsala maintained, "he's always been pretty loyal to me over the years. He is that way with the people that he trusts." And Peek concurred: "He always took care of us. I always felt safe and secure with Chuck, no matter what foreign country we might be in or whatever," no mean feat considering that Berry always traveled without any of the personnel that accompany today's rock stars.

In the mid-1970s, after his stint with Chuck Berry, Peek went on to play with Rod Stewart's band while the singer was enjoying the heights of popularity, and the difference between the touring styles of the two entertainers was remarkable. "Rod's got the whole entourage," the guitarist observed. "He's got a road manager, and a tour manager, and he's got his own manager, you know, and jillions of roadies. He's very protected. Chuck will go out to these gigs, it's just Chuck and us. Sometimes an agent might be there, but it's all taken care of with Chuck."

The overwhelming success of *The London Chuck Berry Sessions* proved hard to follow. Chuck Berry's next studio album and single, 1973's *Bio*, did not fare well, despite the fact that Berry was teamed up with Elephant's Memory, a band whose previous studio work appeared on *Sometime in New York City*, John Lennon and Yoko Ono's controversial social-protest album released in June 1972. *Bio* was damned with faint praise, at least by *Rolling Stone* reviewer Tony Glover; although he praised several songs—most notably the title track, "Hello Little Girl Goodbye," and the instrumental "Woodpecker"—and the country-influenced "Rain Eyes" was described as having "all the evocative power and charm of the Berry songs of old," the rest of the set was viewed as barely acceptable. "I don't know how much longer, " Glover wrote, "Berry can get away with putting out albums that are just all right. . . . Mediocrity is such a bore." In fact, the only thing Glover found truly praiseworthy was the album's package, which features pictures of Berry as a child and of his early music career. There are shots of him in Harry Davis's darkroom, with Ebby Hardy and Johnnie Johnson, and several stills from *Go, Johnny, Go*, many of which had never been seen before. These pictures and the title track were the closest Berry came to revealing his personal life to the world until *The Autobiography* was published some 16 years later.

And once again, it was Berry's personal life that was taking the spotlight; specifically, it was Berry Park, which now seemed to be a small anarchic island in a sea of conformity. Inspired by the hippie ideal of the late 1960s, Berry seems to have let the public have almost free run of the place. One fan, John Etheredge, claimed Berry extended an open invitation for all to stay free of charge during a 1968 appearance on the *Tonight Show*; testing out the invitation two year later, Etheredge was elated to be asked to stay first at the lodge on the grounds at Berry Park and then, when the lodge was full, to sleep on the sofa in Berry's house in the park. "Chuck goes out of his way to make me feel at ease," Etheredge was to write years later. "I offer to pay for my food and lodging, but he [Berry] is adamant that the treat is on him."

After his appearances at the 1968 Miami Pop Festival and the Toronto Rock Festival in 1969, and inspired by the growing successes of the big outdoor music festivals at the beginning of the 1970s, Berry decided to use the park as a venue for a series of self-produced festivals, the first of which was held over the last weekend of August 1970. On a warm, muggy weekend, 500 people paid $2 each to hear several local bands and Chuck Berry, backed by Billy Peek's band. That same weekend, Jimi Hendrix and Jim Morrison were making the final appearances of their lives and Bob Dylan was making his comeback at the Isle of Wight Festival in England.

Berry's second festival, in July 1972, was slightly more ambitious, although it again featured mostly local acts. Disregarding the lessons of history, or at least the Rolling Stones' experience at the Altamont Speedway a few years earlier, Berry hired local bikers as security, and for one brief moment it looked as if history might repeat itself. At some point during the festivities, one of guards, George Clark, fired a shotgun into a small group of festival goers "in an attempt to maintain order." Clark hit and injured John Greenwalt; a year later, Greenwalt and his mother filed suit against Berry, Themetta Berry, and Clark for $100,000. Interestingly, Berry's account of the incident in *The Autobiography* has the shooting occurring between two boys attending a dance at Berry Park. Berry claims that he settled with Greenwalt and his mother (who both remain nameless in *The Autobiography*), paying $450 for medical services and an $800 attorney bill; in fact, the suit was finally settled out of court three years after the incident, with neither party disclosing the actual amount paid.

But it was the final festival, held on July 4, 1974, that forced Berry to rethink his *laissez-faire* policy for the park. A far more ambitious affair than the previous two, it was to feature a number of national acts—including the Band, Leon Russell, Dave Mason, Peter Frampton, and REO Speedwagon— and seven local bands. Berry had entered into an agreement with local promoter Ed Hindelang to lease the park for the day. The first signs of trouble occurred the day before the show when Monarch, a New York company hired by Hindelang to take care of the show production, backed out of the show when they did not receive payment. On the morning of the show, ticket takers at the gate at Berry Park began taking tickets from concert goers; instead of ripping them in half, however, they kept them intact, resold them to others, and pocketed the money. Without adequate supervision of ticket sales at the gate nearly half of the estimated 20,000 crowd entered the park without paying. With less money than anticipated to pay for security, Hindelang left the site at 4:30 that afternoon; more importantly, all of the headliners except the Band and REO Speedwagon canceled just before they were due to go on stage.

Fortunately, the quality of the show was strong enough to appease the crowd that sat through the sweltering heat. Merril Brown of *The St. Louis Post-Dispatch* commented that the "sound system, believe it or not, was quite good," and found much to praise in the appearance of the Hillman, Furay, Souther Band. After a series of other, less memorable appearances by Atlanta's Hydra, the Sons of Champlain from San Francisco, the female band Isis, and Jo Jo Gunne (an aptly named band, given the host), Brown found the "warmth and vigor" of the Band and the hard-rocking well-received set of REO Speedwagon to be the real highlights in an otherwise disastrous day. Although a few members of the crowd were angered by the last-minute cancelations and broke windows in the living quarters at the park, most were well-behaved. But the organizational problems, as well as litter and traffic problems, were enough to convince Berry that there would be no more such events at Berry Park. In typical fashion, however, The *St. Louis Post-Dispatch* reported that Berry managed to be "one of the few nonperformers who was paid anything near what was due him," receiving only $2,900 less than the agreed upon amount for the lease of the property (which, Hindelang maintained, was an "under-the-table" agreement for $20,000).

But if Berry was quick to learn from his mistakes in the rock-festival business, it was probably one of the few successful decisions he made in managing Berry Park during that time. Just a month later, on August 11, Marsha, Bridgette, and Michelle Walters (ages 14, 11, and 10) with their friend, 13-year-old Deira (Dede) Cross, waded into the deep part of the guitar-shaped swimming pool. The girls were not good swimmers, and in the absence of any markers or signs indicating how deep they were venturing, they began to struggle. There were no lifeguards on duty at the park—St. Charles County ordinances did not require any at that time—nor were there ordinances requiring depth markers, even though it was a public pool. It was only the screams of one of the girls that alerted anyone to the fact that there was a problem. Clyde Peterson, who was close by playing volleyball, was the first on the scene, and was able to save Marsha; Michelle, too, was rescued; but, despite the efforts of the Wentzville Volunteer Fire Department and the National Ambulance Service, who worked on the other girls for 30 minutes, both Dede and Bridgette died.

It was not the first time someone had drowned in the pool at Berry Park. In 1968, Jacob Young, a 21 year-old St. Louis man, had drowned, leading to a lawsuit filed in 1970 against Berry for $50,000. That suit was settled out of court for $3,000 in November 1974, but not before Berry Park had attracted so much attention that the St. Charles County prosecuting attorney's office felt that the time had come to shut the operation down. On August 24, 1974, some 40 officers raided the park during one of the Saturday night dances, marking the culmination of two years of observation and a two-week undercover operation. Altogether, the officers arrested nearly 20 adults and nine juveniles, including some as young as 12, for various drinking and drug offenses. One of those arrested was Francine Gillium, who was charged with allowing alcohol to be present after 10:00 P.M. in the club (the club was not licensed and had a "BYOB" policy, which, under local law, meant that all drinking had to be over by 10:00) and contributing to the delinquency of a minor. Finally, about two weeks later, the Park was closed down for six months, with St. Charles County Circuit Judge William M. Turpin on September 9 citing "liquor and narcotics violations . . . one shooting, three rapes and several other violations." Less than a week later, Berry was hit with another lawsuit, this time for $100,000 by Bridgette Walters's parents.

By the time Berry Park was allowed to reopen in May 1975, hippie idealism had given way to hard-nosed pragmatism. Berry was forced to acknowledge that he could no longer take a hands-off approach to managing the park in the increasingly litigious times. In fact, although Chuck Berry himself cannot be held directly responsible for any of the events that occurred at the park during the mid-1970s, his lack of attention to the day-to-day running of his business affairs was another reminder of his poor judgment in so many areas of his personal life. From then on, Berry Park was open by invitation only, home to various family functions and private parties; it began a long, slow decline through the next 15 years, culminating in further scandal in the early 1990s.

All of the domestic events of 1974 seemed to have little effect on Berry, however. Less than two days after the raid on Berry Park, Berry was in New York for a three-day recording session that resulted in the last album he would make for his old record label. Titled simply *Chuck Berry*, it proved to be a fitting swansong for the label, however, with delightful surprises throughout. The original songs, although still not approaching the great songs of the past, were better than the offerings on *Bio*, with some fine vocal support from daughter Ingrid and, on "Sue Answer," some nice piano work from Berry himself. Even two potentially bad choices of cover material, "South of the Border" and "You Are My Sunshine," fared well, the latter again with some nice piano touches by Berry.

But it is the cover material that made the album worth the price of admission, as Berry revisited his rock-and-roll past, particularly the legacy of songs associated with Chicago and Chess Records. The album included fine readings of two Willie Dixon tunes, the 1954 Muddy Waters classic "I Just Want to Make Love to You" and a funked-up version of Little Walter's hit "My Babe" from the following year. Added to them was a driving version of "Hi Heel Sneakers," first recorded by Chess labelmate Tommy Tucker in 1964; a version of "Baby, What You Want Me to Do," another great Chicago blues tune recorded by Jimmy Reed for Vee Jay in 1960; and, perhaps most appropriate of all, a version of "Shake, Rattle and Roll," with lyrics outdoing Big Joe Turner's original in typical Berry style: "You ain't been wearing no bra, you just let them boogie choogie bop."

The album was released in February 1975, but met with no success, even though American-roots rock and roll was experiencing an upsurge in popularity at the time. With the first rumblings of punk and disco still on the musical horizon, this was the time of Bruce Springsteen's *Born to Run* and, a year later, Bob Seger's *Night Moves*, which featured the song "Old Time Rock and Roll," an homage to Berry and the music of the 1950s. Certainly, GRT must take some of the blame; their management of the Chess catalog, which began so disastrously with Leonard Chess's death, had never been more than perfunctory. Consequently, by the end of 1975, GRT sold the Chess catalog, and under new owner Joe Robinson, *Chuck Berry* and the entire Chess catalog languished for nearly a decade, with little or no effort made to promote the product or the artists still under contract to the label. Eventually, in 1986, Robinson's company, All-Platinum, went bankrupt, and the Chess catalog was finally acquired by MCA, a major corporate label. But Chuck Berry had long since disappeared from the label; after Robinson's acquisition of the label, Berry negotiated a settlement with the company, leaving him free to record for another company but leaving his extensive and remarkable recorded legacy behind. Sadly, however, it was a legacy that would be overshadowed by more personal issues over the course of the rest of his life.

The Whole World Knows the Music, Nobody Knows the Man

He's the most difficult person I've ever worked with and probably ever will. When Chuck says, "Okay, I'll do it," he'll do it to some percentage of what he says he'll do. He's always going to throw you a curve. . . . He's an enigmatic, very complex guy . . . and underneath all that, I came out really liking him after this experience.

—Taylor Hackford, 1987

For African Americans, the post-Civil Rights era in America was a contradictory mix of advancements and setbacks. Institutionalized Jim Crow segregation had been dismantled, although the gains were often long in coming; the St. Louis school system, for example, did not fully integrate until 1980, 26 years after the *Brown v. Board of Education* decision. Simultaneously, the black working class was still being crushed by the burden of poverty. By the 1970s, for example, East St. Louis—where Chuck Berry had begun his rise to stardom just three decades earlier—had, according to the U.S. Department of Housing and Urban Development, become "the most distressed small city in America." By 1971, the population had declined from a postwar high of 80,000 to 50,000; by the 1980s, 98 percent of the city's population was black, "a third of its families live[d] on less than $7,500 a year," and "75 percent of its population live[d] on welfare of some form." Smoke and pollution blanketed the city from the nearby Pfizer and Monsanto chemical plants, raw sewage seeped into the local high school on a constant basis, and the city ranked higher than Chicago or any other city in Illinois in fetal deaths and premature births. It was, according to the chairman of the Illinois State Board of Education, "simply the worst possible place I can imagine to have a child brought up."

At the same time, the black population of East St. Louis was coping with such oppressive poverty, blacks elsewhere were enjoying significant gains in working-class and professional occupations, and black consciousness was rising considerably in the media. Nevertheless, acts of brutal racism were never far from view: Yusef Hawkins's shooting in the white New York neighborhood of Bensonhurst in 1989; Rodney King's beating at the hands of Los Angeles police in 1991 and the riot the next year that followed the acquittal of the officers involved; and the 1998 death of James Byrd, Jr., after being dragged behind a pickup truck in Jasper, Texas, were just three vivid reminders that racism still thrived in post-Civil Rights America.

In some ways, Chuck Berry's post-Chess Records career mirrored this larger, contradictory picture. Freed from the poverty that endured in the black community and firmly a member of the black upper class, Berry still remained a target for many unscrupulous whites. And, although he began to reap the awards and honors that come with longevity in the entertainment business, he continued to feel the need to jealously guard his private life, concentrating much of his energy in hiding himself from the world outside of Wentzville in Berry Park.

At no time were these contradictions more evident than in 1979, when nearly every facet of Berry's life and career seemed to converge in a few short months. That February, Berry assembled several of his old cohorts, including Johnnie Johnson and bassist Jim Marsala, to record material for what would become the last studio album he would release to date. The session progressed in a similar fashion to the sessions that produced *Concerto in B. Goode*, *San Francisco Dues*, and many of the songs on *Bio* and *Chuck Berry*; Berry had total control of the material from its conception to its final mix. Jim Marsala remembers that the entire album was put together over two days in the clubhouse studio of Berry Park in a very matter-of-fact way:

> Chuck had been working on the songs for quite a while. When he got the ideas down, he would put a certain amount of that in the tracks and then call me. And I would listen to the tracks and I'd go over the stuff. He'd kinda say "Well, I'd like you to try to do this or do that," you know. And that was how we did it; he'd say, "Play what you want to play," and then start picking that apart. . . . "Do this here, do that there," that kind of thing.

In the cyclical world of music, Berry's method of recording the album, which had been so anachronistic and worked against him in the late 1960s and early 1970s, now seemed up-to-date. After all, in the era of punk rock, this do-it-yourself approach had resulted in a number of acts becoming noticed by the record companies; the kind of independence that had enabled Berry to survive for so long in the music business was now being adopted by a whole new generation of musicians. According to Jim Marsala, Berry took the tapes of the February sessions and sold them to Atco, a division of the Atlantic label, with little or no input from the company. "When most of the recording was done," Marsala remembered, "I think he took that to the record company. And they got interested in it and they came along and I guess they made him an offer that was acceptable to him."

The end result, an album that became known as *Rockit*, like most of Berry's later Chess recordings, was pleasant enough, although it broke little new musical ground. "Move It," the album's lead cut, for example, lyrically reprised "Brown Eyed Handsome Man" with its references to a bases-loaded ballgame and a woman the singer desires, although this time she was not the Venus De Milo but a more contemporary disco queen. The tension between Berry's minor-key guitar chords and Johnson's major-key triplets added a real spark to the piece; in fact, Johnson's contributions to the whole album showed him to be back in form after his disastrous contributions to the Mercury recordings over a decade before. "O What a Thrill" and "I Need You Baby" also made musical and lyrical references to other, older Berry songs ("Back in the U.S.A." and "It Hurts Me Too," respectively); a remake of "Havana Moon," with its hi-hat driven disco treatment, was far less subtle than the original, with Berry's more pronounced faux-Jamaican accent tending to obscure the humor of the lyrics.

In all, it was a polished performance, although the references to the current disco-music trend were not enough to make the material sound new or contemporary. Still, Tom Carson's review in *Rolling Stone* was generally positive. Carson felt that Chuck Berry had at last "made an album that displays all his old skills in fine form. Indeed," he went on to say, "Berry makes the role of old master seem less musty and more spirited than ever."

The satisfaction of having completed the album was to fade all too quickly, however; on June 11 Chuck Berry, pled guilty to tax evasion, marking the end of a five-year investigation by the Internal Revenue Service. A month earlier, Berry had surrendered himself to the U.S. District Court in downtown St. Louis to answer three federal indictments, all from 1973; the first involved a charge of evading taxes, and the second two involved filing false tax returns, the first for himself and Themetta, and second for Chuck Berry Music, Inc. The charges were substantial. In the tax evasion charge, for example, the IRS claimed that the Berrys had attempted to evade about $109,000 in taxes. Added to the two false filing charges, Chuck Berry faced maximum charges of 11 years in prison and fines up to $20,000.

According to Chuck Berry, the charges stemmed from two separate sources of income during 1973. The first was the January tour of England, where Berry maintains a mistake by the promoter led to only half of his fee for the tour appearing on the contract. The other half—up-front money that had already been paid, along with cash payments for two hastily arranged concerts at the tour's conclusion—was never accounted for on the agreement; all told, the discrepancy was somewhere in the order of $45,000. The second came from under-the-table arrangements with Richard Nader for an unspecified number of concerts. These payments immediately aroused IRS agents' suspicions as, on the tax forms for that year, Berry's performance fees fluctuated wildly, from his usual guarantee of $10,000 a night to a union scale wage of $280 for many of the Nader shows.

Berry has never suggested publicly that the charges were not justified. In 1983, for example, he told John Etheredge of *Goldmine*, "This tax thing that I was in was no bum rap. It was straight, true. It was a bum rap in the sense that . . . it was about fifteen percent that they added, but that's nothing to kick about. In other words, they were 85 percent right and 15 percent wrong." And in *The Autobiography*, Berry was frank about his willingness to take cash-only payments. Speaking of his relationship with Richard Nader, Berry wrote that the promoter had often called at the last minute "quoting me one fee for our contract . . . and another amount to be handed under the table." This arrangement Berry christened "malparamanopo . . . my word for 'bad-two-person-operation,'" suggesting that Chuck Berry was an all-too-willing partner in the enterprise.

Even so, the investigation and subsequent conviction were not without irregularities. Billy Peek, for example, now playing guitar for Rod Stewart's band, noted the ferocity of the government's prosecution when he was called in to talk to the Attorney General of Missouri at some point the following year. At first, Peek was reluctant to talk to him, and called his former boss. Chuck Berry, he recalled, was more worried about his friend than himself: "Chuck says to me, 'Well, go on down there, Billy, and talk to them, 'cause if you don't they'll subpoena you.' And he says, 'You can't hurt me.'"

When Peek finally arrived at the Attorney General's office, "it went down just like I thought it would. They were asking me: 'Well, did you ever see any money change hands between Chuck Berry and promoters? How much do you think somebody like Chuck Berry makes?'" Out of loyalty, but also out of honesty, Billy Peek couldn't answer their questions. "I just told them, 'You gotta understand. I don't see money change hands, I don't know what he makes.' I said, 'That is not my interest. My interest is, Chuck comes to me, he says, "Billy, I want you to go on a European tour." He tells me how much he is willing to pay me, and I say yes or no. That's my interest.'"

In addition to trying to get Billy Peek to entrap his former employer, Peek also sensed that one IRS investigator especially was out to get Chuck Berry. "There was this one guy," Peek remembered, "He was one of the investigators, he was like an underling. And he was hot and heavy to get Chuck; he said, 'We're going to try and prosecute him here in Missouri, he can get eleven years for this.'"

Billy Peek also remembers that Berry was wary of going through another court battle in his hometown. The bitterness of the Mann Act conviction, the illegality of the St. Charles police search 20 years earlier, and the hassles from the St. Charles county police over the recent incidents at Berry Park had convinced him that he was not going to get a fair trial in St. Louis. Additionally, Peek recalled Berry feeling that it would be better to "get tried by people who know what show business is like"; consequently, because Berry owned a home in Los Angeles, the case was moved there.

In the end, Chuck Berry entered into a plea bargain with federal prosecutors; in exchange for dropping the two false filing charges, Berry agreed to plead guilty to a single charge of evading $110,000 in income tax. The judge in the case, Judge Harry Pragerson, suspended a three-year sentence and instead sentenced Berry to 120 days in federal prison and four years' probation, during which he was to prove 1,000 hours of community service. According to a UPI report, during the sentencing on July 10, Berry "appeared nervous during the court session and twice broke into tears" as he made his plea.

But the greatest irony of the whole affair, one that seemed to perfectly illustrate the vagaries of Chuck Berry's career and of blacks in the post-Civil Rights era, was that, only three days earlier, Chuck Berry had played on the White House lawn for a gathering of the Black Music Association, President Jimmy Carter, and the first family. It was, by all accounts, a truly humbling experience for Berry. As he stepped up to the microphone, a broad smile made its way across his face. "Mr. President, Mrs. Carter," spoke Berry in subdued tones and without a hint of irony, "and especially Amy, for it's your generation that caused my career to spiral where it is, I am deeply glad to be here, and honored to be here. A very warm feeling for my country came over me when I heard the President call my name. Believe me, I think I'm a different person." Then, with a grin, he added, "I'll try to entertain you now," before launching into "Roll Over Beethoven."

The moment was captured on tape by a BBC camera crew that had been following Berry around for the past few weeks for a documentary. It was really the first in-depth look at the enigmatic entertainer's life to that point; although he had given a handful of interviews throughout the years, this was one of the first times anyone had ever really tried to capture his essence on camera. The film, eventually aired in 1980 under the name "Johnny B. Goode," was a low-budget affair, directed by Ted Clisby for the British current-affairs show *Omnibus*, and shot mostly on location in Wentzville and at two live shows at the Keystone Club in Palo Alto, California, and the Apollo Delman Theater in Tulsa, Oklahoma. What made the hour-long show compelling, however, were two telling segments that revealed Berry's distrust of promoters and his unwillingness to let details of his private life become public.

The first segment, captured at the show in Palo Alto, showed Berry haranguing the concert promoter from the stage. Clearly, the promoter had not read Berry's contract closely and had failed to secure the Dual Showman amplifiers that were always stipulated. Sheepishly, the promoter announced to the crowd, "We got one minor problem. The agent who booked the show explained to us what the equipment was that we needed, so we supplied the equipment that was specified and it was not specified properly what was needed. So Mr. Berry's going to perform with about half of what he normally does."

At that, Chuck Berry turned to the younger man and admonished him. "Uh-uh," he said, just out of range of the microphone, "don't say that." Then, Berry took off his guitar and began animatedly talking into the promoter's ear. Eventually, Berry broke off the conversation, and telling the promoter to "Come on," he backed away to give the promoter a chance to redeem himself to the crowd. Quietly, he began, "We did not supply the amplifiers that we should have ... " to which Berry retorted, "Say it again!" Then, louder, the promoter repeated his announcement. "We did not supply the amplifiers that we should have," he said, "and I hope you enjoy the show as it is."

Significantly, although the scene was played out in public on stage, the encounter did not seem to be an overtly hostile confrontation on Berry's part; Berry was, it must be said, in control at all times, speaking in normal tones throughout the incident. It was also not a moment when Berry held the promoter hostage to get what he wanted; the demands of the contract, while unusual, were not unreasonable. The promoter's double talk and unwillingness to admit his mistake from the outset clearly irked Berry, who went on to execute a fine performance despite the handicap of playing on substandard equipment and the ill-feeling the promoter had caused. It led Ted Clisby to edit in a segment to the documentary, shot in the Berry Park studio, where Berry once again explained his business philosophy. "I have tried to curb the manners by which I have been ripped off," he said to the camera, "so that it don't happen again, which has given me a reputation of being, cynical is it? It's not that I'm distrustful, it's just that if the same type of dog comes up and you think that he'll bite you, well move out."

Then, Clisby himself found himself on the receiving end of Chuck Berry's subdued anger. Toward the end of the film, Clisby turned to the Mann Act conviction, something that Berry had now begun to deny in public. In 1972, for example, in the same *Rolling Stone* interview with William Patrick Salvo in which he discussed the making of the *London Chuck Berry Sessions*, Berry told Salvo that he had never been to prison for the incident. "Nothing really came of it," he told the journalist, referring to the 1959 arrest. "You see, there were two or three different trials, and one was thrown out of the courts because the judge was fairly biased and finally I was acquitted, you see." And, he went on, "take a look at any of the local papers and you will see that I was acquitted. I never went to jail."

In the documentary, Clisby asks Berry about an encounter they had had earlier with an Officer Medley, whom Berry had led Clisby to believe was the officer who had arrested him in St. Charles in 1958. Berry, who had been staring motionless at the speaker, immediately responded. "That's a lie," he said in hushed tones, "I did not say that to you, and if you're trying to invoke some sort of a response from me from that. . . . Now when we stopped and took pictures, because I take pictures of an officer [it] does not mean I was arrested by him." And, to punctuate the point, there was a long, uncomfortable silence broken by Berry's accusing, "Well?"

Clisby, out of camera range, quietly responded, "Well, you said 'That was the man back in '59.'" To which the still impassive, staring Berry shot back, "You're repeating yourself." Clisby, realizing the situation was becoming increasingly awkward, laughed nervously. "Well," he said, "that's what you said to me."

"Well," repeated Berry, calmly, "I'll have to call you a liar again."

"So you don't want to talk about that area?" Clisby asked.

"There was no talk of the area," Berry quietly responded, as he leaned toward the the camera.

"Well," Clisby continued, "we talked about the Mexican girl."

And at this, Chuck Berry stood up, and with a "We're finished," walked out of the Berry Park recording studio. It was a moment of pure drama, one that would be repeated again in seven years time when another director, in the same location, would get a similar response to equally probing personal questions.

But if Chuck Berry could duck questions about his last jail sentence, he could not avoid the reality of his next term. On August 10, 1979, after being granted permission to play a 12-date European tour, Berry entered Lompoc Federal Correctional Institute, a little over an hour's drive north of Los Angeles. To those who knew him at the time, the sentence seemed hardly to affect him; Jim Marsala noted, "he just doesn't let stuff like that bother him." In fact, the bassist explained to Billy Peek, Berry was even "glad of it because he needed a rest." In fact, according to Berry, it was in Lompoc that he finally decided to write his autobiography, handwriting the first parts of the draft and mailing it back to Wentzville for Francine Gillium to type.

Between his release from Lompoc in November of 1979 and the publication of *The Autobiography* in October of 1987, Chuck Berry's career seemed to slow down significantly. In *The Autobiography*, Berry maintains that he played a little more than 300 concerts in that time; an average of about 40 shows a year for the eight year period. The shows garnered mixed reviews, well to be expected for a performer in his 50s, although there were still occasional flashes of brilliance. In 1981, a show at the Ritz in New York was well received; Stephen Holden, reviewing the show for the *New York Times*, wrote that Berry "performed impressively" and praised his "loose-limbed acrobatics and his unquenchably sassy attitude toward his songs."

But the Ritz show would be remembered more for an incident that occurred backstage. As Keith Richards of the Rolling Stones told it in 1986:

> [It] was in the dressing room. . . . I went up to say "hello," and he was just leaving with a little bit of white tail. And I made the mistake of tapping him on the shoulder; I said, "Hey, Chuck, don't rush off without saying hello. . . . " And he just turned round and just gave me a full shot right in the face. I was very proud of the fact I didn't go down. He's the only guy that hit me that I never got back.

A year later, however, a show at the same venue illustrated just how erratic Chuck Berry's live performances had become. Fred Rothwell, reviewing a bootleg performance of the show, accused Berry of turning in a "perfunctory performance . . . peppered with off-schedule notes." Perhaps the show's only redeeming feature occurred in Berry's introduction of Keith Richards to the New York crowd; as the Stones guitarist sat in on the last few numbers of Chuck Berry's set, Berry announced from the stage "For the bo-bo I did, I publicly apologize. This is my main man!"

For some reason, however, the rivalry between the two guitarists—which had begun during Berry's first visit to England in 1964 and that simmered in 1972, when Berry kicked Keith Richards off the stage at a Hollywood concert when Richards began to play too loudly—continued unabated. Two years after the incident at the Ritz, Berry's reaction to encountering Richards again at the Los Angeles airport was to light a match and throw it down Richards's shirt. As Richards saw it, "Every time him and me got in contact, whether it's intentional or not, I end up getting wounded." But, because Richards was still such a disciple and a confirmed fan of Chuck Berry's, it seemed only natural that the honor of inducting Berry into the Rock and Roll Hall of Fame during its first-ever ceremony should fall to the Rolling Stones' guitarist. Fittingly, Richards acknowledged in his speech that, "It's hard for me to induct Chuck Berry, because I lifted every lick he ever played!"

Sharing the same table as Berry and Richards at the luxurious Waldorf Astoria Hotel in New York City that night in January 1986 was a young English literary agent and film producer named Stephanie Bennett. At some point that evening, the talk turned to Berry's impending 60th birthday that year, and the idea of filming a concert in St. Louis, with Richards playing in and leading an all-star band behind Berry, started to take shape. For Richards, it was the beginning of a ten-month odyssey that would ultimately frustrate and anger him, yet satisfy his burning urge to pay the ultimate tribute to the man who had inspired him to a life in music. As he was to say later in *Chuck Berry: Hail! Hail! Rock 'n' Roll*, the movie that was eventually made from the concert, "I wanted to serve Chuck up with a good band. I never heard him play in tune. I've been so disappointed with Chuck Berry's live gigs for years and years and years every time I've seen him. . . . But if anybody was going to do it, I wanted it to be me."

For several months, Bennett's production company, Delilah Films; Taylor Hackford, the director she had chosen for the project; Keith Richards; and Chuck Berry planned the concert and movie. Eventually, one afternoon in mid-September a small Nissan pickup truck loaded down with sound equipment wound its way south from the Wentzville exit of Interstate 70 and along Buckner Road to Berry Park. Its driver, Mark Slocombe, could not believe he was making the trip. A local musician, music store and recording studio owner, and an experienced sound engineer for over 15 years, he had been hired by Tom Adelman of Delilah Films to provide equipment and run sound for rehearsals for an upcoming movie. When Adelman called several weeks earlier, Slocombe was convinced it was one of his customers playing a prank. "Imagine," he was to remember years later, "getting a phone call from some mild-mannered East Coast guy saying 'Yeah, we're shooting a film with Eric Clapton and Keith Richards and Chuck Berry there in your area and we're looking for someone to help us out!'"

Within five minutes of entering the clubhouse at Berry Park, however, Slocombe came face to face with the park's owner; it was a meeting that, for Slocombe at least, was something of a shock. "He had a bandanna tied around his head," the soundman remembered of his first meeting with Chuck Berry:

> He looked like an old hippie, and he was carrying a mop. There was a leak in the roof of the bathroom; you could see sunlight pouring in back there. And we had had some pretty heavy rain so there was a lot of water laying on the floor, and he headed back to the bathroom to mop it up.

Most of all, Slocombe remembered from that first encounter the hand he had just shaken: "His hands were all crippled up. As I was shaking his hand I was thinking that his fingers just felt so old and arthritic, the skin on his hand was just so limp."

Keith Richards's reaction on encountering Chuck Berry at his home for the first time was, like Mark Slocombe's, something of a shock. Arriving in Wentzville for the first time that July to begin planning the rehearsals, Richards was surprised to find that Berry's living room contained "two large video screens. One played whatever he selected. The other ran constant footage of naked white girls throwing pies at each other and falling over." A month later, Richards invited Berry to his home in Jamaica, where Berry began to behave "like a fish out of water, flipping about enigmatically. One minute he was enthusiastic and entertaining the next—poof!—he would withdraw into a stony silence." They were indications of Chuck Berry's deep discomfort around other people and of his dependence on the safety of Berry Park, where his inner nature could be given free reign.

But as Mark Slocombe had noticed, the fabric of Berry Park had crumbled to an alarming degree. In addition to the gaping hole in the bathroom ceiling, there were holes elsewhere in the roof of the clubhouse. One room had been outfitted as a recording studio, and at one point early in the rehearsals Chuck Berry invited director Taylor Hackford and several others to listen to some new songs he had been working on. In the room, Slocombe remembered, there was an "MCI 24-track recorder, real nice MCI automated mixing console. And there were holes in the roof just like in the bathroom, and it's been raining on this equipment." So wet was the equipment that, as Berry turned up the volume on the console, Slocombe and Hackford witnessed "this roaring blast of static and crackle." Worse, the dampness had got into the recording tape, causing the magnetic surface of the tape to separate from its backing. As Chuck Berry began to play the songs for Hackford, Mark Slocombe watched as "giant hunks of oxide began spraying off of the tape, peeling off like an orange peel!" Then, when Berry put his hand onto the tape to stop it from disintegrating, "a big head gate, that comes up on the play-back head [of the tape recoder] to cut down hum, snaps shut and almost cut his fingers off."

Elsewhere around the park, Mark Slocombe witnessed even more drastic signs of decay. The small, overnight guest rooms built behind the stage of the clubhouse "hadn't been used in a long time, there was crap piled up all over the place, stuff thrown in there stored." Beer glasses sitting on glass shelves in the bar area "were piled with dead bugs and spider webs"; the guitar-shaped swimming pool "was half full of brown muck and dead frogs"; and "out back of the place there was a whole bunch of mobile homes that looked like they got dropped from helicopters, crushed and folded up."

Against this backdrop, the band began their rehearsals for the shows; initially, the sessions seemed to be fairly relaxed and amicable. Mark Slocombe remembers hooking up a turntable to the sound system he had installed in the clubhouse and listening to Berry's old Chess recordings while Steve Jordan, drummer for the *Late Night with David Letterman* band, wrote down charts for all the potential songs. An old sofa was moved in front of the stage, and for most of the proceedings, Chuck Berry sat or lay on the couch and played and sang along. Then, with a week to go before the film crew's arrival, Berry left rehearsals for Pittsburgh to play a show at Three Rivers Stadium after a Pirates baseball game. It was to be the highlight of a dismal, losing season for the ball club; to make up for their 62–94 record, the club had hired Berry and the Four Tops to give their fans something to cheer about during their last home game. But as fate would have it, the game went into extra innings, past the time Berry was contracted to play. As was now his established custom in situations like this, Berry got back into his rented Cadillac and headed back to the Pittsburgh airport without playing a note.

On the Monday following the game, Berry stormed into the clubhouse where the band was taking a break between rehearsals. According to Mark Slocombe, Berry began pacing around the room, shouting, "I'm going to beat that rap; they're not going to take me down." Then, just as abruptly as he came, Berry left, and all the musicians in the room turned to look at Johnnie Johnson. And the piano player, who had been found and brought back to play with his old bandmate for this special show, just shrugged his shoulders and uttered, in Mark Slocombe's words, "one of the funniest lines I've ever heard. They're all looking at Johnnie Johnson and Johnnie Johnson says, 'Hey, you all know Chuck just as good as I do; I've just known him longer!'" Slocombe immediately realized the significance of the comment: Nobody, not even someone who had known him for thirty years, truly knew the man.

A little over a week after that incident, Taylor Hackford and his crew arrived in St. Louis to begin filming in earnest. Problems began immediately. The first day of the shoot called for a trip out to the Algoa Reformatory in Jefferson City, where Chuck Berry had been imprisoned in 1944. On a previous trip with Hackford several weeks earlier, Berry had nearly caused a riot; according to Hackford, Berry had turned up with a "female friend with a miniskirt up to her pupick," and an impromptu concert caused the guards and administration to become very concerned. But Berry backed out from the shoot at the last minute and, although he promised to talk about the incident, "He just kept putting it off. In the end," Hackford said, he "just reneged," just as he had done with Ted Clisby several years before.

After that, shooting ran a little more smoothly. Planned shots of Berry Park and the shots at the Fox Theater box office went off without a hitch, as did interior shots at the Cosmopolitan Club, although the film crew had to work around the clock to get the place to look like even a shadow of its former self. By the time Mark Slocombe and the sound crew arrived, the crew had spent "about seventy hours getting ready for it—shoveling out about two feet of mud, putting a drop ceiling in, putting in a bar. They really brought the place back to life, it was just a dilapidated piece of crap before we went there." Then, later on the same day of the Cosmo shoot, Berry hopped a plane to Columbus, Ohio, to play a show, scheduled at the last minute, with Hackford and a three-man crew tagging along to film the proceedings.

The following day, it was back to the Cosmo to film three songs for the movie, then two more days of filming final rehearsals at Berry Park. It was at this point that tensions between Chuck Berry and his guests came to a boil; with Taylor Hackford's cameras rolling, they were captured for the world to see. The tensions began over Berry's guitar sound. The first bone of contention, Mark Slocombe maintained, was over the fact that Berry was charging Delilah Films to rent his Fender Dual Showman amplifiers for the duration of the shoot. "The film was having to pay him, I forget, $800 a day or something to rent this equipment for him to use," according to Slocombe, causing a rift between Berry and the lesser-paid members of the crew. Then, Berry insisted on running his guitar the way he had always done—which would not allow it to be recorded properly. Slocombe noticed that Berry had "set everything on the amplifier on 9—volume, treble, bass, middle, put it all on 9—and set the volume so far down on the guitar if you turned it down anymore it would go off." On the kind of guitar Chuck Berry uses, a Gibson ES-355, Slocombe noted, "this wrecks the tone. The high frequencies all completely go away; it's very dull sounding when you've got it turned down that low."

Consequently, Slocombe, as the sound engineer for the rehearsals, Dave Hewitt, the recording engineer for the movie, and Alan Rogan, Keith Richards's guitar technician, all decided something should be done. Without consulting Berry, whenever Slocombe and Rogan would walk on stage,

> we'd turn the amplifier volume down on him to about 5. And that would cause him to pull his guitar volume up, and then the sound would get brighter. We kept doing this to get the tone to be better, and finally the shit hit the fan. I had just turned the volume down on his amp again, and he turned and looked at Alan Rogan and I and he started yelling, he just went into a tirade. 'I'm Chuck Berry. This is Chuck Berry's club. This is a Chuck Berry movie, and I don't know who's messing with my stuff. . . . ' And off he went, and the film company's running around and they're shooting this and they're trying to capture that.

By the time Taylor Hackford managed to get his cameras rolling, Keith Richards had jumped in to defend both Alan Rogan, his own employee, and Mark Slocombe, who, Richards realized, as an independent contractor could have been fired instantly. Consequently, when the movie was released the following year, the argument seemed to be solely between Berry and Richards; and the end result was just that, as the two found themselves drawn into yet another confrontation. The part that movie audiences saw began with Berry shouting, "Leave the amp as I set it. It's my amp and I'm setting it the way I wish it." To that Richards responded, "That's going to be how it sounds on the film . . . Why it's being done is because it's not recording well." Fittingly, at least this time, it was Chuck Berry who had the last word. "If it winds up on the film," he said, staring at Richards, "that's the way Chuck Berry plays it. You understand?"

On another occasion, Richards walked Berry through the arrangement he had in mind for "Carol," a song Richards had performed many years before with the Rolling Stones. In negotiating the guitar parts for the song, Richards told Berry he wanted him to play the rhythm part; looking Berry in the eye, he said, "It'll be too much for you to sing and play the lead fills as well." Quickly, Berry sardonically replied, "Well, it wasn't." Clearly, like the argument over the amplifier settings, the situation had crossed over into Berry's personal space. At this point, Berry began to needle Richards, having him go over the tricky two-string prebend and vibrato that introduces the song's chorus a number of times. Then, after several false starts to the section of the song, Berry turned on Richards and chastised him: "If you want to get it right," he said pointedly to his pupil, "get it right!"

Not surprisingly then, "over the course of the film," as Mark Slocombe has maintained, "most of the people involved in the film grew to hate Chuck Berry." Aside from the constant outbursts, there were many other incidents that irritated those involved: "The renting of the amplifiers. . . . picking out the songs; he was putting his will into this and not making the best decisions for the film at any one of those steps. So everybody pretty much grew to hate him." But Keith Richards, acutely aware of his mentor's eccentricities, fully understood that this was a manifestation of Berry's discomfort at the situation unfolding all around him. "I feel sorry for him," Richards said later. "He's a very lonely man. . . . After living that secluded one-man show for so many years, he probably wasn't prepared himself for how he was gonna act."

Stephanie Bennett, too, realized that the issue was one of privacy. "I think it was stunning for him to have people all over his property," she told *Rolling Stones*'s Vince Aletti when the film was eventually released, "he's an *extremely* private person." And as Keith Richards put it in the movie, "He decided to write a book and make a movie, right, and he opened a door and he thought he could just let a few people in and goddammit the whole world came in." Clearly, in Stephanie Bennett's and Keith Richards's minds, the reason for the difficult behavior described by Mark Slocombe and captured by Taylor Hackford was all too clear, especially now that literally hundreds of strangers had invaded his park.

By the time the Fox shows came around, Chuck Berry was emotionally and physically spent. The pressure of performing in front of the cameras, the long hours of rehearsal, and the immense energy needed to keep the world at arm's length had all taken their toll. Berry had sufficiently alienated the band and crew that Mark Slocombe was the only one who would work on his equipment, presenting Slocombe with an opportunity to set up a separate amplifier that could be recorded on the soundtrack, without Berry's knowledge. As the crew set up the day before for the technical rehearsal, "I was the one that had to wire up Chuck's gear," he confessed years later, "everybody else was so pissed off at him nobody would have anything to do with him. I unplugged the chords that went into his amp and sent lines out to the mobile recording truck; the truck in turn turned those around and sent them a couple of levels down in the Fox—they had one of Keith Richards's Mesa Boogie amps down there. And that's mic'ed and that's what's on the tape."

With that act of subterfuge taken care of, Slocombe was free to watch the events unfold on the Fox stage. "We rehearsed in the afternoon before the first show, and Chuck was rewriting the songs on the fly. And at one point he stops the band and he's going, 'No! No! No! That's not how it goes! This is how it goes!'" At this point, Steve Jordan, who had faithfully transcribed the songs from the original Chess albums back at Berry Park weeks before, "started to say something, and Chuck just starts yelling at him, 'These are my songs! These are Chuck Berry songs! I'm Chuck Berry, we're going to do it my way!' So at that point," Slocombe recalled sadly, "all six weeks of rehearsal goes right out the window. Whatever he pulls out of his hat on stage, go with it."

Keith Richards later described the same sinking feeling watching Chuck Berry cast aside all the hard work done on the stage of the Berry Park clubhouse. In the movie, Richards remembers that once the show began, any control he might have had over the proceedings evaporated: "Everybody's lookin' at me on stage once we got up there, totally different arrangements, some in different keys, and I just looked at them, you know—'Wing it, boys!'"

Not only that, Mark Slocombe recalled, "We had so many false starts; you know, they'd intro the band, the curtain opens, the crowd goes wild, and we'd get halfway into the song, Chuck'd muff it so bad we've got to stop, clear the stage, close the curtain, do it all over. We did that like six times in that one concert."

"So about five or six songs into it," Slocombe maintained, "Keith Richards sent a message back for Robert Cray and all of a sudden Robert Cray, with no rehearsal, jumps onto the stage, comes out, now he's part of the band." Cray was one of several special guests scheduled to sing just one song that evening, but he stayed on stage after singing his song, "Brown-Eyed Handsome Man," for most of both shows. "And I was standing behind his amp for most of the show," Mark Slocombe continued, "and I could hear, it was an open-back amp, I could really hear what he's playing, and I'm just hearing him nail this stuff."

With Cray now helping to anchor the band, things began to get less tense; by the time of "Roll Over Beethoven," to hear Richards tell it, "Chuck comes over to me in the middle of the solo and says 'After this we're going to change key'—we were in C at the time—'to B Flat.'" At the time, Richards was mortified by the thought, and the film captures a look of horror and consternation passing over his face. But then Chuck Berry walked away from Richards with an impish grin, suggesting that this was not another confrontational moment, but a playful and mischievous way of getting back at Richards for the grueling rehearsal regimen he had subjected Berry to.

After several more songs, the show moved toward its climax as, one by one, some of the biggest names in rock and R&B made their entrances and showed, in several cases, just what an enormous debt they and popular music owed to Chuck Berry. First up was Julian Lennon, son of the late Beatle, whose version of "Johnny B. Goode," while lacking in finesse, was full of playful energy. Next, Eric Clapton led the band though a soulful rendition of "Wee Wee Hours," which featured such a fluid and expressive solo that Berry knelt in mock-homage at his feet and then entreated him to solo for another twelve measures.

Then, with three numbers to go before the end of the first show, Linda Ronstadt came out to sing "Back in the U.S.A.," a song she had covered and turned into a huge U.S. hit in 1978. Ronstadt, however, had not rehearsed with the band until the afternoon before the show; given that and Chuck Berry's own unpredictability, another disaster was just around the corner. "We rehearsed it in C," Mark Slocombe remembered,

> which is really high but that's where she wanted to sing it at. We get to the stage, they bring her out, they strike the first chord, but instead of playing it in C Chuck plays it in G. And the band is so hot you never hear it in the film; the band autocorrects and we're now in G. Linda Ronstadt's such a pro, you really don't hear her strain or muff it. But I will tell you, she was so pissed off when she walked off that stage she went right through the Green Room, right out the stage door, climbed into her limo and never came back for the second show. I heard that they had a hard time getting her to sign the release for the song because she was so pissed off.

The audience, however, remained oblivious to the backstage drama as Etta James took the stage to belt out a spirited version of "Rock and Roll Music" before the band wrapped up the first show with "Reelin' and Rockin'."

Between shows, according to Daniel Brogan of the *Chicago Tribune*, Keith Richards "took charge. First he won a promise from Hackford that there would be no more than three technical breaks in the second show. Then he got Berry to concede their weeklong battle for control of the band." The result, according to Brogan and the rest of the audience, "was like night and day," with the band stretching out on some improvisational jams and even attempting such live rarities as "Havana Moon" and "Jo Jo Gunne." Finally, in the early hours of October 17, the second show ended with Chuck Berry fittingly wheeled onto the stage in the back of a convertible cherry-red Cadillac as the band started up "School Day," the song that made him the legend now being celebrated amid a storm of confetti on the Fox Theater stage. In the end, the 60th birthday celebration had become a triumph, and Taylor Hackford could begin the long, slow process of constructing his portrait of Chuck Berry.

Wentzville
and St. Charles

Berry's name is listed six times in the Wentzville telephone directory. "Quite rightly so," said the sandy-haired attendant at the Sinclair service station. "Yes sir, that Berry drives his Caddy through town 'bout once a week, then turns around and heads back to 'is farm; thinks he owns the place."
—William Patrick Salvo, 1972.

"If I can be very frank, there is an element in town that probably doesn't like Chuck Berry."
—Mike Roscoe, Wentzville City Coordinator, 1987

In October 1987, *Chuck Berry: Hail! Hail! Rock 'n' Roll* and *The Autobiography* were both released to critical acclaim, and the increased visibility precipitated another renaissance for Chuck Berry's career. Response to the movie was, for the most part, very positive. Richard Harrington, writing in the *Washington Post*, found much to praise. While criticizing its length, calling the two hours "long and unwieldy," Harrington felt that Hackford had hit the mark, saying that "it's probably the most revealing look we'll ever get of its subject, and the most loving evocation of his music." Vince Aletti's review for *Rolling Stone*, although it focused more on the way the movie was produced than on the quality of the final product, also was strongly positive. Aletti called the movie "a vivacious narrative history"and praised the "glimpses of Berry's dark side that make Hackford's portrait so engaging."

Indeed, perhaps the two most dramatic moments in the movie are those in which Chuck Berry successfully hides his private life from Hackford. In scenes reminiscent of the one enacted in front of Ted Clisby during the filming of the *Omnibus* documentary seven years earlier, Berry twice interrupts the filming when Hackford's questions probe a little too deeply into his past; both interruptions, significantly, occur in sequences filmed at Berry Park. The first begins when Hackford suggests that Berry has been less than faithful to his long-time wife, Themeta. In a section focusing on Francine Gillium, he details her history as Berry's assistant, which hints at a relationship far deeper than employer and employee. This is immediately followed by a sequence showing Berry discussing his devotion to Themetta; "I have been married since October 28, 1948," Berry says, stumbling over the dates with the excuse that "it's hard for a man to remember these things." Quickly, though, he adds, "And I guess it will be until 2000 before I even think of separating."

Then Hackford, off camera, asks, "But for all rock-and-roll stars on the road, there's twenty million girls screaming and yelling for them. Is that hard?"

And Berry, whose face has been stony as if he was anticipating Hackford's question, cracks a smile and laughs. "Is what hard?" he jokes before getting serious again. "No, it's not hard. If you have a conviction at your home, if you keep the home fires burning, you do what you wanna do. And as I always said, use discretion, be sensible about it, keep the home fires burning." This is, at the very least, an ambiguous statement, neither admitting to on-road liaisons nor explicitly condemning them.

At this point, we hear Themetta Berry's voice while pictures of the Berrys' wedding appear on the screen. "My name is Themetta Suggs Berry," she says as the film cuts to her with Berry Park as her backdrop. "I have been married to Charles Berry for thirty-eight years. We have had a wonderful marriage; we love each other as much as we did the day we met."

Then Hackford, again out of view, asks, "You had been married for about five years . . . " and, before she has time for an answer, Chuck, who is also off camera, says, "Come on." At this, Themetta Berry looks toward Chuck expectantly, waiting to see what she should say next; however, Chuck abruptly exclaims, "Next!" and the scene ends just as quickly.

The next nonmusical segment has a similar beginning and end. The scene moves back to the Berry Park offices, where Francine Gillium and Chuck Berry are again listening to Taylor Hackford's off-camera questions. "Chuck has had a couple of run-ins with the law," Hackford begins, and before he can elaborate, Berry breaks in. "Come on, come on," Berry says indignantly and, as Hackford attempts to clarify, Berry breaks in again, "I don't wanna, I don't wanna hear about it." Hackford quickly backs down, saying "All right," before Berry jumps back in one last time, "I don't wanna hear about it. We'll talk about that at the proper place, not over a desk." And the scene is once again abruptly cut. But, Hackford, as director, was able to have the last word, a little joke at Berry's expense. The musical segment he chose to cut in between the two awkward and uncomfortable confrontations is Berry's "Too Much Monkey Business," that litany of trials and tribulations that now becomes Hackford's metaphor for Berry's own life.

The most negative review of the movie and the accompanying *Autobiography* came, unsurprisingly, from Berry's hometown. *The Riverfront Times*, which had been unmerciful in its criticism of the Fox shows the year before, once again attacked the hometown hero. In a piece entitled, "Hail! Hail! The Bankroll," the author, Cliff Froelich, criticized Berry for his love of money, rather than treating the movie on its own merits. The review was rather contradictory; rightly condemning "rockumentaries" of this sort as often turning into "self-glorifying record advertisements," Froelich then criticized Taylor Hackford for turning the film into "more critique than celebration." He then argued that the major theme of the movie was Berry's greed and criticized Hackford for not being explicitly critical of Berry's "penuriousness," while simultaneously acknowledging that Hackford made the theme explicit by returning to it "again and again." Once again, the mean spirit of St. Louis toward its native son was exposed.

Froelich's article also went on to criticize *The Autobiography*, but here Froelich found himself out of step with the critics who almost unanimously praised the work, both for the quality of the writing and for the depth of its content. Don McLeese, for example, writing in the *New York Times Book Review*, found much to praise in Berry's "breezy word-play, obsessive rhyming and alliteration." So did Bob Greene of the *Chicago Tribune*, who found that "the language, the cadence and the rhythm of the sentences were as fascinating and unique as the lyrics to 'Johnny B. Goode.'" Froelich, in contrast, saw only "a puerile, badly written and often nonsensical ramble."

In terms of the book's content, most praised Berry's willingness to be far more candid than he was in Hackford's movie, although all felt Berry had stopped short of revealing everything about himself. As Vince Aletti put it, "what's intriguing about . . . Berry's crazy quilt self-portrait is how much remains unsaid. . . . What Chuck keeps buried between the lines of *The Autobiography* could fill another volume or two." Don McLeese's criticisms, too, suggested another missing element: self-reflection. McLeese wrote, "another writer might have given a more balanced view of his life and legacy," and that Berry "makes his transgressions sound mischievous rather than malevolent." But criticizing Berry for being evasive and self-serving is to point at the fundamental weakness of *all* autobiography, a point especially missed by Cliff Froelich. While praising Berry for being more open in the book than in the movie, Froelich condemned Berry for obscuring the incidents that he describes. "Berry details the sexual and criminal past he refused to discuss in the film," the critic wrote, "but his clotted purplish prose, self-righteousness, and maddening obtuseness place a dark veil over the face of every truth."

Froelich's use of the term "dark veil," whether conscious or not, immediately evokes one of the great metaphors of African-American literature made famous in W. E. B. Du Bois's seminal work on race in America, *The Souls of Black Folk*. Written in 1903, the work begins by describing Du Bois's first encounter with racism while a young boy in school—a white girl's refusal of his visiting card. Of the encounter, Du Bois wrote, "Then it dawned upon me with a certain suddenness that I was different from all the others; or like, mayhap, in heart and life and longing, but shut out from their world by a vast veil." But, rather than attempting to remove or lift the veil, Du Bois is insistent that he "had thereafter no desire to tear down the veil, to creep through." It is a significant realization. For Du Bois, knowledge of the veil did not, as it did for Booker T. Washington, lead to a desire for assimilation; Du Bois categorically did not want to part the veil and strive to be white. Instead, he "simply wishes to make it possible for a man to be both a Negro and American." Thus, Du Bois seems to argue that the veil between the races is necessary, as it allows for this duality, or "double consciousness" as Du Bois calls it, to take place without impunity. The veil becomes important because it protects the individual from "the eyes of others" and prevents others from "measuring one's soul by the tape of a world that looks on in amused contempt and pity." In this sense, it is a metaphor close to Dunbar's mask; it is only when they are hidden, both authors seem to say, that African Americans can truly express their own identity.

What started out as a criticism, then, becomes a way to read Berry's autobiography. There is no doubt that the book is silent or willfully deceptive on many key moments in Berry's personal and professional life. Key events and significant figures are ignored: There is no mention of Alan Freed's "Big Beat" tour of 1958, for example, and no mention of Berry's feuds with Jerry Lee Lewis or the so-called Boston Riot. In fact, there is little or no mention of Berry's contemporaries: Buddy Holly is absent from the pages; Elvis Presley is mentioned once, and that only in death; Jerry Lee Lewis makes a brief appearance, described as being drunk at a German rock festival in 1973; and Bo Diddley is mentioned briefly twice. Only Little Richard makes anything more than a cameo appearance, although that too is limited to an anecdote, a brief dressing-room encounter hinting that Richard made a pass at Berry. Berry's key relationships of the 1950s—with Johnnie Johnson, Leonard Chess, Alan Freed—are all viewed in monochrome: Johnson is portrayed as a drunk and a liability on the road, rather than as a bandmate and fellow musician; Chess is portrayed as deceptive and a cheat, rather than as a mentor and advisor; Freed, too, is portrayed as a cheat and a drunk, rather than as a promoter of Berry's career and a business associate. In part, the omissions are self-serving, because they refuse to acknowledge the key roles others had in shaping Berry's career. But the omissions also serve to protect Berry's own business interests and, in some cases, point to his unwillingness to "kiss and tell," to participate in low-level celebrity gossip.

Later musical relationships are similarly handled: Producer Esmond Edwards is noticeable by his absence, and the discussion surrounding the recording and subsequent release of "My Ding-a-Ling" counters other statements Berry had made publicly on the topic. There is also no mention of any relationship with executives from Mercury or Atco. Keith Richards is mentioned once, and only in connection with the 60th birthday concert. Again, this could be interpreted as a gesture of loyalty toward Richards; there is no mention of the fights in rehearsal, and the only negative thing Berry describes about the whole experience was the length of the first show.

This mixture of self-interest and loyalty also finds its way into many of the names of the characters Chuck Berry chooses to portray. His first two managers are renamed: Jack Hooke becomes "Jack Hook" and, with delicious irony, Teddy Reig becomes "Teddy Roag." Whatever the reason for the misspelling, characterizing Reig as a "rogue" has a poetic justice typical of Berry's fondness for wordplay. A significant number of other names are changed or misspelled, either through poor editing or faulty memory or, most likely, to hide the characters from any further investigation, especially when their relationship to Berry is personal: Janice Escalanti becomes "Janice Escalante"; Joan Mathis is never referred to by Bates or Rolf, the other names by which she was identified in the court documents stemming from the 1958 arrest in St. Charles; and Theresa Schmitt, one of Berry's many female companions in the 1980s, is mentioned by another of her names, Yvonne Cumbie. In fact, it is in the area of personal relationships that the omissions take on great significance. In his discussion of the Mann Act incident, for example, Chuck Berry never admits to having any kind of sexual relationship with Janice Escalanti, even though the trial transcripts strongly point to such a relationship and Berry would not, at the time of writing, have suffered from disclosing the information. Similarly shrouded are Berry's relationships with Francine Gillium and with his wife Themetta; in fact, there is never an overt admission of a sexual relationship with anyone outside of his own marriage, although numerous passages allude to this side of Berry's life.

His description of the relationship he enjoyed with Candace Mossler, the Houston millionairess immortalized in the song "Promised Land," is typical. Here again, a sexual relationship is only hinted at; his descriptions of his encounters with her are loaded with euphemisms. "Another kiss and my curiosity was standing straight up in need of her effective attention," he writes at one point, later adding that he "heard minute moans of a million-dollar approval" after another encounter. But Berry takes great pains to hide from the reader the scandals in which Mossler had become involved during their relationship. Shortly before her death in 1976, *Esquire* magazine dubbed her "the all-time, all-American femme fatale" for being implicated in the murder of her husband Jacques, who had been stabbed and beaten to death in June 1964. Both she and her lover, her nephew Melvin Lane Powers, were arrested and charged with the murder; the subsequent trial was, according to her obituary in *Newsweek*, the "Trial of the Decade," resulting in the sensational acquittal of both Mossler and Powers. The two subsequently parted, but Mossler's next husband, Wade Garrison, almost suffered the same fate as Jacques Mossler, falling from the roof of Candace's Houston mansion in 1972 under mysterious circumstances. Berry's silence on Mossler's life, like the euphemisms and the name changes, simultaneously obscures and protects both Berry and his acquaintances. Berry's refusal to let his readers see behind the veil once again indicates a deep loyalty to others and a need for self-preservation.

The release of both the movie and the book, however, ensured that 1987 ended on a high note. Berry was awarded a star on Hollywood Boulevard, and on November 5 he made a legendary appearance on *The Tonight Show*. Here, after an out-of-tune "Memphis" in which Berry faked out Tommy Newsome and the Tonight Show Band on the song's ending, Berry appeared charming and comfortable as he discussed both the book and the movie. Even a prompt by Carson about his jail time, albeit a superficial one, was met with light talk-show one-liners. A rousing, in-tune "Roll Over Beethoven" followed, and the audience's reaction was so enthusiastic that Carson made a mid-show decision to cancel his two remaining guests and, for one of the few times in Carson's tenure in the chair of *The Tonight Show*, Berry was invited to remain for the whole show. And Berry returned the compliment with an impromptu "Johnny B. Goode" that, Carson revealed at the show's end, was greeted by the studio audience with a standing ovation.

In conversation with Johnny Carson that night, Berry repeated a prediction that he had already written in *The Autobiography*. In his book, he noted that each of his major offenses were symmetrically spaced 17 years apart (1944, 1957, 1974), and predicted that his next one would occur after his release from Lompoc on the tax-evasion charges sometime in 1996. On Carson, his math was somewhat less erratic, as he predicted he had only 4 years to go until the next major controversy in his life; in fact, in less than six weeks, Chuck Berry's personal life was once again in the news. On December 18, while staying at the Gramercy Park Hotel in New York, Chuck Berry was involved in a disturbance that eventually led to his arrest on assault charges. Little is known about the circumstances surrounding the incident; Berry himself has never spoken about it publicly. All that is known is that Berry hit a woman, Marilyn O'Brien Boteler, in the face; the blow was hard enough, according to documents filed in New York Supreme Court, to cause "lacerations of the mouth, requiring five stitches, two loose teeth, [and] contusions of the face."

The following month, an arrest warrant was issued after Berry failed to appear to answer the charges in Manhattan Criminal Court; meanwhile,

Boteler filed a lawsuit against Berry for $5 million. Berry again failed to appear in court when the hearing was rescheduled for June 5. Finally, on November 22, 1988, Berry pleaded guilty, not to the original charge of assault, which could have resulted in a year in jail and a $1,000 fine, but to a lesser charge of harassment, which cost him a mere $250.

Meanwhile, back in Wentzville, Berry purchased and began renovation on the Southern Air, a landmark restaurant in St. Charles County. It was a purchase that was as much symbolic as it was economic, as Berry had described buying food at the kitchen window of the former Jim Crow restaurant (in his autobiography) on the trip to Kansas City in 1944 that ended in his first brush with the law. Renovations on the restaurant were completed, and it opened for business on September 12, 1988; in an interview with *Post-Dispatch* reporter Ralph Dummit shortly after the opening, Berry described his plans for the restaurant, including international cuisine and music three nights a week. The piece described Berry's contracting skills, developed with his brother and his father in the 1940s and honed for years on the construction of Berry Park; Dummit described Berry stripping insulation from a speaker wire and measuring carpet. But, a year later, Berry's plans for the restaurant were overshadowed by his past. His federal convictions in 1944 and 1961, and the 1974 raid on and arrests at Berry Park, were all cited as reasons for denying Chuck Berry Communications Systems a liquor license for the renovated restaurant. To circumvent the ruling, Berry decided to lease the operation to Francine Gillium; it was an act that was to prove academic, however, because within months the restaurant was to close its doors for good.

One of the waitresses hired to work at the Southern Air was Hosana Huck, the wife of another employee, Vincent, who had worked for Berry for a number of years. Unknown to Berry, Vincent Huck also was working as an investigator for St. Charles attorney Ronald Boggs; together, in the opinion of Richard Schwartz, one of Berry's lawyers for the lawsuits that were to follow, the two began a "coordinated movement to force Chuck Berry to turn over his wealth." It began a few months before the opening of the Southern Air, in June 1988, when Huck began providing information to the Drug Enforcement Agency (DEA) that Chuck Berry was smuggling drugs in his guitar case on his way to and from shows. According to Schwartz, Huck "was constantly trying to get the Feds to seize the guitar cases because he believed that he [Berry] was transporting cocaine in them." They were, in Schwartz's opinion, "just absurd allegations." The information led to increased DEA surveillance of Berry, and on March 12, 1989, Berry was stopped at Lambert Field by drug enforcement agents when a drug-sniffing dog indicated the presence of cocaine in Berry's suitcase and guitar case. However, a subsequent search of Berry's possessions failed to find any drugs at all, and for the time-being the DEA did nothing.

Vincent Huck, however, continued to watch Berry. In September, he claimed to have received an anonymous phone call that led him to discover a number of the so-called "bathroom tapes." These videotapes, which "'contained numerous photographs of women urinating and defecating' . . . were allegedly made with cameras hidden in the air ducts above the stalls in the women's restroom at Southern Aire [sic]." Richard Schwartz, however, believed that Huck obtained the tapes in an entirely different way. "Vincent Huck," Schwartz maintained, "was taken into a position of semi-confidence and was given access" to Berry Park by Chuck Berry himself. One evening, according to Schwarz and to testimony Huck would give later, "he sneaked back on to the farm. There was a small house on the grounds, it was probably one of the old farmhouses that Chuck had done an awful lot of work on and it was just where he went to be alone, his personal playroom." Huck, Schwartz stated, "broke into the house and then jimmied open the lock on a chest inside that house and stole somewhere between dozens and hundreds of porno tapes." Pornographic books, magazines, and photographs—essentially, in Richard Schwartz's words, Berry's "self-created, personal porn collection"—were also taken during the burglary, leaving Chuck Berry vulnerable and in a precarious position.

Some months after, the Hucks used Vincent's haul to their advantage. On December 27, 1989, Hosana Huck filed a lawsuit in the St. Charles County Circuit Court. The suit charged that Chuck Berry "intentionally and without just cause or excuse intruded upon Huck's seclusion and privacy without her permission by surreptitiously making or manufacturing videotapes depicting Huck undressing and dressing and using the toilet at the [Southern Air] restaurant." The suit also claimed that "other female employees and customers were videotaped in the bathroom." Almost simultaneously, the January edition of *High Society*, a soft-core pornographic magazine, printed eight pictures of Berry with a number of female companions. In the photographs, Berry and the women, all white, were naked, although none of the pictures depicted any kind of sexual activity; in each picture, a smiling Berry is seen with his arms around the women. They were clearly personal souvenirs of private sexual encounters. Now, in an outrageous invasion of personal privacy, they were available to the world courtesy of, in *High Society*'s words, "the only magazine with the balls to show Chuck's berries."

Immediately, Chuck Berry hired celebrity West Coast attorney Melvin Belli, who initiated a $10 million lawsuit against the magazine in the Superior Court of San Francisco on January 17. Not surprisingly, the suit specifically named Vincent Huck as the person who stole the photographs and sold them to the magazine. Then, Wayne Schoeneberg, a flamboyant personal injury attorney (with a penchant for Harley Davidson motorcycles) from nearby O'Fallon, Missouri, filed the first of a number of countersuits to Hosana

Huck's original suit, aimed at either deterring or wearing down Berry's accusers. This first countersuit was filed on April 27 against Hosana Huck and her attorney, Thomas Jones, accusing them of invading Berry's privacy and "publicly disclos[ing] private matters concerning Charles E. Berry without his permission or without privilege." Berry was requesting the return of the videotapes that he believed were stolen on September 9, 1989, the same time that the *High Society* pictures and other documents were taken.

Meanwhile, Vincent Huck's continued surveillance of Chuck Berry led Huck to believe that, despite the complete lack of evidence from the March 1989 search of Berry's luggage at Lambert Field, Berry was continuing to traffic in cocaine. He managed to convince Dennis Wichern of the DEA to produce an affidavit to that effect, which was promptly sent to Associate Circuit Judge William T. Lohmaar, who, on the basis of the affidavit, issued a search warrant for Berry Park.

At 5:00 on the morning of Saturday, June 23, members of the St. Charles County Multijurisdictional Enforcement Group raided the park; after a few hours, the search turned up

> two rifles and a shotgun. Two clear plastic bags containing a "green plant material" and a cloth bag containing several plastic bags each containing a green plant material along with "hard dark brown material in aluminum foil." $122,501 in cash. Seven slide trays loaded with pornographic slides. Fifty-nine VHS videotapes. Three paperback books described as "sexual in nature." Four newspapers described as "sexual in content." Films showing "beast/animal sex in nature." An unmarked prescription bottle containing 30 capsules and pills. Berry's Missouri Drivers License. Numerous computer discs.

Quickly, Wayne Schoeneberg seized on the fact that the "huge quantities of cocaine" that were alleged in the affidavit sent to Judge Lohmaar were not there. "Where's the cocaine?" he asked Jo Mannies of the *St. Louis Post-Dispatch*, and at a later press conference he argued that the affidavit had "absolutely no credibility" and that the raid was a "witch hunt." Now, even the DEA was beginning to doubt Vincent Huck's credibility. Kim Neely, a writer for *Rolling Stone*, noted that Huck had already tried to sell his story to the press, and that a source from the St. Charles Police Department "who confirmed Huck was the DEA's main informant noted Huck's apparent willingness to profit from his role in the investigation." The source, Neely stated, believed that Huck "had dollar signs in his eyes. I don't think anybody at the DEA here in St. Louis would admit that they even associate with him." Richard Schwartz also maintains that Huck, motivated by a combination of greed and racism, was the driving force behind the raid. "The raid was instigated by Vincent Huck," the attorney believed, "using a lot of really false and weird allegations. I think he became obsessed. I think there was a lot of racial motivation; he became obsessed with getting a big hunk of Berry's wealth and I think the racial issue bothered him a lot and really further clouded his judgment."

But there was worse to come. Within days, up to 200 more women, all represented by Ronald Boggs, filed a separate class-action suit against Berry that contained the same allegations as Hosana Huck's December 1989 suit: that they had been secretly videotaped while using the bathrooms of the Southern Air and Berry Park. Once again, the ugly specter of racism surrounded the affair; preying on the stereotype of the violent black criminal, Circuit Judge Lester W. Duggan, Jr., ordered the names of the plaintiffs sealed after Boggs argued that, due to Berry's criminal record, his "clients fear[ed] reprisals." With this filing, there was now no doubt in Richard Schwarz's mind that Berry was becoming the victim of a conspiracy that involved Ronald Boggs, Vincent Huck, and a number of people affiliated with the St. Charles judicial and political system. "It seemed to me," the lawyer theorized some years later,

> as though many people in the St. Charles County courthouse and the local polit-
> ical machine were positioning themselves to benefit from the plundering of
> Chuck Berry's estate. Some of the women who worked in the courthouse for the
> judges or in judicial jobs in the clerks' office were claiming that they were also on
> the videotape, and therefore were preparing to become plaintiffs and participate
> in the plunder. It was the anticipation of a feeding frenzy, no question about it.

Later, when other civil lawsuits were filed, "two younger lawyers named Dalton represented plaintiffs in the case," Schwartz said. "They were the son and the nephew of two of the circuit judges in St. Charles County. So this thing was wired in deeply to the courthouse. They were going to have themselves a nice big economic lynching up there in St. Charles County, and I found it all very disturbing."

Indeed, the lawsuit had become so acrimonious that, on the evening the second class-action suit was announced, Berry's lawyer, Wayne Schoeneberg and another lawyer, Rex Burlison, encountered Ronald Boggs and Vincent Huck in Crow's Sport's bar in St. Charles and immediately became involved in a brawl. Schoeneberg, who at the time was on crutches after a skydiving accident, claimed that he was "not about to get into a fight with anybody about anything in that condition," but a police report of the incident mentioned that Huck was hit by a crutch during the fight. In the end, Huck was "treated for a broken rib, a broken nose, and several bruises," and Burlison was charged with misdemeanor assault; Schoeneberg and Boggs, however, were never issued charges related to the incident.

At this point, St. Charles County Prosecuting Attorney William Hannah entered the fray. "Hannah was," in Richard Schwartz's view, "part and parcel of this coordinated movement" to divest Chuck Berry of his wealth. Surprisingly, Hannah was slow to press charges after the June 23rd raid of Berry Park; more than three weeks went by, during which time Berry left to tour Sweden. Finally, four days after a scathing *Post-Dispatch* editorial on July 15, which accused Hannah of "showboating," Berry was formally charged with three charges of child abuse and one charge of possession of over 35 grams of marijuana, all stemming from the items taken in the June 23rd raid. "They charged him with felony child sexual abuse," explained Schwarz, "based upon the videotaping of the female patrons of his restaurant." But, Schwartz maintained, "it's even questionable whether any of it was pornographic because very little of the human body was identifiable. Basically it's a lot of shots from above. But a few of them were young children who would occasionally go in and use the bathroom. That was the basis for filing child sexual abuse charges; nasty, nasty, just deliberately trying to be vicious to this man."

Eleven days later, immediately on his return from Europe, Berry surrendered himself and was released on a $20,000 property bond; unsurprisingly, his career and his music were suffering. The shows in Sweden were heavily criticized in the Swedish press, with one critic calling the opening show of the tour "painful and pathetic" and Berry himself "finished as an artist. Leftover. Finito. Flunked Out." An appearance on the *Tonight Show* and two shows at Knott's Berry Farm in California scheduled for August 11 and 12 were canceled; "all parties," a publicist for the amusement park was quoted as saying, "agreed it was best for him not to be here at this time." Altogether, Chuck Berry played only three shows between July, when the charges were filed, and November, when they were eventually dropped.

Schoeneberg and Schwartz, meanwhile, began to move against Berry's accusers. Following the federal government's return of the money seized in the Berry Park raid on September 28, Schwartz refiled the *High Society* lawsuit on October 29. To consolidate the growing number of suits against Berry, Schwartz requested a change of venue from Los Angeles, where it was originally filed, to St. Louis. One by one, Schwartz explained, "We moved all civil cases down to federal court from St. Charles County under the civil rights jurisdiction. I think that the race factors would have made it impossible to get him a totally or even a moderately fair trial in St. Charles," he reflected several years later, "even without the added inducement that there was so much economic advantage in the situation for the people who were fairly closely tied to the political machine and to the people who ran the courthouses."

Schwartz's next move was even bolder: a deliberate attempt to remove

William Hannah who was facing a tough reelection bid, from the case. The strategy was to file a counter civil suit, seeking $500,000 in actual damages, $100,000 in punitive damages, and a halt to the criminal suit Hannah had brought against Berry. But the suit itself was just a ploy; it was timed for Friday, November 2, just days before Hannah was due to stand for reelection. "We had this all worked out with Chuck," remembered Schwartz,

> approved it with him, and we timed it so that we filed the suit in federal court on the Friday afternoon before the election on the following Tuesday. And we filed it and we made the suit available and I agreed to do interviews with all the major TV stations. And fortunately Hannah refused to comment on or address any of the allegations and simply said that he couldn't comment until he'd seen the case papers. He could have requested any one of the media stations or even called me up to send him a copy, but he didn't. So basically we had the media all to ourselves for the entire period before the election over the weekend. And he was swept out of office big time, and I feel that our case had a lot to do with removing him.

Although Hannah's opponent, Democrat Tim Braun, outspent his opponent five to one, and Hannah was fighting history by becoming the first prosecutor in nearly twenty years to be reelected to office in St. Charles, Schwarz remains convinced that some of Braun's 32,000 votes had come from admirers of the rock-and-roll singer. "I knew we had a lot of Chuck Berry fans out there," Schwartz observed wryly, years later.

The effect on the criminal lawsuit was immediate. "I remember," Schwartz has said, "getting the call almost on the morning after the election—it might have been the day after—but very quickly. I got a call from a lawyer in St. Louis who was representing St. Charles County Prosecutor Hannah wanting to know if we would be willing to dismiss our federal civil rights case against Hannah if Hannah would dismiss the criminal prosecution. So I consulted with Chuck and we accepted their offer. We achieved our objective quickly and cleanly in doing that." On November 20, Chuck Berry agreed to drop the countersuit, make a $5,000 "contribution" to drug and alcohol programs, and accept two years of unsupervised probation for the misdemeanor marijuana charge in return for the dismissal of all three child-abuse charges.

For Chuck Berry, the exoneration on the child-abuse charges was especially sweet. "I feel fantastic," he told a press conference the day before the Thanksgiving holiday, "this is the part that hurt me the most." But almost as quickly as the criminal suit was dropped, new civil suits sprang up. In the week prior to the dismissal, Vincent Huck had filed a libel and slander suit against Berry based on the accusations Berry had made about Huck stealing the videos and *High Society* photographs. Then, on November 27 and again on January 4, 1991, two more invasion of privacy suits were filed by anonymous women. And, adding credence to Wayne Schoeneberg's claim that the whole affair was a witch-hunt, Ronald Boggs announced to the *St. Louis Post-Dispatch* that he was considering asking the St. Charles County court to produce a nationally televised announcement encouraging women who may have been taped to come forward and join the class-action suit against Chuck Berry.

After the flurry of activity in 1990, the civil suits began their slow progress through the courts. As Richard Schwartz continued his battle to move the cases to St. Louis, all of the parties in the cases began the long process of being deposed. "Chuck went through a very long deposition," Schwartz recalled, "about ten or twenty days, it took forever. And he did very well and acquitted himself beautifully." The plaintiffs, however, did not fare so well, and Schwartz remembers that the fabric of the case against Chuck Berry was beginning to unravel. Schwartz remembered, "we deposed a lot of people who were plaintiffs in the civil cases, and we had people making up lies and claiming that they had seen photographs where they could identify themselves by a mole on the buttocks, that it was their buttocks that had been filmed. And then several of the people during the course of their depositions recanted their testimony under cross-examination, and in one of the cases, possibly two, they came back after they gave their depositions, they came back in and said they wanted to change their testimony." Once again, for Schwartz, this was proof that "this was a conspiracy; this was not a real lawsuit, just a conspiracy to split up Chuck Berry's wealth."

Meanwhile, in the St. Charles County Courthouse, rulings were not going in Chuck Berry's favor. "They weren't going to let go of it," Schwartz recalled. "They weren't going to overrule or keep anything out, and they were going to let all the stolen stuff go into evidence." One particular problem was that the plaintiffs refused to produce all the materials they were planning on using in the cases. "They were not allowed to depose Berry until after the production was made in the civil-rights case," remembered Schwartz. "They were supposed to produce everything, but they didn't." So Schwartz continued in his attempts to have the trials transferred to federal court in St. Louis. Berry "decided to hire us to see if we could stop the prosecution in federal court. So we prepared the case alleging prosecutorial misconduct, alleging the protection of First Amendment activity, things of this nature. . . . Basically the personal possession of pornography, if indeed it was pornography, was protected."

In August of 1991, Schwartz filed a motion to consolidate all the lawsuits into one civil suit and have the entire suit moved to the U.S. District Court in downtown St. Louis. "Unfortunately," Schwartz recalled, "the way the clerk's office worked they [the cases] were parceled out, I believe it was, [to] four different judges down there," resulting in slowing down the proceedings even more. For good measure, Schwartz decided to go on the offensive and countersue a number of the plaintiffs in a federal civil rights case. "A matter of days after," said Schwartz, "we initiated a civil rights action against Huck, Boggs, several of the key plaintiffs, to enjoin them from proceeding, with the claims that they were using all this stolen evidence and things like that." In the suit, William Hannah was heavily criticized for his role in the 1990 raid, although, as a result of the agreement reached in November of that year, he was not named as a defendant.

The court deliberated for several months; in March of 1992, they eventually determined that "Berry's claims of civil rights violations fell short of Supreme Court standards allowing federal courts to take cases first filed in state court," leaving Schwartz with no option but to appeal the decision. Fortunately, Schwartz remembered, "The Eighth Circuit set up a very expedited briefing schedule"; the appeal was lodged on June 9 and answered three weeks later. "Unfortunately," Schwartz noted, "rather than deal with the merits of our legal argument, I think they were put off by the scandal. They just wrote a very poorly reasoned opinion, a very short, rough treatment of the legal issues and the constitutional questions raised." To add insult to injury, Schwartz recalled that the opinion was given by a panel of three judges who "didn't put their own names on the opinion. They just called it *per curium* which is Latin for 'by the court.'"

Undeterred, Schwartz decided to take the appeal to the Supreme Court of the United States; meanwhile, illegally produced copies of several of the videotapes were beginning to circulate. Richard Schwartz has alleged that the tapes could only have come from one source: Ronald Boggs. According to Schwartz,

> Boggs launched a new campaign to start to sell some of the materials. We pretty clearly established that Boggs and Huck had launched a new wave of attempting to circulate and trying to sell things. At that point they figured the stuff had probably lost some of its commercial attraction and so they started a new campaign.

Indeed, Schwartz's argument is a compelling one. Late in 1992, Mike Sager, a writer for *Spy* magazine, was invited by Boggs to view one of the tapes in Boggs's St. Charles office. Clearly, Boggs and Huck felt no compulsion whatsoever to keep the material confidential, not only while the court cases were proceeding but also while their rights to the material were still very much in doubt.

The *Spy* magazine article also contained some damaging testimony from Sharissa Kistner, a former resident of a trailer on the Berry Park grounds and a plaintiff in one of the civil suits against Berry, who accused Berry of placing a tiny video camera in a vent above her bed. But, in an attempt to give the incidents some perspective, Sager quoted an unnamed source who pointed out that "there's a guy in a major law firm in St. Louis who won the 'Mr. Leather of America' contest. He's got three rings through his nipple. It's in us. It's in everybody." And, in case Sager's readers missed the point, the byline to the article suggested that the only difference between Chuck Berry and Madonna was that Madonna was getting rich from being naked in front of the camera while Berry was getting into trouble. Indeed, in October 1992, Madonna was publishing nude photos of herself in a lavishly and expensively produced book, appropriately called *Sex*, and releasing an album called *Erotica*. Around St. Louis, however, Chuck Berry was struggling to get work; although work around the country and in Europe was picking up, a planned New Year's Eve Show at the Fox Theater was scrapped, because according to the *St. Louis Post-Dispatch* the advance ticket sales were nonexistent."

The U.S. Supreme Court finally made a decision about the case on February 22, 1993. Once again emphasizing the racial dimensions of the case, Schwartz had "argued that the singer was the victim of St. Charles County officials who were part of a racially motivated conspiracy 'to achieve the financial destruction tantamount to an economic lynching of a uniquely American cultural icon.'" But the Court's decision was not what Schwartz had hoped for; they declined to hear the case at all. For Richard Schwartz, it was a bitter blow. In his opinion, the carefully constructed constitutional arguments about Berry's right to privacy, his right to own pornography under the First Amendment, and the civil-rights issues were all obscured by the scandalous nature of the events. "John Price," believed Schwartz, "a younger lawyer out of Springfield, Missouri, who represented one of the groups who had gone ahead with a reported class action, filed one opposition to it that didn't deal at all successfully with the merits of our constitutional arguments. But he made the argument that this was a smelly case that held a lot of disgusting scandal and that the Court really shouldn't be getting involved in these matters. And I kinda wonder if that sense of propriety may have been the strongest reason why the Court didn't want to take this case."

While the Distirict Court, Appellate Court, and Supreme Court had all summarily dismissed Schwartz's claims about the violation of Chuck Berry's rights in the civil cases, one judge, Edward Filippine, had taken Schwartz's claims very seriously. The federal civil-rights case filed in August of 1991 and now in Filippine's court seemed to present the best hope for an effective counter to the civil charges emanating from St. Charles. But on the morning of March 26, Schwartz remembered, when he "went to the federal court for some sort of in-chambers conference with Ed Filipine, [lawyer] Martin Green was there with his associate Mitch Margo." It was then that Schwartz realized

Chuck Berry had decided to change his legal representation; after almost three years preparing a complex defense for an equally complex series of events, and after masterfully disposing of the child-abuse charges, the services of Richard Schwartz and Wayne Schoeneberg were no longer required.

The reasons for Berry's decision are unclear. Richard Schwartz "never had any indication [that Berry] was dissatisfied." Indeed, Schwartz recalled a show Chuck Berry played at the Bluenote, a club in Columbia, Missouri, when Berry introduced Schoeneberg and Schwartz to the crowd and declared, "I owe my freedom to them. I would be in jail if it weren't for them." But, the attorney sensed, "I know he was disappointed the Supreme Court wouldn't take his case." Schwartz also believed that attorney Martin Green may have influenced Berry tremendously and made him anxious for a speedy resolution to the affair. "Within a matter of weeks," Schwartz recalled, Green had "called me up and said I'd done a good job of protecting Chuck, and that if nothing else we had delayed the whole matter and worn the plaintiffs down for a couple of years. I think he just viewed this as a diversionary tactic. But that wasn't the reason why we started that federal civil-rights litigation, that wasn't why we had kept it going."

But the end result was not what the singer had wanted. "Not very long after we got out," remembered Schwartz, "maybe a month, month and a half, something like that, Fillipine suddenly dismissed the case. I don't know if it was just because he felt that Martin Green and Mitch Margo didn't have any kind of reputation as civil-rights lawyers or what his motivation was, 'cause I was out of it at that point. But as far as I can tell, [Green] didn't appeal Fillipine's ruling." Further, Schwartz was critical of Green's handling of Berry's suit against Drake Publishing, the publishers of *High Society*. "My recollection is that after that, Green just kinda pissed away the invasion of privacy case against *High Society*," Schwartz has argued. "I couldn't tell that he ever did anything. The various other people to whom that material was sold who disseminated it for commercial advantage should have at least been liable to pay damages to Chuck."

Over the next year and a half, Martin Green and Mitch Margo worked to settle the civil suits. On August 23, 1994, the class-action suit was settled for $830,000. As Richard Schwartz had predicted, it was Ronald Boggs and the Hucks who took the lion's share of the settlement; the *Post-Dispatch* reported that Boggs received "about a third" of the settlement, a little over $276,000 "less expenses." Settlements in the suit varied; several awards were made for $17,000, but the majority of women, 59 of the 74 still left in the suit, received $5,000 apiece. In a separate settlement, Hoseana Huck split $310,000 with another woman and their respective attorneys. All told, the four-year ordeal had cost Chuck Berry $1,225,000 plus immense legal fees, amply illustrating Richard Schwartz's metaphor of an "economic lynching." But more disheartening, perhaps, was Berry's decision that it was finally time to leave Wentzville. In June 1993, he purchased a new house in Ladue, a middle-class suburb of St. Louis, near enough to Berry Park to conduct business, yet far enough away from the prying eyes of the suspicious neighbors he must have felt were a part of the St. Charles conspiracy.

In the end, the parallels between the Mann Act incident 30 years earlier and the videotaping lawsuits are truly remarkable. Both were initiated in illegal acts by white men on a successful black man: an illegal search and seizure in the first and a theft of personal property in the second. Both were also the results of Chuck Berry's relentless pursuit and exploitation of women. Both exposed the racism inherent in the American justice system at its many levels. And the lessons from both chapters of Berry's life, too, are many. They give us the example of a man whose detachment from society made him feel immune to its mores and taboos; they also reveal a society whose attitudes toward race and sex remained unchanged, despite years of civil-rights advances. Ultimately, though, both incidents resist easy moralizing, for at their heart they represent an inseparable mix of Berry's personal irresponsibility and the deep prejudice that lies at society's heart. And, sadly, they were not to be the last lawsuits Chuck Berry would face in his life.

Johnson v. Berry

In an oral culture where ... authority is prized above originality, the crucial
issue is not saying something new by saying something first, but in embracing
the paradoxical practice of developing one's voice by trying on someone else's
voice, and thus learning by comparison to identify one's own gift. If imitation
and emulation are the first fruits of ... an oral culture, its mature benefits
include the projection of a unique style—a new style—that borrows from
cultural precedents but finds its own place within their amplifications.

—Michael Eric Dyson,
I May Not Get There With You: The True Martin Luther King Jr.

On November 29, 2000, just days before Chuck Berry was to leave St. Louis
for Washington, D.C., to accept a prestigious Kennedy Center Honor, the
unthinkable happened. In the U.S. Court of the Eastern District of Missouri,
Johnnie Johnson filed suit against Charles E. Berry and Isalee Music,
claiming that he was the coauthor of some 57 songs in the Berry catalog.
The suit claimed Johnson was owed royalties on practically the whole of
Berry's pre-Mercury output, with the exception of "Maybellene" and "Johnny
B. Goode"; one other song, "Wee Wee Hours," Johnson claimed was entirely
his. The amount of royalties owed to Johnson, the lawsuit claimed, went
into the "tens of millions of dollars."

Altogether, the suit listed seven causes of actions. The first five surrounded
the issue of who owned the copyrights. The suit claimed that Berry had
appropriated the music to "Wee Wee Hours," and that Johnson was the
coauthor of all the other Berry songs listed in the suit; that Berry's accounts
should be examined to determine the total amount of royalties Johnson
should have been paid since the two first recorded in 1955; and that Johnson
be awarded damages as a result of not being paid the royalties on the catalog.
The final three claims were that Berry defrauded Johnson in their business
dealings, "taking advantage of Johnson's alcoholism" to make him believe

that he was not entitled to royalties from the songs, causing Johnson to seek further damages against Berry and his corporations. Ironically, Johnson had chosen Mitchell Margo as his lawyer, whereas Berry once again appointed Martin Green as his representative; both lawyers, who had worked together for Berry in settling the videotaping lawsuits, now found themselves on opposing sides of equally acrimonious legal proceedings.

Clearly, the November filing was a cynical attempt to detract from Berry's Kennedy Center Honor and achieve maximum publicity for Johnson. But the question remained as to why the humble and soft-spoken Johnson was filing the suit now, some 34 years after the last song listed in the suit had been recorded.

The answer, essentially, began with an off-hand comment made by an exhausted Keith Richards, slumped in a chair in the Fox Theater dressing rooms minutes after Berry's 60th birthday concert had concluded. The comments, recorded for the *Chuck Berry: Hail! Hail! Rock 'n' Roll* movie, illustrated Richards's belief that it was Johnson who provided the music over which Berry imposed his lyrics. "He's not doing Chuck Berry songs," Richards said of Johnson's piano playing. "No, the way he's playing it, it's his riff; Chuck adapted it to the guitar. I know that, too, because of the key it's in. It's in Johnnie's keys, piano keys. If it was a guitar, if it was rock and roll, you play in A, in E, because you've got open strings." But, added Richards, "On top of everything else, you're playing in piano keys, horn keys, jazz keys, Johnnie Johnson's keys. The minute he does 'School Day,' he ain't copying Chuck's riffs on piano; Chuck adapted them to guitar and put those great lyrics behind them." Then, punctuating his point, Richards added, "But without somebody to give him [Berry] those riffs, Voila! No song! Just a lot of words on paper."

In fact, the songs in the early Chuck Berry canon are in four keys. The majority are in C ("Sweet Little Sixteen," "Little Queenie," "Carol") or G ("School Day," "No Money Down," "Memphis, Tennessee"). Inasmuch as any genre of music can be said to favor certain keys, these keys are typical of folk or country music. But the songs Richards was referring to were in B flat ("Maybellene," "Johnny B. Goode," "Let it Rock') or E flat ("Rock and Roll Music," "Brown Eyed Handsome Man," "Roll Over Beethoven"). They are not typically easy keys for a beginning guitar player, because playing them requires knowing movable chord shapes that can be played up and down the neck; they cannot, as Richards rightly maintained, be played easily in the first position, where the most basic guitar chords exist. But they are keys that are certainly not beyond the average guitar player, and any player who grew up listening to jazz or rhythm and blues, as Berry undoubtedly did, would find the keys familiar enough. Richards's notion that they were not suitable keys for a guitarist thus becomes questionable.

It was this section of the movie, however, that registered most heavily with Houston businessman George Turek. A former Navy pilot and a highly motivated, self-made multimillionaire, he had befriended Johnson after Johnson had played his wedding in 1993. The wedding itself was illustrative of Turek's penchant for hyperbole. An enormous affair for 750 guests, it was held in an aircraft hanger at the Oakland airport in Michigan. Turek's bride-to-be, Linda, arrived in a vintage B-52 bomber and made her entrance wearing a dress from a Guns n' Roses music video. It was this kind of grandiose thinking that Turek was to take into his relationship with the piano player over the following years.

Richards's scene in *Chuck Berry: Hail! Hail! Rock 'n' Roll* was a revelatory moment in Turek's life. He was so moved, he said in Johnson's biography, that he "got off the Stairmaster. . . . I called him [Johnnie Johnson] up right there and then—forget the workout—and asked him point blank, 'Johnnie did you write those songs with Chuck?'" When Johnson replied that he "made up the music" for the songs, "It was like a lightening bolt" to Turek. "That day the lid to the Pandora's box was blown off its hinges." From that simple conversation, Turek was convinced that Johnson was the coauthor of all of Berry's songs and that rock-and-roll history had been built on a lie. After viewing the broadcast of the Rock-and-Roll Hall of Fame Concert with Johnson in September 1995, and feeling that Johnnie Johnson had been slighted by not being included in the show along with Berry, Turek took it upon himself to revise the history books. "Johnnie had been cheated out of his place in history," he declared, and from that day on he would help "Johnnie get the recognition he deserves for the monumental contributions he made to music."

That Turek had no background in music theory or history did not give him pause. "I'm no rock and roll historian," he admitted in Johnson's biography in 1999. "I don't play an instrument, nor can I sing. I am a businessman who just fell into this crazy situation . . . an engineering-type by profession." Instead, he approached his task with the same boundless energy, enthusiasm, and dedication that he had used years earlier to build up his physicians' management business. And his first task was a laudable one: to get Johnnie Johnson elected to the Rock-and-Roll Hall of Fame.

Few could argue that Johnson did not deserve a place in the Cleveland museum. However, unlike sports halls of fame, where the criteria for entrance is based mainly on performance, the criteria for induction to a musical hall of fame has always been less clear. Whereas achievement on the athletic field is measurable and capable of comparison, musical success is not as easy to quantify. Record sales alone do not tell the whole story; measuring the degree of influence of a given artist is equally difficult. Even the definition of what constitutes rock and roll is fluid and arguable. For Johnson personally, satisfying the Hall's most basic requirement, that the artist had to have recorded under his or her own name 25 years or more prior to being inducted, proved impossible. After all, the recordings that got Chuck Berry elected in the first round of inductions in 1986 bore only Berry's name; the first recording to actually bear Johnson's name was a 1989 album named *Cool Hand Johnnie*. Clearly, George Turek faced an uphill task.

The process began in September of 1995, with Turek rounding up a number of musicians and prominent figures in the entertainment field to sign a petition on Johnnie's behalf to have him inducted to the Rock Hall. Keith Richards, Eric Clapton, Dick Clark, and Little Richard leant their names to the endeavor, as did Johnson's old colleagues from the Chess days in Chicago, Bo Diddley, Etta James, and John Lee Hooker. The petition, however, met with no success the following year, because the Johnnie Johnson Nominating Committee (as they had now become known) had missed the deadline for nominations that year (according to Turek, because the Rock-and-Roll Hall of Fame committee had deliberately given him the wrong dates for submitting nominations).

Undeterred, Turek then hired Rogers and Cowan, a major public relations firm, to help spread the word about Johnson and his nomination; true to their reputation, the firm secured television and print exposure for Johnson throughout 1997. But the most significant move on Turek's part that year, one that was not without a degree of hypocrisy and manipulation, was to secure the support of Chuck Berry in the endeavor. In *Father of Rock and Roll: The Story of Johnnie 'B. Goode' Johnson*, Turek makes no attempt to hide his dislike of the man. "I didn't like the guy," he was quoted as saying in the book, accusing him of lying and narcissism in his dealings with Johnson. "I could barely stand to look at him. Everything about the man made me absolutely nauseous. But," he continued, "I figured that I could get more accomplished for Johnnie with Chuck as an ally."

And so Turek went about drafting a letter on Johnson's behalf for Berry to sign and send to Ahmet Ertegun, chairman of Atlantic Records and cochairman of the Rock-and-Roll Hall of Fame Foundation. "I am in full support of Johnnie's nomination," Turek wrote in Berry's name. "Johnnie and I have been friends and musical collaborators for over 40 years. . . . His induction would round out the list of those musicians who made significant contributions during Rock-and-Roll's infancy." Later, Turek was to recall, "I got what I wanted, which was the part about them being 'musical collaborators.' I figured it was pretty gutsy."

To ensure that Berry would sign the letter, Turek then had Johnson call up Berry's office in Wentzville. Berry's response to the letter was magnanimous and not at all in keeping with Turek's characterization of him. Johnson recalled Berry saying, "I'd do anything for you, Johnnie," and then, when there was a delay on Berry's end in signing the letter and Johnson called again, Berry again greeted his old pianist with the generosity reserved only for his friends. Berry told Johnson that he had temporarily misplaced the letter and that he would find it and mail it straight away. "Sure enough," remembered Johnson, "he did. He was real nice about the whole thing and said he hoped I'd get in 'cause I deserved it as much as him."

But even Berry's letter couldn't help his former bandmate, and Johnson's nomination was passed over that year. The pianist and the businessman had to endure the indignity again for two subsequent years until, finally, to Turek's credit, his tenacity and loyalty to his friend secured Johnson a place in the Rock Hall in 2000. This time, Turek had convinced the Rock-and-Roll Hall of Fame committee to open up a new category for sidemen: musicians who had helped record the music but who, for various reasons, had never been given credit for their small yet vital roll. Appropriately, the other sideman inducted with Johnson in that first year of the category was Scotty Moore, whose guitar playing had provided a signature sound for his old boss Elvis Presley, just as Johnson's piano playing had done for Berry.

It was a moment of great triumph for the pair, and rightly so. Johnson could now claim the recognition that for so long had eluded him, and his rightful place in the history of rock and roll had been secured. But for Turek, recognizing Johnson as a sideman simply wasn't enough. In *Father of Rock and Roll*, Turek revealed that his ambition for the piano player went far beyond the Rock-and-Roll Hall of Fame:

> I want him inducted into the Blues Foundation Hall of Fame. He deserves to receive the Lifetime Achievement Award from the Rhythm and Blues Foundation. He should be inducted into the Songwriter's Hall of Fame. He should receive the Lifetime Achievement Award from the Grammys. He should get both the National Medal of Arts Award and induction as a Kennedy Center Honoree. I even think he should receive a Pulitzer Prize for Music. . . . He should have all of these and more.

It was a typically hyperbolic statement from the ambitious Turek, especially as Johnson would always be nothing more or less than a gifted piano player. But in the comment lay the seeds of an even more audacious scheme, one that would combine his love for the genial pianist and his hatred for the man who had taken his friend from the obscurity of an East St. Louis club to the Rock-and-Roll Hall of Fame.

As part of his ongoing campaign to promote Johnson, in 1995 George Turek had approached his 19-year-old stepson, Travis Fitzpatrick, to write Johnnie Johnson's biography. When it eventually saw the light of day in 1999, published by a vanity press out of Turek's hometown of Houston, the book carried the inflated title *Father of Rock and Roll*. Fitzpatrick, unlike his stepfather, exhibited a passing knowledge of rock-and-roll history in the book. However, because it was drawn mostly from first-person interviews, mostly of Johnson himself, the book became a thinly disguised polemic advancing Turek's and Fitzpatrick's claim that Johnnie Johnson had cowritten all of Chuck Berry's songs from 1955 to 1966.

The evidence Fitzpatrick provides is based either on extensive interviews with Johnson or on secondhand speculations by musicians and acquaintances of Berry and Johnson. First, Fitzpatrick dispels Johnson's own provocative statement, first aired in *Chuck Berry: Hail! Hail! Rock 'n' Roll* that, "No, I didn't write the music with him. I'd just be in the room with him sometimes when he was writing." What Johnson meant by "writing" music, however, is critical. Not long after the movie was released, Johnson explained in a phone conversation to George Turek that "I didn't write them [the songs]—I just made up the music for them. . . . Chuck wrote the lyrics and I gave him a lot of the music that he put behind those lyrics to make the song." When Turek pointed out to Johnson that that was writing music, Johnson replied, "No it ain't— that's makin' up music. Writin' music is when you write down what you doing, and I don't know how to write down notes or nothin'." What Johnson meant by "writing," then, is a literal definition of the word: the physical act of placing ideas on paper, rather than the more metaphoric sense of creating. As he was to say several years later in his biography, "Me and Chuck didn't write music. . . . That's 'cause neither one of us can. Can't read music and can't write it."

The book ostensibly advances the theory that Berry was the lyricist and Johnson the creator of the music, and about the first statement there is no argument. Johnson acknowledges that Berry is the sole author of the song lyrics. "The only one doin' any writin' on them songs was Chuck," he said to Fitzpatrick in 1999, "'cause he wrote the words. . . . And he did all that writin' on his own. He never needed anyone's help with words."

But the music was a different matter entirely. In Johnson's recollection, Berry's earlier material—"the hillbilly music," as he referred to it—was pretty much Berry's own creation. "He knew exactly what he wanted to do. He'd get on his guitar with this *umpah-umpah-umpah* and I'd stay right with him. . . . Chuck had those hillbilly songs down." But, continued Johnson, "Blues, boogie, that was my department," adding that "technically, the blues is not hard to play at all. With jazz, you can have up to sixty-four bars with all kinds of tempo and key changes. But in blues you got twelve or eight bars with changes after every eight or four, so you just pick a key and ride it out."

The first thing to acknowledge, then, in any debate about the authorship of the songs is the recognition by Johnson that, musically, the chord structures and the melodies of the songs are based around musical idioms already firmly established. This point, time and time again, has been addressed by Berry himself. In *Chuck Berry: Hail! Hail! Rock 'n' Roll*, for example, right after the scenes in which Keith Richards and Johnnie Johnson discuss song authorship, director Taylor Hackford lets Berry have the last word on the matter. Commenting on the signature guitar riff that opens "Johnny B. Goode," Berry openly admits that "the first time I heard that was in one of Carl Hogan's riffs in Louis Jordan's band." Then, he adds, "You have T-Bone Walker . . . I love T-Bone Walker's slurs and his blues. So put a little Carl Hogan, a little T-Bone Walker, and a little Charlie Christian, the guitarist in Tommy Dorsey's band together. . . . That's what I did in 'Johnny B. Goode' and 'Roll Over Beethoven.'" And, to emphasize the point, the scene concludes with Berry talking about other artists playing Chuck Berry music. "If you can call it my music," he wonders. "But then there's nothing new under the sun."

Johnnie Johnson himself worked in a similar way. One need only remember that Johnson himself had taken his signature tune, "Johnnie's Boogie," from "Honky Tonk Train Blues" by Meade Lux Lewis. Partly, the two were doing what all musicians and artists do: taking elements from different sources and synthesizing them to make an artistic creation that is at once new and derivative. But, in a larger sense, the two also were part of a black cultural tradition that is common to all cultures steeped in an oral rather than print tradition. The oral tradition permits and even encourages the borrowing, credited or uncredited, from other sources. Consider, for example, Michael Eric Dyson's description of how black preachers like he and Dr. Martin Luther King, Jr., learned how to preach:

> Baptist preachers are always ripping each other off and using the stories, illustrations, phrases, verbal tics, mannerisms, phrases—and in some cases, whole sermons—we glean from other preachers. That's how we learn how to preach—by preaching from somebody else until we learn how to preach like ourselves, when our own voices emerge from the colloquy of voices we convene in our homilectical imagination.

It is only when the print tradition dominates a culture that the idea of original expression becomes valued. So for Berry and Johnson, part and parcel of black culture, such wholesale use of other material would not even have been conscious. In this sense, neither Berry nor Johnson can be said to be authors of any of the songs identified with Chuck Berry, inasmuch as no artist can ever claim sole authorship over any artistic creation. Viewed in this way, even Berry's use of Dave Bartholomew's song to create his version of "My Ding-a-Ling" is, arguably, not the egregious plagiarism it seems on the surface. And, it should be noted, it was not Berry but the Chess Brothers and ARC music who sued Brian Wilson for plagiarizing "Sweet Little Sixteen" to make "Surfin' USA."

But in the capitalistic world of modern music, and with huge sums of money at stake, authorship often needs to be precisely determined. Here again, however, Johnson's claim for the co-authorship of the songs is debatable. In *Father of Rock and Roll,* Johnson describes the typical way in which many of the songs were created; it is a section worth quoting at length, because it helps to define the roles the two musicians adopted in the mid-1950s. First, Johnson recognizes that the impetus for the songs always came from Berry:

> Chuck was always the one with the ideas for what the song was going to be about. He'd say somethin' like 'I got this song about going to school.' The he'd read me what he had written. Most of the times he'd write two or three paragraphs of lyrics riding in the car from St. Louis to Chicago or just when we was off the road. When we'd get to the studio, he'd read off what he had written kind of like a poem and we'd try to find some music that would fit. I'd say, 'Well you want it fast or slow?' He might say to try somethin' fast. Sometimes it wouldn't work out that way, so we'd play around 'til we'd find somethin' that'd fit. I'd tell him if I liked somethin', and he'd tell me if he liked somethin'.

So here, at least, Johnson recalls Berry coming up with the lyric and the inspiration for the song, and that his role in the creative process was more as a sounding board, perhaps even a transcriber of some of Berry's ideas. Certainly, by Johnson's own admission, he was not the driving force behind the song's creation.

Then, Johnson continues:

> If he came up with a little tune on his guitar, I'd help him put it together. Sometimes on the road he'd call me to his room when we got to the hotel and play me somethin' he was workin' on. I'd say, "That don't fit," or "try puttin' this here," and Chuck usually listened to what I had to say.

Here, Johnson's role would be more of an arranger, someone who would have taken existing song elements and organized them. Traditionally in the music business this was the kind of work that was paid for on a for-hire basis; Johnson's compensation as a sideman on the Chess recording sessions would thus be appropriate for this level of involvement in the music.

The closest Johnson comes to a claim that he was the creator of the music occurs when he says,

> If he heard me playin' something that he liked he might say "Play that again, man," or "What you got there? Let's see if it will fit these words." Then Chuck would get his guitar and I'd play it over and over until he could get what I was doin' under his fingers. Same as if he had somethin' worked up, I'd play along with what he had and add my stuff to it.

Once again, the issue of Johnson's role is vague; exactly what he was playing when Berry tried to duplicate it on guitar or make it fit some existing lyrics is unclear. Was it a melody line that Berry would use to sing the words? Or was it, as was more likely the case, a chord progression or the kind of generic rhythmic left-hand boogie pattern he had learned from Meade Lux Lewis, Albert Ammons, Pete Johnson, or any of the legions of barrelhouse blues pianists who had preceded him? If so, Johnson's case is, again, not very strong.

Johnson's case is perhaps strongest when he describes another way that the two worked together. In the case of "Maybellene," Johnson has said, Berry "had that already put together when he met me. I added my own little things to it, but he already had the idea." But, the pianist remembered, "'Wee Wee Hours'—that was somethin' I worked up and he just added words to it and kind of strummed along." Here, at least, Johnson's case seems valid; "Wee Wee Hours" was a slow blues, borrowed from hundreds of similar-sounding songs, but Johnson seemed to have brought the idea, if not the progression, to the table, and Berry seems to have superimposed the words.

In the end, however, Johnson concedes that the creative process was too spontaneous to ever really determine exactly who contributed what. "Songs like 'Roll Over Beethoven,'" he remembered, "those were things we did from the start. The words were all his, but can't one of us say we did the music all by ourself. We did that music together." But even in that comment, the argument that Johnson wrote the music, or that the two worked collaboratively as equals, is hard to make. If one agrees that a song is composed of lyrics and a melody line augmented by a chord progression and a rhythm, and that all those elements are then interpreted by one or more musicians on musical instruments, then what part of this music did the two of them together produce? Again, if Berry alone is the author of the songs' lyrics, more than likely as the singer of those lyrics he would have come up with the melody as well. The chord progressions and rhythms, as we have already seen, were preexisting, already a part of the ferment that was 1950s R&B. And the instrumental virtuosity that is used to translate the song's elements to a listening audience—as important as that is and as beautifully as Johnson and Berry managed to execute it in the studio or on the stage—does not constitute authorship of a song.

In truth, if there was merit to Fitzpatrick's argument, then cases could perhaps be made for three songs that Johnson keeps coming back to: "Wee Wee Hours," "Roll Over Beethoven," and "School Day." In all three, Berry had placed his own words over piano patterns that Johnson had been playing prior to Berry's arrival. But, however flawed the argument of *Father of Rock and Roll*, it set the groundwork for what was to come. And although the motives behind the lawsuit appeared genuine enough, there seems to be plenty of evidence to suggest that it was, in no small part, fueled by George Turek's growing vendetta against Chuck Berry.

The first to break the news on the date the suit was filed, two days before the mainstream press broke it on December 1, was johnnie.com, the Johnson website maintained by Spike Longoria, who had been enlisted by Turek to spearhead various media projects attempting to further his crusade on Johnson's behalf. And as the weeks went by, several journalists suggested that it was Turek who had masterminded, and perhaps even bankrolled, the entire suit against Berry. In a piece for the *St. Louis Post-Dispatch* just before Christmas, Ellen Futterman and Tim Bryant questioned the timing and motivation for the suit. "All fingers point to Turek," they wrote, adding that it was Turek who made the initial contact with Mitch Margo, the lawyer who eventually filed the suit on Johnson's behalf. A month later, Dave Hoekstra, writing for the *Chicago Sun-Times*, arrived at a similar conclusion. "Turek helped inspire the suit," he wrote, adding that, in the interview with Johnson that formed the basis of the suit, the pianist came close to admitting that it was Turek, and not he, who filed the suit. "That's who did it," Hoekstra quoted Johnson as saying, although the journalist was quick to point out that Frances, Johnson's wife, had a different take on the suit's origins. "Frances cuts him off," Hoekstra wrote, "and says, 'Yes and no. We all talked about this [the lawsuit]. We all realized it but he [Johnson] didn't. Lately he started seeing the full picture. And it is one of the proudest moments of our life.' "

In fairness, Turek has denied that he was the guiding force behind the suit. "The lawsuit is between Johnnie and his attorneys. I'll pass on that one," Hoekstra quoted him as saying in the same *Chicago Sun-Times* piece, echoing the sentiment expressed in the earlier *Post-Dispatch* article. "It was Johnnie and Frances' [his wife] decision to make," Turek told Futterman and Bryant. But there is no doubt that Johnson, who as late as April 2000 claimed that he "had no animosity" toward Berry about not getting the recognition he deserved, had listened to Turek and others before giving the go-ahead to the suit.

To be sure, there was more than a sense of vindictiveness in the suit. But, like the lawsuits that had gone before, as much as Chuck Berry was a victim, he was also somewhat responsible for his own downfall. Johnnie Johnson's lawsuit had some merit, if only on a moral basis; after all, Berry had profited from the songs throughout the years while his former bandmate had gone on to live in poverty. But whatever merit Johnson's suit had, its existence began to cast a shadow over one of the most important musical legacies of the twentieth century. In truth, however, the arguments that engendered the suit would always be unresolvable; although Johnson's claim had some merit, particularly on a handful of specific songs like "Wee Wee Hours" and "School Day," the truth would always be clouded by one former alcoholic's memory and hidden behind another man's mask.

Epilogue:
Blueberry Hill

On a sultry June evening, University City is bustling. Although it is only a Wednesday, the sidewalks are crowded with people eating at tables in front of the various restaurants or walking in and out of the eclectic stores that line this five-block area of St. Louis known as the Delmar Loop. Many look down at the stars embedded in the sidewalk, the St. Louis Walk of Fame; eventually, they pass the Loop's spiritual home: Blueberry Hill.

The area wasn't always like this. When Joe Edwards took over the restaurant in 1972, this was a neighborhood full of boarded up store fronts; bikers and drug dealers made up the majority of Edwards's first customers. Undeterred, for the next three decades Edwards gave the city a lesson in urban renewal, eventually expanding Blueberry Hill from one store front into an entire city block, installing the Walk of Fame, renovating a 1920s movie theater, and building a state-of-the-art concert venue. Edwards— equal parts hippie idealist, pragmatic businessman, energetic entrepreneur, and collector of music and sports memorabilia—seemed destined to cross paths with Chuck Berry.

The two first came into contact in 1982, when Edwards was eager to try out a new business venture that combined his interests in music and the restaurant business: Rock and Roll Beer. Berry was to be the featured musician on the first "Heroes of Rock and Roll" can, and Edwards contacted Berry to get his approval to use his name and likeness. Edwards's approach was simple, direct, and honest: later, Edwards speculated,

> the reason he even considered the offer and even talked to me further was just the fact that I made a very fair offer. In fact, it was a huge offer for me financially at the time, but I offered what I thought would have been fair; even if I had been rich at the time I think it would have been fair and I think he respected that. And he listened to me as a result and then we talked.

Berry not only agreed to let Edwards go ahead with the scheme but, over the following years, he fostered their relationship beyond a mere business transaction to a genuine friendship. Clearly, Edwards had found a way to get behind the mask, and from that point on, the two enjoyed a relationship similar to the ones Berry had enjoyed with Leonard Chess and Bill Graham. Based on trust and mutual admiration for each other's accomplishments, the relationship allowed Edwards to see a side of Berry that the musician rarely allowed his business acquaintances to see.

For Edwards, the defining moment came several years after the Rock and Roll Beer venture, shortly after Berry's 60th birthday show and the filming of *Chuck Berry: Hail! Hail! Rock 'n' Roll*. Along with his collections of antique Wurlitzer jukeboxes and pop-culture ephemera displayed in the restaurant, including a large collection of memorabilia from the *Howdy Doody Show*, Edwards decided to build a display case devoted to Berry just inside Blueberry Hill's main entrance. According to Edwards, when he mentioned this to Berry, the musician hinted that he would be willing to donate a guitar to the display. "So, I assumed it would just be some old guitar," recalled Edwards several years later, "the kind every guitar player has laying around. But when he brought out the case, I knew right away that it was *the* guitar." What Berry had brought to the restaurant on Delmar that day was the blond Gibson ES-350T guitar that he had used to record "Maybellene" and then used extensively during the first years of his career. Still fixed to the case were the Air Jamaica baggage tags that had been attached when Berry flew down to rehearse at Keith Richards's island home for the movie. The symbolism of the gesture was not lost on Edwards, with his encyclopedic knowledge of rock and roll. "A lot of rock 'n' roll began in that guitar," Edwards realized, adding that, "when he opened it, I was so touched that I couldn't even speak. It was an act of friendship that blew me away. Now, tell me, would a bitter man give that away? The fact that that guitar is here tells you more about him than I ever could."

On June 25, 1989, Edwards found a way to reciprocate. For some time, he and his wife Linda had been working on the idea of a Walk of Fame for Delmar Boulevard. Based on the famous Hollywood tourist attraction, this walk would have a twist to it: The stars embedded in the sidewalks around Blueberry Hill would all honor individuals who could claim a strong connection with St. Louis. After negotiating the University City Council's red tape and putting up $30,000 of his own money for the venture, Edwards then asked a panel of 50 local experts to draw up a list of eligible candidates. All together, 179 names were then placed on a ballot and voted on by a 200-member committee. That June day, ten St. Louisans were inducted; among them, Chuck Berry was honored, with his bronze star and plaque placed in the concrete sidewalk in front of the main entrance to Blueberry Hill. Berry, who had been moved to tears when his star was placed on Vine Street near

Hollywood Boulevard two years earlier, was no less pleased by this home-grown honor. "I am really flattered, as well as honored, and very proud to have this sort of compliment paid to me," he said in his acceptance speech.

Throughout the tumultuous years of the early 1990s, Edwards remained a staunch friend to Berry, accompanying him to events and shows across the country. When it came time for Berry to celebrate his 70th birthday, then, the guitarist chose to avoid the kind of chaos and commotion that had marked his 60th and instead celebrate in the more intimate surroundings of Blueberry Hill. It was a deliberately low-key affair, with little fanfare. The *Post-Dispatch* announced the show a mere two days in advance and, although he could have charged much more, Edwards kept the ticket price down to $10. As it turned out, the show was not one of Berry's best; Chris Dickinson of the *Post-Dispatch* commented that Berry's playing was "sloppy" and "the sound distorted," somewhat typical of Berry's shows in these later years. But Dickinson was quick to add that the emotion of the show, seeing one of rock music's true legends play to a packed crowd in the small basement room, more than compensated for any flaws in the music. "It's good to be among friends, believe me," Dickinson quoted Berry as saying at one point during the performance, adding that the remark appeared absolutely genuine. And when the show finished at the stroke of midnight, ushering in Berry's birthday, the crowd's impromptu version of "Happy Birthday" was, in Dickinson's estimation, completely moving.

For Joe Edwards, still a fan of Berry's as well as a friend, it appeared to be a great moment, never to be relived. But almost immediately after the show, Edwards recalled Berry saying :

> "It would be kind of fun to play in a place the size of the ones I played when I first started out." And it seemed very natural that it be at Blueberry Hill. So I asked him, "How about doing it here?" And I almost hesitated to say it because I didn't want him to say "No," I wanted it to be "Yes" so much. But then again this is a very small venue for someone that's used to playing 5,000 seats on up places and getting paid a fortune to play, whether it's Las Vegas or Atlanta or Europe. And he didn't hesitate at all, just said, "Let's do it."

From then on, Berry decided to play Blueberry Hill on a regular basis. Once a month, on a Wednesday night for the next five years, Berry came to the unpretentious watering hole and played to a capacity crowd. Less than a year after the first show, Edwards bought the old Cicero's nightclub on the western end of the 6500 block of Delmar and immediately set about building better surroundings for Berry's shows. On November 26, 1997, Berry opened the new downstairs room, humorously christened the Duck Room by

Edwards. Amid the duck decoys and the photographs, Berry and his old compatriot Johnnie Johnson were transported back to the days when they first met. With a capacity of 350 and a knee-high, 26 foot stage, for a few moments the room could have been on the other side of the river, the Cosmopolitan Club, almost half a century earlier.

Berry's delight at playing the Duck Room was evident from the start, and continued for every show he has played at Blueberry Hill. On this partic-ular night in June 2001, the show is sold out once again. Six rows of chairs arc around the stage; front row center is reserved for the immediate Berry family, several of whom have come out to see the show tonight. The rest of the audience stands around the sides of the club; they are a mixture of older rock-and-roll fans and younger tourists, nearly all of them white and all eager to see a slice of rock-and-roll history. After an uninspired set of lackluster blues from a local band, the stage is cleared for Berry's entrance. The diminu-tive Edwards—dressed in a pink-striped Oxford shirt, shorts, and sandals, with his familiar blond ponytail and unruly beard—steps up to the micro-phone, obviously pleased that yet again Blueberry Hill would play host to his friend and hero. "Last week," he begins, "the man you are about to see was in Chicago. He threw out the first pitch at Wrigley Field, sang 'Take Me Out to the Ball Game,' during the seventh inning stretch, then played at the Chicago Blues Festival in front of 70,000 people. We are fortunate once again to have him play here at Blueberry Hill, in his hometown, in front of 350 people. Please welcome, the great Mr. Chuck Berry!"

At this, Berry walks out onto the stage with his familiar limber, bouncing gate, and hugs Edwards centerstage. He turns to the audience, a broad smile on his face. "I apologize for the late start," he says into the microphone, referring to the fact that he is ten minutes late. "I ran out of gas on the way here. Happens to all of us!" And, with a nod toward the laughing Edwards standing on the side of the stage, he adds, "The boss is going to kill me!"

Then, with a few tentative strums on his guitar, he rips into the opening chords of "Roll Over Beethoven," to the delight of the crowd. Behind him, bass player Jim Marsala, now a veteran of almost three decades of Berry shows, pianist Bob Lohr, and drummer Bob Kuban—himself a St. Louis celebrity, having scored three national hits including "The Cheater" in 1965 and 1966 with his group the In-Men—jump in on cue. On this occasion, the three are joined, as they have been for most of the Blueberry Hill shows, by two of Berry's children. Charles, Jr., known to the world as "Butch," follows along quietly yet competently on guitar, staring out into the crowd with a look on his face that is part concentration and part scowl. Seated on the side of the stage, Berry's oldest daughter Ingrid, veteran of many of her dad's shows, sits waiting for her cue. Once on stage, she looks for all the world like a high-school student in her first talent show, mugging to the audience and acting as a foil to her father's every gesture. Her slender frame and flawless features belie her age; she, like her father, is taking great delight in the family's presence on stage tonight.

Midway through the opening number, Berry's guitar strap comes off, leading to general confusion on stage for a few long moments before Marsala steps in to help straighten everything out. It is a moment that sets the tone for the earlier part of the show, as the song temporarily falls apart before coming back together. The song, its tempo slow and uneven, and Berry's guitar, a little out of tune, make for a ragged opening, and the following songs, "Let It Rock," with some nice blues-harp touches from Ingrid, Jimmy Reed's "Honest I Do," and "Memphis, Tennessee" are equally ragged. A shortened "My Ding-a-Ling" with some new suitably risque lyrics, is next, its familiar call-and-response chorus eagerly sung by the crowd every time Berry thrusts his head out and to the side of the microphone. It is followed by "Carol" and "Little Queenie," a medley Berry has been performing for a number of years but which sounds like it is still being rehearsed.

Then, a surprise addition to the Berry canon, a country waltz that takes the audience back to Berry's so-called hillbilly roots. The song is Tony Joe White's "3/4 Time," which, judging by Kuban's quiet, tentative drumming, is new to the band. Two weeks after the Blueberry Hill show, Berry will play the song again at the Hootenanny Festival in Irvine, California; the song's significance would not be lost on *Los Angeles Times* reviewer Randy Lewis. Pointing to the lyrics (where the narrator describes a "mean old world" where "none of us gonna get out alive," then defiantly vows "while I'm still kickin'/I'm gonna keep pickin'"), Lewis will realize that the song is Berry's "respectful nod to mortality."

Next up is Jazz Gillum's "Key to the Highway" (the Big Bill Broonzy standard) which, to Chuck Berry's pleasure, gives daughter Ingrid a chance to stretch out. Despite, or perhaps because of, the loss of her husband and long-time musical partner Chuck Clay earlier in the year, Ingrid pours everything she has into the song, with some inspired blues-harp playing thrown in for good measure. Two more Berry songs, "Around and Around" and "Rock and Roll Music" follow, then it is time for Butch to take his turn in the spotlight on Little Walter's "Mean Old World." His solo, while not as distinctive as his father's, is certainly fluid and capable; once again, Berry himself wanders to the side of the stage to quietly admire his offspring's musicianship.

A little over an hour has gone by, and now the 74-year-old is ready to wind up the evening's performance. What follows is nothing short of transcendent rock and roll, the kind of goosebump-raising, hair-standing-on-the-back-of-your-neck moment that makes forgiving the earlier mistakes very easy. It begins with a "Johnny B. Goode." Although Berry forgets the words to the second verse, offering the crowd a reminder that he is not the agile 32-year-old he was when the song was first released, the duck-walk enhanced lead in the middle of the song brings the crowd to its feet. An extended "Reelin' and Rockin,'" complete with new off-color lyrics for the new millenium, finishes the show, as it has done for many years. At the song's conclusion, in what has by now become a ritual, Berry invites the audience to come on stage and dance with him. Hesitantly at first, two women in their mid-20s take him up on the offer; once the ice is broken, the audience swarms onto the stage. Slowly and deliberately, still playing his guitar, Berry winds his way through the dancers. Out of the dressing room door, stage left, an attractive, middle-aged white blond watches as he inches his way toward her. Then, she and Joe Edwards hold the door open, Berry walks in, and the show is over.

For a few minutes, bedlam reigns. Bob Kuban tries desperately to make his way through the crowd, while Jim Marsala and Butch Berry guard the equipment. Slowly, two bouncers restore order and the dancers form an orderly line on the stage and wait patiently for the next ten minutes to visit briefly with the man. Inside the dressing room, a visibly exhausted Berry signs autographs and shakes hands with everyone for the next twenty minutes. But the stage smile is replaced with a stony, pensive stare when one fan's request for him to pose for a photograph is quickly put down: "No, I don't wanna. The flash hurts my eyes," he says curtly. The fan leaves disappointed; one could argue he had no right to make those kinds of demands on anyone, even a celebrity. But for the sake of a second's worth of discomfort, the star could have given a lifetime of pleasure to his fan. Even in an innocuous moment such as this, Chuck Berry keeps his mask firmly in place.

Slowly, the crowd dissipates into the muggy St. Louis night as Berry signs the last album sleeve and then heads up the stairs and into his Cadillac for the ten-minute drive back to Ladue. He will do this again in a month's time, will continue to do it until who-knows-when. Amid the chairs strewn across the floor and the sticky residue of spilled beer, Joe Edwards has a contented smile on his face. He, at least, has seen beneath the mask and has been able to enjoy another Chuck Berry, the happy, joking, generous-to-a-fault Berry whom few present this night could or would ever see. He stands talking with Butch Berry and several others, and the talk this night is of two pressing issues.

The first is the Johnson lawsuit. Rumor is circulating that some sort of decision has made its way down from the court; and, true enough, on the Monday prior to the Blueberry Hill show, the lawsuit has moved in a strange way. Initially, the ruling seemed to favor Berry; Judge Donald T. Stohr had thrown out the allegations that Berry had infringed on Johnson's copyrights. But the judge had kept in the charges that Berry had defrauded Johnson, taking advantage of the pianist's alcoholism to lead him into believing that he had no right to any songwriter's royalties. Additionally, the judge ruled, there was some question as to whether the statute of limitations could be invoked in the case, given the 40-year gap between the alleged fraud and the suit. Berry's lawyers had contended that there was a three-year limit for someone filing a copyright-infringement suit. Even so, the judge concluded, Johnson's suit could go ahead. Johnson could attempt to show why the statute of limitations should not apply; further, Johnson's attorneys could take depositions and investigate Berry's financial records to determine the amount of royalties Berry had been paid on the songs in question. The judge also requested that the two parties select a mediator and explore the possibility of an out-of-court settlement.

It was difficult to know how to interpret the ruling. Martin Green, Berry's lawyer, was quick to claim victory, claiming that the judge, by dismissing the copyright claims, had dismissed "the substantive base of the suit in the first place." But in a way, he had not. By allowing the fraud issue to remain on the table, the ruling seemed to indicate that the issue of who had written the songs had not been resolved. After all, if Berry had defrauded Johnson, what else could he have defrauded him of *except* his right to claim royalties on the songs? And, if Johnson was entitled to royalties, he must therefore have cowritten the songs. So, in a sense, the copyright issue had not been dismissed. And although Joe Edwards also put a positive spin on the decision, it was, at best, a troublesome and contradictory ruling.

But Edwards's optimism about the other topic of discussion this night is perhaps a little more well-founded. Stories that had been circulating for years about the possibility of a new Chuck Berry album now appeared true, and Edwards, who had been invited to some of the studio sessions, was ecstatic at the possibility of an October release to coincide with Berry's 75th birthday. Such rumors had been circulating since the release of Berry's last studio album, *Rockit*, in 1977. Berry had claimed that the fire that destroyed his recording studio at Berry Park in March of 1989 had taken master tapes for a proposed double album with it. Jim Marsala, interviewed for Johnson's biography, recalls recording material in 1993 for an album that was to be part studio compositions and part live recordings from a 1982 show at the Roxy in Los Angeles with Tina Turner. Berry himself had hinted at it in a 2000 interview with authors and historians Stephen Ambrose and Douglas Brinkley for a *USA Today* series on the Mississippi River. In the interview, he claimed 13 songs were ready for release, including "Lady B. Goode," which Berry maintained was not at all like its predecessor, and "Loco Joe," which Berry had premiered at several European dates as early as 1995. (Paul DuNoyer described it as a "trite, smutty number about a traveling salesman sung in cod-Mexican" in a piece for *Q* magazine that year.) But by Berry's birthday, appropriately celebrated at Joe Edwards's new showcase club, the Pageant, several blocks east of Blueberry Hill, the promised album had yet to see the light of day.

Regardless of what the future holds for Berry—whether it be a long, drawn-out lawsuit or a new recording, or (more likely) both—one thing remains: As the last of the crowd filters out of the Duck Room, Joe Edwards muses about the show that has just ended and the Blueberry Hill shows in general. With a fan's sense of pride, he says,

> These monthly shows are legendary because every show is different. No one knows for sure what song is coming next; in fact, Chuck doesn't know what song is coming next until about three seconds before he starts to play it. On a given night, anything could happen. You never know what you're going to see or hear at a Chuck Berry concert.

It's now after midnight, and Edwards is exhausted. But as he climbs the stairs to go back to his office and conclude the day's business at the restaurant, he pauses to give one final review of the night's show, a review that might also stand as a metaphor for Chuck Berry's life.

> I love the fact that he doesn't do encores. There's nothing wrong with encores; if a musician or a band puts on a great show and it's one of those spontaneous encores that is deserved, the way it was first started or was meant to be, I have no problem with that. But it's kind of a yawner I think to have a band not play a certain hit because they're going to do that during the encore. It doesn't make the concert itself as real and spontaneous. I think it works for him, too, at this age especially it's wonderful to put that kind of energy all the way. He just gives everything, and then when it's gone and he's exhausted, then he wraps it up and you've seen a great show that way.

Discography

Below is a list of significant U.S. and U.K. releases. For more comprehensive information, see Fred Rothwell's *Long Distance Information* and Morton Reff's discography in Howard Dewitt's *Chuck Berry: Rock and Roll Music*. *Chuck Berry: The Autobiography* and Michel Ruppli's *The Chess Labels* are also important sources of discographical information.

1. Pre-Chess Recording

1954

Single
Oh Maria/I Hope These Words Will Find You Well (Joe Alexander and the Cubans) (Ballad M-5008)
    (Re-released on Spindle Records SPN-2001 in 1995)

2. The Chess Recordings 1955-1966

1955

Singles
Maybellene/Wee Wee Hours (Chess 1604)
Thirty Days/Together We Will Always Be (Chess 1610)
No Money Down/Downbound Train (Chess 1615; **UK** London HLU-8275, released in 1956)

1956

Singles
Roll Over Beethoven/Drifting Heart (Chess 1626; **UK** London HLU-8428, released in 1957)
Too Much Monkey Business/Brown Eyed Handsome Man (Chess 1635)
You Can't Catch Me/Havana Moon (Chess 1645; **UK** London HLN-8375, released in 1957)

EP
Rhythm and Blues with Chuck Berry (**UK** London RE-U-1053)
    Maybellene/Wee Wee Hours/Thirty Days/Together We Will Always Be

Album
Rock, Rock, Rock (Chess 1425; CD Chess CHD 31270)
    Maybellene/Thirty Days/You Can't Catch Me/Roll Over Beethoven
        (Soundtrack album from the movie of the same name also featuring songs by the Flamingos, the Moonglows and Bo Diddley)

1957

Singles
School Day (Ring! Ring! Goes the Bell)/Deep Feeling (Chess 1653; **UK** Columbia DB-3951)
Oh Baby Doll/La Juanda (Chess 1664)
Rock and Roll Music/Blue Feeling (Chess 1671; **UK** London HLM-8531)

EPs
After School Session (Chess 5118)

School Day/Wee Wee Hours/Too Much Monkey Business/Brown Eyed Handsome Man
Rock and Roll Music (Chess 5119)
Rock and Roll Music/Blue Feeling/School Day/Deep Feeling (Later re-released with "Oh Baby Doll" and "La Juanda" replacing "School Day" and "Deep Feeling")

Album
After School Session (Chess 1426; CD Chess CHD 9284)
School Day/Deep Feeling/Too Much Monkey Business/Wee Wee Hours/Roly Poly/No Money Down/Brown Eyed Handsome Man/Berry Pickin'/Together We Will Always Be/Havana Moon/Downbound Train/Drifting Heart

1958

Singles
Sweet Little Sixteen/Reelin' and Rockin' (Chess 1683; **UK** London HLM-8585)
Johnny B. Goode/Around and Around (Chess 1691; **UK** London HLM-8629)
Beautiful Delilah/Vacation Time (Chess 1697; **UK** London HL-8677)
Carol/Hey Pedro (Chess 1700; **UK** London HL-8712)
Sweet Little Rock and Roller/Jo Jo Gunne (Chess 1709; **UK** London HLM-8767)
Merry Christmas Baby/Run Rudolph Run (Chess 1714)

EPs
Sweet Little Sixteen (Chess 5121)
Sweet Little Sixteen/Rockin' At The Philharmonic/Reelin' and Rockin'/Guitar Boogie
Pickin' Berries (Chess 5124)
Beautiful Delilah/Vacation Time/Carol/Hey Pedro
Sweet Little Rock and Roller (Chess 5126)
Sweet Little Rock and Roller/Jo Jo Gunne/Johnny B. Goode/Around and Around

Album
One Dozen Berries (Chess 1432; **UK** London HA-M2132, released 1959)
Sweet Little Sixteen/Blue Feeling/La Juanda/Rockin' At The Philharmonic/Oh Baby Doll/Reelin' And Rockin'/Ingo/Rock And Roll Music/How You've Changed/Low Feeling/It Don't Take But A Few Minutes ("Low Feeling" is "Blue Feeling" recorded at half-speed and with a section omitted) (*One Dozen Berries* and *Juke Box Hits* re-released on **UK** CD BGO Records BGOCD458)

1959

Singles
Anthony Boy/That's My Desire (Chess 1716)
Almost Grown/Little Queenie (Chess 1722; **UK** London HLM-8853)
Back in the USA/Memphis, Tennessee (Chess 1729; **UK** London HLM-8921)
Broken Arrow/Childhood Sweetheart (Chess 1737)
Say You'll Be Mine/Let Me Sleep Woman (The Ecuadors with Chuck Berry) (Argo 5353)

EP
Reelin' and Rockin' (**UK** London RE-M-1188)
Sweet Little Sixteen/Rock and Roll Music/Reelin' and Rockin'/Guitar Boogie

Album
Chuck Berry Is On Top (Chess 1435; CD Chess CHD-31260)
Almost Grown/Carol/Maybellene/Sweet Little Rock And Roller/Anthony Boy/Johnny B. Goode/Little Queenie/Jo Jo Gunne/Roll Over Beethoven/Around And Around/Hey Pedro/Blues For Hawaiians (**UK** CD Chess CHLD-19250. Additional tracks: Down the Road Apiece/No Money Down/Downbound Train/Jaguar and Thunderbird/The Things I Used To Do/No Particular Place To Go/Fraulein/Nadine (Is It You?)

1960

Singles

Too Pooped To Pop/Let It Rock (Chess 1747; **UK** London HLM-9069)
Bye Bye Johnny/Worried Life Blues (Chess 1754; **UK** London HLM-9159, B-side is
"Mad Lad")
I Got To Find My Baby/Mad Lad (Chess 1763)
Jaguar and the Thunderbird/Our Little Rendezvous (Chess 1767)

Album

Rockin' At The Hops (Chess 1448; CD Chess CHD-9259)
   Bye Bye Johnny/Worried Life Blues/Down The Road Apiece/Confessin'
   The Blues/Too Pooped To Pop/Mad Lad/I Got To Find My Baby/Betty
   Jean/Childhood Sweetheart/Broken Arrow/Driftin' Blues/Let It Rock

1961

Singles

I'm Talking About You/Little Star (Chess 1779; **UK** Pye International 7N.25100)
Come On/Go Go Go (Chess 1799; UK Pye International 7N.25209, released in 1963)

Album

New Juke Box Hits (Chess 1456; CD Chess CHD-9171; **UK** Pye International NPL-
28019, released as *Juke Box Hits* in 1962)
   I'm Talking About You/Diploma For Two/Thirteen Question Method/Away From
   You/Don't You Lie To Me/The Way It Was Before/Little Star/Route 66/Sweet
   Sixteen/Run Around/Stop And Listen/Rip It Up (*Juke Box Hits* and *One Dozen Berries*
   re-released on **UK** CD BGO Records BGOCD458)

1962

Album

Chuck Berry Twist (reissued as *More Chuck Berry* in 1963) (Chess 1465)
   Maybellene/Roll Over Beethoven/Oh Baby Doll/Around And Around/Come On/Let
   It Rock/Reelin' And Rockin'/School Day/Almost Grown/Sweeet Little Sixteen/Thirty
   Days/Johnny B. Goode/Rock And Roll Music/Back In The U.S.A.

1963

Singles

Diploma for Two/I'm Talking About You (Chess 1853)
Sweet Little Sixteen/Memphis, Tennessee (Chess 1866; **UK** Pye International 7N.25218,
   A-side is "Let It Rock")
Run, Rudolph, Run/Johnny B. Goode (**UK** Pye International 7N.25228)

EPs

Chuck Berry (**UK** Pye International NEP-44011)
   Johnny B. Goode/Oh Baby Doll/School Day/Back in the USA
This is Chuck Berry (**UK** Pye International NEP-44013)
   Bye Bye Johnny/Rock and Roll Music/Childhood Sweetheart/Broken Arrow

Album

Chuck Berry On Stage (Chess 1480; **UK** Pye International NPL-28027)
   Go, Go, Go/Memphis, Tennessee/Maybellene/Surfin' Steel/Rockin' On The Railroad
   (Let It Rock)/Brown Eyed Handsome Man (alternate take)/Still Got The Blues/Sweet
   Little Sixteen/Jaguar and Thunderbird/I Just Want To Make Love To You/All
   Aboard/Trick Or Treat/The Man And The Donkey/How High The Moon (All studio
   cuts with overdubbed audience)
Chuck Berry (**UK** Pye International NPL-28024)
   Maybellene/Down The Road Apiece/Mad Lad/School Day/Sweet Little
   Sixteen/Confessin' The Blues/Back In The U.S.A./Johnny B. Goode/Oh Baby
   Doll/Come On/I Got To Find My Baby/Betty Jean/Around And Around/Almost
   Grown

More Chuck Berry (**UK** Pye International NPL-28028)
   Sweet Little Rock and Roller/Anthony Boy/Little Queenie/Worried Life
   Blues/Carol/Reelin' and Rockin'/Thirty Days/Brown Eyed Handsome Man/
   Too Much Monkey Business/Wee Wee Hours/Jo Jo Gunne/Beautiful Delilah (*Chuck
   Berry* and *More Chuck Berry* re-released on **UK** CD BGO Records BGOCD394)

1964

Singles

Nadine (Is It You?)/O Rangutang (Chess 1883; **UK** Pye International 7N.25236)
No Particular Place To Go/You Two (Chess 1898; **UK** Pye International 7N.25242, B-
   side is "Liverpool Drive")
You Never Can Tell/Brenda Lee (Chess 1906; **UK** Pye International 7N.25257)
Little Marie/Go Bobby Soxer (Chess 1912; **UK** Pye International 7N.25271)
Promised Land/Things I Used To Do (Chess 1916; **UK** Pye International 7N.25285
   released in 1965)

EPs

The Best of Chuck Berry (**UK** Pye International NEP-44018)
   Memphis, Tennessee/Roll Over Beethoven/I'm Talking About You/Sweet Little
   Sixteen
Chuck Berry Hits (**UK** Pye International NEP-44028)
   Johnny B. Goode/Nadine (Is It You?)/No Particular Place To Go/Memphis,
   Tennessee
Blue Mood (**UK** Pye International NEP-44033)
   Drifting Blues/Lonely All The Time/Things I Used To Do/Fraulein

Albums

Chuck Berry's Greatest Hits (Chess 1485)
   Roll Over Beethoven/School Day/Rock And Roll Music/Too Much Monkey
   Business/Johnny B. Goode/Oh Baby Doll/Nadine (Is It
   You?)/Maybellene/Memphis/Sweet Little Sixteen/Thirty Days/Brown Eyed
   Handsome Man
Two Great Guitars (With Bo Diddley) (Checker 2991; CD Chess CHD 9170; **UK** Pye
   International NPL-28047 released 1965)
   Liverpool Drive/Chuck's Beat/When The Saints Go Marching
   In/Bo's Beat (Additional track on the CD release: Chuckwalk)
St. Louis To Liverpool (Chess LP-1488; CD Chess CHD 31261))
   Little Marie/Our Little Rendezvous/No Particular Place To Go/You Two/Promised
   Land/You Never Can Tell/Go Bobby Soxer/The Things I Used To Do/Night
   Beat/Merry Christmas Baby/Brenda Lee
The Latest And The Greatest (**UK** Pye International NPL-28031)
   Nadine (Is It You?)/Fraulein/Guitar Boogie/Things I Used To Do/Don't You Lie To
   Me/Drifting Blues/Liverpool Drive/No Particular Place To Go/Lonely All The
   Time/Jaguar And The Thunderbird/O Rangutang/You Two/Deep Feeling/Bye Bye
   Johnny
You Never Can Tell (**UK** Pye International NPL-28039; re-released as Marble Arch MAL-
   702 in 1967)
   You Never Can Tell/Diploma For Two/The Little Girl From Central/The Way It
   Was/Around and Around/Big Ben/Promised Land/Back in the USA/Run
   Around/Brenda Lee/Reelin' and Rockin'/Come On (*The Latest And The Greatest* and
   You Never Can Tell re-released on **UK** CD BGO Records BGOCD428)

1965

Singles

I Got A Booking/Lonely School Days (**UK** Chess CRS 8006)
Dear Dad/Lonely School Days (slow version) (Chess 1926; **UK** Chess CRS 8012, B-side
   is "I Got A Booking")
It Wasn't Me/Welcome Back Pretty Baby (Chess 1943; **UK** Chess CRS 8022; B-side is
   "It's My Own Business")

EPs

The Promised Land (**UK** Chess CRE-6002)
   You Never Can Tell/Brenda Lee/Promised Land/Things I Used To Do
Come On (**UK** Chess CRE-6005)
   Come On/Reelin' and Rockin'/Around and Around/
   Don't You Lie To Me

Albums

Chuck Berry In London (Chess 1495; **UK** Chess CRL-4005)
   My Little Love Light/She Once Was Mine/After It's Over/I Got A Booking/Night
   Beat/His Daughter Caroline/You Came A Long Way From St. Louis/St. Louis
   Blues/Jamaica Farewell/Dear Dad/Butterscotch/The Song Of My Love/Why Should
   We End This Way/I Want To Be Your Driver
Fresh Berry's (**UK** Chess CRL-4506; Chess LP-1498, released 1966)
   It Wasn't Me/Run Joe/Every Day We Rock and Roll/One For My Baby/Sad Day,
   Long Night/It's My Own Business/Right Off Rampart Street/Vaya Con Dios/Merrily
   We Rock and Roll/My Mustang Ford/Ain't That Just Like A Woman/Wee Hours
   Blues ("Welcome Back Pretty Baby" replaces "Sad Day, Long Night" on the US
   release) (*Chuck Berry In London* and *Fresh Berry's* re-released on CD **UK** BGO Records
   BGOCD395)

1966

Singles

Ramona Say Yes/Lonely School Days (fast version) (Chess 1963; **UK** Chess CRS 8037)
   (Later re-released in the US with "Havana Moon" replacing "Lonely School Days")
Johnny B. Goode/Sweet Little Sixteen (**UK** Chess CRS 8075)
No Particular Place To Go/It Wasn't Me (**UK** Chess CRS 8089)

EPs

I Got A Booking (**UK** Chess CRE-6012)
   I Want To Be Your Driver/St. Louis Blues/Dear Dad/I Got A Booking
You Came A Long Way From St. Louis (**UK** Chess CRE-6016)
   You Came A Long Way From St. Louis/His Daughter Caroline/My Little Love
   Light/Jamaica Farewell

1967

Album

Chuck Berry's Golden Decade (Chess LP-1514D)
   Maybellene/Deep Feeling/Johnny B. Goode/Wee Wee Hours/Nadine (Is It
   You?)/Brown Eyed Handsome Man/Roll Over Beethoven/Thirty Days/Havana
   Moon/No Particular Place To Go/Memphis, Tennesee/Almost Grown/School
   Day/Too Much Monkey Business/Oh Baby Doll/Reelin' And Rockin'/You Can't
   Catch Me/Too Pooped To Pop/Bye Bye Johnny/Around And Around/Sweet Little
   Sixteen/Rock And Roll Music/Anthony Boy/Back In The U.S.A.

3. The Mercury Recordings (1967-1969)

1967

Singles

Laugh and Cry/Club Nitty Gritty (Mercury 72643; **UK** Mercury MF-958, released 1966)
Back to Memphis/I Do Really Love You (Mercury 72680; **UK** Mercury MF-994)
Feelin' It/It Hurts Me Too (Mercury 72748)

Albums

Golden Hits (Mercury SR-61103; **UK** Mercury 20102 SMCL; CD Mercury 826 256–2)
   Sweet Little Sixteen/Memphis, Tennessee/School Day/Maybellene/Back In The
   U.S.A./Johnny B. Goode/Rock And Roll Music/Roll Over Beethoven/Thirty
   Days/Carol/Club Nitty Gritty (Additional tracks on the CD release: Around and
   Around, Brown Eyed Handsome Man, Let It Rock, Reelin' and Rockin')

In Memphis (Mercury SR-61123; **UK** Mercury 20110 SMCL; CD Mercury 836 071–2)
    Back to Memphis/I Do Really Love You/Ramblin' Rose/Sweet Little Rock and
    Roller/My Heart Will Always Belong To You/Oh Baby Doll/Check Me Out/It Hurts
    Me Too/Bring Another Drink/So Long/Goodnight, Well It's Time To Go
    Additional track on the CD release: Flying Home
Live At The Filmore (Mercury SR-61138; **UK** Mercury 20112 SMCL; CD Mercury 836
072–2)
    Rocking At The Filmore/Every Day I Have The Blues/C.C. Rider/Driftin'
    Blues/Feelin' It/Flying Home/Hoochie Coochie Man/Filmore Blues/It Hurts Me
    Too/Wee Baby Blues/Johnny B. Goode (Additional tracks on the CD release: Good
    Morning Little Schoolgirl/Bring Another Drink/Worried Life Blues/Reelin' and
    Rockin'/My Ding-A-Ling)

1968

Single
Louie to Frisco/Ma Dear (Mercury 72840; **UK** Mercury MF-1057)

Albums
From St. Louis To Frisco (Mercury SR-61176; CD Mercury 836 073–2)
    Louie to Frisco/Ma Dear/The Love I Lost/I Love Her, I Love Her/Little Fox/Rock
    Cradle Rock/Soul Rockin'/I Can't Believe/Misery/My Tambourine/Oh Captain/
    Mum's the Word (Additional tracks on the CD release: Almost Grown/Laugh and
    Cry/Campus Cookie/Song Of My Love)

1969

Single
Good Looking Woman/It's Too Dark In There (Mercury 72963)
Back to Memphis/Roll Over Beethoven (**UK** Mercury MF-1102)

Album
Concerto In B. Goode (Mercury SR-61233; **UK** Mercury 20162 SMCL; CD Mercury 836
074–2)
    Good Looking Woman/My Woman/It's Too Dark In There/Put Her
    Down/Concerto In B. Goode

1972

Album
St. Louis To Frisco to Memphis (Mercury SRM 2–6051; **UK** Phillips International 6619008)
    Double album set containing entire recording of *Live At The Filmore*, plus St. Louie To
    Frisco/Ma Dear/Soul Rockin'/Check Me Out/Little Fox/Back To Memphis/My
    Tambourine/Misery/It's Too Dark In There/I Do Really Love You/I Can't Believe/My
    Heart Will Always Belong To You/So Long

4. The Later Chess/GRT Recordings (1970-1975)

1970

Single
Tulane/Have Mercy Judge (Chess 2090)

Album
Back Home (Chess LPS-1550; **UK** Chess 6310113)
    Tulane/Have Mercy Judge/Instrumental/Christmas/Gun/I'm A
    Rocker/Flyin' Home/Fish And Chips/Some People

1971

Single
Sweet Little Sixteen/Guitar Boogie (**UK** Chess 6078 707)

Album

San Francisco Dues (Chess CH-50008; **UK** Chess 6310115)
Oh Louisiana/Let's Do Our Thing Together/Your Lick/Festival/Bound To
Lose/Bordeux In My Pirough/San Francisco Dues/Viva Viva Rock And Roll/My
Dream/Lonely School Day

1972

Singles

My Ding-A-Ling/Johnny B. Goode (Chess 2131; **UK** Chess 6145 019, B-side is "Let's
Boogie")
Reelin' and Rockin'/Let's Boogie (Chess 2136; **UK** Chess 6145 020,
B-side is "I Will Not Let You Go," released 1973)

Album

The London Chuck Berry Sessions (Chess CH-60020; CD CHESS CHD-9295; **UK** Chess
6310122; **UK** CD CDRED-20) (Studio)
Let's Boogie/I Will Not Let You Go/Mean Old World/I Love You/London Berry
Blues/(Live) Reelin' And Rockin'/My Ding-A-Ling/Johnny B. Goode

1973

Singles

Bio/Roll 'Em Pete (Chess 2140)
South of the Border/Bio (**UK** Chess 6145 027)

Albums

Chuck Berry's Golden Decade Volume 2 (Chess 2CH-60023; **UK** Chess 6641058)
Carol/You Never Can Tell/No Money Down/Together We Will Always Be/Mad
Lad/Run Rudolph Run/Let It Rock/Sweet Little Rock And Roller/It Don't Take But
A Few Minutes/I'm Talking About You/Driftin' Blues/Go Go Go/Jaguar And
Thunderbird/Little Queenie/Betty Jean (alternate take)/Guitar Boogie/Down The
Road Apiece/Merry Christmas Baby/Promised Land/Jo Jo Gunne/Don't You Lie To
Me/Rockin' At The Philharmonic/La Juanda/Come On
Bio (Chess CH-50043; **UK** Chess 6499650; CD Chess CHD-91510)
Bio/Hello Little Girl, Goodbye/Woodpecker/Rain Eyes/Aimlessly Driftin'/Got It And
Gone/Talkin' About My Buddy

1974

Album

Chuck Berry's Golden Decade Volume 3 (Chess 2CH-60028; **UK** Chess 6641177)
Beautiful Delilah/Go Bobby Soxer/I Got To Find My Baby/Worried Life Blues/Rolli
Polli/Downbound Train/Broken Arrow/Confessin' The Blues/ Driftin'
Heart/Ingo/Man And The Donkey/St. Louis Blues/Our Little Rendezvous/Childhood
Sweetheart/Blues For Hawaiians/Hey Pedro/My Little Love Light/Little
Marie/County Line/Viva, Viva Rock And Roll/House Of Blue Lights/Time Was/Blue
On Blue/Oh Yeah ("Do You Love Me" and "Berry Pickin'" replace "Time Was" and
"Viva Viva Rock And Roll" on the **UK** release)

1975

Single

Shake Rattle and Roll/Baby What You Want Me To Do (Chess 2169; **UK** Chess 6145
038, B-side is "I'm Just A Name")

Album

Chuck Berry (Chess CH-60032; **UK** Chess 9109101)
Swanee River/I'm Just A Name/I Just Want To Make Love To You/Too Late/South
Of The Border/Hi Heel Sneakers/You Are My Sunshine/My Babe/Baby, What You
Want Me To Do/A Deuce/Shake Rattle And Roll/Sue Answer/Don't You Lie To Me

5. Significant Post-Chess Recordings and Releases

1977

Album

Motorvatin' (**UK** Chess 9286 690)

Johnny B. Goode/Roll Over Beethoven/School Day/Maybellene/Rock and Roll Music/Oh Baby Doll/Too Much Monkey Business/Carol/Let It Rock/Sweet Little Rock And Roller/Bye Bye Johnny/Reelin' and Rockin'/No Particular Place To Go/Thirty Days/Sweet Little Sixteen/Little Queenie/Memphis, Tennessee/You Never Can Tell/Brown Eyed Handsome Man/Promised Land/Back In The U.S.A.

1978

Albums

American Hot Wax (A&M SP-6500)

Reelin' and Rockin'/Roll Over Beethoven/Sweet Little Sixteen

(Soundtrack album from the movie of the same name also featuring songs by Jerry Lee Lewis and Screamin' Jay Hawkins. "Reelin' and Rockin'" and "Roll Over Beethoven" were recorded live for the movie)

Live In Concert (Magnum MR-703)

Rock And Roll Music/Nadine (Is It You?)/School Day/Wee Wee Hours/Hoochie Coochie Man/Medley: Johnny B. Goode—Carol—Promised Land/Sweet Little Sixteen/Memphis/Too Much Monkey Business/My Ding-A-Ling/Reelin' And Rockin'/Johnny B. Goode/Maybellene

(This is the complete performance of the 1969 Toronto Rock and Roll Revival. Selections have been re-released on numerous other albums and CDs).

1979

Single

California/Oh What A Thrill (Atco 7203; **UK** Atlantic K-11354)

Album

Rock It (Atco SD 38–118; **UK** Atlantic K-50648; CD Atlantic 7567–80759–2; **UK** CD Magnum Force CDMF-065)

Move It/Oh What A Thrill/I Need You Baby/If I Were/House Lights/I Never Thought/Havana Moon (Re-recording)/Wuden't We/California/Pass Away

1982

Album

The Great Twenty-Eight (Chess CH-8201; CD Chess CHD-92500)

Maybellene/Thirty Days/You Can't Catch Me/Too Much Monkey Business/Brown-Eyed Handsome Man/Roll Over Beethoven/Havana Moon/School Day/Rock And Roll Music/Oh Baby Doll/Reelin' And Rockin'/Sweet Little Sixteen/Johnny B. Goode/Around And Around/Carol/Beautiful Delilah/Memphis, Tennessee/Sweet Little Rock And Roller/Little Queenie/Almost Grown/Back In The USA/Let It Rock/Bye Bye Johnny/ I'm Talking About You/Come On/Nadine (Is It You?)/No Particular Place To Go/I Want To Be Your Driver

1986

Album

Rock and Roll Rarities (Chess 2–92521; CD Chess CHD 92521)

No Particular Place To Go (stereo remix)/Rock And Roll Music (alternate take)/It Wasn't Me (alternate take)/Reelin' And Rockin' (demo)/Come On (alternate take)/Little Queenie (alternate take)/You Never Can Tell (stereo remix)/Sweet Little Sixteen (alternate take)/County Line/Run Rudolph Run/Nadine (Is It You?) (stereo remix)/Betty Jean/I Want To Be Your Driver (stereo remix)/Beautiful Delilah (alternate take)/Oh Yeah/Johnny B. Goode (alternate take)/Bye Bye Johnny (stereo remix)/Little Marie (stereo remix)/Time Was (alternate take)/Promised Land (stereo remix)

More Rock and Roll Rarities (Chess 9190)

Ain't That Just Like A Woman (stereo remix)/Rock And Roll Music (demo)/Down The Road Apiece (stereo remix)/Brown Eyed Handsome Man (second version stereo remix)/Route 66 (alt. take)/Sweet Little Rock And Roller (alternate take)/My Mustang Ford (stereo remix)/Sweet Little Sixteen (demo)/I Got To Find My Baby (stereo remix)/I'm Talking About You (stereo remix)/House Of Blue Lights/Go Go Go (stereo remix)

1987

Album

Chuck Berry Hail! Hail! Rock And Roll (Original Motion Picture Soundtrack) (MCA 6217; CD MCA MCAD-6217; **UK** CD MCA DMCF-3411)

Maybellene/Around and Around/Sweet Litttle Sixteen/Brown Eyed Handsome Man (guest performer: Robert Cray)/Memphis, Tennessee/Too Much Monkey Business/Back In The U.S.A. (guest performer: Linda Ronstadt)/Wee Wee Hours (guest performer: Eric Clapton)/Johnny B. Goode (guest performer: Julian Lennon)/Little Queenie/Rock and Roll Music (guest performer: Etta James)/Roll Over Beethoven/I'm Through With Love

1989

CD

Rock And Roll Rarities (**UK** Chess CDCHESS-1005)

Rock and Roll Music (demo)/Rock and Roll Music (alternate take)/Sweet Little Sixteen (demo)/Sweet Little Sixteen (alternate take)/Reelin' and Rockin' (alternate take)/Johnny B. Goode (alternate take)/Beautiful Delilah (alternate take)/Oh Yeah/House of Blue Lights/Time Was (fast version)/Sweet Little Rock and Roller (alternate take)/Run, Rudolph, Run/Little Queenie (alternate take)/Betty Jean/County Line/Bye Bye Johnny (stereo remix)/I Got To Find My Baby (stereo remix)/Come On (alternate take)/Go Go Go (stereo remix)/Brown Eyed Handsome Man (stereo remix)/Nadine (Is It You?) (stereo remix)/You Never Can Tell (stereo remix)/Promised Land (stereo remix)/No Particular Place To Go (stereo remix)

1990

CD

Missing Berries—Rarities Volume 3 (Chess CHD 9318)

Childhood Sweetheart (alternate take)/Do You Love Me (alternate take)/Big Ben Blues/Man and the Donkey/One O'Clock Jump/Little Girl From Central/Instrumental/Let Me Sleep Woman (with The Ecuadors)/That's My Desire/Blue on Blue/Vacation Time/21 Blues

1994

CD

Live On Stage (**UK** Magnum Force CDMF 092)

School Day/Sweet Little Sixteen/Roll Over Beethoven/Everyday I Have The Blues/Bio/Maybellene-Mountain Dew/Let It Rock/Carol-Little Queenie/Keys to the Highway (with Ingrid Berry)/Got My Mojo Working (with Ingrid Berry)/ Reelin' and Rockin' (with Ingrid Berry)/Johnny B. Goode (Complete live performance from a 1983 show at the Wirrina Sports Stadium in Peterborough, England)

1997

CD

Live (Columbia River Entertainment Group VMK-1154)

Roll Over Beethoven/School Day/Sweet Little Sixteen/Nadine (Is It You?)/Let It Rock/Promised Land/Memphis, Tennessee/Johnny B. Goode/Brown Eyed Handsome Man/Too Much Monkey Business/Carol—Little Queenie/Rock and Roll Music (with Tina Turner)/Instrumental/Reelin' and Rockin' (with Ingrid Berry)

(Complete live performance from a 1982 show at the Roxy Theatre in Los Angeles)

In 1985, MCA obtained the rights to the Chess catalog and systematically set about re-releasing much of the material for the new, burgeoning compact disc market. Among the more significant releases of Chuck Berry recordings were 1988's *Chess Box* (MCA CH6; CD CHD3–80), a three-disc box set; 1997's *His Best, Volume 1* (Chess 9371) and *Volume 2* (Chess 9381); 1999's *The Best of Chuck Berry: 20th Century Masters: The Millennium Collection* (MCA 11944); and 2000's two-disc set *Chuck Berry: The Anthology* (MCA 112 304). Each one varies slightly in scope and song selection.

In 1994, MCA successfully sued Charly Records in a dispute over the European rights to the Chess catalog, forcing Charly to immediately withdraw two other significant UK releases, the comprehensive nine-disc set *The Chess Years* (Charly CD RED BOX 2), originally released in 1991, and the 1994 four-disc collection *Poet of Rock'n'Roll* (Charly CDDIG 1).

Notes

Prologue

"Boy," he began: *Chuck Berry: Hail! Hail! Rock 'n' Roll*, Delilah Films, 1987.

"It made me think": *Chuck Berry: Hail! Hail! Rock 'n' Roll*, Delilah Films, 1987.

The trouble started: Deborah Peterson and Bill Smith, "Berry Goes Strong at Birthday Bash," *St. Louis Post-Dispatch*, October 17, 1986.

Members of Local 6 Stagehands: "Berry's Birthday Bash Criticized," UPI, October 14, 1986 A.M. Cycle.

At an open rehearsal: Daniel Brogan, "Birthday Concert Turns into a Party on Second Try," *Chicago Tribune*, October 19, 1986.

The tensions, evidently: Susan Hegger, "The Hottest Ticket in Town to the Worst Show of the Year," *Riverfront Times*, October 22–28, 1986.

An appearance by Bob Dylan: Hegger, "Hottest Ticket."

"a flood of missed cues": Brogan, "Birthday Concert."

"off-key, off-tempo and off the mark": Hegger, "Hottest Ticket."

"Revolt! Don't stand (up) for this ripoff": Peterson and Smith, "Berry Goes Strong."

With names such as Paul McCartney: Hegger, "Hottest Ticket."

the first show was "derailed": Robert Palmer, "Chuck Berry at 60," *New York Times*, October 18, 1986.

"It was a rock 'n' roll spectacle": Harper Barnes and Dick Richmond, "Reelin' & Rockin': The Chuck Berry Tribute Was Part Spectacle, Part History—All Rock and Roll," *St. Louis Post-Dispatch*, October 19, 1986.

"this is not just a rock 'n' roll show": Bill Smith, "Berry Fans Enjoy a Goode Time," *St. Louis Post-Dispatch*, October 19, 1986.

Robert Palmer went on to call it "inspirational": Palmer, "Chuck Berry at 60."

"cruising like the hot-rod Fords": Brogan, "Birthday Concert."

"on its feet, cheering [and] clapping": Barnes and Richmond, "Reelin' & Rockin'."

"much higher energy level": C. B. Adams, "Chuck Berry Turned 60 With a Lot of Help From Friends and Fans," *St. Louis Globe-Democrat*, October 18–19, 1986.

the singer, "visibly touched, uttered a quiet 'thank you'": Adams. "Chuck Berry Turned 60."

Chapter 1: The Ville

They'd been chastened since birth: Ntozake Shange, *Betsey Brown* (New York: Picador, 1985), 91–92.

"There were restaurants, movies, nightclubs, and schools": Vida "Sister" Prince, "That's the Way It Was: Human Responses to Racism in Everyday Life," in Gerald Early (ed.), *Ain't But a Place* (St. Louis: Missouri Historical Society Press, 1998), 382.

"Everybody lived in the Ville": Doris Wesley and Ann Morris, *Lift Every Voice and Sing: St. Louis African Americans in the Twentieth Century* (Columbia: University of Missouri Press, 1999), 45.

"As children," the engineer remembered: Wesley and Morris, *Lift Every Voice*, 61.

"When we moved to . . . the outskirts of the Ville": Wesley and Morris, *Lift Every Voice*, 159.

just a few years after Cellie Johnson . . . and Charles Henry Banks: Chuck Berry, *The Autobiography* (New York: Simon and Schuster, 1987), xviii, xxi.

Chief Justice Roger B. Taney: Don E. Fehrenbacher, *The Dred Scott Case: Its Significance in American Law and Politics* (New York: Oxford University Press, 1978), 343.

Negroes, according to Taney: Fehrenbacher, *Dred Scott*, 347.

"altogether unfit to associate": Fehrenbacher, *Dred Scott*, 350.

In 1870, for example, Cellie Johnson: Berry, *Autobiography*, xix.

The three major downtown department stores: Early, *Ain't But a Place*, 383.

The Cardinals, one of St. Louis' major league baseball teams: Arnold Rampersad, *Jackie Robinson: A Biography* (New York: Ballantine, 1997), 122.

the Cardinal players threatened to strike: Rampersad, *Jackie Robinson*, 174.

The five major St. Louis movie theaters: "Movies Here Hold Color Line: No Progress Despite Discussions," *St. Louis Argus*, October 9, 1953.

Hotels too, including the Jefferson, Statler ... and Chase: "Billy Eckstine Is Given Hotel Freeze: Balladier Unable to Break Ban," *St. Louis Argus*, May 1, 1953. Rampersad, *Jackie Robinson*, 178.

Until 1923, blacks traveling through St. Louis: "Argus History Shows Longtime Record of Crusade Against Bigotry and Intolerance Here," *St. Louis Argus*, March 15, 1957, 13.

Berry himself recalls: Berry, *Autobiography*, 90.

as a quadrangle "whose sides are represented": Herman H. Long and Charles S. Johnson, *People vs. Property: Race Restrictive Covenants in Housing* (Nashville: Fisk University Press, 1947), 30.

"openings in the buffer line of defense": Long and Johnson, *People vs. Property*, 30.

This "permitted Negro settlement": Long and Johnson, *People vs. Property*, 30.

the Ville had become home to some 6,000 residents: Sandra Perlman Schoenberg and Patricia L. Rosenbaum, *Neighborhoods That Work: Sources for Viability in the Inner City* (New Brunswick, NJ: Rutgers University Press, 1980), 121.

"a nicely kept area": Berry, *Autobiography*, xxii.

"brick and frame cottages with well-cared lawns": Carolyn Hewes Taft, *The Ville: The Ethnic Heritage of an Urban Neighborhood* (St. Louis: Social Sciences Institute, Washington University, 1975), 14.

"the hub of the Ville": Taft, *The Ville*, 15.

their faces had been "whitened from fear" Berry, *Autobiography*, 6.

"Daddy's strategy to have Mother at home": Berry, *Autobiography*, xxii.

write "sophisticated dialect verse": Joanne M. Braxton, *The Collected Poetry of Paul Laurence Dunbar* (Charlottesville: University Press of Virginia, 1993), x.

Henry becoming a deacon at Antioch Baptist: Berry, *Autobiography*, 2–3.

Melba Sweets, recalled him as being: Gregory Freeman, "Retired Columnist Revels in Recalling an 'Interesting Life,'" *St. Louis Post-Dispatch*, February 28, 1999.

"She's a Baptist, but she was like a Catholic nun in the classroom": Cynthia Todd, "Pioneer ... Educator Julia Davis is Honored as She Nears 100," *St. Louis Post-Dispatch*, November 17, 1991.

"These were things that weren't even mentioned." Todd, "Pioneer."

"something that makes the white man partly dependent": Booker T. Washington, *The Future of the American Negro*, in Louis R. Harlan and Raymond W. Smock (eds.), *The Booker T. Washington Papers, Vol. 5: 1899–1900* (Urbana, IL: University of Illinois Press, 1976), 335.

through "the trades, the commercial life: Washington, *American Negro, Papers*, 335.

"my most Christian and most boring": Berry, *Autobiography*, 22.

She "had a profound effect": Berry, *Autobiography*, 8.

"couldn't cope with the strict religious rule": Berry, *Autobiography*, 49.

"struggling to reach my junior year": Berry, *Autobiography*, 49.

the "school auditorium exploded with applause," Berry, *Autobiography*, 33–34.

"There were a lot of wealthy Negro kids at Sumner": Dick Gregory, Excerpt from *Nigger*, in Early, *Ain't But a Place*, 192.

"Sumner High was all black": Tina Turner, Excerpt from *I, Tina*, in Early, *Ain't But a Place*, 223.

the defendant "waives formal judgement": *State of Missouri v. Charles Berry*, Circuit Court of Boone County, Missouri, November 16, 1944.

Berry had not "heretofore been convicted of a felony": *State of Missouri v. Charles Berry*, 1944.

Chapter 2: "De Sun Do Move"

St. Louis! The town where Scott Joplin: Langston Hughes, "In Racial Matters in St. Louis, 'De Sun Do Move'," *Chicago Defender*, May 1, 1954.

38,000 black workers found their way to St. Louis during the 1940s: George Lipsitz, *A Life in the Struggle: Ivory Perry and the Culture of Opposition*, rev. ed. (Philadelphia: Temple University Press, 1995), 65–66.

"one of the grimmest years": Tom Cowan and Jack Maguire, *Timelines of African-American History: 500 Years of Black Achievement* (New York: Perigee, 1994), 209.

"he did climb to the rank of lieutenant": Berry, *Autobiography*, 36.

Cleo Wright, a black oil worker: Dominic J. Capeci, *The Lynching of Cleo Wright* (Lexington: University of Kentucky Press, 1998), 67.

one of six recorded nationwide that year: Cowan and Maguire, *Timelines*, 209.

On July 23, at the Barea Presbyterian Chuch: "Lucy Ann Berry Wins Chance for Fame in Music Festival," *St. Louis Argus*, June 30, 1944.

"an ALL STAR million dollar show": Arnold Rampersad, *The Life of Langston Hughes, Volume II: I Dream a World* (New York: Oxford University Press, 1988), 88.

The story, which carried the headline: "Music Festival Star to Appear," *St. Louis Argus*, December 8, 1944.

"a Polynesian princess": Merle Silverstein, interview with the author, St. Louis, March 28, 2000.

Some protests, like the one at the Katz Drug Store: Richard Dudman, "St. Louis Silent Racial Revolution: Newspapers Did Not Cover Campaign to Integrate Lunch Counters," *St. Louis Post-Dispatch*, June 11, 1990.

The American was the first to desegregate: "Movies Here Hold Color Line: No Progress Despite Discussions," *St. Louis Argus*, October 9, 1953.

it was followed by the Ambassador: "No Racial Incident at Ambassador," *St. Louis Argus*, November 13, 1953.

"When we changed trains there to go into Arkansas and Texas": Hughes, "In Racial Matters."

But one particularly ugly racial incident did occur in St. Louis at this time: Lorenzo J. Greene, Antonio F. Holland, and Gary Kremer, "The Role of the Negro in Missouri History, 1719–1970," http://www.umsl.edu/services/library/blackstudies/civrits.htm.

One statistic suggests that in 1950: Greene, Holland, and Kremer, "Role of the Negro."

Two jobs as a factory worker: *United States v. Charles Edward Anderson Berry*, District Court of the United States. Eastern District of Missouri, Eastern Division, 59 CR 322, (1) 1960.

Frederick Douglass: Joe William Trotter, "From Hard Times to Hope," in James Oliver Horton and Lois E. Horton (eds.), *A History of the African American People* (Detroit: Wayne State University Press, 1997), 123.

"I remember," said Hooke, "it had his picture on it": Jack Hooke, interview with the author, New York, October 31, 1997.

"Barbershops, and beauty parlors": Trotter, "From Hard Times to Hope," 123.

the stockyards and packing plants: Eliot Rudwick, *Race Riot at East St. Louis: July 2, 1917* (Urbana: University of Illinois Press, 1982), 5.

the black population had more than doubled: Rudwick, *Race Riot*, 217

The resulting death toll: Rudwick, *Race Riot*, 217

Johnnie Johnson recalled: Johnnie Johnson, interview with the author, St. Louis, March 30, 2000.

"It should have been named the 'Bucket of Blood'": Johnnie Johnson, interview with the author, St. Louis, March 30, 2000.

"He'd walk out in the middle of a crowd": Travis Fitzpatrick, *Father of Rock and Roll: The Story of Johnnie "B. Goode" Johnson* (Houston: Thomas, Cooke, 1999), 67.

In a park on the opposite side of the street: Fitzpatrick, *Father of Rock and Roll*, 67–68.

The Sir John's Trio played mostly pop standards: Johnnie Johnson, interview with the author, St. Louis, March 30, 2000.

an instrumental virtuoso piano piece Johnson called "Johnnie's Boogie": Fitzpatrick, *Father of Rock and Roll*, 78, 119.

"Muddy Waters, Elmore James, Big Joe Turner": Berry, *Autobiography*, 88.

"The people seemed to really get a kick out of it": Fitzpatrick, *Father of Rock and Roll*, 63.

"They were doing kind of a variety": Johnnie Johnson, interview with the author, St. Louis, March 30, 2000.

a country shuffle called "Mary Jo": Fitzpatrick, *Father of Rock and Roll*, 76.

"The Buggy Ride": Fitzpatrick, *Father of Rock and Roll*, 78.

"Chuck brought something to the group that was missin'": Fitzpatrick, *Father of Rock and Roll*, 75.

"The people loved him": Fitzpatrick, *Father of Rock and Roll*, 76–77.

"He got this look on his face, cold as ice": Fitzpatrick, *Father of Rock and Roll*, 80–81.

At some point in 1954: Berry, *Autobiography*, 91–93.

A Native of New Orleans: Chick Finney, "Calypso Joe," *St. Louis Argus*, March 13, 1953.

On August 13: Liz Eck and Duane Marburger, "Pre-Chess Chuck Berry," *Goldmine* 76, September 1982, 25.

the American Federation of Musicians' recording contract: Eck and Marburger, "Pre-Chess Chuck Berry," 25.

Would Berry consider coming back to his old gig at the Cosmo?: Berry, *Autobiography*, 93.

"Nobody ever thought about making records": Fitzpatrick, *Father of Rock and Roll*, 83.

Chapter 3: Maybellene

"You could tell right away": Peter Guralnick, *Feel Like Going Home: Portraits in Blues and Rock and Roll* (New York: Outerbridge & Deinstfrey, 1971), 197.

A single-story red brick building: Nadine Cohodas, *Spinning Blues into Gold: The Chess Brothers and the Legendary Chess Records* (New York: St. Martin's, 2000), 89.

Several days earlier, Berry had driven to Chicago: Berry, *Autobiography*, 97.

It is entirely possible that he began at Mercury: See, for example, Leonard Chess's comments in Ray Brack and Earl Paige, "Chess and the Blues: From the Street to the Studio," *Billboard*, June 24, 1967, 20.

By the early fifties: Charlie Gilett *The Sound of the City: The Rise of Rock and Roll* (New York: Pantheon, 1983), 6–9.

some recordings, such as Bessie Smith's "Down Hearted Blues": Francis Davis, *The History of the Blues: The Roots, The Music, The People from Charlie Patton to Robert Cray* (New York: Hyperion, 1995), 76.

By the late 1940s they constituted a visible market for black music: Gillett, *Sound of the City*, 14.

A million and a quarter: Gilett, *Sound of the City*, 10.

sales of a hit blues record: Guralnick, *Feel Like Going Home*, 185.

over a hundred by 1952: Gilett, *Sound of the City*, 10.

a respectable rhythm and blues hit: John Jackson, *Big Beat Heat Alan Freed and the Early Years of Rock and Roll* (New York: Schirmer, 1991), 60.

"First place he went was Vee Jay": Fitzpatrick, *Father of Rock and Roll*, 84–85.

"See Leonard Chess": Berry, *Autobiography*, 98.

Nine years Chuck Berry's senior: Cohodas, *Spinning Blues*, 8.

At Cut-Rate Liquor, he had witnessed a knifing: Cohodas, *Spinning Blues*, 28–29.

In the Macomba Lounge: Pete Golkin, "Blacks, Whites, and Blues; The Story of Chess Records," *Living Blues*, November/December 1989, 24.

The bar business was "a rough fuck": Golkin, "Blacks, Whites, and Blues," 24.

Marshall recalls musicians sending his father Mother's Day cards: Ray Topping, "Marshall Shoots the Breeze," *Blues Unlimited* 142, Summer 1982, 16.

"the convergence of outsiders": Cohodas, *Spinning Blues*, 2.

"They didn't come into the country with any prejudice": Golkin, "Blacks, Whites, and Blues," 28.

"You gotta remember one thing": Guralnick, *Feel Like Going Home*, 181.

Aside from his business ventures in the world of alcohol: Cohodas, *Spinning Blues*, 11–13.

"A Jew would rather earn five dollars a week": Cohodas, *Spinning Blues*, 2.

"my father and him had a very close relationship": Marshall Chess, interview with the author, November 4, 1998.

"He never used profanity while doing business with me": Berry, *Autobiography*, 185.

He booked time at a local studio: Cohodas, *Spinning Blues*, 33–34, 37.

By the end of 1949: Cohodas, *Spinning Blues*, 50.

When the Macomba burnt down in the Fall of 1950: Cohodas, *Spinning Blues*, 51, 56.

using arguably the first ever echo chamber: Brack and Paige, "Chess and the Blues," 21.

The song was a hit: Brack and Paige, "Chess and the Blues," 21.

"Rolling Stone" was also a modest hit: Guralnick, *Feel Like Going Home*, 185.

driving 5,000 miles every three months: Brack and Paige, "Chess and the Blues," 21.

"That's different; it just might sell.": Robert Palmer, *Rock and Roll: An Unruly History* (New York: Harmony, 1995), 30.

For the sake of venturing a few hundred dollars: Tony Palmer, *All You Need Is Love: The Story of Popular Music* (New York: Penguin, 1977), 159.

Variety reported that over 260 radio stations nationwide were programming R&B music: Jackson, *Big Beat Heat*, 49.

An R&B dance promoted by Freed in August: Jackson, *Big Beat Heat*, 55.

Freed's "Moondog House" show was being taped and rebroadcast on WNJR: Jackson, *Big Beat Heat*, 59.

the previous year, he had been introduced to Cleveland group: Jackson, *Big Beat Heat*, 55–6.

"Nadine" was released by Chess: Jackson, *Big Beat Heat*, 57–8.

Although a second Coronets single: Jackson, *Big Beat Heat*, 61.

In September 1954, Freed left his disc jockey position at WJW: Jackson, *Big Beat Heat*, 65.

though he had been heard in the New York area: Jackson, *Big Beat Heat*, 59.

Their first release, "Sincerely": Jackson, *Big Beat Heat*, 77.

a white cover of the song by the McGuire Sisters: Jackson, *Big Beat Heat*, 77.

Leonard renamed "Uncle John" and the guitar player Bo Diddley: George White, *Bo Diddley: Living Legend* (Chessington, Surrey: Castle, 1995), 55.

the song eventually went on to sell over a million copies: White, *Bo Diddley*, 62.

"Mannish Boy" also provided Chess with another huge single: White, *Bo Diddley*, 71.

"the businesslike way I'd talked to him": Berry, *Autobiography*, 100.

he described the song as being "nothing complicated": Fitzpatrick, *Father of Rock and Roll*, 96.

"Different. Different from Bo": Fitzpatrick, *Father of Rock and Roll*, 89.

"You could feel it. You could tell it was crossing over": Guralnick, *Feel Like Going Home*, 198.

"The big beat, cars, and young love": Guralnick, *Feel Like Going Home*, 198.

"The first time Chuck Berry came there, we knew 'Maybellene' could be a crackshot hit": Willie Dixon with Don Snowden, *I Am the Blues: The Willie Dixon Story* (New York: Da Capo, 1989), 90.

"Chuck had it sounding more like a country & western tune": Dixon and Snowden, *I Am the Blues*, 90.

The versions Chuck Berry may well have been familiar with: Fred Rothwell, *Long Distance Information: Chuck Berry's Recorded Legacy* (York, England: Music Mentor Books, 2001), 23.

the lyrics to the song were inspired by "Hot Rod Race": Rothwell, *Long Distance Information*, 23.

which inspired Shibley to make four sequels that year: http://www.rockabilly.com/HotRodLncln.html.

On May 21, Berry wrote in the *Autobiography*: Berry, *Autobiography*, 100. See also Rothwell, *Long Distance Information*, 22. For this and subsequent recording session dates, I have followed Rothwell's chronology.

Berry recalled doing thirty-five takes of the song: Berry, *Autobiography*, 103.

"we didn't have anything to compare it to": Fitzpatrick, *Father of Rock and Roll*, 95.

"couldn't tell the difference between most of them": Fitzpatrick, *Father of Rock and Roll*, 95.

"We started puttin' our heads together": Fitzpatrick, *Father of Rock and Roll*, 90.

"We had to change the spellin'": Fitzpatrick, *Father of Rock and Roll*, 90.

The song, according to the *Autobiography*: Berry, *Autobiography*, 103.

"when Chess asked us for another song": Fitzpatrick, *Father of Rock and Roll*, 96.

union scale of $42.50 for the session: Dixon and Snowden, *I Am the Blues*, 98.

"We could cut a record": Topping, "Marshall Shoots the Breeze," 16.

"I was going to New York anyway": Michael Lydon, "Chuck Berry," *Rock Folk: Portraits from the Rock and Roll Pantheon* (New York: Dial, 1971), 10.

he played it for over two hours : Jackson, *Big Beat Heat*, 106.

By the time Leonard Chess returned to Chicago: Brack and Paige, "Chess and the Blues," 20.

"Chess would never get over 1,000 or 2,000 records": Dixon and Snowden, *I Am the Blues*, 91.

Due to Freed's influence, the song caught on in the Northeast: "Buy of the Week," *Billboard*, July 30, 1955, 44.

"way ahead of pop versions by Jim Lowe on Dot and Johnny Long on Coral": Paul Ackerman, "R&B Notes," *Billboard*, September 3, 1955, 18.

"the tune has apparantly brought back 'answer' songs": Ackerman, "R&B Notes," *Billboard*, September 3, 1955, 18.

In the *Autobiography*, Berry maintained: Berry, *Autobiography*, 110.

Marshall Chess disagreed: Topping, "Marshall Shoots the Breeze," 16.

the "cost of doing business. A start-up cost": Marshall Chess, interview with the author, New York, November 4, 1998.

Later, Leonard Chess confided to Jack Hooke: Jack Hooke, interview with the author, New York, October 31, 1997.

"We didn't have much money in those days," Topping, "Marshall Shoots the Breeze," 16.

"Russ probably paid Chuck money for that," Marshall Chess, interview with the author, New York, November 4, 1998.

Chapter 4: Breaking White

"We used to say that if he would have been white": Topping, "Marshall Shoots the Breeze," 16.

interest in "Maybellene" "was unusually high": "This Week's Best Buys," *Billboard*, July 30, 1955, 44.

"I'd only been in the business since '54": Jack Hooke, interview with the author, New York, October 31, 1997.

The average fee for a solo or small combo: Galen Gart, *First Pressings: The History of Rhythm & Blues, Vol. 5: (1955)* (Milford, NH: Big Nickel, 1990), 106.

Berry's claim that the contract offered $40,000 a year: Berry, *Autobiography*, 105.

Berry recalled a conversation with Tim Gale: Robert Hilburn, "Chuck Berry Sets the Record Straight," *Los Angeles Times*, October 4, 1987.

"He was overjoyed, naturally": Jack Hooke, interview with the author, New York, October 31, 1997.

The first series of bookings: Berry, *Autobiography*, 107–108. See also Gart, *First Pressings, Vol. 5*, 95.

Berry, who was at the wheel at the time, "was passing cars in the tunnel": Johnnie Johnson, interview with the author, St. Louis, March 30, 2000.

Equally surprising to Berry: Berry, *Autobiography*, 112, 116.

"He wanted to be everything but a St. Louisan": Johnnie Johnson, interview with the author, St. Louis, March 30, 2000.

By the end of the first day, Bennett complained of throat problems: Jackson, *Big Beat Heat*, 101.

A life-size cardboard cutout of Bennett that had graced the Paramount's lobby: Jackson, *Big Beat Heat*, 100.

according to Leroy Kirkland, musical director of the band: Jackson, *Big Beat Heat*, 101.

the Brooklyn Paramount shows grossed $154,000: Abel Green, "Alan Freed's Rock 'n' Roll Troup Pulls Spectacular 154G at B'klyn Par," *Variety*, September 14, 1955, 49.

"it never took the shape of anything worse than they wanted to sit down front": Green, "Alan Freed's Rock 'n' Roll Troup," 49.

"We are not anti-Rock 'n Roll," he wrote in his review of the Freed show: Franklin, "Brooklyn After Dark," *New York Age-Defender*, September 17, 1955, 7.

"When the curtain went up and we saw the big band": Franklin, "Brooklyn After Dark," 7.

"We got the biggest kick out of the audience": Franklin, "Brooklyn After Dark," 7.

the show at Pittsburgh's Soldier and Sailors Memorial Hall: "Strip Ads Snarl Pit 'Rock 'n' Roll,'" *Variety*, September 21, 1955, 61.

enroute from a date in Houston to a show in Beaumont, Texas: "Two Johnson Sidemen Nabbed in Reefer Raps," *Variety*, October 5, 1955, 49. See also Berry, *Autobiography*, 128.

"A lot of times," Johnson explained, "we couldn't find no place to sleep or eat": Fitzpatrick, *Father of Rock and Roll*, 98.

"A lot of times we had to play two shows for the price of one": Fitzpatrick, *Father of Rock and Roll*, 99.

At a date in Jacksonville, Florida, Berry recalls ropes being tied down the center aisle: Berry, *Autobiography*, 123.

"although they still had the audiences together in the building, they were *there* together": Charles White, *The Life and Times of Little Richard, The Quasar of Rock* (New York: Harmony, 1984), 69.

It "had a lot to say sociologically in our country": White, *Little Richard*, 69.

"We knocked both these records off in no time flat": Fitzpatrick, *Father of Rock and Roll*, 105–106.

"Some of the hecklers at the Apollo": Berry, *Autobiography*, 117.

"There's no opportunity either to take rhythm & blues or leave it alone": "House Reviews," *Variety*, November 23, 1955, 53.

"playing one song," as Johnnie Johnson remembered it: Johnnie Johnson, interview with the author, St. Louis, March 30, 2000.

"He weighed about 400 pounds," remembered Jack Hooke: Jack Hooke, interview with the author, New York, October 31, 1997.

"he reminded you of a big old fat moose": Johnnie Johnson, interview with the author, St. Louis, March 30, 2000.

"I hate to say it but I have to": Jack Hooke, interview with the author, New York, October 31, 1997.

"Teddy was selling Chuck Berry to a promoter for $5000": Jack Hooke, interview with the author, New York, October 31, 1997.

"**We were two street guys**": Jack Hooke, interview with the author, New York, October 31, 1997.

"**Leonard was a dear friend of mine**": Jack Hooke, interview with the author, New York, October 31, 1997.

"**The first few jobs we had**": Jack Hooke, interview with the author, New York, October 31, 1997.

"**I called Leonard**," remembered Hooke: Jack Hooke, interview with the author, New York, October 31, 1997.

"**After a concert in Lynn, Massachusetts, in 1955**": Berry, *Autobiography*, 109.

"**After he found out that Teddy ripped him off with his money**": Johnnie Johnson, interview with the author, St. Louis, March 30, 2000.

"**Chuck Berry was at the Stage Lounge when he first came out with 'Maybellene'**": Bill Greensmith, "Red Holloway" (Part 2), *Blues Unlimited*, March/April, 1976, 9–14.

"**Here am I**," he noted indignantly: White, *Bo Diddley*, 81.

"**I went through a spendthrift era, buying a lot of crap**": White, *Bo Diddley*, 160.

"**A lot of people will say—Chuck Berry this, Chuck Berry that**": John M. McGuire, "Our Father of Rock: 'The Thrill Is Gone,' Berry Says, Still an Attraction at Age 72," *St. Louis Post Dispatch*, November 15, 1998.

"**'Enjoy it?'**" **Chess replied to Guralnick's question**: Guralnick, *Feel Like Going Home*, 197.

"**You have to look at that '50s period**," he once said: Golkin, "Black, White, and Blues" (Part 2), 16.

There were shows in Chicago . . . then shows on December 2 and 3: Gart, *First Pressings, Vol. 5*, 140–141.

"**a pre-holiday treat**": "One Night Only . . . A Pre-Holiday Treat," *St. Louis Argus*, December 16, 1955, 22.

"**'Maybellene' [sic] has skyrocketed St. Louis' own Chuck Berry**": Chick Finney, "Chick Finney's Blue Notes," *St. Louis Argus*, December 23, 1955, 22.

"**On January 3, the Chuck Berry Combo was booked for a week-long engagement**": Gart, *First Pressings, Vol. 5*: 140.

"**this was followed by a swing down the West Coast in February**": Galen Gart, *First Pressings: The History of Rhythym & Blues, Vol. 6 (1956)* (Milford, NH: Big Nickel, 1991), 9.

Billboard, in proclaiming the song its "Buy of the Week": "Buy of the Week," *Billboard*, February 11, 1956, 47.

"**showing increasing deficiencies in their performances due to their drinking**": Berry, *Autobiography*, 138.

"**It got to where we didn't socialize much on stage**": Fitzpatrick, *Father of Rock and Roll*, 129.

"**When we started puttin' music together for 'Beethoven'**": Fitzpatrick, *Father of Rock and Roll*, 125.

In the "Vox Jox" column of May 19: June Bundy, "Vox Jox," *Billboard*, May 19, 1956.

In a piece entitled "The Up-Town Klans" in the April 20 edition of the *St. Louis Argus*: A. Scott Pride, "The Up-Town Klans," *St. Louis Argus*, April 20, 1956, 14.

At the end of March, 1956, Carter spoke out against anyone who played the music: "Segregationists Would Ban All Rock, Roll Hits," *Billboard*, April 7, 1956, 130.

Chapter 5: Deliver Me from the Days of Old

"**We've set up a twenty-man committee**": Asa Carter, "Renegades," *Rock & Roll* Episode 1, PBS, September 24, 1995.

"**Grunt and groin**," one critic labeled it: Peter Guralnick, *Last Train to Memphis: The Rise of Elvis Presley* (Boston: Little, Brown, 1994), 285.

an "aboriginal mating dance": In Alfred Wertheimer, *Elvis '56:In the Beginning* (London: Pimlico, 1994), 26.

"**Whisky flowed like water**": "Drunk-in-Dixie," *Variety*, June 6, 1956, 43.

Disorders "at or near" the Armory: "Farewell to Armory," *Variety*, June 6, 1956, 43.

another Haley show at Miami's Dinner Key Auditorium: "Rock 'n' Roll Called 'Worm 'n' Wiggle' as Censors Rap 'Delinquent' Beat," *Variety*, June 6, 1956, 43.

"**following a knock-down fight at Convention Hall**," "R&R Battered 'n' Badgered," *Variety*, July 16, 1956, 41–46.

there was a riot in San Jose: "R&R Battered 'n' Badgered," 41–46.

and "a near riot" at a youth dance in Minneapolis: "Not 'Proper' Entertainment," *Variety*, July 16, 1956, 46.

During July and August, Berry joined Carl Perkins: Gart, *First Pressings, Vol. 6*, 71.

On July 14, the package, with Little Richard as an added attraction: Gart, *First Pressings, Vol. 6* (1956), 104–105.

Eight teenagers were arrested outside of the auditorium: "The Rocks Keep Rolling at R&R; Pittsburgh Is Latest Rioting Locale," *Variety*, July 25, 1956, 111.

A day later, almost a third of the population of Canton, Ohio: Gart, *First Pressings, Vol. 6*, 104–5.

At Carr's Beach Amphitheater, 8,000 people crammed into the shows: Gart, *First Pressings, Vol. 6*, 91.

Variety reported that the shows were as successful as any on the tour: " 'Record Stars' 18G, St. L." *Variety*, August 1, 1956, 45.

"The terrific sounds of rhythm and blues," wrote Finney: Chick Finney, "Rock 'N' Roll Scored," *St. Louis Argus*, August 3, 1956.

"The jump for joy mood": Finney, "Rock 'N' Roll scored."

"They wanted me to play all 'gut-bucket' music": "Fire anti-R&R Jockey," *Variety*, July 16, 1956, 46.

Freed immediately booked artists represented by all of his close business associates: Jackson *Big Beat Heat*, 149.

"the total number of rhythm and blues LPs available": Gary Kramer, "Rhythm and Blues Notes," *Billboard*, January 19, 1957, 49.

the publishing, however, went to Snapper Music: Jackson, *Big Beat Heat*, 152.

After being introduced to Freed through their mutual friend Jack Hooke: Jackson, *Big Beat Heat*, 85.

George Goldner, a cash-strapped compulsive gambler: Frederick Dannen, "The Godfather of Rock and Roll," *Rolling Stone*, November 17, 1988, 93.

"Whenever he [Chess] was about to do something that was not in your favor": Berry, *The Autobiography*, 130.

"When he came back from his first trip, we hooked up together": Johnnie Johnson, interview with the author, St. Louis, March 30, 2000.

as critics like Fred Rothwell have argued: Rothwell, *Long Distance Information*, 31.

"a fictional condition always appreciated in a baseball game": Berry, *Autobiography*, 151.

"this club that we were playing in Little Rock": Little Aaron Mosby, interview with the author and Bill Greensmith, East St. Louis, April 1, 2000.

"Later on Chuck run to the Cadillac": Little Aaron Mosby, interview with the author and Bill Greensmith, East St. Louis, April 1, 2000.

After agreeing on a fee of $750: Krista Reese, *Chuck Berry: Mr. Rock and Roll* (New York: Proteus, 1982), 41.

"She had everything down there," Nader recalled Berry saying: Reese, *Chuck Berry*, 41.

"It's a country dance and we had no idea that 'Maybellene' was recorded by a niggra man": Berry, *Autobiography*, 136.

the publicity shots he had furnished to the Gale Agency had been underexposed: Berry, *Autobiography*, 135.

the "most impressive act in the picture": Gary Kramer, " 'Rock, Rock, Rock' Jumbo Size Disc Talent Package," *Billboard*, December 8, 1956, 22.

On October 24, *Variety*'s front page: "Elvis a Millionaire in One Year," *Variety*, October 24, 1956, 1.

Domino was well on the way to having 16 gold records: "Million-aires: Champion 'Gold Record' Winner Is Fats Domino," *Ebony*, February 1959, 127.

Berry heard the rumor that Domino was earning $10,000 a week: Berry, *Autobiography*, 163.

"You just can't go right into a shuffle": Fitzpatrick, *Father of Rock and Roll*, 141–142.

"to emphasize the jumps and changes I found in classes in high school": Berry, *Autobiography*, 152.

some, including Fred Rothwell, have argued that it is too commercially calculated: Rothwell, *Long Distance Information*, 41.

Billboard correctly predicted that the song "can't miss": Jay Warner, *Billboard's American Rock 'n' Roll in Review* (New York, Schirmer, 1997), 17.

the song had become "the biggest thing we ever had": Galen Gart, *First Pressings: The History of Rhythym & Blues, Vol. 7 (1957)*, (Milford, NH: Big Nickel, 1993), 54.

The tune had caught on locally like a "house-a-fire": Gart, *First Pressings, Vol. 7*, 54.

as "an energetic guitar-strumming Negro singer": "New Acts," *Variety*, February 6, 1957, 62.

two sell out shows at Syria Mosque in Pittsburgh: Gart, *First Pressings, Vol. 7*, 37.

"no one was injured" at the show: Buddy Lonesome, "3,500 Shriek for Fats Domino and other R&R Stars," *St. Louis Argus*, March 1, 1957.

Feld took the unusual step of chartering two Convair planes: Gart, *First Pressings, Vol. 7* (1957), 37.

In Portland at the Civic Auditorium on March 5: "Fats Big $16,700 Port.," *Variety*, March 13, 1957, 44.

when the show returned to the Syria Mosque in Pittsburgh: "Domino Unit Fat 18G in Return to Pit," *Variety*, April 17, 1957, 45.

that the front few rows tried to "virtually beseige" the stage: "House Reviews," *Variety*, July 10, 1957,, 119.

The *New York Times*, however, under the headline "Rock 'n' Rollers Collect Calmly": Jackson, *Big Beat Heat*, 167.

"his taste is limited and seeming without the imagination to give it [rock and roll] a wider base": Review, *Variety*, July 10, 1957, 119.

At a show at the Kiel Auditorium on August 12: "Dragnet Out For Slayer in Murder at Kiel Auditorium," *St. Louis Argus*, August 16, 1957, 1.

It seems as if the Negro parents in this city: Buddy Lonesome," Community Shows Apathy at Issue," *St. Louis Argus*, July 5, 1957, 1.

"Brown Eyed Handsome Man" and "Roll Over Beethoven" were both featured songs: Ellis Amburn, *Buddy Holly: A Biography* (New York: St. Martin's, 1995), 97.

it is unlikely, however, that the frugal Berry ever shot craps: Amburn, *Buddy Holly*, 97.

occasionally, he would take along Holly's bassist: Amburn, *Buddy Holly*, 97.

11 of the first 21 dates: "'Biggest Show of Stars' Wham 400G 1st Three Wks: Drop 'Whites' in Dixie,'" *Variety*, October 2, 1957, 59.

But after the show in Raleigh, North Carolina: "'Biggest Show of Stars' Wham 400G," 59.

there were "'no incidents of any kind in the south,'": "'Biggest Show of Stars' Wham 400G," 59.

The Crickets and Paul Anka rejoined the tour: Amburn, *Buddy Holly*, 99.

At the November 6 show at the Kiel Auditorium: "Free Rock and Roller of Local Holdup Charges," *St. Louis Argus*, November 15, 1957, 1.

"a 28-man police detail, assigned to keep order, made 12 arrests": "Hub Chief Justice Rocks 5 Taken in Tow After Hot Fats Domino Roller," *Variety*, November 20, 1957, 62.

"a good thing for someone, but terrible for Boston": "Hub Chief Justice," 62.

Chapter 6: Windermere Place

Because my mouth: Langston Hughes, "Minstrel Man," *The Collected Works of Langston Hughes Volume 1: The Poems 1921–40*, Ed. Arnold Rampersad (Columbia: University of Missouri Press, 2001), 171.

Most were built of red brick in the Colonial Revival style: *http://stlouis.missouri.org/visitation-park/winder.htm.*

The Berrys' next door neighbors, the Williams: John A. Wright, *Discovering African American St. Louis: A Guide to Historical Sites* (St. Louis: Missouri Historical Society Press, 1994), 67.

Their daughter Paulette: Kimberly J. McLarin, "At Home with Ntozake Shange: Native Daughter," *New York Times* November 24, 1994, C1.

in the twenty years between 1950 and 1970: Perlman and Rosenbaum, *Neighborhoods That Work*, 47.

In the ten years between the passage of the ruling and the Berry family's move: Tim Fox, *Where We Live: A Guide to St. Louis Communities* (St. Louis: Missouri Historical Society Press, 1995), 136.

The first and most obvious source for the song, as Johnnie Johnson has observed: Fitzpatrick, *Father of Rock and Roll*, 143.

But other sources, including "Around the Clock Blues": Rothwell, *Long Distance Information*, 51.

"the first song where Leonard had me rip the keys": Fitzpatrick, *Father of Rock and Roll*, 143.

"I don't usually do that," Johnson explained: Fitzpatrick, *Father of Rock and Roll*, 143–44.

"I 'bout tore my thumbnail off": Fitzpatrick, *Father of Rock and Roll*, 145.

The scene of a young fan: Berry, *Autobiography*, 154.

ABC estimated his audience: John Jackson, *American Bandstand: Dick Clark and the Making of a Rock 'n' Roll Empire* (New York: Oxford University Press, 1997), 67.

the *Argus* had published a letter: "American Bandstand," *St. Louis Argus*, January 3, 1958, 2B.

the paper launched the first of a two-part attack: "Does 'Bandstand' Have Two Standards?" *St. Louis Argus,* January 10, 1958, 1, and "Rock and Roll: American Bandstand Not American at All," *St. Louis Argus,* January 17, 1958, 1.

Clark's version of the story: Dick Clark and Richard Robinson, *Rock, Roll, and Remember* (New York: Thomas Y. Crowell, 1976), 72–73.

It us unlikely, as Chuck Berry has maintained: Berry, *Autobiography,* 185.

Clark made the decision not to book Berry: Berry, *Autobiography,* 185.

"Chuck Berry saved $100,000 the first year": Greensmith, "Red Holloway (Part 2)," 9–14.

Berry hired Robert Goldenhersh of Rosenblum, Goldenhersh, and Silverstein: Berry, *Autobiography,* 203.

He maintained that they met in 1956: Berry, *Autobiography,* 163.

the two became friends over the course of a year: Berry, *Autobiography,* 164–165.

"He needed a secretary and I needed a change": *Chuck Berry: Hail! Hail! Rock 'n' Roll,* Delilah Films, 1987.

"I was twenty-one," Gillium recalled: *Chuck Berry: Hail! Hail! Rock 'n' Roll,* Delilah Films, 1987.

But one of her first tasks as Berry's new employee: Berry, *Autobiography,* 163.

Marshall Chess, who had turned sixteen on March 13, was working in the back room: Cohodas, *Spinning Blues into Gold,* 154.

"He sort of had this persona of wanting to be Hawaiian": Marshall Chess, interview with the author, New York, November 4, 1998.

"I think that something with his being Hawaiian was knowing that he could be more successful": Marshall Chess, interview with the author, November 4, 1998.

Referring to the other acts on the bill: "House Reviews," *Variety,* March 12, 1958, 71.

The *Argus* reported that several black teenagers had gone to the St. Louis Arena: "St. Louis Hop: Say Arena Doorman Insulted Teenagers," *St. Louis Argus,* January 31, 1958.

SMILING CHUCK BERRY, rock and roll star: "SMILING CHUCK BERRY," *St. Louis Argus,* March 28, 1958, 3C.

the "'Johnny' in the song is more or less myself": Berry, *Autobiography,* 156.

the third verse, inspired, according to Berry, by his own mother's prediction: Berry, *Autobiography,* 155.

Berry has admitted that he "wrote it intending it to be a song for Johnnie Johnson": Berry, *Autobiography,* 156.

the title, according to the pianist, came "from when we used to tour": Fitzpatrick, *Father of Rock and Roll,* 101.

"a man of the black masses with provincial concerns": Donna Sullivan Harper, *Not So Simple: The 'Simple' Stories by Langston Hughes* (Columbia: University of Missouri Press, 1995), 40.

That would require, among other things, giving him a name: Harper, *Not So Simple,* 121.

a coach boy "on the L. & N. down to New Orleans": Langston Hughes, *The Best of Simple* (New York: Hill and Wang, 1961), 19.

Hughes was "deconstructing other typical images of the African-American male": Hans A. Ostrom, *Langston Hughes: A Study of the Short Fiction* (New York: Twayne, 1993), 44.

"holding up the mirror to urban working-class African-American men": Ostrom, *Langston Hughes,* 44.

"it would be biased to white fans to say 'colored boy' and changed it to 'country boy'": Berry, *Autobiography,* 157.

united "in all things essential to mutual progress": Booker T. Washington, *Up From Slavery,* in Louis R. Harlan and Raymond W. Smock (eds), *The Booker T. Washington Papers, Vol. I: The Autobiographical Writings* (Urbana, IL: University of Illinois Press, 1976), 332.

many of the stopped string bends: Tom Wheeler, "Chuck Berry: The Interview," *Guitar Player,* March 1988, 58.

The 12-day run over the previous Christmas holiday: Jackson, *Big Beat Heat,* 179.

The story most often told: See, for example, Nick Tosches, *Hellfire* (New York: Delacorte, 1982),145–146.

The account gained credibility when it was revealed: *Great Balls of Fire,* MGM, 1989.

"when I would tell him [Berry] 'you're third on the show": Jack Hooke, interview with the author, New York, October 31, 1997.

"even after the frantic acts that preceded him": "R&R at B'klyn Par, or Alan Freed's 'Big Beat' Loaded with Amateurs," *Variety,* April 2, 1958, 65.

"a talented songwriter and singer with a regular, pronounced beat": "R&R at B'klyn Par," *Variety,* April 2, 1958, 65.

Even so, the tour began prosperously: "R&R at B'klyn Par," *Variety*, April 2, 1958, 65.

On April 6, in Cleveland: Jackson, *Big Beat Heat*, 191.

Chuck sat at the piano, "trying it out, and Jerry Lee comes over": Jack Hooke, interview with the author, New York, October 31, 1997.

"We're not going to continue the show with that cracker": Jack Hooke, interview with the author, New York, October 31, 1997.

Berry was joined on tour by Joan Mathis: Motions of Defendant, February 12, 1960. District Court of the United States Eastern Division of Missouri, Eastern Division, 60 CR 18 & 19.

who had begun an affair with Berry the previous Christmas: Berry, *Autobiography*, 195.

Competing with two other tours that spring: Jackson, *Big Beat Heat*, 190.

On the Monday following the Toledo show: Amburn, *Buddy Holly*, 159.

The next day in St. Louis, Buddy Holly's guitar was stolen: Amburn, *Buddy Holly*, 160.

A week later, at Waterloo, Wisconsin, Jerry Lee failed to show: Amburn, *Buddy Holly*, 160.

Only a show in Minneapolis on April 25 produced any real cheer for the entourage: "Freed Rock 'n' Roller Grosses 10G in MPLS," *Variety*, April 30, 1958, 84.

the second half of the show had to be interrupted several times: Jackson, *Big Beat Heat*, 193–195.

That night, Chuck Berry was scheduled to close the show: Jackson, *Big Beat Heat*, 195–6.

The *New York Times* reported multiple stabbings: Jackson, *Big Beat Heat*, 199.

"We finished the show; we felt bad that the kids had to see it in the bright lights": Jack Hooke, interview with the author, New York, October 31, 1997.

Though a date at the Lewiston Armory in Maine: "Boston Common to Hoot Mon Belt They Rock 'N' Riot Out of This Veldt," *Variety*, May 7, 1958, 1.

"These so-called music programs are a disgrace": "Boston Common" 58.

Over the Memorial Day Weekend, Berry and Joan Mathis: 60 CR 18 & 19, Miscellaneous court documents.

Berry pulled the car off the new Interstate 70 and onto Highway 94: CR 18 & 19 Motions of Defendant, February 12, 1960.

"The officer," noted Weber, "went up to where the man was voluntarily stopped": 60 CR 18 & 19 Motions of Defendant, February 12, 1960.

Because the car was parked about fifty feet outside the St. Charles city limits: 60 CR 18 & 19 Motions of Defendant, Feb. 12, 1960.

After a round of questioning from Neumann and St. Charles Police Chief Earl Humphrey: 60 CR 18 & 19 Motions of Defendant, February 12, 1960.

Immediately, Karrenbrock fined Berry $30 for having an expired driving license: "Chuck Berry Faces Weapons Charge," *St. Louis Post-Dispatch*, June 3, 1958, 5B.

"the bail was no problem, however, for Chuck Berry peeled off $1,250 in cash": "Rock and Roller Chuck Berry 'All Tore Up,' " *St. Louis Argus*, June 6, 1958, 1.

The night before Berry was due to appear in St. Charles: "Rock 'n' Roll Star's Pink Caddy Reels on Road and He's Roped," *St. Louis Globe Democrat*, July 12, 1958, 1.

"Dressed for the court in an eggshell-white suit": "Rock 'n' Roll Star's Pink Caddy," 1.

"I was not a rock and roll addict": Merle Silverstein, interview with the author, St. Louis, March 28, 2000.

"without a warrant and was not incident to an arrest": Merle Silverstein, interview with the author, St. Louis, March 28, 2000.

The incident should be taken "under advisement": "Weapons Charge Hearing for Rock and Roll Singer," *St. Louis Post-Dispatch*, July 12, 1958, 7A.

Judge Lewis fined Chuck Berry a further $15: "Rock 'n' Roll Singer Fined for Rock 'n' Roll Driving," *St. Louis Post-Dispatch*, July 17, 1958, 3A.

"I called Merle," remembered Mayer, "and told him what had been reported to us": Frederick Mayer, interview with the author, June 22, 2000.

Mayer "discussed the charges against him": Frederick Mayer, interview with the author, June 22, 2000.

"And that," according to Frederick Mayer, "was basically the start of it": Frederick Mayer, interview with the author, June 22, 2000.

Both the *Argus* in its June 27 piece: "Chuck Berry Postponement Until July 11," *St. Louis Argus*, June 27, 1958, 1.

Berry in *The Autobiography*: Berry, *Autobiography*, 196.

"because nobody even knew what she was doing with him": Merle Silverstein, interview with the author, St. Louis, March 28, 2000.

within weeks was blacklisted by Dick Clark and, worse, by top-40 radio: Colin Escott with Martin Hawkins, *Good Rockin' Tonight: Sun Records and the Birth of Rock and Roll* (New York: St. Martin's, 1991), 201.

"to demonstrate the links among jazz, blues, and rock": John Hammond with Irving Townsend, *John Hammond on Record: An Autobiography* (New York: Penguin, 1981), 301.

"the bleacher brigade," as *Variety* dubbed the teenagers there, "went wild": "Jazz Purists Razz Berry at Newport," *Variety*, July 9, 1958, 53.

"Chuck Berry received the biggest response from the crowd": As quoted in Rothwell, *Long Distance Information*, 64.

"There was nearly a riot and the police were called": Hammond, *Hammond on Record*, 301.

"fights broke out and the local gendarmes had their hands full": "Jazz Purists Razz Berry," 53ff.

Only the biblical references in the song's chorus: Rothwell, *Long Distance Information*, 59.

"All you could hear was Bobby": Palmer, *All You Need Is Love*, 229.

Chapter 7: Club Bandstand

THAT'S GOOD NEWS Shouted the enthusiastic music lover: Chick Finney, "Chick Finney's Blue Notes," *St. Louis Argus*, March 27, 1959.

the audience's "enthusiastic response was nipped somewhat": "House Reviews," *Variety*, September 3, 1958, 54, 63.

"Unlike the show biz era in the past": "House Reviews," *Variety*, September 3, 1958, 54, 63.

a "standout . . . who breaks it up [with] 'Carol,' 'Schoolday,' and 'Go, Johnny, Go' [sic]": "House Reviews," *Variety*, September 3, 1958, 54, 63.

but the brothers had set up their own record pressing plant in Chicago: Cohodas, *Spinning Blues into Gold*, 160.

their new company, L&P Broadcasting: Cohodas, *Spinning Blues into Gold*, 212.

"At this time," he was to write in *The Autobiography*: Berry, *Autobiography*, 191.

"ran through a bunch of cover tunes and galloped over a few lyrics": Berry, *Autobiography*, 191.

Berry claims that he first heard "Signifying Monkey" in Algoa: Berry, *Autobiography*, 161.

"The Signifying Monkey," Gates writes, "invariably repeats to his friend, the Lion, some insult": Henry Louis Gates, Jr., *The Signifying Monkey: A Theory of African-American Literary Criticism* (New York: Oxford University Press, 1988), 55.

a "'language of implication . . . the language of trickery'": Roger D. Abrahams, as quoted by Gates, *Signifying Monkey*, 54.

"'complimentary remarks may be delivered in a left-hand fashion'": Claudia Mitchell-Kernan, as quoted by Henry Louis Gates, *Signifying Monkey*, 85.

Deep down in the jungle so they say: Roger D. Abrahams, *Deep Down in the Jungle: Negro Narrative Folklore from the Streets of Philadelphia* (Hatboro, PA: Folklore Associates, 1964), 149–50.

the original, Berry admits, was "naughty . . . and funnier": Berry, *Autobiography*, 161.

it "is often a part of [black] adolescent education": Gates, *Signifying Monkey*, 75.

"In the midst of the unsubtle, heart-pounding and walloping singing": "House Review," *Variety*, December 31, 1958, 44.

"who is no improvement over Alan Freed": "House Reviews," *Variety*, December 31, 1958, 44.

"they threw a script at me and we started shooting the next day": Greil Marcus, "Roll Over Chuck Berry," *Rolling Stone*, June 14, 1969, 15.

"I have to assume that Chuck got frightened": Jack Hooke, interview with the author, New York, October 31, 1997.

"they've got that whole script, they've got a whole plan here to do a movie": Jack Hooke, interview with the author, New York, October 31, 1997.

"They're going, they're coming," he told Hooke: Jack Hooke, interview with the author, New York, October 31, 1997.

"I took him, I said, 'Chuck, you don't have to read these lines all the way through'": Jack Hooke, interview with the author, New York, October 31, 1997.

"That Johnny Melody, he can really put over a Chuck Berry number": *Go, Johnny, Go*, Hal Roach Studios, 1959.

"He's gotta be six-feet tall," says Freed: *Go, Johnny, Go*, Hal Roach Studios, 1959.

"You know, we dig him the same way": *Go, Johnny, Go*, Hal Roach Studios, 1959.

"I remember that session pretty well": Fitzpatrick, *Father of Rock and Roll*, 152.

Johnson recalls playing "the little rip up and down the keys": Fitzpatrick, *Father of Rock and Roll*, 152.

"it just wasn't much different from what we had been doin'": Fitzpatrick, *Father of Rock and Roll*, 152.

"CHUCK BERRY NITE CLUB on Grand Boulevard [sic]": Chick Finney, "Chick Finney's Blue Notes," *St. Louis Argus*, January 9, 1959.

"'THIS IS IT!' CHUCK BERRY CLUB BANDSTAND": Advertisement, *St. Louis Argus*, March 13, 1959.

a second advertisement announced a Gala Floor Show beginning at 8:00: Advertisement, *St. Louis Argus*, March 20, 1959.

"He was trying to get a carbon copy of Dick Clark's thing": Johnnie Johnson, interview with the author, St. Louis, March 30, 2000.

an expression that is a part of nature and should be given its freedom: Francine Gillium, "I Like Rock and Roll," *Monthly Journal*, March 1959.

during the 1920s and 1930s the Midtown area surrounding Grand Avenue: Tim Fox, *Where We Live*, 94.

"I had a nightclub in St. Louis that was predominantly catered to by the white populace of St. Louis": Hilburn, "Chuck Berry Sets the Record Straight."

a showing of the black-themed movie "St. Louis Blues": http://www.fabulousfox.com/played-fox.asp.

"he was just another member of the Musician's Local 197": Chick Finney, "Chick Finney's Blue Notes," *St. Louis Argus*, January 30, 1959.

Tillman, Finney wrote, "is set for the bigtime": Chick Finney, "Chick Finney's Blue Notes," *St. Louis Argus*, March 13, 1959.

Years later, Peek remembered "when Russ Carter, the MC of the show": Billy Peek, interview with the author, St. Louis, March 29, 2000.

"one of the girls threw her arms around me and hung a soul-searching kiss": Berry, *Autobiography*, 197.

"this nigger asked my sister for a date!": Berry, *Autobiography*, 198.

"the sergeant," he wrote, "suggested that the entire seven hundred dollars they had relieved me of": Berry, *Autobiography*, 199.

The Meridian Star, claiming to present "conflicting accounts" of what happened: "Negro Singer Jailed After Dance 'Incident,'" *Meridian Star*, August 28, 1959.

The girl, the *Star* declared in no uncertain terms, "was on the verge of hysteria": "Negro Singer Jailed."

Berry, the Star reported, told Paul Busby, the County Attorney: "Negro Singer Jailed.

he "was first taken to the police station": "Negro Singer Jailed After Dance 'Incident,'" *Meridian Star*, August 28, 1959.

On the morning of December 1: The account of the incident that follows is taken from the court documents of *United States v. Berry* 59CR322.

Chapter 8: The Mask

We wear the mask that grins and lies: Paul Laurence Dunbar, "We Wear the Mask," *Collected Poems of Paul Laurence Dunbar*, Edited and With an Introduction by Joanne M. Braxton (Charlottesville: University of Virginia Press, 1993).

that she had been transported to this City from Texas: Report 59 275 678, Police Department, City of St. Louis, December 22, 1959.

The legislation was part of the so-called Progressive Movement: David J. Langum, *Crossing Over the Line: Legislating Morality and the Mann Act*. The Chicago Series on Sexuality, History and Society, edited by John C. Fout (Chicago: University of Chicago Press, 1994), 6.

any person who shall knowingly transport or cause to be transported: As quoted in Langum, *Crossing Over the Line:* 261–262.

Wilson v. United States in 1914, helped shape the idea: Langum, *Crossing Over the Line*, 70–71.

Caminetti v. United States, also in 1914, seemed to be a response to public opinion of the day: Langum, *Crossing Over the Line*, 120.

"Basically," he recalled, "with the Indian girl it was age": Frederick Mayer, interview with the author, June 22, 2000.

"the defendant has been denied the rights to a speedy trial": *United States of America v. Charles Edward Anderson Berry*, 60CR 18, Motion to Dismiss Indictments, February 10, 1960.

"there were only three [live] jobs that February": Berry, *Autobiography*, 204.

On February 25, four days before the first of Chuck Berry's Mann Act Trials: Jackson, *Big Beat Heat*, 278.

"management in accordance with a policy of racial segregation is a violation of Constitution and laws of the United States": "Housing Case Meant Much to Veteran's Family: Public Housing Bias is Set Back," *St. Louis Argus*, December 30, 1955.

they "had that 'nigra' out there": William J. Shore, "Why Judge McMillian Worries," *St. Louis Post-Dispatch*, August 11, 1991.

"One day," he remembered, Moore "was having criminal arraignments": Merle Silverstein, interview with the author, St. Louis, March 28, 2000.

Themetta, who, according to the *Argus*, "sat calm throughout the entire trial": "Mrs. Chuck Berry Breaks as Husband Is Convicted," *St. Louis Argus*, March 11, 1960, 3B.

Berry too "seemed unpurturbed [sic] by the serious charges resting against him": "Chuck Berry Says Charges Not True," *St. Louis Argus*, March 4, 1960, 1.

"I felt she was telling the truth": Frederick Mayer, interview with the author, June 22, 2000.

"Is he a white man or a Negro?": *United States v. Berry* 59CR322 (1), 8.

"Who was Johnny [sic] Johnson?" he asked her: *United States v. Berry* 59CR322 (1), 10.

with these outbursts Moore "made a mockery of Chuck's race": Merle Silverstein, interview with the author, St. Louis, March 28, 2000.

his "mild voice" and "weakly sounded objections": Berry, *Autobiography*, 207.

"To confront him and say, 'You can't do this in front of a jury'": Merle Silverstein, interview with the author, St. Louis, March 28, 2000.

the most difficult decision a "trial lawyer faces during the trial": Merle Silverstein, interview with the author, St. Louis, March 28, 2000.

"In my opinion," Frederick Mayer would later say: Frederick Mayer, interview with the author, June 22, 2000.

if she understood what he meant when he spoke of "sexual intercourse": *United States v. Berry* 59CR322 (1), 18.

"another sexual relationship" in the back of Berry's Cadillac: *United States v. Berry* 59CR322 (1), 26–27.

At the Drexel Hotel, too, she recalled another sexual encounter: *United States v. Berry* 59CR322 (1), 30.

Escalanti recalled having sex with Berry "just about every night": *United States v. Berry* 59CR322 (1), 39.

matters concerning "conversations between her and this Negro": *United States v. Berry* 59CR322 (1), 64.

"I'm sure that it was on the second day, but not unless I'm mixed up it isn't": *United States v. Berry* 59CR322 (1), 71.

"There is no question involved about persuasion in this case": *United States v. Berry* 59CR322 (1), 79.

it had "big entrance gates" and that it was "a fine looking place": *United States v. Berry* 59CR322 (1), 87.

"By Mr. Berry, do you mean this Negro, the defendant?" *United States v. Berry* 59CR322 (1), 129.

"in the bed closest to the door" and with "the covers up to her neck": *United States v. Berry* 59CR322 (1), 131.

"Is that hotel patronized by the white?": *United States v. Berry* 59CR322 (1): 175.

"I dislike very much to inconvenience anybody else": *United States v. Berry* 59CR322 (1), 176.

"She was a very homely person," Merle Silverstein was to recall: Merle Silverstein, interview with the author, St. Louis, March 28, 2000.

He offered several reasons for inviting the girl to travel with him: *United States v. Berry* 59CR322 (1), 230.

Moore interrupted by asking Berry not to "tell us what she wanted": *United States v. Berry* 59CR322 (1), 226.

he recalled that he "must have dressed" for the show: *United States v. Berry* 59CR322 (1), 268.

"No. Don't tell me usually": *United States v. Berry* 59CR322 (1), 236.

"I discovered that I had asked for a double bed": *United States v. Berry* 59CR322 (1), 262.

Berry could only guess that it "had to be between": *United States v. Berry* 59CR322 (1), 275.

there was "none, other than if—I mean": *United States v. Berry* 59CR322 (1), 245.

"'Yes, you know, we had a romantic attachment to each other'": Merle Silverstein, interview with the author, St. Louis, March 28, 2000.

"I think if he had taken that position," he maintained: Frederick Mayer, interview with the author, June 22, 2000.

"not what she seemed to do": *United States v. Berry* 59CR322 (1), 285.

It occurred when Mayer accused Berry: *United States v. Berry* 59CR322 (1), 304.

without hesitation, Berry replied, "No sir": *United States v. Berry* 59CR322 (1), 313.

"She made this advancement, sir, if you call it an advancement": *United States v. Berry* 59CR322 (1), 314.

"It didn't matter too much whether I could trust her": *United States v. Berry* 59CR322 (1), 316–317.

"to some people" he was a favorite there: *United States v. Berry* 59CR322 (1), 324.

"Mr. Berry, I am going to show you now": *United States v. Berry* 59CR322 (1), 326.

Escalanti "didn't seem to pay attention very well": *United States v. Berry* 59CR322 (1), 361.

Gillium overheard her say, "What am I supposed to do": *United States v. Berry* 59CR322 (1), 362.

her husband "met a Spanish-speaking Indian girl": *United States v. Berry* 59CR322 (1), 381.

Escalanti "had been angry with him for trying to send her home": *United States v. Berry* 59CR322 (1), 385.

Mayer asked Brown "had you seen the defendant on any prior occasion?": *United States v. Berry* 59CR322 (1), 387.

"And was Mr. Berry staying at the Drexel Hotel in October?": *United States v. Berry* 59CR322 (1), 389.

"Did you," he said directly to Oliver Brown, "hear Mr. Berry refer to that woman": *United States v. Berry* 59CR322 (1), 389.

"Is there any doubt in your mind," Mayer continued relentlessly: *United States v. Berry*, 59CR322 (1), 390.

Silverstein simply asked, "The words that you can remember him saying": *United States v. Berry* 59CR322 (1), 391.

I used the statement referred to": *United States v. Berry* 59CR322 (1), 391.

He demanded of Judge Moore that "this witness's entire rebuttal testimony be stricken": *United States v. Berry* 59CR322 (1), 392.

"When he got to St. Louis," Mayer recalled for the court": *United States v. Berry* 59CR322 (1), 401.

"Here is a famous performer, a TV and record idol": *United States v. Berry* 59CR322 (1), 402.

"This is a terribly bad evening," he told them: *United States v. Berry* 59CR322 (1), 423.

everyone on the jury "glared at one specific guy": Merle Silverstein, interview with the author, St. Louis, March 28, 2000.

the *Argus* the following week described the rest of the courtroom: "Mrs. Chuck Berry Breaks, 3B.

Chapter 9: St. Louis Blues

I got the St. Louis Blues, just as blue as I can be: W. C. Handy, "St. Louis Blues," 1914.

"It is a shameful story that was unfolded": *United States v. Berry* 59CR322 (1), 436–7.

"You came into this courtroom," Moore continued: *United States v. Berry* 59CR322 (1), 437.

According to your own testimony, you have been very successful: *United States v. Berry* 59CR322 (1), 438.

"He was very upset," recalls Merle Silverstein: Merle Silverstein, interview with the author, St. Louis, March 28, 2000.

"Stand up," he boomed: *United States v. Berry* 59CR322 (1), 438.

"There is no sentence," he intoned gravely: *United States v. Berry* 59CR322 (1), 439.

"There will be no bail set by this court": *United States v. Berry* 59CR322 (1), 439–40.

the comments were, quite simply, "atrocious": Merle Silverstein, interview with the author, St. Louis, March 28, 2000.

"The case was so infiltrated with prejudice at points": Merle Silverstein, interview with the author, St. Louis, March 28, 2000.

She was described in a small piece in the *St. Louis Post-Dispatch*: "Chuck Berry Acquitted in Case Involving Woman," *St. Louis Post-Dispatch*, June 2, 1960, 17A.

"On the stand," recalled Merle Siverstein: Merle Silverstein, interview with the author, St. Louis, March 28, 2000.

"Joan answered slowly and deliberately": Berry, *Autobiography*, 206.

Berry is described as having "denied an intent to violate the law": "Chuck Berry Acquitted," 17A.

"As intent," he writes in one: Miscellaneous court documents, 60 CR 18 & 19.

Judge Weber defined "debauchery and other immoral practices": Miscellaneous court documents, 60 CR 18 & 19.

the evidence did not "show the intent necessary": *Berry v. United States,* U.S. Court of Appeals, Eighth Circuit, October 28, 1960, 283 F.2d 466.

the judge "erred in certain rulings on evidence": *Berry v. United States,* U.S. Court of Appeals, Eighth Circuit, October 28, 1960, 283 F.2d 466.

"conducted in an atmosphere of complete hostility": "Appeals Court Remands Case Over Questions by Judge Moore," *St. Louis Post-Dispatch,* October 28, 1960, 5.

"to emphasize the racial aspects of the case": "Appeals Court Remands Case," 5.

"There was ample circumstantial evidence of his intent": *Berry v. United States,* U.S. Court of Appeals, Eighth Circuit, October 28, 1960, 283 F.2d 466.

However, "what has given us concern," the judges went on: U.S. Court of Appeals, Eighth Circuit, October 28, 1960, 283 F.2d 466.

"a trial judge who, in the presence of the jury": *Berry v. United States,* U.S. Court of Appeals, Eighth Circuit, October 28, 1960, 283 F.2d 467.

In Merle Silverstein's estimation, Harper was "tough": Merle Silverstein, interview with the author, St. Louis, March 28, 2000.

"We had one heck of a time finding Janice": Frederick Mayer, interview with the author, June 22, 2000.

"the second time I knew what she [Escalanti] was going to say": Merle Silverstein, interview with the author, St. Louis, March 28, 2000.

"I can't remember no four or five times": *United States v. Berry* 59CR322 (2), 93.

"You remember those questions and answers being asked you": *United States v. Berry* 59CR322 (2), 96.

"Didn't you make a statement to her, 'Somebody is going to pay for this'?": *United States v. Berry* 59CR322 (2), 100.

if Berry was "going to act dirty then I might as well act dirty too": *United States v. Berry* 59CR322 (2), 100.

"I meant like that when he acts like he don't care whether I have the ticket or not": *United States v. Berry* 59CR322 (2), 105.

"Well, if he is going to be stuck up and treat people mean": *United States v. Berry* 59CR322 (2), 106.

"Dear Chuck," he read aloud: *United States v. Berry* 59CR322 (2), 110.

"two pork chops . . . a milkshake: *United States v. Berry* 59CR322 (2), 120–121.

"During the night recess, gentlemen of the jury": *United States v. Berry* 59CR322 (2), 12.

the *St. Louis Globe-Democrat* published a short piece on the trial: "Berry Lured Her to St. Louis, Girl, 14, Says." *St. Louis Globe-Democrat,* March 14, 1961, 15.

"In my opinion," Harper stated, "I thought she told a pretty straight story": *United States v. Berry* 59CR322 (2), 179.

"She started an argument about wanting to go to Yuma": *United States v. Berry* 59CR322 (2), 289.

Berry "had picked her up in El Paso": *United States v. Berry* 59CR322 (2), 332.

"the United States of America versus Charles Edward Anderson Berry": *United States v. Berry* 59CR322 (2), 348.

"If you believe," he argued to the jury: *United States v. Berry* 59CR322 (2), 350.

the crux, that is the main, that is virtually the only issue": *United States v. Berry* 59CR322 (2): 350.

"This girl is not so dumb," he told them: *United States v. Berry* 59CR322 (2), 352.

It was, he argued, a "preposterous story": *United States v. Berry* 59CR322 (2), 354.

"Why," he asked, "is this girl doing this?": *United States v. Berry* 59CR322 (2), 369.

"This defendant's actions," he twice maintained during his summation: *United States v. Berry* 59CR322 (2), 369, 374.

"Remember," he told them, "this is Charles Berry": *United States v. Berry* 59CR322 (2), 370.

"I learned an old rule when I was young": Merle Silverstein, interview with the author, St. Louis, March 28, 2000.

In less than a year, both the Department of Justice and the FBI: Langum, *Crossing Over the Line,* 242.

Chapter 10: "Never Saw a Man so Changed"

Repeatedly some writers claim that I have a bitter attitude: Berry, *Autobiography*, 321.

"for what," he wrote later, "I was convicted of just having the intention of doing": Berry, *Autobiography*, 211.

the first public announcement occurred on June 16: Advertisement, *St. Louis Argus*, June 16, 1961.

the Double H's Labor Day celebration in 1960: Advertisement, *St. Louis Argus*, August 19, 1960.

Judge Harper's instructions in the trial were "adquate, fair, and accurate:" U.S. Eighth Court of Appeals 295 F.2d 192 (1961), January 8, 1962.

the "'long established policy that maintains the secrecy of the grand jury proceedings in the federal courts'": U.S. Eighth Court of Appeals 295 F.2d 192 (1961), January 8, 1962.

"It never went to a lawsuit," Marshall Chess recalled: Marshall Chess, interview with the author, November 4, 1998.

"I made this deal with Pye Records": Marshall Chess, interview with the author, November 4, 1998.

It was seeing a copy of the rare album: Bill Wyman with Ray Coleman, *Stone Alone: The Story of a Rock and Roll Band* (New York: Signet, 1991), 117.

"We began all over again," remembered Marshall Chess: Marshall Chess, interview with the author, November 4, 1998.

"His side of it related to the financial aspect": Marshall Chess, interview with the author, November 4, 1998.

"He carried a little electric plate in his suitcase": Topping, "Marshall Shoots the Breeze," 14.

If he had changed, Chess maintained, it was "nothing that I recognized": Marshall Chess, interview with the author, November 4, 1998.

"I took the top hits of my past and re-shaped them": Max Jones, "Berry's Formula—Old Songs With a New Sound," *Melody Maker*, November 14, 1964, 13.

"the city took on a new mood, a mood which was a bit nasty and yet zany": Hank Harrison, *The Dead* (Millbrae CA: Celestial Arts, 1980), 44.

Phil Chess, "frequently grinned and laughed during the recording": Guy Stevens, "A Chuck Berry Recording Session," *Jazzbeat*, April 1964: 14.

"We've been friends for eighteen years," she told *Esquire* magazine: Mark Goodman, "The Further Misadventures of Candy," *Esquire*, June 1976, 93.

an unrehearsed jam that Berry did "for about ten minutes with the other musicians: Stevens, "A Chuck Berry Recording Session," 14.

On stage, he "came through with all the strength of his recorded work": Chris Roberts, "Great, Chuck, Just Great!" *Melody Maker*, May 16, 1964, 3.

"Hey, listen, man," Burdon recalls Berry screaming: Eric Burdon, *I Used to Be an Animal But I'm All Right Now* (Boston, Faber and Faber, 1986), 60.

"Chuck was a little unsure of his backing band": Roberts, "Great, Chuck, Just Great!" 3.

Chuck, according to Ted "Kingsize" Taylor, tried to fool the drummer whenever he had the chance: Rothwell, *Long Distance Information*, 123.

"posing pleasantly for a knot of photographers": Roberts, "Great, Chuck, Just Great!" 3.

"Although we passed messages to him," Wyman remembered: Bill Wyman, *Stone Alone*, 255.

The two Rolling Stones "were in a hotel elevator": Bill Wyman, *Stone Alone*, 260.

The two impressarios were "on their knees peeling off single pound notes": Eric Burdon, *I Used to Be an Animal*, 61–62.

"Did you get the money yet?" Berry asked Peter Grant: Eric Burdon, *I Used to Be an Animal*, 61.

He "was usually alone before a show": James Craig, "When Chuck Snubbed the Rolling Stones," *Record Mirror*, April 2, 1965, 7.

"Chuck changed," Johnson recalled in 1999: Fitzpatrick, *Father of Rock and Roll*, 185–6.

"Never saw a man so changed": Michael Lydon, "Chuck Berry," 21.

Some, such as veteran music journalist Robert Christgau: Robert Christgau, "Chuck Berry," *Rolling Stone History of Rock and Roll*, 3rd ed, Anthony DeCurtis and James Henke with Holly George-Warren (New York, Random House, 1992), 64.

In a 1983 interview with Kim Plummer: Kim Plummer, "Daughter of Legend Wants Own Career in Rock 'n' Roll," *St. Louis Globe-Democrat*, March 22, 1983, 1B.

in 1998, the couple celebrated their golden wedding anniversary: McGuire, "Our Father of Rock."

"Berry himself walked in and stayed a long while chatting about amps and things": Bill Wyman, *Stone Alone*, 274–275.

A "full-scale riot" took place: Buddy Lonesome, "Neighborhood Hostile After Leffingwell Riot," *St. Louis Argus*, July 10, 1964,1.

The rest of the performance "fell flat": Rod Harrod, "Chuck Berry Getting Too Old?" *Record Mirror*, January 16, 1965.

"If everything you had was as big as your mouth, you wouldn't have to work": Chris Welch, "Backstage With Chuck," *Melody Maker*, January 16, 1965.

Berry started to get moody and "change keys in the middle of songs": Chick Kattenhorn, "Chuck by Chick," *Melody Maker*, February 20, 1965.

"'Oh well, I suppose we'll have to do some commercial things'": Kattenhorn, "Chuck by Chick."

"The usual Berry contract called for two Fender Dual Showman amps": Cub Koda, "Chuck Berry: And the Joint Was Rockin'," *Goldmine*, December 13, 1991, 16.

Chapter 11: Mercury Falling

"When I left to go to Mercury": Marcus, "Roll Over Chuck Berry," 15.

they had signed the composer of "'Maybelline' [sic], 'Roll Over Beethoven,' and 'Johnny B. Goode.'": "Mercury Signs Chuck Berry," *Billboard*, August 6, 1966, 52.

"there were no bad feelings. We just shook hands": Norman Jopling, "Rock Lives!" *Melody Maker*, March 4, 1967, 7.

"it was actually a very amicable thing": Marshall Chess, interview with the author, November 4, 1998.

Mercury's "drive to become a major factor in r&b": "Mercury Signs Chuck Berry," *Billboard*, August 6, 1966, 52.

"I might as well," he told Greil Marcus: Marcus, "Roll Over Chuck Berry," 15.

Berry had revised the figure down to $60,000: Berry, *Autobiography*, 226.

"I have witnessed many recording sessions that went into as many as 30 takes": Jim Delehant, "How an Innovator Lasts Forever," *Hit Parader*, March 1967.

Berry posed for a picture with Peek: Dick Richmond, "Billy Peek: He Backed the Stars," *St. Louis Post-Dispatch*, December 4, 1981, 3D.

"That was what was so great about Chuck": Billy Peek, interview with the author, St. Louis, MO, March 29, 2000.

"by that time," the guitarist remembered: Billy Peek, interview with the author, St. Louis, MO, March 29, 2000.

"I was scared to death," Peek remembered: Richmond, "Billy Peek," 3D.

"he started coming in and hanging around again": Billy Peek, interview with the author, St. Louis, MO, March 29, 2000.

"Finally after coming in there for quite a few times": Billy Peek, interview with the author, St. Louis, MO, March 29, 2000.

"It was a great place to be": Billy Peek, interview with the author, St. Louis, MO, March 29, 2000.

"This guy had gotten drunk or something": Billy Peek, interview with the author, St. Louis, MO, March 29, 2000.

"When I was in Wentzville": Billy Peek, interview with the author, St. Louis, MO, March 29, 2000.

"Chuck wouldn't even come out to the airport to meet me": Bill Graham and Robert Greenfield, *Bill Graham Presents: My Life Inside Rock and Out* (New York, Doubleday, 1992), 178–179.

"He didn't move or speak": Graham and Greenfield, *Bill Graham Presents*, 179.

"'You want cash or a check?'": Graham and Greenfield, *Bill Graham Presents*, 179.

"He said, 'Let's go.' It was like, 'You want me to fight ten rounds?'": Graham and Greenfield, *Bill Graham Presents*, 179.

"Chuck, listen to that applause": Graham and Greenfield, *Bill Graham Presents*, 180.

"That short thirty seconds was pure genius thought": Graham and Greenfield, *Bill Graham Presents*, 180.

"It's a ritual every time Chuck plays here": Lydon, "Chuck Berry," 22.

"musicians who learned from him, grown up and migrated": "Review of *Chuck Berry: Live at the Fillmore*," *Rolling Stone* November 9, 1967.

"You meet him as a person and you don't forget him": Chuck Berry, *Live at the Fillmore*, sound recording, Mercury SR-61138, 1967.

Berry recalls, he "suggested she leave": Berry, *Autobiography*, 231.

The town residents, Berry argues, "were unable to cope": Berry, 230.

"I go to a record store once a year": Peter Meadon, "Berry Favourites," *Record Mirror*, April 4, 1965, 8.

"Chuck was off in his own world. . . . I never saw him": Fitzpatrick, *Father of Rock and Roll*, 204.

"Berry Park captivates quite a bit of my time": Marcus, "Roll Over Chuck Berry," 15.

Berry Park "has been his favorite place" of all the property he has owned: Billy Peek, interview with the author, St. Louis, MO, March 29, 2000.

"I have no idea how they got them there": Bob Baldori, interview with the author, Toronto, February 7, 1998.

Berry, according to *Billboard*'s reviewer Ed Ochs, "incited fans to riots of ecstasy": Ed Ochs, "Berry the Berries at Fillmore," *Billboard*, June 21, 1969, 36.

While banning "Chuck Berry and other rock and roll acts" from the hall: "Ban on Rock! At London's Royal Albert Hall." *Melody Maker*, July 19, 1969, 1.

it was, in the critic's estimation, "a record worthy of his reputation": Lester Bangs, Review of "*Concerto in B. Goode, Rolling Stone*", August 9, 1969.

Billy Peek's own review of the album, that it was simply "a terrible record": Billy Peek, interview with the author, St. Louis, March 29, 2000.

"I shall be going back, soon, to Chess": Marcus, "Roll Over Chuck Berry," 15.

The rumors that the Chess brothers had decided to sell their business: Cohodas, *Spinning Blues into Gold*, 294.

As Chess was driving to a business appointment in Chicago: Cohodas, *Spinning Blues into Gold*, 299.

Chapter 12: Back Home

"After I left [Chess Records] he had the biggest hit that he ever had": Marshall Chess, interview with the author, November 4, 1998.

"anybody that played rock and roll was like scum": William Patrick Salvo, "Chuck Berry Speaks!" *Melody Maker*, December 16, 1972, 34.

things "were a mess": Bob Baldori, interview with the author, Toronto, Canada, February 7, 1998.

"It was surprising to me": Bob Baldori, interview with the author, Toronto, February 7, 1998.

"I don't recall it at all," Edwards has maintained: Esmond Edwards, telephone interview with the author, December 14, 1998.

"Chuck has got the fucking art . . . of always keeping up with the times": Guralnick, *Feel Like Going Home*, 199.

"He called me up and said 'I'll come up'": Bob Baldori, interview with the author, Toronto, February 7, 1998.

"He spent a week [in the studio]": Bob Baldori, interview with the author, Toronto, February 7, 1998.

the album was "a marginal effort" and that it was "abominable": Salvo, "Chuck Berry Speaks!" 34.

"there was all these politics involved with it": Bob Baldori, interview with the author, Toronto, February 7, 1998.

"We go to a gig in Indianapolis," the pianist recalls: Bob Baldori, interview with the author, Toronto, February 7, 1998.

according to *Rolling Stone* over a thousand tried unsuccessfully: Jan Hodenfeld, "Rock and Roll Revived," *Rolling Stone*, November 29, 1969, 38.

"1969's own dear trendies": Hodenfeld, "Rock and Roll Revived," 38.

"In the last few years of rock concerts": Mike Jahn, "'Rock Revival' Audience Cheers Bill Haley and 15-Year-Old Hit," *New York Times* October 20, 1969: 61.

Haley was "glad to get the money": Reese, *Chuck Berry*, 85.

"as exciting as almost anything heard lately": Jahn, "'Rock Revival'": 61.

the band resembled "a winning bowling team": Hodenfeld, "Rock and Roll Revived": 38.

Even getting him there had been a struggle: Reese, *Chuck Berry*, 85.

"tired then, he is exhausted now": Hodenfeld, "Rock and Roll Revived": 38.

Nader was to maintain that he was paying Berry under-the-table: Reese, *Chuck Berry*, 96–7.

"Just fucking *play*, Chuck": Reese, *Chuck Berry*, 85.

"I can't deny that it turned out okay": Berry, *The Autobiogrpahy*, 259–60.

"Chuck Berry is no battered old relic": Charles Shaar Murray, "Big Cars, Little White Chicks, and the Chuck Berry Lick," *Creem*, March 1972: 27.

Berry was "the highlight of the first house": Tony Stewart, "One of the Most Adventurous Bills Ever," *New Musical Express*, February 12, 1972: 30.

the crowd began "to bounce in perfect time": Murray, "Big Cars": 26.

"The way the audience reacted, with incessant calls for more": Stewart, "One of Most Adventurous Bills Ever," 30.

"We really didn't have enough adequate or audible material": William Patrick Salvo, "Chuck Berry," In Herbst, Peter (Ed).*The Rolling Stone Interviews: Talking With the Legends of Rock and Roll 1967–80*. NY: St. Martin's Rolling Stone Press, 1981: 230.

"Listen, please! Please! He's overrun fifteen minutes": Chuck Berry, *The London Chuck Berry Sessions*, sound recording, Chess CH60020, April 1972.

"what happened was that some DJ's latched on to 'My Ding-A-Ling'": Esmond Edwards, telephone interview with the author, December 14, 1998.

"the thing that sold," according to the song's producer, "was the spontaneity": Esmond Edwards, telephone interview with the author, December 14, 1998.

"comes across as what it essentially is: a silly little ditty": Fred Rothwell, *Long Distance Information*, 176.

"I had heard that there was a suit brought against Chuck for plagiarizing that tune": Esmond Edwards, telephone interview with the author, December 14, 1998.

"I understand that he doesn't mention my name in his autobiography": Esmond Edwards, telephone interview with the author, December 14, 1998.

The $250,000 royalty check Berry claims he received: Berry, *The Autobiography*, 261.

"What he was doing," Peek felt, "was saying, 'Look, I'll do a show here for you'": Billy Peek, interview with the author, St. Louis, MO, March 29, 2000.

"We came in the afternoon for rehearsal": Billy Peek, interview with the author, St. Louis, MO, March 29, 2000.

"You're never gonna work in Vegas, you're never gonna do this": Billy Peek, interview with the author, St. Louis, MO, March 29, 2000.

"You're gonna get paid," he told Peek, "don't worry about it": Billy Peek, interview with the author, St. Louis, MO, March 29, 2000.

"I'm just about to go to sleep," Peek recalled: Billy Peek, interview with the author, St. Louis, MO, March 29, 2000.

"Yeah," Billy Peek, said. "We can get over there": Billy Peek, interview with the author, St. Louis, MO, March 29, 2000.

"I don't know what went down, but that entertainment director was really nice to Chuck": Billy Peek, interview with the author, St. Louis, MO, March 29, 2000.

"he was dressed to the nines, he had the cape": Billy Peek, interview with the author, St. Louis, MO, March 29, 2000.

"The guy just lost it, you know": Billy Peek, interview with the author, St. Louis, MO, March 29, 2000.

"Chuck," Peek recalled, "was having a problem with a contract again: Billy Peek, interview with the author, St. Louis, MO, March 29, 2000.

"I thought Chuck looked at me funny": Billy Peek, interview with the author, St. Louis, MO, March 29, 2000.

"I said, 'Well, I've been had'": Billy Peek, interview with the author, St. Louis, MO, March 29, 2000.

"The promotion was horrible": Billy Peek, interview with the author, St. Louis, MO, March 29, 2000.

"I've never seen Chuck do this much": Billy Peek, interview with the author, St. Louis, MO, March 29, 2000.

"He's pretty loyal": Jim Marsala, interview with the author, St. Louis, MO, March 29, 2000.

"all the evocative power and charm of the Berry songs of old": Tony Glover, review of *Bio*, *Rolling Stone* Nov 22 1973: 79.

"Chuck goes out of his way to make me feel at ease": John Etheredge, "Chuck Berry: A Conversation With Mr. Rock 'n' Roll," *Goldmine* November 1983: 6.

500 people paid $2 each to hear several local bands: Charlene Prost, "Rock Festival Held in Chuck Berry's Park," *St. Louis Post-Dispatch*, August 31, 1970, 3E.

"in an attempt to maintain order": "Suit Against Singer Settled," *St. Louis Post-Dispatch*, October 2, 1975.

Berry's account of the incident in *The Autobiography* has the shooting occurring between two boys: Berry, *Autobiography*, 250.

Berry had entered into an agreement with local promoter Ed Hindelang: Richard K. Weil, Jr., "Festival in the Red, Promoters Are Blue," *St. Louis Post-Dispatch*, July 5, 1974, 1.

the "sound system, believe it or not, was quite good": Merrill Brown, "Rock Festival a Disaster in Almost Every Way," *St. Louis Post-Dispatch*, July 5, 1974, 4B.

"one of the few nonperformers who was paid anything near what was due him": Weil, "Festival in the Red," 1.

Just a month later, on August 11: "2 Girls Drown in Park Pool," *St. Louis Post-Dispatch*, August 12, 1974, 9A.

In 1968, Jacob Young, a 21-year-old St. Louis man, had drowned: "Settlement in Wrongful Death Suit," *St. Louis Post-Dispatch*, November 28, 1974.

On August 24, 1974, some 40 officers raided the park: Leo Fitzmaurice, "St. Charles County Seeks to Close Club," *St. Louis Post-Dispatch*, August 27, 1974.

"liquor and narcotics violations. . . . one shooting, three rapes and several other violations.": "Rock Concert Site Is Ordered Closed," *St. Louis Post-Dispatch*, September 11, 1974.

Berry was hit with another lawsuit: "Suit on Drowning at Berry Park," *St. Louis Post-Dispatch*, September 18, 1974.

Chapter 13: The Whole World Knows the Music, Nobody Knows the Man

"He's the most difficult person I've ever worked with": Vince Aletti, "Chuck Berry Tells All—Sort Of," *Rolling Stone*, December 4, 1987, 74.

"the most distressed small city in America": Jonathan Kozol, *Savage Inequalities: Children in America's Schools* (New York: Crown, 1991), 7.

"a third of its families live[d] on less than $7,500 a year": Kozol, *Savage Inequalities*, 7.

and the city ranked higher than Chicago: Kozol, *Savage Inequalities*, 20.

"simply the worst possible place I can imagine": Kozol, *Savage Inequalities*, 25.

"Chuck had been working on the songs for quite a while": Jim Marsala, interview with the author, St. Louis, March 29, 2000.

"When most of the recording was done": Jim Marsala, interview with the author, St. Louis, March 29, 2000.

Chuck Berry had at last "made an album that displays all his old skills": Tom Carson, "Review of *Rockit*," *Rolling Stone*, January 24, 1980.

A month earlier, he had surrendered himself to the U.S. District Court: "Rock Singer 'Chuck' Berry Charged With Tax Evasion," *St. Louis Post-Dispatch*, May 14, 1979: 3A.

The first was the January tour of England: Berry, *Autobiography*, 271.

Berry's performance fees fluctuated wildly: Reese, *Chuck Berry*, 96.

"This tax thing that I was in was no bum rap": Etheredge, "Chuck Berry," 13.

"quoting me one fee for our contract": Berry, *Autobiography*, 270.

"Chuck says to me, 'Well, go on down there, Billy'": Billy Peek, interview with the author, St. Louis, March 29, 2000.

"it went down just like I thought it would": Billy Peek, interview with the author, St. Louis, March 29, 2000.

"There was this one guy," Peek remembered: Billy Peek, interview with the author, St. Louis, March 29, 2000.

it would be better to "get tried by people who know what showbusiness is like": Billy Peek, interview with the author, St. Louis, March 29, 2000.

Berry "appeared nervous during the court session and twice broke into tears": "Chuck Berry Draws Jail Term," *St. Louis Post-Dispatch*, July 11, 1979, 8D.

"Mr. President, Mrs. Carter," spoke Berry in subdued tones": "Johnny B. Goode," *Omnibus*, BBC TV, 1980.

"We got one minor problem": "Johnny B. Goode," *Omnibus*, BBC TV, 1980.

"I have tried to curb the manners by which I have been ripped off": "Johnny B. Goode," *Omnibus*, BBC TV, 1980.

"Nothing really came of it," he told the journalist: Salvo, "Chuck Berry," 234.

"That's a lie, I did not say that to you": "Johnny B. Goode," *Omnibus*, BBC TV, 1980.

"he just doesn't let stuff like that bother him": Jim Marsala, interview with the author, St. Louis, March 29, 2000.

Berry was even "glad of it": Billy Peek, interview with the author, St. Louis, MO, March 29, 2000.

Berry "performed impressively": Stephen Holden, "Chuck Berry Rocks Them at the Ritz," *New York Times,* June 28, 1981, 48.

"it was in the dressing room": *Chuck Berry: Hail! Hail! Rock 'n' Roll,* Delilah Films, 1987.

a "perfunctory performance . . . peppered with off-schedule notes": Rothwell, *Long Distance Information,* 235.

"For the bo-bo I did, I publicly apologize": Rothwell, *Long Distance Information,* 235.

"Every time him and me got in contact": Victor Bockris, *Keith Richards: The Biography* (New York: Poseidon, 1992), 360–361.

"It's hard for me to induct Chuck Berry": http://www.rockhall.com/hof/inductee.asp?id=67.

"I wanted to serve Chuck up with a good band": *Chuck Berry: Hail! Hail! Rock 'n' Roll,* Delilah Films, 1987.

"imagine," he was to remember years later, "getting a phone call: Mark Slocombe, telephone interview with the author, February 7, 2002.

"He had a bandanna tied around his head": Mark Slocombe, telephone interview with the author, February 7, 2002.

Berry's living room contained "two large video screens": Bockris, *Keith Richards,* 361.

"like a fish out of water, flipping about enigmatically: Bockris, *Keith Richards,* 361.

there was an "MCI 24-track recorder: Mark Slocombe, telephone interview with the author, February 7, 2002.

The small, overnight guest rooms built behind the stage: Mark Slocombe, telephone interview with the author, February 7, 2002.

Berry left rehearsals for Pittsburgh: "Pirates Foiled as Chuck Ducks," *Chicago Tribune,* October 1, 1986.

"I'm going to beat that rap; they're not going to take me down": Mark Slocombe, telephone interview with the author, February 7, 2002.

a "female friend with a miniskirt up to her pupick": Aletti, "Chuck Berry Tells All," 74.

"He just kept putting it off": Aletti, "Chuck Berry Tells All," 74.

the film crew had spent "about seventy hours getting ready for it": Mark Slocombe, telephone interview with the author, February 7, 2002.

"The film was having to pay him, I forget, $800 a day": Mark Slocombe, telephone interview with the author, February 7, 2002.

"we'd turn the amplifier volume down on him": Mark Slocombe, telephone interview with the author, February 7, 2002.

"Leave the amp as I set it": *Chuck Berry: Hail! Hail! Rock 'n' Roll,* Delilah Films, 1987.

"It'll be too much for you to sing and play the lead fills as well": *Chuck Berry: Hail! Hail! Rock 'n' Roll,* Delilah Films, 1987.

"Over the course of the film": Mark Slocombe, telephone interview with the author, February 7, 2002.

"I feel sorry for him," Richards was to say later: Bockris, *Keith Richards,* 361.

"I think it was stunning for him to have people all over his property": Aletti, "Chuck Berry Tells All," 74.

"He decided to write a book and make a movie, right": *Chuck Berry: Hail! Hail! Rock 'n' Roll,* Delilah Films, 1987.

"I was the one that had to wire up Chuck's gear": Mark Slocombe, telephone interview with the author, February 7, 2002.

"We rehearsed in the afternoon before the first show": Mark Slocombe, telephone interview with the author, February 7, 2002.

"Everybody's lookin' at me on stage": *Chuck Berry: Hail! Hail! Rock 'n' Roll,* Delilah Films, 1987.

"We had so many false starts; you know": Mark Slocombe, telephone interview with the author, February 7, 2002.

"Chuck comes over to me in the middle of the solo": *Chuck Berry: Hail! Hail! Rock 'n' Roll,* Delilah Films, 1987.

"We rehearsed it in C": Mark Slocombe, telephone interview with the author, February 7, 2002.

Keith Richards "took charge": Brogan, "Birthday Concert," 5C.

Chapter 14: Wentzville and St. Charles

Berry's name is listed six times in the Wentzville telephone directory: Salvo, "Chuck Berry," 226.

"If I can be very frank, there is an element in town": Robert Hilburn, "Private Chuck Berry Still Calling the Tunes at 60," *Los Angeles Times*, October 26, 1986.

calling the two hours "long and unwieldy": Richard Harrington, "Hail! Hail! Good Times With Berry," *Washington Post*, October 9, 1987, B2.

"a vivacious narrative history": Aletti, "Chuck Berry Tells All," 71.

"I have been married since October 28, 1948": *Chuck Berry: Hail! Hail! Rock 'n' Roll*, Delilah Films, 1987.

"But for all rock and roll stars on the road": *Chuck Berry: Hail! Hail! Rock 'n' Roll*, Delilah Films, 1987.

"My name is Themetta Suggs Berry": *Chuck Berry: Hail! Hail! Rock 'n' Roll*, Delilah Films, 1987.

"Chuck has had a couple of run ins with the law": *Chuck Berry: Hail! Hail! Rock 'n' Roll*, Delilah Films, 1987.

"self-glorifying record advertisements": Cliff Froelich, "Hail! Hail! The Bankroll," *The Riverfront Times*, October 14–20, 1987, 4B.

"breezy word-play, obsessive rhyming and alliteration": Don McLeese, "The Spirit of a Rocker," *New York Times*, October 18, 1987.

"the language, the cadence and the rhythm of the sentences": Bob Greene, "A Star's Dim View of His Own Luster," *Chicago Tribune*, January 6, 1988, C1.

"a puerile, badly written and often nonsensical ramble": Froelich, "Hail! Hail! The Bankroll," 8B.

"what's intriguing about . . . Berry's crazy quilt self-portrait": Aletti, "Chuck Berry Tells All," 71.

"another writer might have given a more balanced view of his life and legacy": McLeese, "The Spirit of a Rocker."

"Berry details the sexual and criminal past he refused to discuss": Froelich, "Hail! Hail! The Bankroll," 8B.

"Then it dawned upon me with a certain suddenness": W.E.B. DuBois, *The Souls of Black Folk* (New York: Signet, 1968), 44.

"had thereafter no desire to tear down the veil": DuBois, *The Souls of Black Folk*, 44.

"simply wishes to make it possible for a man to be both a Negro and American": DuBois, *The Souls of Black Folk*, 45.

it protects the individual from "the eyes of others": DuBois, *The Souls of Black Folk*, 45.

"Another kiss and my curiosity was standing straight up": Berry, *Autobiography*, 237.

he "heard minute moans of a million-dollar approval": Berry, *Autobiography*, 239.

"the all-time, all-American femme fatale": Mark Goodman, "The Further Misadventures of Candy," *Esquire*, June 1976, 91.

the "Trial of the Decade": Pete Axelrod, "Candy," *Newsweek*, November 8, 1976, 93.

"lacerations of the mouth, requiring five stitches": Barbara Goldberg, "Woman Slugged by Berry Needed Stiches," UPI, June 6, 1988.

Boteler filed a lawsuit against Berry for $5 million: Barbara Goldberg, "Chuck Berry Sued for $5 Million in Alleged Assault," UPI, June 14, 1988.

Berry again failed to appear in court: Mark Perkiss, "Rock Pioneer Chuck Berry Stands Up Police," UPI, June 5, 1988.

on November 22, 1988, Berry pleaded guilty: "Chuck Berry Fined," *St. Louis Post-Dispatch*, November 26, 1988.

Berry described his plans for the restaurant: Ralph Dummit, "Chuck Berry Opens Doors: Rock and Roll Idol Turns Restaurateur," *St. Louis Post-Dispatch*, September 22, 1988.

His federal convictions in 1944 and 1961: Lisha Gayle, "Thwarted Chuck Berry's Restaurant Can't Get Liquor License," *St. Louis Post-Dispatch*, September 29, 1989.

the two began a "coordinated movement to force Chuck Berry to turn over his wealth": Richard Schwartz, interview with the author, St. Louis, March 31, 2000.

Huck began providing information to the Drug Enforcement Agency: Kim Neely, "DEA Targets Chuck Berry," *Rolling Stone*, August 23, 1990, 34.

Huck "was constantly trying to get the Feds to seize the guitar cases: Richard Schwartz, interview with the author, St. Louis, March 31, 2000.

he claimed "to have received an anonymous phone call": Neely, "DEA Targets Chuck Berry," 34.

"Vincent Huck," Schwartz maintained, "was taken into a position of semi-confidence: Richard Schwartz, interview with the author, St. Louis, March 31, 2000.

"'intentionally and without just cause or excuse": Ralph Dummit, "Chuck Berry Taped Women, Suit Charges" *St. Louis Post-Dispatch*, December 27, 1989.

"the only magazine with the balls to show Chuck's berries": *High Society*, January 1990, 3.

the suit specifically named Vincent Huck as the person who stole the photographs: *Berry v. Drake Publishers, Inc*, Circuit Court of the City of St. Louis, Case No. 902–10071.

"'publicly disclos[ing] private matters concerning Charles E. Berry": "Berry Files Suit to Get Toilet Videotapes Back," *St. Louis Post-Dispatch*, May 3, 1990.

"two rifles and a shotgun. Two clear plastic bags": Marianna Riley, "Berry Upstages Accuser. Items in Drug Raid Planted, He Says," *St. Louis Post-Dispatch* June 29, 1990.

"Where's the cocaine?" Jo Mannies, "Drug Unit Raids Chuck Berry Estates, Seized Items," *St. Louis Post-Dispatch*, June 28, 1990.

"the affidavit had "absolutely no credibility": Neely, "DEA Targets Chuck Berry," 34.

"a source from St. Charles Police Department": Neely, "DEA Targets Chuck Berry," 34.

"The raid was instigated by Vincent Huck": Richard Schwartz, interview with the author, St. Louis, March 31, 2000.

due to Berry's criminal record his "clients fear reprisals": Marianna Riley, "Women Sue Berry, Charge He Took Bathroom Videos," *St. Louis Post-Dispatch*, June 30, 1990.

"It seemed to me," the lawyer theorized: Richard Schwartz, interview with the author, St. Louis, March 31, 2000.

he was "not about to get into a fight with anybody": Marianna Riley, "Bar Brawlers Said to Include Lawyers in Chuck Berry Suit," *St. Louis Post-Dispatch*, July 4, 1990.

"Hannah was," in Richard Schwartz's view: Richard Schwartz, interview with the author, St. Louis, March 31, 2000.

after a scathing *Post-Dispatch* editorial on July 15: "The Prosecutor and the Performer," *St. Louis Post-Dispatch*, July 15, 1990.

"They charged him with felony child sexual abuse": Richard Schwartz, interview with the author, St. Louis, March 31, 2000.

one critic calling the opening show of the tour "painful and pathetic": Marianna Riley, "Berry, on Tour in Sweden, Denies Charges Against Him," *St. Louis Post-Dispatch*, July 4, 1990.

An appearance on the *Johnny Carson Show*: Marianna Riley, "Chuck Berry Unburdened by Resolution of Charges," *St. Louis Post-Dispatch*, November 23, 1990.

"all parties," a publicist for the amusement park was quoted as saying: Randy Lewis, "Knott's Cancels Berry Concerts," *Los Angeles Times*, July 26, 1990, F3.

Chuck Berry played only three shows: Marianna Riley, "Child-Abuse Charges Dropped in Chuck Berry Plea Bargain," *St. Louis Post-Dispatch*, November E. 22, 1990.

"We moved all civil cases down to federal court": Richard Schwartz, interview with the author, St. Louis, March 31, 2000.

"We had this all worked out with Chuck": Richard Schwartz, interview with the author, St. Louis, March 31, 2000.

"I remember," Schwartz recalls, "getting the call almost on the morning after the election": Richard Schwartz, interview with the author, St. Louis, March 31, 2000.

"I feel fantastic": "Child Abuse Charges Dropped Against Chuck Berry," UPI, November 21, 1990.

Vincent Huck had filed a libel and slander suit against Berry: Riley, "Chuck Berry Unburdened."

Ronald Boggs announced to the *St. Louis Post-Dispatch*: Robert Manor, "Use TV Ads in Tapes Case, Lawyer Opposing Berry Says," *St. Louis Post-Dispatch*, December 3, 1990.

"Chuck went through a very long deposition": Richard Schwartz, interview with the author, St. Louis, March 31, 2000.

"They weren't going to let go of it": Richard Schwartz, interview with the author, St. Louis, March 31, 2000.

"Unfortunately," Schwartz recalled, "the way the clerk's office worked": Richard Schwartz, interview with the author, St. Louis, March 31, 2000.

"Berry's claims of civil rights violations fell short": "St.Charles County Rock Star's Appeal Is Rejected by U.S.," *St. Louis Post-Dispatch*, July 1, 1992.

"The Eighth Circuit set up a very expedited briefing schedule": Richard Schwartz, personal interview, St. Louis, March 31, 2000.

"Boggs launched a new campaign to start to sell some of the materials": Richard Schwartz, interview with the author, St. Louis, March 31, 2000.

"there's a guy in a major law firm in St. Louis": Mike Sager, "Sex and Drugs and Rock 'n' Roll," *Spy*, February 1993, 60.

"because the advance ticket sales were nonexistent": Jerry Berger, "Companions Quail When Lawyer Fires," *St. Louis Post-Dispatch*, December 9, 1992.

"to achieve the financial destruction tantamount to an economic lynching": "High Court Rejects Berry's Appeal in Videotapings Suits, *Los Angeles Times*, February 23, 1993.

"John Price," believed Schwartz, "a younger lawyer": Richard Schwartz, interview with the author, St. Louis, March 31, 2000.

when he "went to the federal court for some sort of in-chambers conference": Richard Schwartz, interview with the author, St. Louis, March 31, 2000.

"never had any indication he was dissatisfied": Richard Schwartz, interview with the author, St. Louis, March 31, 2000.

"Not very long after we got out," remembers Schwartz: Richard Schwartz, interview with the author, St. Louis, March 31, 2000.

Boggs received "about a third" of the settlement: Nordeka English, "Most Women in Berry Settlement Will Get $5,000, *St. Louis Post-Dispatch*, May 24, 1995.

In June 1993, he purchased a new house in Ladue: Jerry Berger, "Berry Is Departing Wentzville for Ladue," *St. Louis Post-Dispatch*, June 22, 1993.

Chapter 15: Johnson v. Berry

In an oral culture where . . . authority is prized above originality: Michael Eric Dyson, *I May Not Get There With You: The True Martin Luther King, Jr.* (New York: Touchstone, 2001), 143.

"tens of millions of dollars": *Johnnie Johnson v. Charles E. Berry and Isalee Music Company*, U.S. District Court, Eastern District of Missouri, Eastern Division, 4:00CV01891DJS, 5.

"taking advantage of Johnson's alcoholism": *Johnson v. Berry*, 5

"He's not doing Chuck Berry songs": *Chuck Berry: Hail! Hail! Rock 'n' Roll*, Delilah Films, 1987.

"got off the Stairmaster": Fitzpatrick, *Father of Rock and Roll*, 330–331.

"Johnnie had been cheated out of his place in history": Fitzpatrick, *Father of Rock and Roll*, 335.

"I'm no rock and roll historian": Fitzpatrick, *Father of Rock and Roll*, 370–371.

the Rock and Roll Hall of Fame committee had deliberately given him the wrong dates: Fitzpatrick, *Father of Rock and Roll*, 342.

Turek then hired Rogers and Cowan: Fitzpatrick, *Father of Rock and Roll*, 350.

"I didn't like the guy": Fitzpatrick, *Father of Rock and Roll*, 355.

Everything about the man made me absolutely nauseous: Fitzpatrick, *Father of Rock and Roll*, 353.

"I figured that I could get more accomplished for Johnnie: Fitzpatrick, *Father of Rock and Roll*, 355.

"I am in full support of Johnnie's nomination": http://www.johnnie.com/c-lett.html.

"I got what I wanted, which was the part about them being 'musical collaborators'": Fitzpatrick, *Father of Rock and Roll*, 357.

"I'd do anything for you, Johnnie": Fitzpatrick, *Father of Rock and Roll*, 357.

"Sure enough," remembered Johnson, "he did": Fitzpatrick, *Father of Rock and Roll*, 358.

I want him inducted into the Blues Foundation Hall of Fame: Fitzpatrick, *Father of Rock and Roll*, 369.

"No, I didn't write the music with him": *Chuck Berry: Hail! Hail! Rock 'n' Roll*, Delilah Films, 1987.

"I didn't write them [the songs]": Fitzpatrick, *Father of Rock and Roll*, 331.

"Me and Chuck didn't write music": Fitzpatrick, *Father of Rock and Roll*, 122.

"The only one doin' any writin' on them songs was Chuck": Fitzpatrick, *Father of Rock and Roll*, 122.

"He knew exactly what he wanted to do": Fitzpatrick, *Father of Rock and Roll*, 123.

"technically, the blues is not hard to play": Fitzpatrick, *Father of Rock and Roll*, 55.

"the first time I heard that was in one of Carl Hogan's riffs": *Chuck Berry: Hail! Hail! Rock 'n' Roll*, Delilah Films, 1987.

Baptist preachers are always ripping each other off: Michael Eric Dyson, *I May Not Get There With You*, 139.

"Chuck was always the one with the ideas": Fitzpatrick, *Father of Rock and Roll*, 125–6.
"If he came up with a little tune on his guitar": Fitzpatrick, *Father of Rock and Roll*, 126.
If he heard me playin' something that he liked": Fitzpatrick, *Father of Rock and Roll*, 126.
"Songs like 'Roll Over Beethoven' ": Fitzpatrick, *Father of Rock and Roll*, 126.
"All fingers point to Turek," they wrote: Ellen Futterman and Tim Bryant, "Key Issue in Suit Against Rock Star Is Whether It Was Filed Too Late: Case Causes Rift Between Ex-Partners Chuck Berry and Johnnie Johnson," *St. Louis Dispatch*, December 22, 2000, A1.
"Turek helped inspire the suit": Dave Hoekstra, "Goode Times, Bad Times," *Chicago Sun-Times*, January 21, 2001.
"The lawsuit is between Johnnie and his attorneys": Hoekstra, "Goode Times, Bad Times."
he "had no animosity" toward Berry: Johnnie Johnson, interview with the author, St. Louis, March 30, 2000.

Epílogue: Blueberry Híll

the reason he even considered the offer: Joe Edwards, interview with the author, St. Louis, March 30, 2000.
"So, I assumed it would just be some old guitar": Hilburn, "Chuck Berry Sets the Record Straight."
"I am really flattered, as well as honored": Lorraine Kee Montre, "Ten St. Louis Stars Make 'Walk of Fame,' " *St. Louis Post-Dispatch*, June 26, 1989.
Berry's playing was "sloppy" and "the sound distorted": Chris Dickinson, "Still Rockin' Chuck Berry Packs House on 70th Birthday," *St. Louis Post-Dispatch*, October 20, 1996.
"It would be kind of fun to play": Joe Edwards, interview with the author, St. Louis, March 30, 2000.
Judge Donald T. Stohr had thrown out the allegations: Tim Bryant, "Judge Dismisses Claim of Infringement in Lawsuits Against Chuck Berry by His Longtime Pianist," *St. Louis Post-Dispatch*, June 16, 2001.
"the substantive base of the suit": Bryant, "Judge Dismisses Claim of Infringement."
he claimed thirteen songs were ready for release: Stephen E. Ambrose and Douglas Brinkley, "Berry Met Flow of American Life in St. Louis: Pioneer Has No Place He'd Rather Go Than the Source of His Inspiration," *USA Today*, August 2, 2000.
a "trite, smutty number about a traveling salesman": Paul DuNoyer, "The Life of a Ladies Man," *Q*, May 1995, 67.
"These monthly shows are legendary": Joe Edwards, interview with the author, St. Louis, March 30, 2000.
"I love the fact that he doesn't do encores": Joe Edwards, interview with the author, St. Louis, March 30, 2000.

Works Cited

Books

Abrahams, Roger D. *Deep Down in the Jungle: Negro Narrative Folklore from the Streets of Philadelphia*. Hatboro, PA: Folklore Associates, 1964.

Amburn, Ellis. *Buddy Holly: A Biography*. New York: St. Martin's, 1995.

Berry, Chuck. *The Autobiography*. New York: Simon and Schuster, 1987.

Bockris, Victor. *Keith Richards: The Biography*. New York: Poseidon, 1992.

Braxton, Joanne M., ed. *The Collected Poetry of Paul Laurence Dunbar*. Charlottesville: University Press of Virginia, 1993.

Burdon, Eric. *I Used to be an Animal but I'm All Right Now*. Boston: Faber and Faber, 1986.

Capeci, Dominic J. *The Lynching of Cleo Wright*. Lexington: University of Kentucky Press, 1998.

Clark, Dick, and Richard Robinson. *Rock, Roll, and Remember*. New York: Thomas Y. Crowell, 1976.

Cohodas, Nadine. *Spinning Blues into Gold: The Chess Brothers and the Legendary Chess Records*. New York: St. Martin's, 2000.

Cowan, Tom, and Jack Maguire. *Timelines of African-American History: 500 Years of Black Achievement*. New York: Perigee, 1994.

Davis, Francis. *The History of the Blues: The Roots, The Music, The People from Charlie Patton to Robert Cray*. New York: Hyperion, 1995.

Dewitt, Howard. *Chuck Berry: Rock and Roll Music*. 2d ed. Ann Arbor, Michigan: Pierian, 1985.

Dixon, Willie, with Don Snowden. *I Am the Blues: The Willie Dixon Story*. New York: Da Capo, 1989.

DuBois, W. E. B. *The Souls of Black Folk*. New York: Signet, 1968.

Dyson, Michael Eric. *I May Not Get There With You: The True Martin Luther King Jr.* New York: Touchstone, 2001.

Early, Gerald. *Ain't But A Place: An Anthology of African American Writings about St. Louis*. St. Louis: Missouri Historical Society Press, 1998.

Escott, Colin with Martin Hawkins. *Good Rockin' Tonight: Sun Records and the Birth of Rock and Roll*. New York: St. Martin's, 1991.

Fehrenbacher, Don E. *The Dred Scott Case: Its Significance in American Law and Politics*. New York: Oxford UP, 1978.

Fitzpatrick, Travis. *Father of Rock and Roll: The Story of Johnnie "B. Goode" Johnson*. Houston: Thomas, Cooke, 1999.

Fox, Tim. *Where We Live: A Guide to St. Louis Communities*. St. Louis: Missouri Historical Society Press, 1995.

Gart, Galen. *First Pressings: The History of Rhythm & Blues Vol 5 (1955)*. Milford, NH: Big Nickel, 1990.

———. *First Pressings: The History of Rhythm & Blues Vol. 6 (1956)*. Milford, NH: Big Nickel, 1991.

———. *First Pressings: The History of Rhythm & Blues Vol. 7 (1957)*. Milford, NH: Big Nickel, 1993.

Gates Jr., Henry Louis. *The Signifying Monkey: A Theory of African-American Literary Criticism*. New York: Oxford University Press, 1988.

Gilett, Charlie. *The Sound of the City: The Rise of Rock and Roll*. New York: Pantheon, 1983.

Graham, Bill, and Robert Greenfield. *Bill Graham Presents: My Life Inside Rock and Out*. New York, Doubleday, 1992.

Guralnick, Peter. *Feel Like Going Home: Portraits in Blues and Rock and Roll*. New York: Outerbridge and Dienstfrey, 1971.

———. *Last Train to Memphis: The Rise of Elvis Presley.* Boston: Little, Brown, 1994.

Harper, Donna Sullivan. *Not So Simple: The "Simple" Stories by Langston Hughes.* Columbia. MO: University of Missouri Press, 1995.

Harrison, Hank. *The Dead.* Millbrae CA: Celestial Arts, 1980.

Hammond, John, with Irving Townsend, *John Hammond on Record: An Autobiography.* New York: Penguin, 1981.

Herbst, Peter, ed. *The Rolling Stone Interviews: Talking With the Legends of Rock and Roll 1967–80.* NY: St. Martin's Rolling Stone Press, 1981.

Hughes, Langston. *The Best of Simple.* New York: Hill and Wang, 1961.

———. *The Collected Works of Langston Hughes. The Poems 1921–40, Vol. 1,* ed. Arnold Rampersad. Columbia: University of Missouri Press, 2001.

Horton, James Oliver, and Lois E. Horton, eds. *A History of the African American People.* Detroit:Wayne State University Press, 1997.

Jackson, John. *Big Beat Heat Alan Freed and the Early Years of Rock and Roll.* New York: Schirmer, 1991.

———. *American Bandstand: Dick Clark and the Making of a Rock 'n' Roll Empire.* New York: Oxford University Press, 1997.

Kozol, Jonathan. *Savage Inequalities: Children in America's Schools.* New York: Crown, 1991.

Langum, David J. *Crosssing over the Line: Legislating Morality and the Mann Act.* The Chicago Series on Sexuality, History and Society, ed. John C. Fout. Chicago: University of Chigago Press, 1994.

Lipsitz, George. *A Life in the Struggle: Ivory Perry and the Culture of Opposition.* Rev. ed. Philadelphia: Temple University Press, 1995.

Long, Herman H., and Charles S. Johnson. *People vs. Property: Race Restrictive Covenants in Housing.* Nashville: Fisk University Press, 1947.

Ostrom, Hans A. *Langston Hughes: A Study of the Short Fiction.* New York: Twayne, 1993.

Palmer, Robert. *Rock and Roll: An Unruly History.* New York: Harmony, 1995.

Palmer, Tony. *All You Need Is Love: The Story of Popular Music.* New York: Penguin, 1977.

Rampersad, Arnold. *Jackie Robinson: A Biography.* New York: Ballantine, 1997.

———. *The Life of Langston Hughes. Vol. 2: I Dream A World.* New York: Oxford University Press, 1988.

Reese, Krista. *Chuck Berry: Mr. Rock and Roll.* New York: Proteus, 1982.

Rothwell, Fred. *Long Distance Information: Chuck Berry's Recorded Legacy.* York, England: Music Mentor Books, 2001.

Rudwick, Eliot. *Race Riot at East St. Louis: July 2, 1917.* Urbana, Il: University of Illinois Press, 1982.

Ruppli, Michel. *The Chess Labels.* 2 Vols. Westport, Connecticut: Greenwood, 1983.

Shange, Ntozake. *Betsey Brown.* New York: Picador, 1985.

Schoenberg, Sandra Perlman, and Patricia L. Rosenbaum. *Neighborhoods That Work: Sources for Viability in the Inner City.* New Brunswick, NJ: Rutgers UP, 1980.

Taft, Carolyn Hewes. *The Ville: The Ethnic Heritage of an Urban Neighborhood.* St. Louis: Social Sciences Institute, Washington University, 1975.

Tosches, Nick. *Hellfire.* New York: Delacorte, 1982.

Warner, Jay. *Billboard's American Rock 'n' Roll in Review.* New York: Schirmer, 1997.

Washington, Booker T. *The Future of the American Negro.* Edited by Louis R. Harlan and Raymond W. Smock. *The Booker T. Washington Papers. Vol. 5: 1899–1900.* Urbana, Il: University of Illinois Press, 1976.

———. *Up From Slavery.* Edited by Louis R. Harlan and Raymond W. Smock. *The Booker T. Washington Papers. Vol. 1: The Autobiographical Writings.* Urbana, Il: University of Illinois Press, 1972.

Wertheimer, Alfred. *Elvis '56: In the Beginning.* London: Pimlico, 1994.

Wesley, Doris, and Ann Morris. *Lift Every Voice and Sing: St. Louis African Americans in the Twentieth Century.* Columbia: University of Missouri Press, 1999.

White, Charles. *The Life and Times of Little Richard, the Quasar of Rock.* New York: Harmony, 1984.

White, George R. *Bo Diddley: Living Legend.* Chessington, Surrey: Castle, 1995.

Wright, John A. *Discovering African American St. Louis: A Guide to Historical Sites*. St. Louis: Missouri Historical Society Press, 1994.

Wyman, Bill, with Ray Coleman, *Stone Alone: The Story of a Rock and Roll Band*, New York: Signet, 1991.

Newspaper and Periodical Articles

Ackerman, Paul. "R&B Notes." *Billboard*, September 3, 1955.

Adams, C. B. "Chuck Berry Turned 60 With a Lot of Help From Friends and Fans." *St. Louis Globe-Democrat*, October 18–19, 1986.

Advertisement. *St. Louis Argus*, March 13, 1959.

Advertisement. *St. Louis Argus*, March 20, 1959.

Advertisement. *St. Louis Argus*, June 16, 1961.

Advertisement. *St. Louis Argus*, August 19, 1960.

Aletti, Vince. "Chuck Berry Tells All—Sort Of." *Rolling Stone*, December 4, 1987:74.

Ambrose, Stephen E. and Douglas Brinkley. "Berry Met Flow of American Life in St. Louis: Pioneer Has No Place He'd Rather Go Than the Source of His Inspiration." *USA Today*, August 2, 2000.

"American Bandstand." *St. Louis Argus*, January 3, 1958.

"Appeals Court Remands Case over Questions by Judge Moore." *St. Louis Post-Dispatch*, October 28, 1960.

"Argus History Shows Longtime Record of Crusade Against Bigotry and Intolerance Here." *St. Louis Argus*, March 15, 1957.

Axelrod, Pete. "Candy." *Newsweek*, November 8, 1976.

"Ban on Rock! At London's Royal Albert Hall." *Melody Maker*, July 19, 1969.

Bangs, Lester. Review of *Concerto in B. Goode*. *Rolling Stone*, August 9, 1969.

Barnes, Harper and Dick Richmond. "Reelin' & Rockin': The Chuck Berry Tribute Was Part Spectacle, Part History—All Rock and Roll." *St. Louis Post-Dispatch*, October 19, 1986.

Berger, Jerry. "Companions Quail When Lawyer Fires." *St. Louis Post-Dispatch*, December 9, 1992.

———. "Berry is Departing Wentzville For Ladue." *St. Louis Post-Dispatch*, June 22, 1993.

"Berry's Birthday Bash Criticized." UPI, October 14, 1986.

"Berry Files Suit to Get Toilet Videotapes Back." *St. Louis Post-Dispatch*, May 3, 1990.

"Berry Lured Her to St. Louis, Girl, 14, Says." *St. Louis Globe-Democrat*, March 14, 1961.

"'Biggest Show of Stars' Wham 400G 1st Three Wks: Drop 'Whites' in Dixie." *Variety* October 2, 1957.

"Billy Eckstine Is Given Hotel Freeze: Balladier Unable to Break Ban." *St. Louis Argus*, May 1, 1953.

Brack, Ray and Earl Paige. "Chess and the Blues: From the Street to the Studio." *Billboard*, June 24, 1967: 20.

"Boston Common to Hoot Mon Belt They Rock 'N' Riot out of this Veldt." *Variety*, May 7, 1958: 1.

Brown, Merrill. "Rock Festival A Disaster in Almost Every Way." *St. Louis Post-Dispatch*, July 5, 1974.

Brogan, Daniel. "Birthday Concert Turns Into A Party On Second Try." *Chicago Tribune*, October 19, 1986.

Bryant, Tim. "Judge Dismisses Claim of Infringement in Lawsuits Against Chuck Berry By His Longtime Pianist." *St. Louis Post-Dispatch*, June 16, 2001.

Bundy, June. "Vox Jox." *Billboard*, May 19, 1956.

"Buy of the Week." *Billboard*, July 30, 1955: 44.

"Buy of the Week." *Billboard*, February 11, 1956: 47.

Carson, Tom. "Review of *Rockit.*" *Rolling Stone*, January 24, 1980.

"Child Abuse Charges Dropped Against Chuck Berry." UPI, November 21, 1990.

Christgau, Robert. "Chuck Berry." *Rolling Stone History of Rock and Roll*. 3rd ed. Ed. Anthony DeCurtis and James Henke with Holly George-Warren New York, Random House, 1992: 60–66.

"Chuck Berry Acquitted In Case Involving Woman." *St. Louis Post-Dispatch*, June 2, 1960.

"Chuck Berry Draws Jail Term." *St. Louis Post-Dispatch*, July 11, 1979.

"Chuck Berry Faces Weapons Charge." *St. Louis Post-Dispatch*, June 3, 1958.

"Chuck Berry Fined." *St. Louis Post-Dispatch*, November 26, 1988.

"Chuck Berry Postponement Until July 11." *St. Louis Argus*, June 27, 1958: 1.

"Chuck Berry Says Charges Not True." *St. Louis Argus*, March 4, 1960: 1.

Craig, James. "When Chuck Snubbed the Rolling Stones." *Record Mirror*, April 2, 1965.

Dannen, Frederick. "The Godfather of Rock and Roll." *Rolling Stone*, November 17, 1988: 93.

Delehant, Jim. "How an Innovator Lasts Forever." *Hit Parader*, March 1967.

Dickinson, Chris. "Still Rockin' Chuck Berry Packs House on 70th Birthday." *St. Louis Post-Dispatch*, October 20, 1996.

"Does 'Bandstand' Have Two Standards?" *St. Louis Argus*, January 10, 1958.

"Domino Unit Fat 18G In Return To Pit." *Variety*, April 17, 1957: 45.

"Dragnet Out For Slayer In Murder At Kiel Auditorium." *St. Louis Argus*, August 16, 1957.

"Drunk-in-Dixie." *Variety*, June 6, 1956: 43.

Dudman, Richard. "St. Louis Silent Racial Revolution: Newspapers Did Not Cover Campaign to Integrate Lunch Counters." *St. Louis Post-Dispatch*, June 11, 1990.

Dummit, Ralph. "Chuck Berry Opens Doors: Rock and Roll Idol Turns Restaurateur." *St. Louis Post-Dispatch*, September 22, 1988.

———. "Chuck Berry Taped Women Suit Charges." *St. Louis Post-Dispatch*, December 27, 1989.

DuNoyer, Paul. "The Life Of A Ladies Man." *Q*, May 1995: 67.

Eck, Liz and Duane Marburger. "Pre-Chess Chuck Berry." *Goldmine* 76 (September 1982): 25.

"Elvis a Millionaire in One Year." *Variety*, October 24, 1956: 1.

English, Nordeka. "Most Women in Berry Settlement Will Get $5,000," *St. Louis Post-Dispatch* May 24, 1995.

Etheredge, John. "Chuck Berry: A Conversation with Mr. Rock 'n' Roll." *Goldmine*, (November 1983): 6.

"Farewell to Armory." *Variety*, June 6, 1956: 43.

"Fats Big $16,700 Port." *Variety*, March 13, 1957: 44.

"Fats Domino Unit 52G in 4 N. California Dates." *Variety*, October 23, 1957: 55.

Finney, Chick. "Chick Finney's Blue Notes." *St. Louis Argus*, December 23, 1955: 22.

———. "Chick Finney's Blue Notes." *St. Louis Argus*, January 9, 1959.

———. "Chick Finney's Blue Notes." *St. Louis Argus*, January 30, 1959.

———. "Chick Finney's Blue Notes." *St. Louis Argus*, March 13, 1959.

———. "Chick Finney's Blue Notes." *St. Louis Argus*, March 27, 1959.

———. "Calypso Joe." *St. Louis Argus*, March 13, 1953.

———. "Rock N Roll Scored." *St. Louis Argus*, August 3, 1956.

"Fire anti-R&R Jockey." *Variety*, July 16, 1956: 46.

Fitzmaurice, Leo. "St. Charles County Seeks to Close Club." *St. Louis Post-Dispatch*, August 27, 1974.

Franklin, Buddy. "Brooklyn after Dark." *New York Age-Defender*, September 17, 1955: 7.

"Free Rock and Roller of Local Holdup Charges." *St. Louis Argus*, November 15, 1957.

"Freed Rock 'n' Roller Grosses 10G in MPLS." *Variety* April 30, 1958: 84.

Froelich, Cliff. "Hail! Hail! The Bankroll." *The Riverfront Times*, October 14–20, 1987.

Futterman, Ellen and Tim Bryant. "Key Issues In Suit Against Rock Star Is Whether It Was Filed Too Late: Case Causes Rift Between Ex-Partners Chuck Berry and Johnnie Johnson," *St. Louis Dispatch*, December 22, 2000.

Gayle, Lisha. "Thwarted Chuck Berry's Restaurant Can't Get Liquor License." *St. Louis Post-Dispatch*, September 29, 1989.

Gillium, Francine, "I Like Rock and Roll." *Monthly Journal*, March 1959.

Glover, Tony. Review of *Bio. Rolling Stone*, November 22, 1973: 79.

Green. Abel. "Alan Freed's Rock 'n' Roll Troup Pulls Spectacular 154G at B'klyn Par." *Variety*, September 14, 1955: 49.

Greensmith, Bill. "Red Holloway (Part 2)."*Blues Unlimited*, (March/April 1976): 9–14.

Goldberg, Barbara. "Woman Slugged By Berry Needed Stiches." UPI, June 6, 1988.

———. "Chuck Berry Sued For $5 Million in Alleged Assault." UPI, June 14, 1988.

Golkin, Pete. "Blacks, Whites, and Blues: The Story of Chess Records." *Living Blues*, (November/December 1989): 24.

Goodman, Mark. "The Further Misadventures of Candy." *Esquire*, June 1976: 93.

Greene, Bob. "A Star's Dim View of His Own Luster." *Chicago Tribune*, January 6, 1988.

Harrington, Richard. "Hail! Hail! Good Times With Berry." *Washington Post*, October 9, 1987.

Harrod, Rod. "Chuck Berry Getting Too Old?" *Record Mirror* January 16, 1965.

Hegger, Susan. "The Hottest Ticket in Town to the Worst Show Of The Year." *Riverfront Times*, October 22–28, 1986.

Hilburn, Robert. "Chuck Berry Sets the Record Straight." *Los Angeles Times*, October 4 1987.

———. "Private Chuck Berry Still Calling The Tunes At 60." *Los Angeles Times*, October 26, 1986.

"High Court Rejects Berry's Appeal In Videotapings Suits." *Los Angeles Times*, February 23, 1993.

High Society, January 1990: 3.

Hodenfield, Jan. "Rock and Roll Revived." *Rolling Stone*, November 29 1969: 38.

Hoekstra, Dave. "Goode Times, Bad Times." *Chicago Sun-Times*, January 21, 2001.

Holden, Stephen. "Chuck Berry Rocks Them at The Ritz." *New York Times*, June 28, 1981.

"House Reviews." *Variety*, November 23, 1955: 53.

"House Reviews." *Variety*, July 10, 1957: 119.

"House Reviews." *Variety*, March 12, 1958: 71.

"House Reviews." *Variety*, September 3, 1958: 54, 63.

"House Reviews." *Variety*, December 31, 1958: 44.

"Housing Case Meant Much to Veteran's Family: Public Housing Bias is Set Back." *St. Louis Argus*, December 30, 1955.

"Hub Chief Justice Rocks 5 Taken in Tow After Hot Fats Domino Roller." *Variety*, November 20, 1957: 62.

Hughes, Langston. "In Racial Matters in St. Louis, 'De Sun Do Move.'" *Chicago Defender*, May 1, 1954.

Jahn, Mike. "'Rock Revival' Audience Cheers Bill Haley and 15-Year-Old Hit." *New York Times*, October 20, 1969: 61.

"Jazz Purists Razz Berry At Newport." *Variety* July 9, 1958, 53+.

Jones, Max. "Berry's Formula—Old Songs With A New Sound." *Melody Maker* November 14, 1964.

Jopling, Norm. "Rock Lives!" *Melody Maker*, March 4, 1967.

Kattenhorn, Chick. "Chuck by Chick." *Melody Maker*, February 20, 1965.

Kramer, Gary. "Rhythm and Blues Notes." *Billboard*, January 19, 1957: 49.

———. "'Rock, Rock, Rock' Jumbo Size Disc Talent Package." *Billboard*, December 8, 1956: 22.

Koda, Cub. "Chuck Berry: And the Joint Was Rockin'." *Goldmine*, December 13, 1991: 16.

Lewis, Randy. "Knott's Cancels Berry Concerts." *Los Angeles Times*, July 26, 1990.

Lonesome, Buddy. "3,500 Shriek for Fats Domino and other R&R Stars." *St. Louis Argus*, March 1, 1957.

———. "Community Shows Apathy at Issue." *St. Louis Argus*, July 5, 1957.

———. "Neighborhood Hostile After Leffingwell Riot." *St. Louis Argus*, July 10, 1964.

"Lucy Ann Berry Wins Chance For Fame in Music Festival." *St. Louis Argus*, June 30, 1944.

Lydon, Michael. "Chuck Berry." In *Rock Folk: Portraits from the Rock and Roll Pantheon*. New York: Dial, 1971: 1–23.

Marcus, Greil. "Roll Over Chuck Berry." *Rolling Stone* June 14, 1969: 15.

Mannies, Jo. "Drug Unit Seizes Raids Chuck Berry Estates, Seized Items." *St. Louis Post-Dispatch*, June 28, 1990.

Manor, Robert. "Use TV Ads In Tapes Case, Lawyer Opposing Berry Says." *St. Louis Post-Dispatch*, December 3, 1990.

McGuire, John M. "Our Father of Rock: 'The Thrill is Gone,' Berry Says, Still an Attraction at Age 72." *St. Louis Post Dispatch*, November 15, 1998.

McLarin, Kimberly J. "At Home With Ntozake Shange: Native Daughter." *New York Times*, November 24, 1994.

McLeese, Don. "The Spirit Of A Rocker." *New York Times*, October 18, 1987.

Meadon, Peter. "Berry Favourites." *Record Mirror*, April 4, 1965.

"Mercury Signs Chuck Berry." *Billboard*, August 6, 1966: 52.

"Million-aires: Champion 'Gold Record' Winner is Fats Domino." *Ebony*, February 1959: 127.

Montre, Lorraine Kee. "Ten St. Louis Stars Make 'Walk Of Fame.'" *St. Louis Post-Dispatch*, June 26, 1989.

"Movies Here Hold Color Line: No Progress Despite Discussions." *St. Louis Argus*, October 9, 1953.

"Mrs. Chuck Berry Breaks as Husband is Convicted." *St. Louis Argus*, March 11, 1960.

Murray, Charles Shaar. "Big Cars, Little White Chicks, and the Chuck Berry Lick." *Creem*, March 1972: 27.

"Music Festival Star to Appear." *St. Louis Argus*, December 8, 1944.

Neely, Kim. "DEA Targets Chuck Berry." *Rolling Stone*, August 23, 1990: 34.

"Negro Singer Jailed After Dance 'Incident.'" *Meridian Star*, August 28, 1959.

"New Acts." *Variety*, February 6, 1957: 62.

"No Racial Incident at Ambassador." *St. Louis Argus*, November 13, 1953.

"Not 'Proper' Entertainment." *Variety*, July 16, 1956: 46.

Ochs, Ed. "Berry the Berries at Fillmore." *Billboard*, June 21, 1969: 36.

"One Night Only . . . A Pre-Holiday Treat." *St. Louis Argus*, December 16, 1955.

Palmer, Robert. "Chuck Berry at 60." *New York Times*, October 18, 1986.

Perkiss, Mark. "Rock Pioneer Chuck Berry Stands Up Police." UPI, June 5, 1988.

Peterson, Deborah and Bill Smith. "Berry Goes Strong at Birthday Bash." *St. Louis Post-Dispatch*, October 17, 1986.

"Pirates Foiled as Chuck Ducks." *Chicago Tribune*, October 1, 1986.

Plummer, Kim. "Daughter of Legend Wants Own Career in Rock 'n' Roll." *St. Louis Globe-Democrat*, March 22, 1983.

Pride, A. Scott. "The Up-Town Klans." *St. Louis Argus*, April 20, 1956.

Prost, Charlene. "Rock Festival Held in Chuck Berry's Park." *St. Louis Post-Dispatch* August 31, 1970.

"R&R at B'klyn Par, or Alan Freed's 'Big Beat' Loaded With Amateurs." *Variety* April 2, 1958: 65.

"R&R Battered 'n' Badgered." *Variety* July 16, 1956: 41–46.

"'Record Stars' 18G, St. L." *Variety*, August 1, 1956: 45.

Review of *Live at the Fillmore*. Rolling Stone, November 9, 1967.

Richmond, Dick. "Billy Peek: He Backed the Stars." *St. Louis Post-Dispatch*, December 4, 1981.

Riley, Marianna. "Bar Brawlers Said to Include Lawyers in Chuck Berry Suit." *St. Louis Post-Dispatch*, July 4, 1990.

———. "Berry, On Tour in Sweden, Denies Charges Against Him." *St. Louis Post-Dispatch*, July 4, 1990.

———. "Berry Upstages Accuser. Items in Drug Raid Planted, He Says." *St. Louis Post-Dispatch*, June 29, 1990.

———. "Child-Abuse Charges Dropped in Chuck Berry Plea Bargain." *St. Louis Post-Dispatch*, November 22, 1990.

———. "Chuck Berry Unburdened by Resolution of Charges." *St. Louis Post-Dispatch*, November 23, 1990.

———. "Women Sue Berry, Charge He Took Bathroom Videos." *St. Louis Post-Dispatch*, June 30, 1990.

Roberts, Chris. "Great, Chuck, Just Great!" *Melody Maker*, May 16, 1964: 3.

"Rock and Roll: American Bandstand Not American At All." *St. Louis Argus*, January 17, 1958.

"Rock and Roller Chuck Berry 'All Tore Up.'" *St. Louis Argus*, June 6, 1958.

"Rock Concert Site is Ordered Closed." *St. Louis Post-Dispatch*, September 11, 1974.

"Rock 'n' Roll Called 'Worm 'n' Wiggle' As Censors Rap 'Delinquent' Beat." *Variety*, June 6, 1956: 43.

"Rock 'n' Roll Singer Fined for Rock 'n' Roll Driving." *St. Louis Post-Dispatch*, July 17, 1958.

"Rock 'n' Roll Star's Pink Caddy Reels on Road and He's Roped." *St. Louis Globe Democrat*, July 12, 1958.

"Rock 'n' Roll Troupe Rolls Up 21G In Pitt." *Variety*, September 16, 1957: 54.

"Rock Singer 'Chuck' Berry Charged With Tax Evasion." *St. Louis Post-Dispatch*, May 14, 1979.

Sager, Mike. "Sex and Drugs and Rock 'n' Roll, Especially Sex." *Spy*, February 1993: 60.

Salvo, Patrick William. "Chuck Berry." In *The Rolling Stone Interviews: Talking With the Legends of Rock and Roll 1967–80*. Ed. Peter Herbst New York: St. Martin's Rolling Stone Press, 1981. 224–34.

———. "Chuck Berry Speaks!" *Melody Maker*, December 16, 1972: 34.

"Segregationists Would Ban All Rock, Roll Hits." *Billboard*, April 7, 1956: 130.

"Settlement in Wrongful Death Suit." *St. Louis Post-Dispatch*, November 28, 1974.

Shore, William J. "Why Judge McMillian Worries." *St. Louis Post-Dispatch*, August 11, 1991.

"SMILING CHUCK BERRY." *St. Louis Argus*, March 28, 1958.

Smith, Bill. "Berry Fans Enjoy A Goode Time." *St. Louis Post-Dispatch*, October 19, 1986.

"St. Charles County Rock Star's Appeal Is Rejected By U.S." *St. Louis Post-Dispatch*, July 1, 1992.

"St. Louis Hop: Say Arena Doorman Insulted Teenagers," *St. Louis Argus*, January 31, 1958.

Stevens, Guy. "A Chuck Berry Recording Session." *Jazzbeat* April 1964: 14.

Stewart, Tony. "One of the Most Adventurous Bills Ever." *New Musical Express*, February 12, 1972: 30.

"Strip Ads Snarl Pit 'Rock 'n' Roll.'" *Variety*, September 21, 1955: 61.

"Suit Against Singer Settled." *St. Louis Post-Dispatch*, October 2, 1975.

"Suit on Drowning at Berry Park." *St. Louis Post-Dispatch*, September 18, 1974.

"The Prosecutor and the Performer," *St. Louis Post-Dispatch*, July 15, 1990.

"The Rocks Keep Rolling at R&R; Pittsburgh is Latest Rioting Locale." *Variety*, July 25, 1956: 111.

"This Week's Best Buys." *Billboard*, July 30, 1955: 44.

Todd, Cynthia. "Pioneer . . . Educator Julia Davis is Honored as She Nears 100." *St. Louis Post-Dispatch*, November 17, 1991.

Topping, Ray. "Marshall Shoots the Breeze." *Blues Unlimited*, 142 (Summer 1982): 16.

"2 Girls Drown in Park Pool." *St. Louis Post-Dispatch*, August 12, 1974.

"Two Johnson Sidemen Nabbed in Reefer Raps." *Variety*, October 5, 1955: 49.

"Weapons Charge Hearing for Rock and Roll Singer." *St. Louis Post-Dispatch*, July 12, 1958.

Weil Jr., Richard K. "Festival in the Red, Promoters Are Blue." *St. Louis Post-Dispatch*, July 5, 1974.

Welch, Chris. "Backstage With Chuck." *Melody Maker*, January 16, 1965.

Interviews

Bob Baldori, interview with the author, Toronto, Canada, February 7, 1998.

Marshall Chess, interview with the author, New York, November 4, 1998.

Esmond Edwards, telephone interview with the author, December 14, 1998.

Joe Edwards, interview with the author, St. Louis MO, March 30, 2000.

Jack Hooke, interview with the author, New York, October 31, 1997.

Johnnie Johnson, interview with the author, St. Louis MO, March 30, 2000.

Jim Marsala, interview with the author, St. Louis, MO, March 29, 2000.

Frederick Mayer, video interview with the author, June 22, 2000.

Little Aaron Mosby, interview with the author and Bill Greensmith, East St. Louis, IL, April 1, 2000.

Billy Peek, interview with the author, St. Louis, MO, March 29, 2000.

Richard Schwartz, interview with the author, St. Louis, March 31, 2000.
Merle Silverstein, interview with the author, St. Louis MO, March 28, 2000.
Mark Slocombe, telephone interview with the author, February 7, 2002.

Court Documents and Police Reports

State of Missouri vs. Charles Edward Berry. Circuit Court of Boone County, Missouri, November 16, 1944.

United States v. Charles Edward Anderson Berry. 60 CR 18 & 19, miscellaneous court documents. District Court of the United States, Eastern District of Missouri, Eastern Division.

United States v. Charles Edward Anderson Berry. 60 CR 18 & 19, Motions of Defendant. District Court of the United States, Eastern District of Missouri, Eastern Division, Feb 12, 1960.

United States v. Charles Edward Anderson Berry. 59CR322 (1). District Court of the United States, Eastern District of Missouri, Eastern Division.

United States v. Charles Edward Anderson Berry. 59CR322 (2). District Court of the United States, Eastern District of Missouri, Eastern Division.

Police Department Report 59 275 678. City of St. Louis, December 22, 1959.

United States v. Charles Edward Anderson Berry. 283 F.2d 466. United States Court of Appeals, Eighth Circuit, October 28, 1960.

United States v. Charles Edward Anderson Berry. 295 F.2d 192. United States Court of Appeals, Eighth Circuit, January 8, 1962.

Berry v. Drake Publishers, Inc. 902–10071. Circuit Court of the City of St. Louis.

Johnnie Johnson v. Charles E. Berry and Isalee Music Company. 4:00CV01891DJSUS. District Court of the United States, Eastern District of Missouri, Eastern Division.

Movies, Television, and Audio Recordings

Berry, Chuck. *Live at the Filmore.* Sound recording, Mercury SR-61138. November 1967.
——. *The London Chuck Berry Sessions.* Sound recording, Chess CH60020. April 1972.
Chuck Berry: Hail! Hail! Rock 'n' Roll. Delilah Films, 1987.
Go, Johnny, Go. Hal Roach Studios, 1959.
Great Balls of Fire. MGM, 1989.
"Johnny B. Goode." *Omnibus,* BBC TV, 1980.
"Renegades." *Rock & Roll.* Episode 1. PBS. September 24, 1995.

Web Sites

Berry, Chuck. Letter to Ahmet Ertegun. January 13, 1997. *http://www.johnnie.com/c-lett.html*
Chuck Berry. Rock and Roll Hall of Fame Inductees. *http://www.rockhall.com/hof/inductee.asp?id=67*
Fox Theater. "Everyone Played the Fox." *http://www.fabulousfox.com/played-fox.asp*
Greene, Lorenzo J. Antonio F. Holland, and Gary Kremer. "The Role of the Negro in Missouri History, 1719–1970." *http://www.umsl.edu/services/library/blackstudies/civrits.htm*
"Homes of Windermere Place." *http://www.stlouis.missouri.org/visitationpark/winder.htm*
Wajgel, Joe. "A Short History and Evolution of 'Hot Rod Lincoln.'" *http://www.rockabilly-hall.com/HotRodLncln.html*

Index